THE CAMBRIDGE (
POETRY AND

MW00779173

The Cambridge Companion to American Poetry and Politics since 1900 shows how American poets have addressed political phenomena since 1900. This book helps students, teachers, and general readers make sense of the scope and complexity of the relationships between poetry and politics. Offering detailed case studies, this book discusses the relationships between poetry and social views found in works by well-established authors such as Wallace Stevens, Langston Hughes, and Gwendolyn Brooks, as well as lesser known, but influential figures such as Muriel Rukeyser. This book also emphasizes the crucial role contemporary African American poets such as Claudia Rankine and leading spoken word poets play in documenting political themes in our current moment. Individual chapters focus on specific political issues – race, institutions, propaganda, incarceration, immigration, environment, war, public monuments, history, technology – in a memorable and teachable way for poetry students and teachers.

DANIEL MORRIS is Professor of English at Purdue University. He is author of *The Writings of William Carlos Williams: Publicity for the Self* (University of Missouri Press, 1995), *Remarkable Modernisms: Contemporary American Authors on Modern Art* (University of Massachusetts, 2002), *The Poetry of Louise Glück: A Thematic Introduction* (University of Missouri Press, 2006; 2020), *After Weegee: Essays on Contemporary Jewish American Photographers* (Syracuse University Press, 2011), *Lyric Encounters* (Bloomsbury Academic, 2013), *Not Born Digital: Poetics, Print Literacy, New Media* (Bloomsbury Academic, 2016), and *Kenneth Goldsmith's Recent Work on Paper* (Fairleigh Dickinson University Press, 2019). He has also edited or coedited four other books as well as published four volumes of poetry, including *Hit Play* (Marsh Hawk Press, 2015) and *Blue Poles* (Marsh Hawk Press, 2019).

A complete list of books in the series is at the back of the book.

THE CAMBRIDGE
COMPANION TO

AMERICAN POETRY AND POLITICS SINCE 1900

EDITED BY

DANIEL MORRIS

Purdue University

CAMBRIDGE
UNIVERSITY PRESS

CAMBRIDGE
UNIVERSITY PRESS

Shaftesbury Road, Cambridge CB2 8EA, United Kingdom

One Liberty Plaza, 20th Floor, New York, NY 10006, USA

477 Williamstown Road, Port Melbourne, VIC 3207, Australia

314–321, 3rd Floor, Plot 3, Splendor Forum, Jasola District Centre, New Delhi – 110025, India

103 Penang Road, #05–06/07, Visioncrest Commercial, Singapore 238467

Cambridge University Press is part of Cambridge University Press & Assessment, a department of the University of Cambridge.

We share the University's mission to contribute to society through the pursuit of education, learning and research at the highest international levels of excellence.

www.cambridge.org
Information on this title: www.cambridge.org/9781009180023

DOI: 10.1017/9781009180047

First published 2023

A catalogue record for this publication is available from the British Library.

Library of Congress Cataloging-in-Publication Data
NAMES: Morris, Daniel, 1962– editor.
TITLE: The Cambridge Companion to American Poetry and Politics since 1900 / edited by Daniel Morris.
DESCRIPTION: Cambridge ; New York : Cambridge University Press, 2023. | Series: Cambridge companions to literature | Includes bibliographical references and index.
IDENTIFIERS: LCCN 2022045403 (print) | LCCN 2022045404 (ebook) | ISBN 9781009180023 (hardback) | ISBN 9781009180030 (paperback) | ISBN 9781009180047 (epub)
SUBJECTS: LCSH: American poetry–20th century–History and criticism. | Politics and literature–United States–History–20th century. | Political poetry, American–History and criticism. | Politics in literature. | LCGFT: Literary criticism.
CLASSIFICATION: LCC PS310.P6 C36 2023 (print) | LCC PS310.P6 (ebook) | DDC 811/.509358–dc23/eng/20220930
LC record available at https://lccn.loc.gov/2022045403
LC ebook record available at https://lccn.loc.gov/2022045404

ISBN 978-1-009-18002-3 Hardback
ISBN 978-1-009-18003-0 Paperback

Contents

Notes on Contributors

Stephanie Burt is Professor of English at Harvard University. Her most recent books include *We Are Mermaids* (Graywolf, 2022), *After Callimachus: Poems and Translations* (Princeton University Press, 2020), and *Don't Read Poetry: A Book about How to Read Poems* (Basic, 2019). With Alfred Bendixen, she coedited the *Cambridge History of American Poetry* (Cambridge University Press, 2014). She lives in Belmont, Massachusetts, with three humans, two cats, one dog, and too many X-Men comics.

Matthew Calihman is Professor of English at Missouri State University. He is the coeditor, with Gerald Early, of *Approaches to Teaching Baraka's Dutchman* (MLA, 2018) and the coeditor, with Tracy Floreani and A Yẹmisi Jimoh, of the Ralph Ellison Special Issue of *American Studies* (2015), and he has published articles and book chapters on Baraka, Ellison, and John A. Williams.

Michael S. Collins is the author of an intellectual biography, *Understanding Etheridge Knight* (University of South Carolina Press, 2012); a book of poems, *The Traveling Queen* (Sheep Meadow Press, 2013); and many uncollected essays and poems that have appeared in venues ranging from *Harper's Magazine* to *The Best American Poetry 2003*. His current projects include a book on affirmative action that is forthcoming from the University Press of Kansas, and a second, paperback edition of *Understanding Etheridge Knight* (University of South Carolina Press, 2013). He teaches at Texas A & M University.

Maria Dikcis is a College Fellow in the Department of English at Harvard University. Previously, she was an American Council of Learned Societies Emerging Voices Fellow at the University of Chicago, where she served as a Postdoctoral Researcher and Mass Incarceration and Policing Fellow at the Pozen Family Center for Human Rights. Her current book project traces a comparative literary history examining how African American, Asian American, and Latinx poets have used a range of print, audio, broadcast, and digital technologies to innovate new forms of racial representation and political critique throughout the post-1965 era. Her scholarly work has appeared in *ASAP/Journal* and *Chicago Review*, where she was a member of the poetry editorial board. She holds a PhD in English from Northwestern University and an MA in Humanities from the University of Chicago.

Dallas Donnell is a PhD candidate in the Department of American Studies at the University of Maryland. He received his BA in Comparative Race and Ethnic Studies from the University of Chicago. He is also a former organizer and communications professional for a variety of racial and social justice organizations, including the Black Youth Project, Color of Change, and ROC United. His research interests include Black radicalism, theories of social death, and Black music and popular culture.

Sarah Ehlers is Associate Professor of English at the University of Houston. She is the author of *Left of Poetry: Depression America and the Formation of Modern Poetics* (University of North Carolina Press, 2019) as well as numerous essays on modern and contemporary poetics.

Ann Fisher-Wirth is Emeritus Professor of English and Director of the Interdisciplinary Minor in Environmental Studies at the University of Mississippi. She is the author of six books of poems, most recently *The Bones of Winter Birds* (Terrapin Books, 2019) and *Mississippi*, a poetry/photography collaboration with Maude Schuyler Clay (Wings Press, 2018). With Laura-Gray Street, she coedited the groundbreaking *Ecopoetry Anthology* (Trinity University Press, 2013). A senior fellow of the Black Earth Institute, she has received Fulbrights to Switzerland and Sweden, and poetry residencies to Djerassi, Hedgebrook, the Mesa Refuge, and Camac/France.

Florian Gargaillo is Associate Professor of English at Austin Peay State University. He is the author of *Echo & Critique: Poetry and the Clichés of Public Speech* (Louisiana State University Press, 2023). His articles on modern and contemporary poetry have appeared in such venues as *Modern Language Quarterly*, *Essays in Criticism*, *Genre*, *Modernism/modernity*, *Journal of Modern Literature*, *Twentieth-Century Literature*, and *The Journal of Commonwealth Literature*.

Loren Glass is Professor and Chair of English at the University of Iowa, specializing in twentieth- and twenty-first-century literatures and cultures of the United States, with an emphasis on book history and literary institutions. He is the author of *Counterculture Colophon: Grove Press, the* Evergreen Review, *and the Incorporation of the Avant-Garde* (Stanford University Press, 2013) – republished in paperback by Seven Stories Press under the title *Rebel Publisher: Grove Press and the Revolution of the Word* – and the editor of *After the Program Era: The Past, Present, and Future of Creative Writing in the University* (University of Iowa Press, 2016). He is currently working on a literary history of Iowa City. He is a member of the Post45 collective and coedits their book series.

Alec Marsh is a Professor of English at Muhlenberg College. He has written widely on twentieth-century American poetry, especially on Ezra Pound and William Carlos Williams.

J. Peter Moore is Clinical Assistant Professor and Director of Creative Inquiry in the Honors College at Purdue University. He is completing a book manuscript, "Vernacular Poetics in an Era of Vernacular Studies," which traces the emergence of the term "vernacular" in the years after the Second World War as a site of contested engagement with the limits of formal knowledge production. Chapters on Amiri Baraka and Robert Duncan have appeared in *American Literature* (Duke University Press, 2017) and *Sillages Critiques* (Centre de Recherche "Texte et Critique de Texte," 2019). He is also at work on a second project about avant-gardism and the American South, an excerpt of which, on the films of Arthur Jafa, has appeared in *Revisiting the Elegy in the Black Lives Matter Era* (Routledge, 2020). He has authored two poetry collections, *Southern Colortype* (three count pour, 2013) and *Zippers & Jeans* (selva oscura, 2017).

Daniel Morris is author of seven books on twentieth- and twenty-first-century poetry and visual culture, editor or coeditor of four previous essay collections, and author of four books of poetry. Recent titles include *Not Born Digital* (Bloomsbury, 2016), *Blue Poles* (Marsh Hawk Press, 2019), and a paperback reissue of his study of Nobel Laureate Louise Glück (University of Missouri Press, 2021). He has taught at Purdue since 1994.

Wanda O'Connor is an Associate Lecturer and Honorary Associate at the Open University in Wales. She is coeditor of the *Journal of British and Irish Innovative Poetry* and a member of the Critical Poetics Research Group at Nottingham Trent University. Her creative work has appeared in journals and anthologies such as *The Best Canadian Poetry 2014* (Tightrope Books, 2014), *Wretched Strangers* (Boiler House Press, 2018), *The World Speaking Back ... to Denise Riley* (Boiler House Press, 2018), and *Bad Kid Catullus* (Sidekick Books, 2017).

Kathy Lou Schultz is the Catherine and Charles Freeburg University Professor and Director of the Women's and Gender Studies Program at the University of Memphis. Her books include *The Afro-Modernist Epic and Literary History: Tolson, Hughes, Baraka* (Palgrave, 2013), as well as four collections of poems, including *Biting Midge: Works in Prose* (Belladonna, 2008) and *Some Vague Wife* (Atelos, 2002). Her work is anthologized in *Some Other Blues: New Perspectives on Amiri Baraka* (The Ohio State University Press), *The Companion to Modernist Poetry* (Wiley, 2014), *From Our Hearts to Yours: New Narrative as Contemporary Practice* (ON Contemporary Practice, 2017), and *Efforts and Affections: Women Poets on Mentorship* (University of Iowa Press, 2008). Schultz's poems are published in *Bombay Gin, Cleaver Magazine, Fence, Hambone, Marsh Hawk Review, Miracle Monocle, Mirage #4/ Period(ical), New American Writing*, and other journals. She has performed poetry with musicians in Memphis and on the CD, *The Colored Waiting Room*, by Dr. Guy's MusiQology.

Christopher Spaide is a Junior Fellow in the Society of Fellows at Harvard University. His book project, "Lyric Togetherness," examines the plural pronouns and collective voices of American poetry from 1945 to today. His essays, reviews, and poems have appeared in *College Literature, Contemporary Literature, Harvard Review, Poetry*, and *The Yale Review*.

Mark Steven is the author of *Red Modernism: American Poetry and the Spirit of Communism* (Johns Hopkins, 2017) and *Splatter Capital* (Repeater, 2017), and editor of *Understanding Marx, Understanding Modernism* (Bloomsbury, 2021). He is also a Senior Lecturer in 20th and 21st Century Literature at the University of Exeter .

Orchid Tierney is an assistant professor of English at Kenyon College. She is the author of *a year of misreading the wildcats* (Operating System, 2019). Her articles have appeared or are forthcoming in *Venti, Substance, Jacket2*, and elsewhere.

Mark W. Van Wienen is a professor of English at Northern Illinois University. He is author of *Partisans and Poets: The Political Work of American Poetry in the Great War* (Cambridge University Press, 1997),

Rendezvous with Death: American Poems of the Great War (University of Illinois Press, 2002), and *American Socialist Triptych: The Literary-Political Work of Charlotte Perkins Gilman, Upton Sinclair, and W. E. B. Du Bois* (University of Michigan Press, 2011). He is editor of *American Literature in Transition, 1910–1920* (Cambridge University Press, 2017) and (with Tim Dayton) of *A History of American Literature and Culture of the First World War* (Cambridge University Press, 2020).

Tyrone Williams teaches literature and theory at Xavier University in Cincinnati, Ohio. He is the author of several chapbooks and seven books of poetry: *c.c.* (Krupskaya, 2002), *On Spec* (Omnidawn 2008), *The Hero Project of the Century* (Backwaters Press, 2009), *Adventures of Pi* (Dos Madres Press, 2011), *Howell* (Atelos Books, 2011*), As Iz* (Omnidawn, 2018), and, with Pat Clifford, *washpark* (Delete Press, 2021). A limited-edition art project, *Trump l'oeil*, was published by Hostile Books in 2017. He and Jeanne Heuving edited an anthology of critical essays, *Inciting Poetics* (University of New Mexico Press, 2019). His website is at www.flummoxedpoet.com/.

Acknowledgments

I am grateful to Ray Ryan, editor at Cambridge University Press, for his faith in me, sharp critiques of my proposals, and ongoing support for this project. Edgar Mendez, also of Cambridge University Press, has collaborated closely with me throughout the process. Edgar has always been friendly, informative, and encouraging. Stephanie Sakson's meticulous copy editing improved this book. Kaye Barbaro, Emma Goff-Leggett, and Vinithan Sedumadhavan provided timely support as the book went into the production and marketing phases. My biggest appreciation for sure goes to Ethan Goffman. Ethan and I worked together on projects before this one, but his rare combination of fine-grained editorial skills and big-picture understandings of what matters in literature, politics, and culture made him an indispensable supporter on this project. Ethan read and commented on all the essays and offered invaluable advice on the overall shape of the project. Monica Wolfe, an advanced PhD candidate in the Purdue English department, offered timely editorial assistance at crunch time. Vincent Leitch, John Duvall, and Leonard Cassuto stand out as sage voices who offered support during the preliminary stages of the project. Family members Joy, Isaac, Aaron, Hannah, George, and Meyer have been in my corner throughout this endeavor. I also want to thank Professor Dorsey Armstrong, head of the Purdue English department, for releasing funds that helped to pay for the index.

Introduction

Daniel Morris

In "Can Poetry Matter?" (1991), Dana Gioia points to a contradictory situation for American poetry:

> Decades of public and private funding have created a large professional class for the production and reception of new poetry comprising legions of teachers, graduate students, editors, publishers, and administrators. Based mostly in universities, these groups have gradually become the primary audience for contemporary verse. Consequently, the energy of American poetry, which was once directed outward, is now increasingly focused inward.

Noting the lack of poetry reviews in newspapers and the rise of the novel as the preeminent literary genre in the United States, Gioia, writing in *The Atlantic*, worries that an insulated subculture has taken custody of poetry: "Even if great poetry continues to be written, it has retreated from the center of literary life. Though supported by a loyal coterie, poetry has lost the confidence that it speaks to and for the general culture." Contra Gioia, the success of US poet laureate Robert Pinsky's 1997 "Favorite Poem Project," to which, as the project website reports, "18,000 Americans wrote in to share their favorite poems – Americans from ages 5 to 97, from every state, representing a range of occupations, kinds of education, and backgrounds" – suggests a strong undercurrent of enthusiastic poetry readers. Similarly, Tracy K. Smith, US poet laureate from 2017 to 2019, "made seven trips across the country in an 'American Conversations' tour, traveling from Alaska to Louisiana, holding readings in rural areas that are not on the typical literary circuit," writes Neely Tucker. Addressing an audience at Georgetown University in 2017, Smith has described poetry as "a perfect vehicle for promoting national conversations" because it "tells us you have to talk but you also have to stop and listen and struggle with what you hear. And honesty, rather than elaborate obfuscation, is the currency of a poem" (qtd. in "U.S. Poet Laureate"). Exploring the claims of Smith,

Pinsky, and Gioia, each of which paints a partial picture, this companion focuses on how American poets since 1900 have (and have not) engaged with politics in the broad sense of the term as defined by Adrienne Rich in a journal entry from 1969: *"politics* is the effort to find a way of humanely dealing with each other – as groups or as individuals – politics being simply process, the breaking down of barriers of oppression, tradition, culture, ignorance, fear, self-protectiveness" (Rich 24, quoting from her own journal entry of 1969).

In June 2020, *Together in a Sudden Strangeness: America's Poets Respond to the Pandemic* was published, gathering "85 poems about isolation, grief, boredom, longing, and hope, including work by Billy Collins, Jane Hirshfield, Kamilah Aisha Moon, Jenny Xie and Matthew Zapruder." The collection was assembled in forty days, published as an e-book with a hardcover edition that November. Contra W. H. Auden's declaration in "In Memory of W. B. Yeats" (1939) that poetry "makes nothing happen," Knopf, the Poetry Society of America, its executive director, Alice Quinn (who edited the volume), *New York Times*, and eighty-five American poets regard poetry as essential personal protective equipment (PPE). It is software to help readers work through COVID-19 trauma. *Together in a Sudden Strangeness* (2020) takes its place alongside *An Eye for an Eye Makes the Whole World Blind: Poets on 9/11* (edited by Allen Cohen, Michael Parenti, et al., 2002), *Cry Out: Poets Protest the (Iraq) War* (2003), *Poetry after 9/11: An Anthology of New York Poets* (edited by Dennis Loy Johnson and Valerie Merians, 2011), and *American Poets in the 21st Century: Poetics of Social Engagement* (edited by Claudia Rankine and Michael Dowdy, 2018) as illustrations of how twenty-first century American poets grapple with unsettling current events.

My opening paragraphs confirm that American poets are engaging with social issues that have inevitably morphed into political conflicts, but Tracy K. Smith (b. 1972) contends that the efforts of her generation lack precedence. In fact, when she honed her craft as an MFA student at Columbia, her teachers discouraged the writing of "political poems":

> In the mid-1990s, when I was a student of creative writing, there prevailed a quiet but firm admonition to avoid composing political poems. It was too dangerous an undertaking, one likely to result in didacticism and slackened craft. No, in American poetry, politics was the domain of the few and the fearless, poets like Adrienne Rich or Denise Levertov, whose outsize conscience justified such risky behavior. Even so, theirs weren't the voices being discussed in workshops and craft seminars. (Smith)

In her poetry, teaching, and criticism, Smith joins "the domain of the few and the fearless" by engaging with a tangle of relationships between poetry and politics: race, sexuality, violations against the fragile human body, civics, war, terrorism, and institutional amnesia in relation to the history of twentieth-century American political poetry.

Smith's essay, however, begs the question that underscores the need for this companion: What *were* the relationships between poets, poems, poetics, and politics throughout the twentieth century in the United States? Contra Smith (and her teachers at Columbia), this companion demonstrates there are instructive, if unsung, stories to tell. Given, as Cary Nelson lamented in 1991, that English professors rarely explain why "the poetry sung by striking coal miners in the 1920s is so much less important than the appearance of *The Waste Land* in *The Dial* in 1922," it remains an uphill task to remember how American poets engaged with politics over the course of the twentieth century (68). This "uphill task" is especially the case when we acknowledge, as do the contributors to this volume, that the range of responses to political issues covers the gamut of ideological perspectives. Further, as contributors demonstrate, individual poets have themselves been of mixed minds about how to address political themes in poems. Writing in 1993, even Adrienne Rich, the legendarily activist poet cited by Smith, admits the impact of New Critical dogma that engraved the autotelic – or "art for art's sake" – nature of poetry on her perception that poetry cannot amend social relations:

> I knew – had long known – how poetry can break open locked chambers of possibility, restore numbed zones to feeling, recharge desire. But I had, more than I wanted to acknowledge, internalized the idea, so common in this country, so strange in most other places, that poetry is powerless, or that it can have nothing to do with the kinds of powers that organize us as a society, as communities within that society, as relationships within communities. (Rich, xiv)

No longer stymied by New Critical pieties, which guided how Radcliffe professors taught poetry to Rich in the 1950s, Smith says that since 9/11 and, subsequently, the Iraq War (2003–2011) opened the door, we may characterize American political poetry by its empathy, ambivalence, and spiritual yearnings. Until recently, however, she considers what has passed for engaged poetry as merely enraged poetry. This companion emphasizes the approach to political poetry practiced by Rich and Smith, but it acknowledges that no poets or critics hold a monopoly over how poetry should or should not relate itself to politics.

Contrarily, as Susan Ehlers observes in Chapter 3, "Depression-Era Poetics and the Politics of How to Read," New Critical formalist assumptions dominated mid-twentieth-century American literary values in part by discouraging poets from doing political work in a direct way. These, in turn, were shaped by "a conservative critical movement that originated with the southern 'fugitive poets' [that] defined itself against the rise of a left cultural front." These earlier "culture wars" were won, at least temporarily, by the faction that wished to squeeze politics out of poetry.

Yet poetry has always had a social and political side, and explicitly political poetry has a long history. At the same time, a primary lesson I have learned from editing this companion is that even when poets are self-consciously writing "political poetry," they bring with them myriad understandings of how poetic language relates to speech acts that compel direct actions such as strikes or demonstrations. As Florian Gargaillo writes in Chapter 2 on poetry and propaganda, most twentieth-century American poets preferred *not* to view their poetry as overt and direct political discourse. Deploying a strategy that he refers to as "echo and critique," Gargaillo attends to poets who suggest their discomfort with overt political discourse by, ironically, including political slogans in their poetry. Their intent is *not* to endorse the sentiments put forward in the slogans, however, but rather to challenge the comprehensibility or validity of the partisan statements. As Gargaillo writes, "For [Denise] Levertov, the goal of a poem – or at least, a good poem – is not to spur readers to action, but instead to sharpen their attentiveness, so they are able to respond more fully and more responsibly to the world, from ordinary sights and sounds to the news of global events." This companion demonstrates that Levertov and Rich, both of whom participated in solidarity movements, were not alone in expressing wariness about regarding their poetry as speech acts comparable to a political leaflet or a rousing speech designed to spur listeners to engage in collective action.

Like Gargaillo, Mark Van Wienen in Chapter 7 regards a key task of American war poets for at least a century as ideological critique, that is, as contesting idealistic rhetoric put forward by national leaders that conceals hard facts on the ground. President Woodrow Wilson declared America's entry into World War I as intended to make "the world safe for democracy," but American poets after 1917 challenged the message: "Yet under the idealistic veneer Wilson's aim was no less than US hegemony in a world capitalist system, in which 'political liberty' would promote an open global marketplace that the United States could dominate. This contradiction between Wilsonian ideals and reality catalyzed, in turn, a body of trenchant antiwar poetry." From William Vaughn Moody's poetry of the Spanish American War to contemporary poets writing about wars in the Persian Gulf and Iraq, the Balkans, or Afghanistan, Van Wienen argues that poets have offered an anti-imperialist critique that flies in the face of sloganeering put forward by government officials. The story of how poets imagined war in their writings, however, is not one-sided. Hundreds of American poets wrote patriotic verses in support of the nation's entry into World War I; female poets wrote elegies lamenting the loss of their sons on the battlefield; mainstream poets such as Carl Sandburg critiqued the war effort by arguing that "economic and political interests ... ultimately propelled the United States into the war," and African American soldier-poets such as Lucian B. Watkins responded to the contradictions between Wilsonian idealism abroad and Wilsonian racism back home. Working in a form recognized for nuanced self-expression, not ham-fisted diatribe, is it a surprise that American poets who wrote about war tended to see martial conflict in shades of gray? Like Van Wienen, Michael Collins, writing in Chapter 11 on three African American poets who endured incarceration, demonstrates that poets often regard their poems as revisionary correctives to public discourse, which they view as a mask to conceal domination and exploitation. The task of such poetry is to encourage readers to think twice about interpreting political language as an assertion of unambiguous meaning. Collins shows how Bob Kaufman, Etheridge Knight, and Reginald Dwayne Betts trouble President Ronald Reagan's version of American history as a "utopian statement because it refers to an America that never existed ... especially [for] those who have been caught up in the legislation written for comic-strip reality rather than the real thing."

In line with Collins and Van Wienen, both of whom align poetry with ideological critique, Christopher Spaide, in Chapter 1, on how American poets have addressed public monuments, notes that the most famous example of the genre, Emma Lazarus' "The New Colossus," negates an "exceptionalist mythos," in this case one associated with a precursor from the ancient world: "Against the classical monumental merits of the Colossus of Rhodes – masculinity, military success, an exceptionalist mythos decorated in 'storied pomp' – this New Colossus offers maternal authority and an unconditional invitation." As Spaide explores in his essay, however, Lazarus' revisionary treatment of the Colossus of Rhodes has itself come to represent an exceptionalist ethos for contemporary poets who wonder if the United States has lived up to the compassionate ideals of "world-wide welcome" in the 120 years since her poem became affixed to the base of Lady Liberty. Spaide writes, "Thanks to Black Lives Matter and related activist movements, it is increasingly common to probe the meaning of monuments, the retrospective narratives they tell, and their connections to settler colonialism, slavery, patriarchal force, and American exceptionalism."

One need not point to a range of American poets representing a specific topic such as propaganda or war or incarceration to notice how ambivalently related are the terms "poetry" and "politics." Individual poets often combine feelings of hope, anger, grief, and despair when confronting a major topic of social import. No individual poet discussed in this companion may be more characterized by a complex relationship to politics in tone and temperament than Wallace Stevens (1879–1955). In Chapter 5, Alec Marsh traces how Stevens negotiated a middle path between aestheticism and political commitment at a moment when influential poets on the Left during the Great Depression "set the agenda; to be useful in the social struggle, art should function as propaganda." In his close reading of "Mr. Burnshaw and the Statue" (1936), Marsh describes how Stevens wrestles with a figure representing Burnshaw, the Marxist critic, to offer "a dialectical dance between things imagined (the future) and things as they are (the past) which may be far apart, but still reflect each other." For Stevens, as for Robert Frost, freedom of thought, liberation of emotion, and the treatment of literary language as a medium for creative play signal personal emancipation from groupthink. At the same time, Stevens accepts the Shelleyan role of the poet as unacknowledged legislator. His task it is to accurately reflect on a social world. As Marsh writes, Stevens' "poems address issues that lie behind the struggle of the poet to make sense of 'things as they are' (*CP* 165), that is, the social responsibilities of the poet, and deeper, expressive responsibilities to the poetic self, struggling in an incorporated world of militant mass politics and economic crisis." Control of thought, whether associated with the politics of the Right or the Left, is, for Stevens, anathema to what Frost called "the freedom of the poet," but, as Marsh shows in his reading of "The Man with the Blue Guitar" (1937), Stevens agrees with the need for social reform, but questions a propagandistic or blatantly political role for the poet, but he is also concerned with the poet's role in representing conflicts within social life and the common cause. Writing on Stevens, a corporate insurance executive who lived and worked in Hartford, Connecticut, and whose finances were secure during the Great Depression, Marsh reminds us of the range of subject positions from which poets regard their art as a forum to represent a contested social text. In Chapter 3, Sarah Ehlers highlights a much more explicitly political poet than Stevens, and even a model for many of today's political poets.

Focusing on Muriel Rukeyser's *The Book of the Dead* (1938), a book-length modernist poem that documents with archival precision the plight of West Virginia coal miners, many of whom were African American, who died in an industrial disaster at Hawk's Nest Tunnel at Gauley Bridge, West Virginia, Ehlers joins contributor Mark Steven in attending to a quintessential, if at times underappreciated, author who believed poetry could awaken readers to human suffering stemming from economic causes and environmental crises. By placing Rukeyser in conversation with a contemporary documentary poet, Susan Briante, Ehlers builds a new literary historiography, one in which, as Paula Rabinowitz has put it, the literary productions of Depression-era leftist writers "must still be reckoned with if we are to comprehend fully what depression means to ... aesthetics."

Like Ehlers, Kathy Lou Schultz in Chapter 12 contributes to a fresh approach to literary history by, in this case, placing Rukeyser in conversation with another leading contemporary poet, Claudia Rankine, who emphasizes how microaggressions are inseparable from structural violence against African Americans. Schultz aligns Rankine's *Citizen: An American Lyric* (2014) to Rukeyser's *The Book of The Dead*. Both are long poems put in the service of historical documentation of social crises involving the mistreatment of individuals by representatives of institutional power. As importantly, Schultz notes that Rukeyser and Rankine understand the political dimension of multimedia aesthetics. Each wanted to combine visual and verbal media to document crises within a social, economic, and political environment characterized by racial division and class conflict.

For Schultz, Rukeyser's and Rankine's interest in photography and other media underscores "the importance of both documentation and social connection as remedies for social injustice." Countervailing ways of recalling history as well as retelling the history of poetic representation are crucial aspects of the story of the politics of American poetry since 1900.

In a separate way from those discussed above, Stephanie Burt in Chapter 6 develops an intersection between poetry and politics by rethinking the history of modern and contemporary American poetry. Rather than recover the long form documentary tradition of a Rukeyser or a Louis Zukofsky, Burt attends to a neglected heritage: the eighteenth-century Augustan tradition of witty poetry associated with English authors such as Alexander Pope. At first, Burt's recovery of "wit" in modernist poets such as Marianne Moore and Langston Hughes; mid-twentieth-century poets such as Richard Wilbur, Randall Jarrell, and James Merrill; and contemporary poets such as Terrence Hayes and Rae Armantrout may seem out of place in a book about the political dimension of poetry. But Burt's point is that "wit" is a political mode of addressing imagined readers. Witty poetry is a social form. It implies an author's respect for the reader's sensibility, one characterized by intellectual flexibility, sense of discovery, and an awareness that there is often more in a statement than what one might at first assume. Witty poetry treats the reader as participant in the complex task of meaning making.

The goal of the witty poet is to facilitate a community of equals between reader and writer. Given the internal divisions, culture wars, and polarizing rhetoric of our current moment in the United States, a moment in which words are too often imagined as things, and thus treated as ways to inflict pain on others, perhaps even spurring violence, Burt's recovery of a "wit" tradition may serve as a corrective model for us to imagine a political discourse and sociability based on trust, empathy, and respect. Witty poetry is not compatible with a conception of the self as inhabiting a separate universe that is unknowable to another. If "wit" moves language in the direction of play, we may remember that playful words are often preferable to fighting words. Burt's essay reminds us that poets may be politically engaged but need not be dogmatic or ideological.

If wit may be an indirect way of touching on political subjects, experimental poets throughout the twentieth century have fused a play of language with an implicit political critique, often made explicit in their theoretical writings. Discussing the legacy of twentieth-century leftist poets such as Zukofsky, Oppen, and, again, Rukeyser, Mark Steven in Chapter 4 argues that an experimental formalism need not suggest apolitical aestheticism. Steven demonstrates that leftist poets from the 1930s "were contemporaneously engaged in a program of aesthetic innovation, producing works not only informed by political commitment and revolutionary imperative but also beholden to the modernist mission of literary reinvention. These poets – writing in their capacity as labor organizers, as insurrectionary agitators, and as comrades at arms – set out to socialize the means of poetic expression, creating verse that is revolutionary in form no less than content." Acknowledging affinities between West Coast Beat poets from the 1950s and Bay Area avant-gardist writings by language poets in the 1970s – ludic, antiestablishment, and anarchistic – Tyrone Williams in Chapter 14 also situates language poets within a long history of "experimental writings and Marxist politics." He notes that while language poets drew on the Objectivists, they remained skeptical about considering distinct poets in terms of group labels. Williams writes, "Louis Zukofsky's and George Oppen's combination of innovative writing and social critique made them especially significant to language poets [Barrett] Watten and [Ron] Silliman, thus the more linear narrative forms deployed by Objectivists like Carl Rakosi, Charles Reznikoff, Muriel Rukeyser, and Lorine Niedecker led to their relative neglect by Watten and Silliman despite their avowal of leftist politics." Further, Williams explains that language poets were influenced by aesthetic developments associated with politically conservative High Modernists such as T. S. Eliot and Ezra Pound, as well as by the documentary long-form tradition favored by many poets on the political Left. Literary experimentation continues to this day, encompassing a growing array of voices and media formats.

Orchid Tierney in Chapter 18 connects early twentieth-century modernism to the most innovative trends in twenty-first-century poetics while emphasizing the politics of new media formats in her essay on digital poetics. She argues that digital modernism builds on language poets' experimentalism while being more explicitly political, and considerably more culturally and racially diverse. She says that digital modernism aligns with strategies of the avant-garde: it challenges traditional expectations about what art is and does. It illuminates and interrogates the cultural infrastructures, technological networks, and critical practices that support and enable these judgments. Following Marshall McLuhan, the philosopher and communications theorist who taught generations to recognize that media are not value neutral, but, as he famously quipped, are the message (or, as his book title from 1967 wittily stated, the massage), Tierney proposes that digital media poets simultaneously address economic themes including who owns a literary work in a hypertext environment – an issue of copyright – and the related issue of authorship in a medium associated with appropriation and the repurposing of "found" materials. As with most essayists in this companion, Tierney teaches us that the questions digital media poets are grappling with today are simultaneously new and not new, forward-looking and backward-glancing, original and unoriginal. Upending Romantic conceptions of the inspired author as individual genius and the modernist division of cultural productions into racial and class-based "brows" – high, middle, and low – Tierney argues that the emphases on proceduralism and assemblage in digital poetics troubles traditional categorizations of creative expression. In Tierney's cultural assemblage, we notice how literary history makes for strange political alliances. Here we have Ezra Pound, the right-wing modernist impresario, recast as a precursor to digital poets who explore the political implications of said technologies in relation to contemporary

issues that range from immigration and environmentalism to racial hierarchies and gender categories of identity.

Wanda O'Connor in Chapter 15 offers another example of strange
alliances in her essay on innovative women poets from the 1970s and
beyond. O'Connor shows that Charles Olson's theory of "field" or "open"
form poetics and his composition of what he called "projective verse,"
developed in the 1940s and published in his epic poem *The Maximus
Poems*, which he composed until his death in 1970, was adapted by
innovative female poets such as Susan Howe, Rachel Blau DuPlessis, and
Kathleen Fraser to claim an archivally rich and yet unbounded documentary situation to account for previously unexplored and unacknowledged
female experiences. O'Connor writes, "*Projective Verse* provided women
poets with the impetus to move into the 'open field' and to explore such
blurring of boundaries on the page. Examples of this practice took shape in
the plurality or difference of the line, in collage-based fragments, and in
palimpsest and supplementary gestures within the textual-visual body. The
shaping of plural forms and contexts often instructed unfixed narratives
and encouraged further impulses toward openness."

Poetic form usually refers to material structures such as the line or the
graphic display of words on a page and to the established patterns poets use
to fit words and syllables into pleasing shapes with memorable lilt. Several
contributors to this companion, however, expand the definition of poetic
form to refer to the frame, context, situation, or medium in which poetry
reaches (or does not reach) potential audiences. In his essay on poems
about public art (Chapter 1), Spaide, for example, reminds us that Lazarus
wrote her iconic Petrarchan sonnet in 1883 as a fundraiser for the
Bartholdi Pedestal Fund and that it was not originally intended to appear
at the base of a pedestal. In further, ironic recastings, Spaide notes,
"beyond the innumerable poems, novels, and children's books responding
to it, you can find Lazarus's sonnet in films by Alfred Hitchcock, Ken
Burns, and Gus Van Sant; songs by Irving Berlin, Joan Baez, Lou Reed,
Patti Smith, and Public Enemy; and even a first-person-shooter video
game, *Wolfenstein II: The New Colossus* (2017). Lazarus never would have
guessed that her fundraising sonnet would be quoted on a commemorative
silver dollar, issued for the statue's centennial in 1986 – a piece of limited-
edition Lazarusiana that sells for upward of twenty dollars today."

In another example of how crucial is context to how poetry is assigned
political meanings, J. Peter Moore in Chapter 10 observes that the significance of a single ode by Gwendolyn Brooks – in this case one she was
originally commissioned to write for a 1965 centennial commemoration of

the death of Abraham Lincoln held in Springfield, Illinois – changed from looking backward to looking forward when she revised her ode – Lincoln's name does not appear in the second version! – for republication in 1987 for a press associated with pan-African and Black Nationalist political movements. Moore's essay speaks to how specific forms of reception may be understood as aesthetic spaces that influence the political valence of poetry.

In Chapter 16 on "transcultural agency," Maria Dikcis builds on Emma Lazarus' vison as well as on the new perspective employed by feminist poets. Dikcis focuses on how geographical context influences the political reception of poetry. By situating American poetry within "comparative, transnational, and cross-hemispheric contexts," Dikcis is able to argue that "transcultural exchange across racial, ethnic, and national boundaries is the very quality that distinguishes American poetry since 1900." Part of the same explosion of new voices and multiculturalism explored by Dikcis, Matthew Calihman in Chapter 9 expands the frame for reading African American political poetries. He reminds readers that the quintessential "Harlem Renaissance" bard, Langston Hughes, was, in fact a poet who embraced a transnational perspective on the Black experience: "Hughes remained an internationalist throughout his career. In much of his work of the 1930s and 1940s, when he was closely identified with the Communist movement, he portrayed the struggle against Jim Crow as part of a transnational, interracial, multiethnic struggle against capitalism and impe-rialism." Calihman also emphasizes the role institutional infrastructures played in the development of African American political poetries.

In Chapter 8, Loren Glass' wide-ranging essay on how cultural institu-tions – from Pound's "ezuversity" to small presses funded by the scions of wealthy industrialists such as James Laughlin, founder of New Directions Press, to the development of poets in the academy (Frost at Amherst College being among the first) to full-fledged MFA degree-granting pro-grams in poetry writing (the University of Iowa being among the first) to the culture of celebrity – has reimagined the frames, contexts, and condi-tions in which poetry is written, published, and consumed – a matcrial aspect of poetry and poetics with political resonances.

Most contributors to this companion focus on the politics of textual forms and publication formats that appeal to the eye of the reader through the visual dimension of poetry. O'Connor's essay on experimental feminist poets who appropriated the open form or "field" poetics of the mid-twentieth-century poet Charles Olson to imagine new experiences and life worlds of unruly women is one example. But Dallas Donnell's Chapter 13, on the political resonances of hip hop and Black performance poetry, addresses the contemporary turn toward oral forms as a political gesture. Blurring or erasing the boundaries between high culture and popular culture, Donnell's attention to recording artists such as Beyoncé is, by itself, a reframing of the scope, and the history, of American poetry, and thus a political gesture.

Ann Fisher-Wirth in Chapter 17 discusses a more recent addition to the ranks of political poetry, works addressing environmental catastrophe (branching off from the long history of the environmental movement). Adding to the complexity, she addresses how the intersections of race, gender, ethnicity, and relationship to citizenship inflect the poet's idiosyncratic response to environmental catastrophe and the interrelatedness between human beings and the nonhuman world. Embracing Adrienne Rich's contention that the personal is the political, Fisher-Wirth shows, for example, the interconnectedness between "personal history, African American history, and the environment" in Camille Dungy's *Trophic Cascade*.

Focusing on Dungy, Brenda Hillman, and Craig Santos Perez, Fisher-Wirth calls attention to the unique features of each poet's work. At the same time, she regards all three as "environmental activists for whom poetry is not separate from political engagement and awareness of the ways in which colonialism, postcolonialism, and industrialism have exploited both humans and nature." As with Maria Dikcis' essay on transnational agency, Fisher-Wirth makes clear that contemporary American poetry is by no means limited to commentary on activities occurring within the geographical borders of the United States. When confronting an existential crisis such as climate change, Fisher-Wirth indicates that Hillman, Dungy, and Santos Perez perceive American poetry as global poetry. Their poems are composed on behalf of the survival of nonhuman beings as well as human beings.

This companion makes evident that some theorists, poets, and critics regard *language, context, occasion, form,* and *association* as political concerns. For some poets and critics, *language* is the fundamental site of political inquiry. For these authors, diction (standard or vernacular); accessibility to readers; disjunction; mimesis; allusivity; the decision to write in English, another language, or a hybrid; and representing language on paper or through spoken word (or sung or rapped) are, at bottom, ideological concerns. For others, *context* reveals political views. Institutional frames, such as publication venue, evaluation principles, methods of preservation, and criteria for reward exhibit political commitments. For others, poetry, to be political, must investigate, witness, or document historical events or the monuments and memorials that W. J. T. Mitchell has argued usually have "a direct reference to violence in the form of war or conquest" (886). For these writers, political poetry is *occasioned* by distinct phenomena: war, labor unrest, poverty, incarceration, sexual assault, peace movement protest, presidential inauguration and assassination, or violence motivated by race, immigration, gender, sexuality, and ethnicity. Others regard poetry's emphasis on *form* – especially unique aspects of the genre such as line length, metrical pattern, and epic, ballad, and lyric modes – as technical dimensions of the art that enact political administration, especially if we regard politics as the method for legislating, distributing, and structuring access to power in a social world. For still others, a poet's *association* with a literary movement, cultural community, pedagogical circle, or ethnic, gendered, or racial group identification is itself a form of political alignment that influences why poets are recognized and how readers receive poetry. For yet another group, political poetry must focus on the body, particularly on the way female bodies are represented and often violated, and on how some bodies are incarcerated. For others, political poetry must pay special attention to how human societies have put stress on the environment to the point that the age of the Anthropocene may be passing away into the time of the post-human.

As editor, I was pleasantly surprised to notice that more contributors celebrated Muriel Rukeyser (1913–1980) as a visionary precursor to current poetry than any other twentieth-century American poet. Why the emergence of this relatively unsung author? Why Rukeyser? Why now? To find out, I asked a prominent Rukeyser scholar, Elisabeth Däumer, to speculate about the poet's enduring importance. Here is what she told me:

> Like the great modernist poets T. S. Eliot, Ezra Pound, and W. C. Williams, Rukeyser believed in poetry as an essential cultural resource. Yet when she published her Ars Poetica *The Life of Poetry* in 1949 it was derided by compatriots and simply ignored by the poetic establishment. Even today, many scholars of American literature do not know, or do not think they ought to know, about her nuanced defense of poetry in relation to a society consumed by wars and their aftermath. Like Pound, Rukeyser wrote poems with history. She sought to establish for poetry a key role in our ability to respond to the present, retrieve the past (in her case, not a canonical one, but the voices of the forgotten, wasted, anonymous), and imagine possible futures. But unlike Pound, and other modernists, she remained a dedicated anti-fascist her entire life and turned to poetry as a force of democratization, not elitism. Her principled optimism – often ridiculed as facile or unearned – speaks with searing intensity to the present

moment, as we find ourselves in the midst of political upheavals, global refugee crises, and climate disaster. In her by now iconic poem, simply entitled "Poem," she writes about making her poems "for others unseen and unborn" and reminds us of "those men and women, / Brave, setting up signals across vast distances, / Considering a nameless way of living, of almost unimagined values." Rowena Kennedy-Epstein concludes her recent book *Unfinished Spirit: Muriel Rukeyser's Twentieth Century* with this stirring assessment:

> "Rukeyser's work, finished and unfinished, is about learning how to be 'receptive' to the world we are living in right now. It asserts that any future worth imagining actually depends on the acceptance of our unfinishedness in the present, on the recurrences of searching, looking, undoing, on the connections we form and in the prodigal waste we are born into and make our way through. The unfinishedness is about learning to be always 'approaching alive and now.'" (Däumer)

Like contributors such as Tyrone Williams, Orchid Tierney, Mark Steven, and Loren Glass, all of whom acknowledge the influence of Ezra Pound on American poetry and politics over the last century, Däumer invokes Pound when discussing Rukeyser. Like Pound, Rukeyser, Däumer notes, understood poetry as an "essential cultural resource" that engages with "history." The crucial difference between what Hugh Kenner termed the "Pound Era" in a famous book from 1971 and what this companion suggests may be regarded as the "Rukeyser Era" is that "she remained a dedicated anti-fascist her entire life and turned to poetry as a force of democratization, not elitism." Of course, these "eras" are and were often going on simultaneously, at cross purposes, but Rukeyser's vision of a poetry that engages with a range of social and political issues and gives voice to the unrepresented has ultimately overtaken Pound, who for decades was taken more seriously and seen as the ideological bedrock of poetry. Having begun this project amid the January 6, 2021, insurrection on the United States Capitol and completed my introduction as the Russian Federation invades Ukraine in April 2022, I hope and pray that American poetry remains dedicated to the values upheld by Rukeyser.

WORKS CITED

"About the Favorite Poem Project." Favorite Poem Project website, www .favoritepoem.org/about.html.

Alter, Alexandra. "Publishers and Writers Race to Depict the Outbreak." *New York Times*, May 19, 2020, B6.

Auden, W. H. *Selected Poems*. Edited by Edward Mendelson. Vintage, 2007.

Däumer, Elisabeth. "On Rukeyser's Enduring Importance." Unpublished essay.

Gioia, Dana. "Can Poetry Matter?" *The Atlantic Monthly*, May 1991. https:// danagioia.com/essays/american-poetry/can-poetry-matter/.

Kennedy-Epstein, Rowena. *Unfinished Spirit: Muriel Rukeyser's Twentieth Century*. Cornell University Press, 2022.

Kenner, Hugh. *The Pound Era*. University of California Press, 1971.

Mitchell. W. J. T. "The Violence of Public Art: 'Do the Right Thing.'" *Critical Inquiry*, vol. 16, no. 4, summer 1990.

Nelson, Cary. *Repression and Recovery: Modern American Poetry & Politics of Cultural Memory*. University of Wisconsin Press, 1991.

Pressman, Jessica. *Digital Modernism: Making It New in New Media*. Oxford University Press, 2014.

Quinn, Alice, ed. *Together in a Sudden Strangeness: America's Poets Respond to the Pandemic*. Knopf, 2020.

Rabinowitz, Paula. "Between the Outhouse and the Garbage Dump: Locating Collapse in Depression Literature," *American Literary History*, vol. 23, no. 1, spring 2011, pp. 32–55.

Rich, Adrienne. *What Is Found There: Notebooks on Poetry and Politics*. W. W. Norton, 2003.

Smith, Tracy K. "Politics & Poetry." *New York Times*. December 10, 2018, p. 1 of the Sunday Book Review, www.nytimes.com/2018/12/10/books/review/ political-poetry.html

Tucker, Neely. "Tracy K. Smith Bids Farewell as U.S. Poet Laureate." April 19, 2019. Library of Congress website, https://medium.com/@librarycongress/ tracy-k-smith-bids-farewell-as-u-s-poet-laureate-715861f2f1dd.

"U.S. Poet Laureate: Deepen Civic Engagement through Poetry." October 30, 2017, www.georgetown.edu/news/u-s-poet-laureate-deepen-civic-engage ment-through-poetry/.

CHAPTER I

The Space of Public Memory
Monuments, Memorials, and American Poetry from "The New Colossus" to Black Lives Matter

Christopher Spaide

When W. H. Auden – thirtysomething poet, English expatriate, and new New Yorker – wrote the words "Poetry makes nothing happen," he was mere miles from a 305-foot-tall counterexample. Poetry didn't build the Statue of Liberty, and didn't notably influence the statue's French sculptor, Frédéric Auguste Bartholdi, or the Americans who funded and built its pedestal. But "The New Colossus" (1883), a sonnet by the Jewish American poet and humanitarian Emma Lazarus, did raise $1,500 at auction for the Bartholdi Pedestal Fund – not much, but for fourteen lines, not bad. In an inestimably greater contribution, "The New Colossus" prospectively transformed the statue into a monument to immigration, a "Mother of Exiles" from whose "beacon-hand / Glows worldwide welcome." In an audacious turn from octave to sestet, from a prophetic future tense ("Here at our sea-washed, sunset gates *shall stand* / A mighty woman with a torch") to a gripping present, Lazarus's sonnet lets the statue speak:

> "Keep, ancient lands, your storied pomp!" cries she
> With silent lips. "Give me your tired, your poor,
> Your huddled masses yearning to breathe free,
> The wretched refuse of your teeming shore.
> Send these, the homeless, tempest-tost to me,
> I lift my lamp beside the golden door!" (58)

Against the classical monumental merits of the Colossus of Rhodes – masculinity, military success, an exceptionalist mythos decorated in "storied pomp" – this New Colossus offers maternal authority and an unconditional invitation. Lifting her lamp for all exiles, whatever their unspecified "lands," this Mother makes a utopian promise: a new home for the homeless. Ingeniously adapting the Petrarchan sonnet, Lazarus reimagines her sestet's interwoven *cdcdcd* rhymes as that perennial American balancing act, unity versus multiplicity. Her end rhymes condense a resolution as much musical as argumentative: *she*, embodying the *free*, greets us as a first-person *me*; the *poor*, hailing from every foreign *shore*, can enter through the golden *door*.

The commonest misapprehension about "The New Colossus" is that Lazarus wrote it after the statue's completion, as a dedication or ode. This puts the cart before the horse, the statue beneath its pedestal. The copper statue was Bartholdi's creation, but the Statue of Liberty, as we still remember that icon today, remains indebted to Lazarus and the contradictory figure she named and animated to stirring speech – a figure mighty and motherly, xenophilic yet nationalist, classical but new. A bronze casting of the poem was placed in the statue's pedestal in 1903, an early step in "The New Colossus" becoming a monument itself. Certainly no other nineteenth-century poem has bequeathed a more adaptable phrase book for what Max Cavitch calls "an American integrationist fantasy . . . of an open and welcoming yet coherent and unified nation" (1). Beyond the innumerable poems, novels, and children's books responding to it, you can find Lazarus's sonnet in films by Alfred Hitchcock, Ken Burns, and Gus Van Sant; songs by Irving Berlin, Joan Baez, Lou Reed, Patti Smith, and Public Enemy; and even a first-person-shooter video game, *Wolfenstein II: The New Colossus* (2017). Lazarus never would have guessed that her fundraising sonnet would be quoted on a commemorative silver dollar, issued for the statue's centennial in 1986 – a piece of limited-edition Lazarusiana that sells for upward of twenty dollars today.

Nothing in the sonnet's legacy is more self-contradictory than its deployment by American politicians, who have enlisted its stockpiled cultural capital to antithetical ends. In his 1958 pamphlet *A Nation of Immigrants*, Senator John F. Kennedy wryly rewrote the poem to protest the "national origins" quotas in place since 1921. "Under present law," he proposed, Lazarus's "Give me your tired, your poor, / Your huddled masses yearning to breathe free" should continue "as long as they come from northern Europe, are not too tired or too poor or slightly ill, never stole a loaf of bread, never joined any questionable organization, and can document their activities for the past two years" (33–34). Lazarus's lines, as written, also appear in a Kennedy presidential campaign ad, read by Eleanor Roosevelt; they recur in the public papers of Jimmy Carter, Ronald Reagan, and Barack Obama, all of whom present Lazarus's story as a prologue for their presidential programs. When, in 2019, Donald Trump's acting director of Citizenship and Immigration Services announced an anti-immigrant regulation expanding the definition of a "public charge," he claimed to be acting in the spirit of "The New Colossus," only to recite words Lazarus never wrote: "Give me your tired and your poor who can stand on their own two feet and who will not become a public charge." What Kennedy dolloped high with sarcasm, the director recited straight-faced. "That it neither rhymes nor scans is the least of our worries," responded Esther Schor, Lazarus's biographer. Preemptively refuting the director's later allegation that the phrase "wretched refuse" referred strictly to European refugees, Schor confirmed that, for Lazarus, "aiding the poor and oppressed of all lands was the mission of all Americans, the mission of America itself."

Like the statue it glorifies, "The New Colossus" stands tall in American history: What does it stand for today? It remains a high point, visible from great distances, transmitted even further through quotations and appropriations, maximized into national icons and miniaturized onto coins. It is neither the first nor last American poem pertaining to monuments or memorials: that tradition extends from Native American chants to Herman Melville's Civil War inscriptions, from modernist immensities to memorials for September 11 and COVID-19. But surely Lazarus's sonnet is our most visible triangulation of poetry, public art, and – in Schor's phrase – "the mission of America," as successive generations have defined and debated it. Thanks to Black Lives Matter and related activist movements, it is increasingly common to probe the meaning of monuments, the retrospective narratives they tell, and their connections to settler colonialism, slavery, patriarchal force, and American exceptionalism. That public attention to monuments has been mirrored, even anticipated, in such twenty-first-century poetry collections as Heid E. Erdrich's *National Monuments* (2008), Jena Osman's *Public Figures* (2012), and Natasha Trethewey's *Monument* (2018); anthologies like Lisa Russ Spaar's *Monticello in Mind: Fifty Contemporary Poems on Jefferson* (2016) and Laren McClung's *Inheriting the War: Poetry and Prose by Descendants of Vietnam Veterans and Refugees* (2018); and the amassing criticism on the poetry of monuments and calls for their removal.

Despite this attention, monuments and memorials remain elusive objects of study. There is no broadly recognized category called "monument poetry" – nor should there be. Any critical mass of monument poetry shuffles together far more clearly defined genres: odes, elegies, epitaphs, ekphrases, travel poetry, erasures, and so-called project books. Equally mistaken would be to assume that monuments are nothing but subject matter, what these poems are "about." Canonically, monuments set culture's high bar, a symbolic benchmark to reach for (W. B. Yeats's "Monuments of unageing intellect") or surpass (Horace, "I have built a monument more lasting than bronze"). In these comparisons, monuments emerge as examples of what Jahan Ramazani calls poetry's others, those neighboring discourses poetry defines itself alongside and against. But unlike poetry's closer cousins, like the news, prayer, or song, monuments generally assume a superhuman stature, both spatial and temporal. The Statue of Liberty stands out not only in New York Harbor but on a global map, as conspicuous to the English expatriate Thom Gunn in "Iron Landscapes (and the Statue of Liberty)" (1976) as to the Chilean poet Nicanor Parra, penning a postcard-poem on the "USA" (1972): "Donde la libertad / es una estatua" ("where liberty / is a statue"). And monuments, of course, are built to outlast – to stay constant amid historical and generational change. The same monument Walt Whitman celebrates in "Washington's Monument, February, 1885" reappears in decade after decade, in poems written by the likes of Carl Sandburg, Ogden Nash, Muriel Rukeyser, Bob Kaufman, James Schuyler, Allen Ginsberg, Rita Dove, and Elizabeth Alexander. Stroll through your local bookstore, and you might spot the Washington Monument on the cover of Claudia Rankine's *Just Us: An American Conversation* (2020). Even obscured behind Rankine's title and an ominous black haze, the obelisk is recognizably itself, lancing across the book's spine like a calcified backbone, or a stake impaling the body politic.

Given their longevity and sprawl, monuments are difficult to file within the standard periods of American literary history. Poems on monuments and memorials have a history all their own, which can be told in four overlapping chapters. First, from "The New Colossus" to the 1920s, poets celebrated distinctly American monuments and interventions into a world canon; their goal was the "new," whether Lazarus's patriotic "new" or the modernist "new" of Ezra Pound's imperative, "MAKE IT NEW." Second, from the Great Depression through World War II, poets invented their own monuments – thought experiments in testing aesthetic and social questions during unprecedented global transformations. Third, postwar poets returned *en masse* to actual monuments, at home and abroad, which they understood as admirable historical artifacts and mirrors for their multidimensional autobiographical speakers. Finally, from the 1970s onward, contemporary poets explored three deviations from the monumental: the countermonumental, the antimonumental, and the documentary.

The modern history of monument poetry begins with American culture lagging behind. At "Thebes or Troy, Carthage or Babylon," the ancient world had its monuments, therefore "You must have Monuments too, O America." That may sound like a preamble to "The New Colossus," or some Whitmanian echo. In truth it comes from one of the 6,175 manuscripts submitted to "the contest for the Official Poem of the New York World's Fair" in 1939: "The World of Tomorrow," by Joan O. Harvey, a farmer from Newtown, Pennsylvania; as one of five runners-up, she received $100 (Academy of American Poets 24, 3). Harvey's line is a needful reminder of how much monument poetry has been occasional poetry, aimed at popular audiences. Its places were the podium, the plaque, the press release, the official program. No occasional poem has endured quite like "The New Colossus"; as the occasional poem that paradoxically struck on permanence, it became a touchstone for more fleeting efforts. In 1956, the Empire State Building Corporation commissioned a prose poem, a "tribute" to the skyscraper's new "Freedom Lights," in the mold of Lazarus's sonnet. In a miffed review titled "Eighty-Six-Storied Pomp," Geoffrey T. Hellman balked at the publicity stunt, with its forced equivalence between international concord and American commercialism: "The Statue of Liberty is a gift from France to this country; its dividends are intangible. If the Empire State is our nation's doorway, so are the Chrysler Building, the Metropolitan Life, and Costello's bar and restaurant, on Third Avenue" (97).

For modernist poets, America needed monuments in a more capacious sense. Monuments (or simply the word "monument," a ubiquitous term of praise) stood for a Western or worldwide tradition initiated millennia before the United States – a tradition modernists sought to join and extend. For T. S. Eliot in "Tradition and the Individual Talent" (1919), the tradition is a constellation of monuments, constantly being redrawn: "The existing monuments form an ideal order among themselves, which is modified by the introduction of the new (the really new) work of art among them" (*Sacred* 44). In *The Waste Land* (1922), Eliot physicalizes that order-making as sifting through "stony rubbish" and "A heap of broken images," amid an unreal city's "Falling towers." "These fragments I have shored against my ruins," he summarizes at the poem's feverish close (10, 11, 49). Ezra Pound, *The Waste Land*'s editor and dedicatee, reworked that last line to open the four Malatesta Cantos (1922–23), an early crux of his unfinished life's work, *The Cantos*. Their name derives from the fifteenth-century nobleman Sigismondo Malatesta, a man consumed by his own unfinished project: the renovation of Rimini's church of San Francesco into the Tempio Malatestiano, complete with a sepulcher for himself and his third wife. In Lawrence S. Rainey's telling, Pound "came to view the church of San Francesco – a sepulchral monument – as a symbol of his own poetic and cultural enterprise"; for readers, the sepulcher "can also epitomize the cultural monument of literary modernism" *tout court* (2). Eliot, Pound, and second-generation modernists like George Oppen (who wrote two poems titled "Monument") were not unique in seeking monuments abroad. Several Harlem Renaissance poets praised European and Asian monuments as sublime testaments to labor, endurance, and societies unblemished by American racism. As though leapfrogging American literary history altogether, those poems ease into centuries-old verse-forms: sonnets like Claude McKay's "Russian Cathedral" (1925) and Countee Cullen's "At the Wailing Wall in Jerusalem" (1927), and Langston Hughes's "Ballads of Lenin" (1933), with its chummy address to the deceased: "Comrade Lenin of Russia, / High in a marble tomb, / Move over, Comrade Lenin, / And give me room" (183).

Early-twentieth-century poets unsatisfied with existing monuments instead consecrated their own, with media ranging from found materials (Robert Frost's woodpile, Wallace Stevens's jar) to towns and cities (Edgar Lee Masters's fictional Spoon River, William Carlos Williams's Paterson). Inasmuch as they stood for regional or national experiences, these unofficial monuments have their politics, too. Few recognized that truth more clearly, or knew better how to obscure it, than the Southern poet and New Critic Allen Tate. In his self-styled "reactionary" criticism, Tate swiftly unearthed the myths he believed were buried inside monuments to modernity. In his eyes, the evolving America of Hart Crane's *The Bridge* (1930) – and, by extension, of the poem's symbolic centerpiece, the Brooklyn Bridge – "stands for a passage into new truths. Is this the meaning of American history? ... Which American history?" (*Reactionary* 33–34). Conversely, as Tate traverses a Southern graveyard in his "Ode to the Confederate Dead" (1927/1937) and mourns "inscrutable infantry" lost in the Civil War, he bookends his grief between universalizing natural imagery: autumn's "splayed leaves," a "casual sacrament / To the seasonal eternity of death," and a "gentle serpent," a "Sentinel of the grave who counts us all!" (*Collected* 21, 20, 23). Which American history is *this*? A revisionist history: Tate wrote his "Ode" after the largest spike in the dedication of new Confederate monuments, from 1900 to the 1920s ("Whose"); like those monuments, it shields a racist history behind whitewashed appeals to heritage and nostalgia. As for Crane, Tate's friend and contemporary? Tate was correct to characterize Crane's America as a "passage," but *The Bridge* is less a departure from tradition than a two-way thoroughfare, permitting passage back and forth through time. In his proem "To Brooklyn Bridge," Crane imagines passageways between the bridge and declaredly *old* truths: that earlier monument, the Statue of Liberty (a seagull "build[s] high / Over the chained bay waters Liberty"), and the traditional arts of sacrament and song (the bridge is hailed as "O harp and altar," suspended on "choiring strings") (33). Yet as strictly as it obeys any formal constraint, *The Bridge* respects the Brooklyn Bridge's innovative architectural contours. In Jake Adam York's reading, "the poem uses those most recognizable elements – the cables, the carrier bars, the monolithic pylons – as the visible boundaries for the conceptual space the poem constructs" (140).

As Crane drafted *The Bridge*, a structure on America's West Coast was transforming into poetry, to nearly no one's knowledge. A year before Lazarus's New Colossus made her "world-wide welcome," the Chinese Exclusion Act became law, necessitating the construction of facilities like the Angel Island Immigration Station in San Francisco Harbor. Of the roughly 100,000 Chinese immigrants who arrived at that major port from 1910 to 1940, over half were detained at Angel Island, for periods ranging from a night to over two years. In 1970, a park ranger noticed Chinese characters carved into the wooden walls of the station's barracks; in time, scholars and activists uncovered engravings of over a hundred original poems. In the hands of these poems' largely anonymous authors, imprisonment itself is refashioned into a makeshift monument. Adapting classical modes, they chronicled their arduous voyages and harrowing detentions, their nostalgia for China and their curbed aspirations for America. Many poems pledge themselves to a time-traveling solidarity: "I write my wild words to let those after me know"; "Leave this as a memento to encourage fellow souls" (Lai et al. 128, 144). Others fix recognizable forms onto bewildering, transient experiences. One example is a *qijue* (quatrain in seven-character lines) labeled "Fifth Day of the Tenth Moon, Xinhai Year, Effusion after Moving to Another Room" ("Xinhai Year" is 1911, the year of the Chinese Revolution):

> I arrived in the wooden building one week ago.
> Whenever someone mentions switching rooms, it distresses me excessively.
> Gathering all my baggage together, I hurriedly run.
> Who would ever know the misery of it all? (Lai et al. 132)

Without replicating the original prosody, this English translation preserves the quatrain's parallelisms of grammar and thought. The first and third lines track restless movements, one transpacific, the other room-to-room. The second and fourth record solitary feelings: distress exceeding the center's claustrophobic rooms, misery incommunicable to anyone, inside or out. Amid the frenzied commotion, this author finds footholds in the title's precise date and the very act of inscribing this spontaneous "effusion" into wood – something to stay put when, inevitably, the poet moves on.

As Angel Island poetry makes its belated way into a multilingual canon, its local, improvised monumentality may become representative of an entire era. Partway through the detention center's operation, American poets found their interest in existing monuments beginning to wane. Instead they invented their own monuments, suited to the Great Depression, World War II, and the era's artistic and social ferment. Whether memorializing specific losses or epitomizing monumentality generally, these fictional monuments were designed both to reflect and to react against unprecedented times. That conflicted response shapes or even deforms the era's poems, manifesting formally in displays of excess or experimentation: multiple voices, contrasting sections, parodic poses, ironic personae.

No American poet invested more imagination into inventing monuments than Wallace Stevens at midcareer. Marble statues and metal sculptures recur throughout his work, but his faith in monumentality grated against a mocking skepticism, evident as early as "The Death of a Soldier" (1918): "Death is absolute and without memorial" (81). In the 1930s, Stevens wrote two topical sequences, utterly dissimilar in approach: "The Man with the Blue Guitar" (1937), which embraced the continual change of musical performance, and *Owl's Clover* (1936), a book-length sequence with a politicized monumentality at its core. For Michael North, the "basic attempt" of *Owl's Clover* is "to replace the failed American monument of rhetoric and bombast with one fabricated of modern materials" (219–20). But that "basic attempt" demands digressive length and a baroque, radial organization – 861 lines over five sections, all revolving around a shapeshifting statue, Stevens's metonym for public art. Each section views that statue from the vantage of a different onlooker or opponent: an Old Woman who represents Depression-era realities, the uncongenial Marxist critic Mr. Burnshaw, culturally remote audiences in Africa, and "sprawlers on the grass" who impose themselves on the statue, "seeing / And feeling the world in which they live" (585). The final section bids "farewell, farewell" to the statue, seen to scale "In hum-drum space," increasingly invisible as night falls (591). For a poet who resolves that "It is only enough / To live incessantly in change" (573), monuments can appear static, unresponsive, calling constantly for replacement. Does that make *Owl's Clover* a "failure," in North's summary of prevailing views

(207)? If so, Stevens didn't disagree, choosing to republish a shorter, safer version a year after its standalone publication. But reread today, *Owl's Clover* seems decades ahead of its time. No modernist poem anticipated more core elements of twenty-first-century poetry on monuments: a rejection of monolithic meanings, a pluralist cast and structure, and an acceptance of the fateful obsolescence of all public artworks, whatever their former significance.

A second, satirical streak of fictional monuments stems from the war-time experiences of W. H. Auden. After immigrating to New York in 1939, he published "In Time of War," a sonnet sequence derived from travels in China during the Sino-Japanese War. "Here war is simple like a monument," opens one sonnet; war, viewed from a civilian's remove, has a statue's smoothness and symbolic unity. Yet we can name precisely where war is otherwise: "maps can really point to places / Where life is evil now: / Nanking; Dachau" (*English* 257). Acclaimed for his sober, authoritative poems at World War II's onset, Auden also inaugurated a mutinous sense of irony, taking the state's ceremoniousness and official lingo as his chief targets. In *Another Time* (1940), his first collection after his transatlantic move, Auden cordoned off a section of "Lighter Poems" – a relative designation. The briefest, "Epitaph on a Tyrant," memorializes a dictator whose cruelties resemble pat, perfect "poetry," something "easy to under-stand." Unlike Auden's multivalent art, this tyrant's poetry insists on coercively uniform meanings: "When he laughed, respectable senators burst with laughter, / And when he cried the little children died in the streets" (82). Next comes "The Unknown Citizen," a mock-memorial dedicated "TO JS/07/M/378," an alphanumeric anonymity, and prefaced with the self-congratulatory credit "THIS MARBLE MONUMENT IS ERECTED BY THE STATE" (83). Intoned in lines of dragging doggerel, "The Unknown Citizen" suggests that monumentality is the very inverse of lyricality; as administrative units from "the Bureau of Statistics" to "our Eugenist" translate this citizen's behavior into quantifiable terms, his interiority remains entirely "unknown": "Was he free? Was he happy? The question is absurd: / Had anything been wrong, we should certainly have heard" (83, 84). Auden sets one sardonic precedent for the era's many antimonumental elegies for American soldiers, including Randall Jarrell's "The Death of the Ball Turret Gunner" (1945). "From my mother's sleep I fell into the State," the fallen airman recalls, with an Audenesque fusion of briskness and brusqueness. His funeral is a mechanical chore; his monument, a ghastly runoff: "When I died they washed me out of the turret with a hose" (144).

One last group of midcentury poets erected fictional monuments purely to pull them apart and toy with the pieces. Their meta-monumental poetry poses teasing questions: Which authorities determine monumentality? Does monumentality stand in for fuzzier virtues and vices – masculine authority, unquestioned narratives, a narrowly representational aesthetics? Elizabeth Bishop's "The Monument" (1939) begins with an even simpler question: "Now can you see the monument? It is of wood / built somewhat like a box." This question is not only a spoof of Bishop's own fine-tuned observations; as Guy Rotella explains, the question concerns "the propriety of placing this particular object within the aesthetic category 'monument'" (27). Bishop flaunts her familiarity with monumental history – and the earliest meaning of *monument*, "[a] tomb, a sepulchre" – when she imagines that her boxy assemblage shelters the remains of some "artist-prince." But her final lines strike on a novel understanding of monuments as generative edifices, demanding our vigilant attention: "It is the beginning of a painting, / a piece of sculpture, or poem, or monument, / and all of wood. Watch it closely" (27). A blunter blow against monumentality arrives in "The Colossus" (1959), the title poem of Sylvia Plath's début collection. The title's Grecian grandeur is a feint – before the first stanza begins, a wrecking ball swings in, breaking the colossus irreparably: "I shall never get you put together entirely, / Pieced, glued, and properly jointed" (129). Some private association between mythic monumentality and clomping patriarchy endures in the virtuoso name-calling of "Daddy" (1962), in which Plath addresses her "Marble-heavy" father as a "Ghastly statue with one gray toe / Big as a Frisco seal." With feet ashore on the Pacific, his "head in the freakish Atlantic," the psychological edifice of Plath's father spans a continental length: a memorably outrageous figure for confessional poetry's mapping of the personal onto the universal (222).

In the postwar era – the era of high modernism's eclipse, the ascension of New Critical pedagogy, and poetry's institutionalization in writing programs and fellowships – monumentality emerged as one virtue for the well-wrought, well-schooled poem. Stanley Kunitz, John Berryman, and May Swenson found monuments across North America, while others, including W. S. Merwin, James Wright, and Gary Snyder, etched monumentality into their free-verse lines, taking inspiration from engravings and translated literature with centuries of proven staying power. The most frequent practice, particularly for white, professionalized poets, was to seek monuments abroad. In Robert von Hallberg's estimation, "three conventional poetic subjects dominated" the 1950s: animals, fine arts, and travel

(62). "Although poets traveled widely," across South America, Asia, and especially Europe, "the poems tend to gather, like pigeons and hawkers, around the sights and monuments ... By fountain, statue, palazzo and piazza, the poets were demonstrating their ability to write intelligently, tastefully about the outward signs of the cultural heritage America was taking over after the war" (71–72). What strikes von Hallberg as a unified wing of cultural imperialism looks more various, and less nefarious, once we concentrate on individual poets. Take the early Richard Wilbur, who viewed Roman monuments as testaments to secular humanism, unobtrusive artifice, and his buoyant yet self-skeptical liberalism. His characteristically patient "For the New Railway Station in Rome" (1956) ends not with assertions but with rhetorical questions: "What is our praise or pride / But to imagine excellence, and try to make it? / What does it say over the door of Heaven / But *homo fecit?*" – that is, *man made it* (351). For Wilbur's fellow formalist James Merrill, monuments inspired culture-crossing identifications and cheeky metaphysical conceits. In "Losing the Marbles" (1986), he sees something of himself in the Parthenon's Elgin Marbles, which he analogizes with the spherical marbles of his childhood and his failing adult memory: "Another / Marble gone" (572).

The tourist poem was squarely mainstream, in every sense relevant to midcentury America: immensely popular, aligned with establishment poets, and glaringly white. Monumentality mattered less for the counter-cultural poets of Donald Allen's *The New American Poetry 1945–1960* (1960), who prized antithetical virtues – process, impulse, chance, dynamism. "How I hate subject matter!" rails Frank O'Hara in one poem in Allen's anthology; his hate extends to "all things that don't change, / photographs, / monuments" (275). Monuments were similarly inessential for the poetry of second-wave feminism, the Black Arts Movement, and the Chicano and Asian American literary movements. Relative to those movements' revolutionary charges, conventional monuments were politically conservative or else literal acts of conservation, freezing social imbalances in place. The era's divergent understandings of monumentality jostle in Gwendolyn Brooks's "Two Dedications," from *In the Mecca* (1968), whose dedication bridges generations and traditions: on one side, the late Langston Hughes; on the other, Brooks's juniors James Baldwin, Amiri Baraka, and Mike Alexandroff. Comprising two occasional poems read twelve days apart – "The Chicago Picasso," for Picasso's untitled steel sculpture commissioned for Daley Plaza, and "The Wall," on the *Wall of Respect* (1967–71), a community mural portraying legendary Black figures in Brooks's neighborhood of Bronzeville – "Two Dedications" flanks aesthetic quandaries from opposite angles. The former poem takes modernist monumentality as an invitation to philosophize on "man," abstractly: "Does man love Art?" (442). The latter looks up from the page and sees Bronzeville's many-colored audience: "hundreds of faces, red-brown, brown, black, ivory, / yield me hot trust, their yea and their Announcement / that they are ready to rile the high-flung ground" (445).

Two dominant themes of postwar political poetry – the problem of the color line and the United States' emergence as a global power – converge in two titanic poems on war memorials. Robert Lowell's "For the Union Dead" (1960), which gave his 1964 collection its title, and Yusef Komunyakaa's "Facing It" (1987), the closing poem of his Vietnam War collection *Dien Cai Dau* (1988), rank among postwar America's most anthologized poems. Among poems on monuments, their only rivals are one another.

The poem famously titled "For the Union Dead" was originally titled "Colonel Shaw and the Massachusetts' 54th." How fitting for a poem whose subterranean subject – the tectonic plate shifting beneath its surface-level topics – is history understood as a never-finished process of writing, reading, and rewriting. The poem, Dan Chiasson explains, inhabits "a world of crossings out and writings over, as many stages of historical time vie for the nearest and outermost plane of representation" (41). One way to rewrite history is to monumentalize it, giving it physical, permanent form. Lowell's central example is Augustus Saint-Gaudens's bronze bas-relief on the Boston Common, which commemorates the 54th Massachusetts Infantry Regiment, the North's first Black regiment in the Civil War, and their volunteer colonel, the white abolitionist Robert Gould Shaw. Saint-Gaudens depicts the regiment marching through Boston with Shaw on horseback, only two months before a doomed charge on Fort Wagner, South Carolina, led to Shaw's death and casualties for nearly half the regiment. Another way to rewrite is to correct others' writing, which Lowell does twice before the poem proper begins. With his title, he wrests away the somber dignity of Tate's "Ode to the Confederate Dead" and recommits it to the Union dead, tragically lost for noble causes. And for his epigraph, he revises the Latin inscription on Saint-Gaudens's monument, changing its verb from singular to plural: *"Relinquunt Omnia Servare Rem Publicam,"* "They leave behind everything to serve the Republic" (376). With a two-letter revision, Lowell prizes open the memorial's intended scope. Like Saint-Gaudens, he esteems Shaw as a singularly Great Man, but he also recognizes the sacrifice that "they," that plural collective, undertook to no acclaim.

Poems, too, can rewrite history, working on their own time, not a textbook's or a political program's. With only a stanza break or semicolon as warning, "For the Union Dead" vaults days and decades, forward and backward. New England from the Puritans to the congested infrastructure of modern Boston, three wars over three centuries (Revolutionary, Civil, World War II), nuclear catastrophe, school desegregation, advertising's ubiquity, television's indispensability, the space race, souped-up conspicuous consumption – extracted from the poem, these topics read like an American history syllabus, but "For the Union Dead" compresses them into seventeen quatrains, all of them elliptically orbiting Saint-Gaudens's monument. In the poem's three innermost quatrains, Lowell modulates from past-tense historiography to an ekphrasis of the bas-relief. Now over sixty years old, the monument still

> sticks like a fishbone
> in the city's throat.
> Its Colonel is as lean
> as a compass-needle.
>
> He has an angry wrenlike vigilance,
> a greyhound's gentle tautness;
> he seems to wince at pleasure,
> and suffocate for privacy.
>
> He is out of bounds now. He rejoices in man's lovely,
> peculiar power to choose life and die –
> when he leads his black soldiers to death,
> he cannot bend his back. (377)

No longer surfacing as a charismatic "I," Lowell stays submerged, an editorializing eye. His observations are precise, his similes outlandishly right, but the ethical lessons he draws remain uncertain. Is that Colonel still magnetized, a moral compass-needle for our directionless present? (What kind of compass needle stands upright, perpendicular to our terrestrial plane, pointing up to heaven, or down to the grave?) Can we model ourselves after a hero who embodies the contradictory extremes of animal intensity ("wrenlike," "a greyhound's gentle tautness") and superhuman responses to stimuli – wincing at pleasure, suffocating for privacy he spurned by volunteering to fight? With him "out of bounds," should we, the living, aspire to obstruct the throats of bureaucracy and hypocrisy, rejoicing to die for our causes? Or is that aspiration an illusion cast by Saint-Gaudens's bas-relief and the unattainable stance of a figure who "cannot bend his back," frozen in bronze and art's timeless present tense?

For later readers, these same quatrains may elicit questions of a different tilt: Why did Lowell follow Saint-Gaudens in devoting more attention to Shaw than to the Black Union dead behind him? After all, didn't "they leave behind everything to serve the Republic"? These are not questions Lowell's contemporaries posed, and they may arise from a later, less triumphant stage in the history of American memorialization, by which time Lowell's poem and its dashed idealism had become monuments themselves, ready to be written over. Saint-Gaudens's monument would in fact be overwritten in 1982, when the names of sixty-two soldiers of the 54th were carved into its granite. The same year saw the dedication of another monumental act of naming: the Vietnam Veterans Memorial in Washington, DC. That memorial is central to Komunyakaa's "Facing It," easily the most anthologized American poem about the Vietnam War, even as it ponders the values (aesthetic, psychological, political) of memorial art generally. It does none of this straightforwardly, communicating instead via superimposed images and deep-seated ambiguities, starting with its title: facing *what*? The war in Vietnam, where Komunyakaa served in 1969–70, earning a Bronze Star for his work as a journalist and newspaper editor? Or the memorial itself, designed by the Chinese American architect Maya Lin – an oblique angle of two black granite walls, half-sunken into the National Mall? Stark, geometric, antirepresentational, the memorial initially drew public controversy, but critics admired its unadorned presentation of names and its interweaving of architecture and landscape. "Everything about it is part of a text," judged Arthur C. Danto (153).

Facing that text means facing oneself, one's imperfect reflection, one's readerly imposition: "My black face fades, / hiding inside the black granite." To then "go down the 58,022 names" (the number has since grown) is to face what was lost in war, including how much of oneself; Komunyakaa reads "half-expecting to find / my own in letters like smoke." To recognize a name and feel its engraving can be to imaginatively "touch" the unforgettable person it denotes – then stung anew by trauma: "I touch the name Andrew Johnson; / I see the booby trap's white flash." More concisely than any critical prose, "Facing It" captures the optical illusion unique to Lin's memorial, its constant confusion of figure and ground. One moment, the eye skims across the granite's glassy surface; the next, it fixes onto an inscription: "Names shimmer on a woman's blouse / but when she walks away / the names stay on the wall." For veterans unable to walk away, the memorial cannot promise healing, or even a reprieve from the social inequities of civilian life: "A white vet's image floats / closer to me, then his pale eyes / look through mine. I'm a window." The encounter happens so fast that Komunyakaa barely has time to process it. Was this "white vet" seeing himself in a fellow veteran, or treating this Black stranger as a transparent nobody, a "window"? When Komunyakaa notices the vet has "lost his right arm / inside the stone," is *he* recognizing a fellow vet and his disabilities – or are the memorial's reflective "stone" and angular geometry playing tricks on him again (63)? His succession of uncertainties and constant readjustments is something like the experience of reading "Facing It," as Komunyakaa alternately fuzzes and focuses our attention with his lines' unpredictable syncopations and whiplashing enjambments.

There is no shortage of ways to measure the vast gulf between "For the Union Dead" and "Facing It," but the correspondences between them are extraordinary. Both poems understand the wars they commemorate within the long history of American conflict: Lowell sees "no statues for the last war," World War II, only an opportunistic advertisement depicting "Hiroshima boiling // over a Mosler safe"; Andrew Johnson, the name Komunyakaa lingers on, belongs to a veteran but also the white-supremacist president who succeeded Abraham Lincoln after the Civil War. Both poems assiduously track their poets' locations – literally, and in Adrienne Rich's extended sense of location as identity, at the pinpointable intersection of nationality, gender, sexuality, race, class, and ability. After mingling personal memory and public memorializing, both poems conclude with images of life going on, whether obliviously, shamefully, or consolingly. In Lowell's Boston, "giant finned cars nose forward like fish; / a savage servility / slides by on grease" – no courageous marching here, not with everyone complacently crammed into their cars. And Komunyakaa, tricked by the memorial's "black mirror," thinks he glimpses a woman "trying to erase names," until his last line's soothing self-correction: "No, she's brushing a boy's hair" (63). Neither poem supplies a prophecy or political program. Instead, they offer a tributary monumentality in their sculpted free-verse forms: Lowell in his polished quatrains, Komunyakaa in his poem's unbroken column, which mirrors the Vietnam Veterans Memorial's "black granite" and enumerated names in its continuous black ink.

By placing their faith, however counterbalanced by doubt and dissent, in national memorials, Lowell and Komunyakaa wrote poetry that is already, strangely, historical. By 1960, Lowell saw the end coming: "We've emerged from the monumental age," he remarked before one reading of "For the Union Dead" (qtd. in Rudman 132). Surely some new age was underway by 1978, when the bicentennial's spike in patriotic poetry crashed, and Mark

Strand published his bewitching book-length poem *The Monument*, with its sped-up cartoon of the poetry world splintering:

> They are back, the angry poets. But look! They have come with hammers and little buckets, and they are knocking off pieces of The Monument to study and use in the making of their own small tombs. (248)

For poetry of the hammer, the knock-off, and the handcrafted tomb, the aptest term is rarely "monumental." One alternative is *countermonumental*, a term Joshua S. Jacobs adheres to Adrienne Rich's late sequence "An Atlas of the Difficult World" (1990–91). The designation is variously apt: Rich's atlas runs counter to conventional monumentality by surveying unheralded landscapes (say, the foggy Northern California that Rich made her late-in-life home), shifting monumentality's center of gravity away from a romanticized Northeast ("no icon lifts a lamp here"), and monumentalizing the "unmonumented," lives written off by reigning social narratives ("prowling Angel Island muffling Alcatraz / poems in Cantonese inscribed on fog") (717, 718). "Countermonument" brings to mind so-called countercelebrations, such as Indigenous Peoples' Day (observed instead of Columbus Day) and Unthanksgiving Day; it suggests the companion term "countermemorial," commemoration in an unconventional or parodic key. Between them, those three terms cover countless late-twentieth-century long poems, including Bernadette Mayer's *Midwinter Day* (1982), Frank Bidart's "Hours of the Night" (1990–present), John Ashbery's *Flow Chart* (1991), and A. R. Ammons's *Garbage* (1993).

Countermonumental poetry values monuments, but it elevates the neglected over the canonical, the local over the central. What about poetry opposed to monumentality altogether? A negatory, anarchic poetry whose hostility to monuments takes shape as fantasies of vandalism, graffiti, and demolition? We could call that poetry not counter- but *antimonumental*. While Jacobs introduces that term for Muriel Rukeyser's feminist manifesto "The Poem as Mask" (1968) – "No more masks! No more mythologies!" (748) – the antimonumental has proven equally indispensable for poets of color, and especially for generations of Black poets. Within that robust history, even poets who seldom agree find common ground in the pursuit of monuments sustained in action and performance rather than set down in stone. When Robert Hayden, in "Frederick Douglass" (1947), remembers that great man "not with statues' rhetoric" but "with the lives grown out of his life" (62), he anticipates a similar desire for a living, mutable legacy in "Black Art" (1965), by his eventual opponent Amiri Baraka: "We want live / Words of the hip world live flesh & / Coursing blood" (149). Twenty-first-century Black poets, in ripostes to canonical

white poets, make their antimonumental thrust explicit. Natasha
Trethewey's *Native Guard* (2006) and Kevin Young's *For the Confederate
Dead* (2007) rededicate the Southern ground of Tate's "Ode to the
Confederate Dead"; Claudia Rankine's *Citizen: An American Lyric*
(2014) identifies monumentality with the supersized "I" of Robert
Lowell, and she lets him know: "Listen, you, I was creating a life study
of a monumental first person, a Brahmin first person" (73). If antimonu-
mentality has a technique, it's erasure, which rebuts official narratives
while recognizing the truths they tell despite themselves. Erasure,
paradoxically, clarifies: for Tracy K. Smith, Reginald Dwayne Betts, and
Nicole Sealey, it makes selective sense out of the Declaration of
Independence, court filings, and the Department of Justice's "Ferguson
report," respectively.

  What if there is no monument to speak of, nothing to celebrate or
protest? What if a poet has nothing but silence and lacunae to work with?
To countermonumental and antimonumental poetry, we could add a third
deviation: *documentary* poetry. Often cast as a strictly twenty-first-century
phenomenon, the term suits centuries of monumentalizing work; indeed,
one early definition of "monument" is "[a] written document or record."
Susan Briante's *Defacing the Monument* (2020) finds examples of documentary poetics from Rukeyser's "The Book of the Dead" (1938) to
Briante's own work with the University of Arizona's Southwest Field
Studies in Writing Program, which sends creative-writing students to
collaborate with activists at the US-Mexico border. Despite her engagement, Briante sees nothing inherently ethical or politically resistant in
documentary poetry, which risks replicating official narratives and "the
elisions of the state." Hence the need, at times, for defacement: "As poets
and documentarians, we can extend the document or deface it to discern
its limits and to situate it against those other sources that broaden its
narrative, reveal its omissions, lay bare its brutality" (34). It's no coinci-
dence that documentary work is particularly freighted for poets who write
about undocumented migrants, trailing losses in linguistic and geographic
translation. In *Guillotine* (2020) – published the same week as *Defacing the
Monument* – Eduardo C. Corral assembles a twenty-five-page sequence,
"Testaments Scratched into a Water Station Barrel," from markings left by
Mexican and Central American migrants at life-sustaining water stations in
the Arizona desert. Entire journeys leave, as evidence, little more than
prayers, grim wisecracks, and unexplained tally marks. "I notch letters into
mesquite," one anonymous voice resolves, in a bilingual "carta abierta"
(open letter) with no readers in sight (35).

"We erect monuments so that we shall always remember, and build memorials so that we shall never forget": Arthur C. Danto's distinction remains useful today, even as commonplace conceptions of monuments and memorials have utterly transformed since Lin's memorial, let alone Lazarus's colossus (152). To march in protest, rename a landmark, reclaim a narrative, question a monument, even tear it down: these are all contemporary modes of remembering and never forgetting, and today's poets know it well. Walking through his hometown of New Orleans, the poet and journalist Clint Smith recalls a line by the historian Walter Johnson: "The whole city is a memorial to slavery" (6). *How the Word Is Passed* (2021), Smith's history of American slavery told through visits to nine historical sites, concludes by recognizing his own family as a living monument: "the past not only is housed in museums, memorials, monuments, and cemeteries but lives in our lineage" (270). Caroline Randall Williams, another Black Southern poet echoing calls for the removal of Confederate monuments, sees blatant evidence against the supposed romance of the Lost Cause in her own "rape-colored skin": "If there are those who want to remember the legacy of the Confederacy, if they want monuments, well, then, my body is a monument. My skin is a monument." Even an instant anthology piece such as Layli Long Soldier's "38" (2015) – named for the thirty-eight Dakota men hanged under orders by Abraham Lincoln, days before the Emancipation Proclamation – asks readers to reconceptualize, sentence by sentence, what a contemporary monument can be. Reflecting on the Dakota 38 + 2 Memorial Ride, an arduous 325-mile journey from South Dakota reservations to stolen lands in Minnesota, Long Soldier speaks equal truths about her own poem: "Often, memorials come in the forms of plaques, statues, or gravestones. // The memorial for the Dakota 38 is not an object inscribed with words, but an *act*" (52). We are many miles from the Statue of Liberty and even further from "The New Colossus," whose best-known phrases ring hollow in Long Soldier's setting (whose "ancient lands"? which "golden door"?). But the ride she describes is an "*act*" as monumental as any copper statue, community mural, or marble wall. So is a poetic act like "38": a chance, for a few renewable minutes of reading or listening, to pause, commemorate, breathe free.

WORKS CITED

Academy of American Poets. *The Official Poem of the New York World's Fair, 1939, and Other Prize Winning Poems.* Bowne & Co., 1939.

Auden, W. H. *Another Time.* Random House, 1940.

The English Auden: Poems, Essays and Dramatic Writings, 1927–1939. Edited by Edward Mendelson, Random House, 1977.

Baraka, Amiri. *S O S: Poems 1961–2013.* Expanded ed. Grove Press, 2015.

Bishop, Elizabeth. *Poems.* Farrar, Straus and Giroux, 2011.

Briante, Susan. *Defacing the Monument.* Noemi Press, 2020.

Brooks, Gwendolyn. *Blacks.* Third World Press, 1987.

Cavitch, Max. "Emma Lazarus and the Golem of Liberty." *American Literary History,* vol. 18, no. 1, Spring 2006, pp. 1–28.

Chiasson, Dan. *One Kind of Everything: Poem and Person in Contemporary America.* University of Chicago Press, 2007.

Corral, Eduardo C. *Guillotine.* Graywolf Press, 2020.

Crane, Hart. *Complete Poems and Selected Letters.* Edited by Langdon Hammer. Library of America, 2006.

Danto, Arthur C. "The Vietnam Veterans Memorial." *The Nation,* August 13, 1985, pp. 152–55.

Eliot, T. S. *The Sacred Wood: Essays on Poetry and Criticism.* Methuen, 1920.

The Waste Land. Boni and Liveright, 1922.

Hayden, Robert. *Collected Poems.* Rev. ed., edited by Frederick Glaysher. Liveright, 1996.

Hellman, Geoffrey T. "Eighty-Six-Storied Pomp." *New Yorker,* May 12, 1956, pp. 95–98.

Hughes, Langston. *The Collected Poems of Langston Hughes.* Edited by Arnold Rampersad, associate editor David Roessel. Vintage, 1995.

Jacobs, Joshua S. "'An Atlas of the Difficult World': Adrienne Rich's Countermonument." *Contemporary Literature,* vol. 42, no. 4, Winter 2001, pp. 727–49.

Jarrell, Randall. *The Complete Poems.* Farrar, Straus and Giroux, 1969.

Kennedy, John F. *A Nation of Immigrants.* Anti-Defamation League of B'nai B'rith, 1958.

Komunyakaa, Yusef. *Dien Cai Dau.* Wesleyan University Press, 1988.

Lai, Him Mark, Genny Lim, and Judy Yung, eds. *Island: Poetry and History of Chinese Immigrants on Angel Island, 1910–1940.* 2nd ed. University of Washington Press, 2014.

Lazarus, Emma. *Selected Poems.* Edited by John Hollander. Library of America, 2005.

Long Soldier, Layli. *WHEREAS.* Graywolf Press, 2017.

Lowell, Robert. *Collected Poems.* Edited by Frank Bidart and David Gewanter with DeSales Harrison. Farrar, Straus and Giroux, 2003.

Merrill, James. *Collected Poems.* Edited by J. D. McClatchy and Stephen Yenser. Knopf, 2004.

"Monument, N." In *Oxford English Dictionary,* September 2022, www.oed.com/view/Entry/121852.

North, Michael. *The Final Sculpture: Public Monuments and Modern Poetry.* Cornell University Press, 1985.

O'Hara, Frank. *The Collected Poems of Frank O'Hara.* Knopf, 1971.

Parra, Nicanor. "USA." Translated by Patricio Lerzundi and Lynne Van Voorhis. In *Antipoems: New and Selected*, edited by David Unger. New Directions, 1985, pp. 114–15.

Plath, Sylvia. *The Collected Poems*. Edited by Ted Hughes. Harper Perennial, 2008.

Rainey, Lawrence S. *Ezra Pound and the Monument of Culture: Text, History, and the Malatesta Cantos*. University of Chicago Press, 1991.

Ramazani, Jahan. *Poetry and Its Others: News, Prayer, Song, and the Dialogue of Genres*. University of Chicago Press, 2013.

Rankine, Claudia. *Citizen: An American Lyric*. Graywolf Press, 2014.

Rich, Adrienne. *Collected Poems: 1950–2012*. W. W. Norton, 2016.

Rotella, Guy. *Castings: Monuments and Monumentality in Poems by Elizabeth Bishop, Robert Lowell, James Merrill, Derek Walcott, and Seamus Heaney*. Vanderbilt University Press, 2004.

Rudman, Mark. *Robert Lowell: An Introduction to the Poetry*. Columbia University Press, 1983.

Schor, Esther. "What the Trump Administration Gets Wrong about the Statue of Liberty." *New York Times*, August 14, 2019, www.nytimes.com/2019/08/14/opinion/ken-cuccinelli-emma-lazarus.html.

Smith, Clint. *How the Word Is Passed: A Reckoning with the History of Slavery across America*. Little, Brown, 2021.

Stevens, Wallace. *Collected Poetry and Prose*. Edited by Frank Kermode and Joan Richardson. Library of America, 1997.

Strand, Mark. *Collected Poems*. Knopf, 2014.

Tate, Allen. *Collected Poems, 1919–1976*. Farrar, Straus and Giroux, 2007.
Reactionary Essays on Poetry and Ideas. Charles Scribner's Sons, 1936.

von Hallberg, Robert. *American Poetry and Culture, 1945–1980*. Harvard University Press, 1985.

"Whose Heritage? Public Symbols of the Confederacy." Southern Poverty Law Center, February 1, 2019, www.splcenter.org/20190201/whose-heritage-public-symbols-confederacy.

Wilbur, Richard. *Collected Poems 1943–2004*. Harcourt, 2004.

Williams, Caroline Randall. "My Body Is a Confederate Monument." *New York Times*, June 26, 2020, www.nytimes.com/2020/06/26/opinion/confederate-monuments-racism.html.

York, Jake Adam. *The Architecture of Address: The Monument and Public Speech in American Poetry*. Routledge, 2005.

CHAPTER 2

Poetry and Propaganda

Florian Gargaillo

Throughout the twentieth century, American poets engaged in a spirited debate about their art's relation to propaganda. Some rejected outright the notion that poetry should advocate for a political cause. To instrumentalize poetry, in this view, would be to degrade its very nature. William Carlos Williams, in a statement intended for the first issue of *Blast: A Magazine of Proletarian Fiction* in 1933, contended that "a dilemma has been broached when the artist has been conscripted and forced to subordinate his training and skill to party necessity for a purpose" (*On Art and Artists* 75). Still, others argued that poets should have freedom to promote a cause. Langston Hughes made this case in the *Chicago Defender* in 1945: "Art in its essence is a path to truth. Propaganda is a path toward more to eat. That the two may be inextricably mixed is not to be denied. That they may often be one and the same is certainly true" (quoted in Rampersad 121). This disagreement can be read as part of a much longer history of poets debating the role of politics in their art and whether poetry should ever be used as propaganda.

While poets of the twentieth century took strong positions on the issue in their prose, they displayed more complex attitudes in their verse, sometimes even going against the principles they laid out elsewhere. For instance, the modernists who argued most adamantly for the separation of poetry and politics used tools like the manifesto to defend and advertise their approach – even though the manifesto, as a public declaration that aims to persuade, is itself a form of propaganda. By the same token, politically minded poets seemed wary of actually using their art as an instrument for mass persuasion and instead found ways to engage in politics without the rhetorical mechanisms of propaganda. The methods they developed were highly diverse. Some composed poems that were oratorical in style but did not advocate for a discernible cause, thus making the poems adaptable to different political contexts. Others described how public events impacted their own individual lives and their communities;

in doing so, they resisted speaking authoritatively for and to a mass audience. Others still viewed their poems as opportunities to foster attention and empathy among their readers without advancing a set program, the hope being that readers with such capacities could then engage more responsibly in the political realm beyond the poem. These attitudes can all be traced back to a shared discomfort with using their poems in the service of a narrow political goal. If propaganda marshals all its rhetoric toward a cause beyond the individual propagandist, poetry affords a more personal, immediate, and nuanced reflection on the political issues that animate the writer. Indeed, propaganda enabled poets to understand more fully how the function of political poetry differs from that of propaganda and to shape their varied approaches accordingly. This essay traces the history of poetry's complex response to propaganda across the twentieth century.

American modernist poetry, as it took shape in the 1910s, initially seemed to reject engaging with politics, let alone embracing the tools of propaganda. Imagism represents one notable example of this phenomenon and its paradoxes. As a discernible movement, Imagism was short-lived. Its program was established in 1912, during a meeting between Ezra Pound, Hilda Doolittle, F. S. Flint, and Richard Aldington. The group had already disbanded by 1917 when Amy Lowell released the anthology *Some Imagist Poets*. Yet the ideas formulated by Imagism continued to exert influence beyond the group's dissolution, as in William Carlos Williams' edict in *Paterson* (1950) that there can be "no ideas but in things" (6). Imagists did not wish poetry to serve as an instrument for sociopolitical causes. Verse, to their mind, should be neither discursive nor persuasive. Instead, the goal of a poem was to *present* a chosen object as fully and accurately as possible.

In the essay "A Retrospect" (1918), Ezra Pound reflected on the rules for Imagism that he, H.D., and Aldington had drawn up. The first was the "direct treatment of the 'thing,' whether subjective or objective" (Pound 3). The word "direct" implies that any object can be isolated from its context and its fundamental properties dissected beyond the sociopolitical uses and biases superimposed on them. The role of the writer, in Pound's formulation, is to represent those fundamental qualities and resist adopting an approach – be it analytical, critical, polemical – that would create a filter between poet and thing, and distort the object. Likewise, Amy Lowell's preface to *Some Imagist Poets* expressed a desire to isolate poetry from the world of politics. Granted, she did not insist quite so readily on the impersonality of the ideal writer. For instance, she took it as a given that good verse would convey "the individuality of a poet." But she also stated that poets should display "absolute freedom in the choice of subject" – the implication being that they should not subordinate their verse to a cause beyond themselves. Her belief that "poetry should . . . not deal in vague generalities, however magnificent and sonorous" stemmed from a deep skepticism toward rhetoric, which extended to political language. Like Pound, she deemed rhetoric empty, bombastic, and manipulative. Poetry should deal instead with "particulars," which she felt were concrete and neutral (Lowell vi–vii).

It is ironic, then, considering Imagism's resistance to propaganda, that its statements usually took the form of manifestos. Both Pound and Lowell offer a list of criteria that authors must follow for their work to qualify. Scholars have picked up on this underlying connection and described the documents in terms of propaganda. Noel Stock, in a 1970 biography of Ezra Pound, writes that the poet "threw himself . . . into propaganda on behalf of Imagism" (121). Hugh Kenner refers to "Imagist propaganda" in *The Pound Era* (191) and Suzanne Juhasz alludes to "that literary movement, or moment, called Imagism, with its accompanying pronouncements, programs, and propaganda" (18). Nor were the Imagists the only modernist group using propaganda tools to defend their principles, advocate for their development, and lay out a set of rules, particularly across the Atlantic in Europe. Modernism is still often described as the era of art manifestos, with declarations issued by groups like Futurists, Surrealists, and Vorticists, which Pound became closely involved in. Propaganda supplied a model for the public work of modernism, even in cases like Imagism, where the goal was precisely to avoid using poetry as a propagandist instrument.

Even as the most prominent modernist groups, like the Imagists, turned away from politics, other writers not affiliated with any particular group continued to write political poetry on the social and economic issues of the era. Yet their relation to propaganda was by no means less complicated. Carl Sandburg stands as a notable example of this, particularly for his 1916 collection *Chicago Poems*. Sandburg was a socialist who did see poetry as part of a broader effort in advancing social equality and justice, but he resisted adopting the methods of political propaganda. It is useful to compare his poetry to Imagism because the two have so often been set in contrast. Amy Lowell, in *Tendencies in Modern American Poetry* (1917), accused Sandburg of falling into a common trap: "Propaganda is the pitfall of poets. So excellently endowed a poet as Mr. Sandburg should beware" (221). To her mind, real poetry is universal and timeless. Political poetry forsakes these qualities by tying itself to historical particulars that will have no resonance to future generations of readers. "Art, nature, humanity, are eternal. But the minimum wage will probably matter as little to the twenty-second century as it did to the thirteenth, although for different reasons" (Lowell 222). As Mark Van Wienen has shown, Lowell was hardly alone in accusing Sandburg of succumbing to propaganda in his poems.[1]

Aware of these criticisms, Sandburg argued that it was the writer's responsibility to address the social issues of their time. Any wholesale rejection of propaganda itself constitutes a political stance, specifically a conservative effort to stem change. Using the poet Stephen Vincent Benét as a model, Sandburg wrote that Benét "knew the distinction between pure art and propaganda in the written or spoken word," and yet at the same time,

> He saw that a writer's silence on living issues can itself constitute a propaganda of conduct leading toward the deterioration or death of freedom. He wrote often hoping that men would act because of his words. He could have been Olympian, whimsical, seeking to be timeless amid bells of doom not to be put off. ("Notes for a Preface" xxvi)

Still, the indirectness of Sandburg's argument is telling. He describes his principles through another author and calls the avoidance of politics "a propaganda" in and of itself, yet he never states directly that poetry ought to function as propaganda and borrow its rhetorical techniques. Indeed, the label applies uneasily to even the most political pieces in *Chicago Poems*. Consider "Child of the Romans."

> "The dago shovelman sits by the railroad track
> Eating a noon meal of bread and bologna.
>   A train whirls by, and men and women at tables
>   Alive with red roses and yellow jonquils,
>   Eat steaks running with brown gravy,
>   Strawberries and cream, eclaires and coffee.
> The dago shovelman finishes the dry bread and bologna,
> Washes it down with a dipper from the water-boy,
> And goes back to the second half of a ten-hour day's work
> Keeping the road-bed so the roses and jonquils
> Shake hardly at all in the cut glass vases
> Standing slender on the tables in the dining cars."

The poem is built around contrasts between "the dago shovelman" and the first-class passengers on the train: "the dry bread and bologna" versus the abundance of "steaks running with brown gravy, / strawberries and crema,

---

[1] See Mark Van Wienen, "Taming the Socialist: Carl Sandburg's Chicago Poems and Its Critics," *American Literature*, vol. 63, no. 1 (March 1991), pp. 94–96.

eclairs and coffee," the unglamorous "road-bed" versus the bouquet of "red roses and yellow jonquils," leisure versus work, movement versus immobility. Sandburg reinforces the distance between the two worlds visually through indentation, only to underline what connects them in the last three lines. The material comfort of the train passengers is said to depend on the work of the shovelman, who creates and sustains the conditions for the travelers' smooth passage. The poet's goal is evidently to provoke sympathy for the worker, as well as righteous anger on his behalf. Sandburg knows that his readers are more likely to be the passengers than the shovelman. Yet it is notable that he refrains from offering a course of action. He describes, but does not issue commands. Nor does he imagine a response from the travelers that could serve as an implicit model. He does play on his reader's emotions, so that one concrete outcome may be a greater willingness to recognize the thankless labor that goes on invisibly in the background of their lives. But what form that realization will take in the field of political action, if it does at all, lies squarely outside the poet's consideration. Despite his defense of poetry mingling with propaganda, Sandburg was reluctant to use the full rhetorical tools of propaganda in his own verse.

That same difficult balance can be found in the poetry of the Harlem Renaissance. During the modernist period, no movement received more attacks for succumbing to propaganda. Yet these attacks simplified a complex relationship to political persuasion. Much of the poetry associated with the Harlem Renaissance can be deemed political in nature, to the extent that it critiques inequality and advocates for the acknowledgment of human dignity in the face of prejudice. Moreover, there are multiple defenses of propaganda in African American thought of this era. W. E. B. Du Bois, in "Criteria of Negro Art" (1926), contended that "all art is propaganda and ever must be, despite the wailing of the purists. I stand in utter shamelessness and say that whatever art I have for writing has been used always for propaganda for gaining the right of black folk to love and enjoy." The only risk, for Du Bois, is the imposition of one group's propaganda to the exclusion of others: "I do not care a damn for any art that is not used for propaganda. But I do care when propaganda is confined to one side while the other is stripped and silent" (259). Du Bois' argument, like many other defenses of this time, originates in the belief that propaganda is essential to the advancement of civil rights, and the fear that attacks on propaganda would be leveraged specifically to suppress African American political advocacy. Still, this does not mean that poets of the Harlem Renaissance aligned their work with propaganda in practice.

Claude McKay is a notable figure in this regard. On the one hand, he defended in prose the propagandist nature of his writing and of literature more broadly. In the essay "Soviet Russia and the Negro" (1924), he described his gradual realization that art does not suffer when it is motivated by a propaganda intent. Even though his early readings in Milton's poetry and prose had "impressed" on the young poet a false notion "that gilt-washed artificiality, *The Picture of Dorian Gray*, would outlive *Arms and the Man* and *John Bull's Other Island* ... inevitably as I grew older I had perforce to revise and change my mind about propaganda." The word "inevitably" does much to frame his later support of propaganda in art as a necessary development: what, in his illustration, all mature minds eventually conclude. Indeed, he later refers to "the childish age of the enjoyment of creative work for pleasurable curiosity." As McKay grew up, "a widening horizon revealed that some of the finest spirits of modern literature – Voltaire, Hugo, Heine, Swift, Shelley, Byron, Tolstoy, Ibsen – had carried the taint of propaganda" ("Soviet Russia and the Negro" 51). Yet four years later, when Du Bois published a negative review of his novel *Home to Harlem* (1928) for catering to white fantasies of "utter licentiousness" among African Americans, McKay wrote a pained letter to Du Bois describing his work negatively in terms of propaganda:

> Certainly I sympathize with and even pity you for not understanding my motive, because you have been forced from a normal career to enter a special field of racial propaganda and, honorable though that field may be, it has precluded you from contact with real life, for propaganda is fundamentally but a one-sided idea of life.... I should not be surprised when you mistake the art of life for nonsense and try to pass off propaganda as life in art! ("Letter to W. E. B. Du Bois" 150)

This time, McKay speaks not of expansion but of reduction. Propaganda offers "but a one-sided idea of life," which has "precluded [Du Bois] from contact with real life." Despite his public defense of propaganda as a serious form of engagement for writers, privately he felt some discomfort with the role of political persuasion in literature, fearing that propaganda might narrow an artist's range and divorce them from the vitality of everyday life.

That tension appears in his poetry. McKay was drawn to political rhetoric and persuasion in verse, yet he resisted the temptation to direct that rhetoric toward a specific cause. His most quoted poem, "If We Must Die" (1919), is an example of this paradox. Of the many sonnets that McKay wrote in the 1910s and 1920s, this most closely imitates the oratory of public speech, and by extension of political propaganda, with the use of the first-person plural, commands, exclamations, and sonorous apostrophes. The rhetoric is elevated, seeking to move and persuade a collective audience – or at least, that appears to be the intent. But it remains ambiguous what specific injustice the speaker decries: racism, colonialism, or poverty and economic inequality? The metaphors – of "hogs," "mad and hungry dogs," "the murderous, cowardly pack" – are broad enough to represent various members of society. McKay wrote the poem so that it could be put to different purposes by different readers. As a result, the sonnet functions not truly as propaganda for a specific target and cause but rather as a fictional script that can feasibly be used for political persuasion by others, not the poet.

McKay's other political poems similarly resist functioning as propaganda. Most are tied to his individual experience as a Jamaican immigrant in the United States, so he rarely speaks from an impersonal voice, let alone one that claims total omniscience. He also tends to express, and reflect on, his own emotional and intellectual response to injustices in America, rather than advocating for a particular course of action. In "The White House," he voices his frustration at the political exclusion that he has encountered in the United States by speaking figuratively to the building that houses the president: "Your door is shut against my tightened face, / And I am sharp as steel with discontent; / But I possess the courage and the grace / To bear my anger proudly and unbent." The poem ends with a stirring injunction, but it is self-directed: "Oh, I must keep my heart inviolate / Against the potent poison of your hate" (*Complete Poems* 148–49). This poem can be considered propaganda only in the broadest sense of fostering self-recognition among readers who have met similar challenges, and sympathy among readers who have not. Some may come to the end of the poem and decide that they wish to demand change, but "The White House" offers no clear program or solution. There is nothing in the text of the poem stating that action should be taken at all save by the speaker, steeling himself against "the potent poison" of injustice. It is not that McKay wishes to shy away from political action, but rather that he believes it lies outside the poem's direct field of action.

In short, at the start of the twentieth century, even politically minded poets hesitated to align their work too closely with propaganda. World War II complicated, but did not reverse, this attitude. Poets who otherwise might have expressed skepticism toward propaganda had trouble questioning its necessity when the cause – the fight against fascism – was so grave. And indeed, many poets were solicited to participate in the "war effort" by applying their rhetorical skills to mass persuasion. For instance, Langston

Hughes was hired to write propaganda for the Department of State, including a broadcast for English-speaking islands in the Caribbean and a script for the morale-boosting variety show *Keep 'em Rolling* (Rampersad 39). Some poets went further than ad hoc commissions and acquired full-time employment in government propaganda. Archibald MacLeish was made head of the Office of Facts and Figures in 1942, and later became assistant director of the Office of War Information in 1945. Still, many poets continued to have contentious responses to propaganda in their own verse. The war saw not a radical change in poetic attitudes but a wider range of approaches.

Some poets absorbed wartime propaganda into the language of their poetry, perhaps not as critically as they should have. One example is "Walking-Sticks and Paperweights and Watermarks" by Marianne Moore, first published in 1936 and then revised in 1941. Her writing before the war had been notable for its precise descriptive style and its incisive analyses. During the conflict, she found herself using one of her preferred techniques, quotation, on the slogans of war propaganda. The result was often to reinforce these phrases rather than to analyze them critically, as in the 1941 version of this poem.

> "Airmail is quick." "Save rags, bones, metals." Hopes are harvest when deeds follow
>
> words postmarked "Dig for victory." (*New Collected Poems* 387)

The first three lines juxtapose advertising ("Airmail is quick"), public service announcements ("Save rags, bones, metals"), and war propaganda ("Dig for victory"). The latter appeared in a campaign encouraging British citizens to ward off food shortages by planting their own fruits and vegetables. The juxtaposition reflects advertising's proximity to propaganda, but erases the distinction between the two genres. Far from analyzing the slogan critically, Moore lends it credibility by developing its central metaphor further. "Digging" for victory produces a "harvest" of "hopes" for a better future. But such hopes are possible only if "deeds follow / words," hence if the slogan is put into practice. The propagandist call to action, absent in the poems of the modernist era we discussed previously, is very much present here.

Moore's poem is part of a broader phenomenon of poets putting their work in the service of Allied propaganda, either by performing their poems in patriotic, morale-boosting radio broadcasts, composing new verse for campaigns, or (as here) by writing poems that favorably evoke the language of the poster, the film short, or the political speech. But this is not to say that the earlier resistance to propaganda fell away entirely. Indeed, other poets during this time resisted the pressure to lend their voice to the "war effort" and echoed specific phrases from war propaganda in order to analyze them critically, drawing out their implications and studying their effects. This new approach – not simply shaping their poetry in opposition to propaganda, but rather engaging with specific instances of its language – is the chief innovation in poets' relationship to propaganda in this period. Consider the following lines from Randall Jarrell's "A Lullaby" (1944):

> For wars his life and half a world away
> The soldier sells his family and days
> He learns to fight for freedom and the State;
> He sleeps with seven men within six feet. (265)

The "fight for freedom" was a common phrase in World War II propaganda. Jarrell echoes it here to then gloss its implications. He does so first by expanding the phrase to "freedom and the State." With the addition of "the State," Jarrell implicitly argues that the patriotic call to defend essential democratic values (such as freedom) is in fact a cover to defend the state, its government, and bureaucracies. That is the real, concrete purpose that propaganda serves to conceal. Second, Jarrell contrasts the phrase "fight for freedom" with a realistic picture of life in the barracks: "He sleeps with seven men within six feet." While many are drawn to the military with the promise of defending and expanding liberty, their actual day-to-day experience is marked by constraints: physical, social, and intellectual. The specific choice of "six feet," with its evocation of the phrase "six feet under," reminds us of the very real risks that soldiers run in the war – and which propaganda, again, conceals behind talk of abstract values.[2]

This practice of echoing specific propaganda phrases and then critiquing them endured long after the end of World War II. The language that preoccupied poets shifted, however, as a rousing yet uniform wartime rhetoric gave way to two major and frequently opposed sources of political persuasion: first, an ever-expanding imperial American state defending its military interventions abroad; second, a variety of social movements operating from the ground up and standing in opposition to the state. Many poets turned a wary eye to both strands of propaganda, even if they sympathized politically with the cause. For Allen Ginsberg in "Howl" (1955), the materials produced by the counterculture of his era were ultimately ineffective. He laments the minds

---

[2] I discuss this poem more fully in "Wistful Lies and Civil Virtues: Randall Jarrell on World War II Propaganda," *JML: Journal of Modern Literature*, vol. 43, no. 3 (Spring 2020), pp. 45–63.

who reappeared on the West Coast investigating the FBI in beards and shorts with big pacifist eyes sexy in their dark skin passing out incomprehensible leaflets,

who burned cigarette holes in their arms protesting the narcotic tobacco haze of Capitalism,

who distributed Supercommunist pamphlets in Union Square weeping and undressing while the sirens of Los Alamos wailed them down . . . (12)

The leaflets here are deemed "incomprehensible," too specialized and obscure to persuade anyone, while the protests and pamphlets are drowned out not only by the chaos of life on the outskirts of acceptable society but also by successful attempts at suppression from those in power. The line culminates in the wailing of police sirens, come to silence the protesters.

Karl Shapiro agreed with Ginsberg on the incomprehensibility of the rhetoric used by the countercultural movements; indeed, he held these groups largely in contempt. In "Sestina of the Militant Vocabulary" (1976), he used echo and critique, as well as the repetitive structure of a sestina, to suggest that the key terms of this rhetoric were doled out with little thought to their meaning.

> The first word you must know is *relevant,*
> The qualifier of *experience.*
> Relevant experience of the *revolution,*
> For instance, trains you to confront the *pigs,*
> The first defense line of the *power structure,*
> Which guards insidiously the *Establishment.*
>
> What we are after is the Establishment,
> Which acts as if we are not relevant
> And forces us to wreck the power structure.
> This confrontation is an experience
> Not only for the people but for the pigs
> Whom we'll win over in the revolution.

The italics in the first stanza signal to the reader that these terms are quoted language drawn directly from the "militant vocabulary." As the words recur in their expected places in the second stanza, we are made to feel that they are deployed out of habit, because they imply a broader political allegiance, with little attention paid to their individual sense. The highly ordered nature of the sestina – the fact that a poet must place the words in a specific position in each stanza – conveys the poet's argument that this vocabulary is deeply rigid and regimented, leaving little room for flexibility of language or thought. In the envoi, he concludes his poem by suggesting that the protesters are hypocritical and protest authority only so that they can eventually claim it for themselves: "While pigs perpetuate the power structure, / Baby, be relevant to the revolution / Till we experience the Establishment" (323–24).

Even poets who also worked as activists in this time resisted using their poems simply to advance a chosen cause. Much like at the start of the century, poets developed more complex understandings of how their writing could be political. Audre Lorde, for instance, was politically active and addressed contemporary social issues in her poetry. Indeed, several poems have titles that evoke propaganda, such as "Movement Song." Nonetheless, she was wary of taking poetry as a *medium* for propaganda, but always returns to the individual, the personal, and the particular when dealing with the political. Her approach recalls that of her contemporary, Adrienne Rich. Both weigh the force of public events on their own sensibility, describing how these external pressures enter into their consciousness and impact their everyday life. If lyric poetry is defined as the expression of an individual perspective, then the political function of poetry can be to register such forces, reflect on them, and through this intuit an experience shared by others in society. Lorde's poem "Sisters in Arms" (1986), for example, begins with a domestic scene shared by the speaker and a Black female South African lover:

> The edge of our bed was a wide grid
> where your fifteen-year-old daughter was hanging
> gut-sprung on police wheels
> a cablegram nailed to the wood
> next to a map of the Western Reserve

It is not possible to keep out the political entirely at such moments, though. Intimations of violence ("hanging," "nailed to the wood"), and police brutality in particular ("gut-sprung on police wheels"), cast a shadow over the scene. The world then enters the home fully through a common route: the daily news.

> I reach for the taste of today
> the *New York Times* finally mentions your country
> a half-page story
> of the first white south african killed in the "unrest"
> Not of Black children massacred at Sebokeng
> six-year-olds imprisoned for threatening the state
> not of Thabo Sibeko, first grader, in his own blood
> on his grandmother's parlor floor
> Joyce, nine, trying to crawl to him
> shitting through her navel (357–58)

The newspaper, though, reflects social biases, revealing who is valued and who is considered dispensable. The hypocrisy of devoting an entire "half-page story" to "the first white south african killed" in the conflict, but making no mention of the many "Black children massacred at Sebokeng," is underscored dramatically by a capitalized "Not." The final description of a murder in the home ("Thabo Sibeko … in his own blood / on his grandmother's parlor floor") brings home to the poet how the (compromised) tranquility of her own domestic space could have been vitiated by injustice and violence – and could still be in the future.

The goal of Lorde's poems, then, is less to persuade or push toward action, and more often to affirm her experience in the face of hostile social forces. Even when she speaks for a collective of outsiders, as in "A Litany for Survival," the oratorical style never claims the function of actual public oratory. In the first stanza, Lorde describes her intended audience:

> For those of us who live at the shoreline
> standing upon the constant edges of decision
> crucial and alone
> for those of us who cannot indulge
> the passing dreams of choice
> who love in doorways coming and going
> in the hours between dawns
> looking inward and outward
> at once before and after
> seeking a now that can breed
> futures
> like bread in our children's mouths
> so their dreams will not reflect
> the death of ours

Together, the elevated tone, the repetition, and the first-person plural give this poem the musical qualities of a speech. The spirit here is not one of petition so much as recitation and dedication. The stanza ends with a semicolon, leaving the sentence unfinished, and the following stanza begins with a reprise: "For those of us / who were imprinted with fear." At this juncture, it becomes clear that Lorde's main interest is in honoring her imagined community through address. She allows herself to indulge in the catalogue of description and delay the ostensible message of the poem. That message, when it does arrive at the end of the second stanza, is a plain statement spoken on behalf of all those who have been marginalized by society: "We were never meant to survive." Lorde voices relief, implicitly and through contrast, that "we" did in fact survive. Yet even this sentence does not galvanize so much as affirm. It is telling that the key verb at the end of the poem is "speak":

> So it is better to speak
> remembering
> we were never meant to survive.[3]

Not "demand," not "urge," not even "encourage," though Lorde was comfortable performing all of these speech acts in her political work outside poetry. But her verse proceeds from the belief that poetry's ideal function is to assert individual and collective experiences in the face of pressure to be silenced. In this sense, Lorde's approach is consonant with W. H. Auden's philosophy in his elegy to W. B. Yeats: "Poetry makes nothing happen . . . it survives, / A way of happening, a mouth" (255–56).

That wariness can be found in poems critical of the Vietnam War. Denise Levertov, one of the most notable responders to the war, condemned the tendency to instrumentalize verse toward political ends, arguing that such a use went against the nature of art itself. In the essay "The Poet in the World" (1972), she posited that "good poets write bad political poems only if they let themselves write deliberate, opinionated rhetoric, misusing their art as propaganda. The poet does not use poetry, but is at the service of poetry" (*New & Selected Essays* 136). In an interview with Jewel Spears Brooker, she developed this idea further, echoing Auden's line from "In Memory of W. B. Yeats":

> I don't think that poetry designed specifically to make things happen would make things happen. Poetry written overtly as propaganda wouldn't be very good poetry, hasn't traditionally been very good poetry and therefore hasn't made things happen. But I think that poetry as it sets in motion parts of people's being that would not be set in motion without it indirectly must make things happen. If a person through reading poetry feels more alive and more aware of things, and just has been reading poetry, then goes out and walks down the street and sees things and feels things he would not otherwise have felt if the poems he's just been reading hadn't stirred them up. (*Conversations* 64)

For Levertov, the goal of a poem – or at least, a good poem – is not to spur readers to action, but instead to sharpen their attentiveness, so they are able to respond more fully and more responsibly to the world, from ordinary sights and sounds to the news of global events. The word "things" is capacious enough to cover that range. Crucially, this does not mean that a good poem cannot be political in nature or effect. Indeed, it encourages a fuller engagement with politics, as with other realms of human life. But poetry does not succeed by simply advocating for a program. It succeeds by shaping and heightening the reader's attention to the world.

---

[3] Lorde, *Collected Poems*, 255–56.

The long poem "An Interim," first published in *Poetry* magazine in November 1968, reflects on this principle even as it puts it into practice. In an early section, the speaker responds to a news report on the Vietnam War. At first, she is overwhelmed by the seeming powerlessness of language, and of poetry, in the face of mass casualties.

> "It became necessary
> to destroy the town to save it,"
> a United States major said today.
> He was talking about the decision
> by allied commanders to bomb and shell the town
> regardless of civilian casualties,
> to rout the Vietcong.
> O language, mother of thought,
> Are you rejecting us as we reject you? ("An Interim" 70)

The US major's report is so matter-of-fact, so bureaucratic in tone and rhythm as to (almost, not quite) conceal the insoluble paradox that it presents to its listeners: destruction as salvation. The use and abuse of rhetoric strikes Levertov so deeply that she thinks of it as a rejection by language itself. Her response initially is to reject language in turn by resisting close attention or artfulness: the lines that follow just after the quote are insistently prosaic ("He was talking about the decision"), devoid of the craft, play, and invention that distinguishes poetry from bureaucratese. When the poet's voice does elevate beyond the prosaic, it is for a lament on the failure of language. "O language, mother of thought . . ." As the poem wears on, however, she recovers an important function of poetry in times of crisis, despite her inability to act.

> Peace as grandeur. Energy
> serene and noble. The waves
> break on the packed sand,
>
> butterflies take the cream o' the foam,
> from time to time a palmtree lets fall
> another dry branch, calmly . . .
>
> The quiet there is
> in listening.
> Peace could be
>
> that grandeur, that dwelling
> in majestic presence, attuned
> to the great pulse. (71–72)

Such a passage could easily be dismissed as a turn away from the violence of war and toward beautiful imaginary landscapes ("butterflies take the cream o' the foam"). But what this moment allows the poet to do is focus her attention, so that she may see and hear more fully. "The quiet there / is in listening." The effect is not deadening, and the poet does not remove herself from harsh realities. The final line suggests that after regaining control, she will be able to return that ear to what is not always peaceful: "the great pulse" of the world. For Levertov, that is the essential function of poetry in time of war. Poetry cannot stop a gunshot or a bomb. It cannot recover the dead. But amid the cacophony of events and news reports, it can teach us how to center our attention so that we may register what is occurring and speak of it more responsibly.

Through all the changes described here, most American poets responded to propaganda in the twentieth century without approval or hostility, preferring to deal with social and political issues in more personal, complex ways. On the one hand, few poets rejected propaganda outright. Indeed, several defended the use of art as propaganda, out of concern that their own political writing might otherwise be dismissed. Some went so far as to participate in government propaganda work at key moments (like World War II) and lend their writing or their voice to those efforts. Yet in practice, even the most politically minded of poets sensed that they could not apply the rhetorical mechanisms of mass persuasion to verse. The very function of propaganda – which is to persuade an audience to believe a given idea, or take a particular course of action, by playing on their emotions, impressions, and assumptions – was too narrowly utilitarian for what most poets wished to achieve in their art. Throughout the twentieth century, American poets found a variety of ways to write politically without shaping their verse within the confines of political propaganda. Carl Sandburg used the tools of poetry to reflect the inequalities of American society, but resisted outlining a program he deemed appropriate. Claude McKay emulated the oratorical style of public speeches but did not define one specific cause, thus allowing his poem to be repeated and adapted in a wide range of contexts. Audre Lorde described her individual response to global events and registered its impact on her everyday life. To her mind, the function of poetry is assertive, not persuasive: poems affirm the experience of a specific individual and the communities to which that individual belongs. For Denise Levertov, though poetry makes nothing happen in the political field, it does help the poet, and the reader, focus their attention so they may respond more fully and more responsibly to the events of the world. These examples make clear that propaganda actually provided a useful point of comparison for poets – one that allowed them to better define how they understood the political nature and function of poetry and refine their own methods by contrast.

WORKS CITED

Auden, W. H. *Selected Poems*. Edited by Edward Mendelson. Vintage, 2007.
Du Bois, W. E. B. "Criteria of Negro Art." In *The New Negro: Readings on Race, Representation, and African American Culture, 1892–1938*. Edited by Henry Louis Gates Jr. and Gene Andrew Jarrett. Princeton University Press, 2007.
Ginsberg, Allen. *Howl and Other Poems*. City Lights Books, 1956.
Jarrell, Randall. "A Lullaby." *Poetry*, vol. 64, no. 5, 1944, p. 265.
Juhasz, Suzanne. *Metaphor and the Poetry of Williams, Pound, and Stevens*. Bucknell University Press, 1974.
Kenner, Hugh. *The Pound Era*. University of California Press, 1971.
Levertov, Denise. *Conversations with Denise Levertov*. Edited by Jewel Spears Brooker. University Press of Mississippi, 1998.
    "An Interim." *Poetry*, vol. 113 no. 2, 1968, pp. 70.
    New & Selected Essays. New Directions, 1992.
Lorde, Audre. *The Collected Poems of Audre Lorde*. Norton, 1997.
Lowell, Amy. "Preface." In *Some Imagist Poets: An Anthology*. Houghton Mifflin, 1915.
McKay, Claude. *Complete Poems*. Edited by William J. Maxwell. University of Illinois Press, 2004.
    Harlem Shadows. Harcourt, Brace, 1922.
    "Letter to W. E. B. Du Bois." In *The Passion of Claude McKay: Selected Poetry and Prose, 1912–1948*. Edited by Wayne F. Cooper. Schocken Books, 1973.
    "Soviet Russia and the Negro." *The Crisis*, vol. 27, no. 2, 1923, pp. 61–65.
Moore, Marianne. *New Collected Poems*. Edited by Heather Cass White. Farrar, Straus and Giroux, 2017.
Pound, Ezra. *Literary Essays of Ezra Pound*. Edited by T. S. Eliot. New Directions, 1968.
Rampersad, Arnold. *The Life of Langston Hughes, vol. 2: 1914–1967, I Dream a World*. Oxford University Press, 2002.
Sandburg, Carl. *Chicago Poems*. Henry Holt and Company, 1916.
    "Notes for a Preface." In *Collected Poems*. Harcourt Brace Jovanovich, 1950.
Shapiro, Karl. *Collected Poems, 1940–1978*. Random House, 1978.
Stock, Noel. *The Life of Ezra Pound*. Routledge, 1970.
Williams, William Carlos. *Paterson*. Edited by Christopher MacGowan. New Directions, 1995.
    William Carlos Williams on Art and Artists. Edited by Bram Dijkstra. New Directions, 1978.

CHAPTER 3

Depression-Era Poetics and the Politics of How to Read

Sarah Ehlers

Reckonings

The contemporary poet Susan Briante's 2016 volume *The Market Wonders* reinvents a poetic strategy employed by the poet Muriel Rukeyser in her 1938 documentary poetic sequence "The Book of the Dead." Influenced by Rukeyser's placement of a newspaper stock price readout within a poem sequence about industrial catastrophe and labor exploitation, Briante crafts an approximation of a stock ticker that runs across the bottom of her poems. "I put some of my life, my love, in a space between numbers, between the values against which they are judged," Briante writes in her poem, "December 19 – The Dow Is Closed"; "I have set a ticker (tick, tick, tick) like Muriel Rukeyser does in 'The Book of the Dead'" (71). Through such repurposing, Briante reimagines, and thus rereads, Rukeyser's formal strategies amid a moment when ideas about poetry's relationship to political commitment remain in flux: *The Market Wonders* was written in response to the 2008 economic recession and the consolidation of mass political movements such as Occupy and Black Lives Matter, and it was published concomitant with the election of Donald Trump. As Michael Dowdy has pointed out, several recent poetry volumes addressing the current landscape of political, economic, and ecological crisis cite Rukeyser as a model (157). I begin with *The Market Wonders*, and with Briante's citation of Rukeyser, to suggest that Rukeyser's Depression-era left milieu has literary historical and critical consequences for thinking about the intersections between poetry and politics beyond influence per se. Briante's reappropriation of Rukeyser reveals how the composition and interpretation of poems is embedded in political, economic, and institutional realities, and it suggests that understanding the limits and possibilities of poetry reading in the present requires a grappling with the past.

Since the 1960s and 1970s, scholars of the US literary Left have challenged canonical literary histories and evaluative methods by recovering and interpreting complex variations of Depression-era poetic practice that were repressed by a Cold War New Critical hegemony.[1] As Michael Thurston observes, the New Critical evaluative assumptions "that dominated American literary institutions for a generation, from the late 1930s until the rise of a newly politicized literary criticism in the 1960s," encouraged adherence to "a seductive corollary" whereby poems that try to do political work in a "direct way" are interpreted as "bad . . . doomed to (poetic and political) failure" (7). Such assumptions often depend on the valuation of formal strategies associated with high modernism over experiments in popular verse genres. It is not simply that the poems of an earlier era have been, to borrow another phrase from Rukeyser, "buried, wasted, lost" – it is that contemporary readers do not fully understand what has been lost in terms of our own parameters for reading them.

This essay on the "politics of how to read" American poetry focuses on the 1930s as a crucial moment in the history of poetry reading. If, as Juliana Spahr suggests, "in order to understand the relationship between literature and politics, one has to attend to specific examples and the nuances of history that shape these specific examples," then the decade of the 1930s is a critical place to start (4). During this moment, the ideological battle between left cultural workers and conservative poets and critics associated with the Southern Agrarian and New Critical movements produced a series of contestations – between art and propaganda, traditional and experimental forms, mass culture and academic institutions – that were foreclosed by the dominance of New Criticism during the Cold War. In the sections that follow, I demonstrate how a return to the Depression moment reveals foreclosed aspects of the politics of poetry reading that have implications for how we take up the "old question about how to understand the vexed and uneven relationship between literature

---

[1] The publications of Daniel Aaron's, *Writers on the Left: Episodes in American Literary Communism*, Alan Wald's *The Revolutionary Imagination: The Poetry and Politics of John Wheelwright and Sherry Magnan*, and Cary Nelson's *Repression and Recovery: Modern American Poetry and the Politics of Cultural Memory* revealed the forces shaping critical views of literary periods and aesthetic movements and established new interpretive paradigms. See also Constance Coiner, *Better Red: The Writing and Resistance of Tillie Olsen and Meridel LeSueur*; Walter Kalaidjian, *American Culture between the Wars: Revisionary Modernism and Postmodern Critique*; Nancy Berke, *Women Poets on the Left: Lola Ridge, Genevieve Taggard, and Margaret Walker*; Alan Filreis, *Counter-Revolution of the Word: The Conservative Attack on Modern Poetry*; John Lowney, *History, Memory, and the Literary Left*; James Smethurst, *The New Red Negro: The Literary Left and African American Writing*; and Michael Thurston, *Making Something Happen: American Political Poetry between the Wars*.

and politics" today (Spahr 5). I begin by outlining debates between left
literary critics and conservative Southern Agrarians. I then use this context
to underscore ways of reading that have become naturalized within mainstream literary institutions as well as to bring to light interpretive methods
that have been obscured. As I show, the ideologies of reading that marked
the interwar period produced not just methods for interpreting poems, but
also ideas about "poetry" and the social roles it fulfills that reverberate in
both obvious and unacknowledged ways.

Poetry Criticism and the 1930s "Culture Wars"

In his account of early-twentieth-century literary culture, *Exile's Return*
(1934), the critic Malcolm Cowley observed that the 1929 Wall Street
Crash precipitated "a new conception of art" that replaced "the idea that it
was something purposeless, useless, wholly individual and forever opposed
to the stupid world" (287). As Cowley suggests, and as scholars of interwar
poetic culture have argued since, the historical, political, and cultural
changes of the 1930s did not just shift the ground on which individual
poems were evaluated; they also altered how "poetry," as an idea, was
thought in relation to political realities. And yet Cowley's narration of the
shift from the 1920s to the 1930s as an abrupt replacement of one ideal of
art with another reproduces narratives about 1920s "high modernism" that
would be codified during the Cold War. Such narratives obscure the
complex terrain on which ideas about the value and social function of
poetry were negotiated during the early twentieth century. As Joseph
Harrington argues, before the 1930s "culture wars" and the subsequent
Cold War–era "high modernist/New Critical hegemony," the term
"poetry" was used to describe "not a genre with a consensus definition,
but a crossing point, an indeterminate and contested space in which new
ways of writing emerged" (3–4). During the Depression, a moment of
economic crisis that shifted the terrain of high literary as well as consumer
culture, debates about how to read poems became sites where ideas about
the role of poetry in political life could be negotiated and stabilized.

The so-called culture wars of the 1930s, in which a conservative critical
movement that originated with the Southern "fugitive poets" defined itself
against the rise of a left cultural front, is a crucial moment in the history of
American poetry reading. The crises of the Depression era – the 1929 Wall
Street crash and its aftermath, the rise of fascism in Europe, and major
shifts in US imperial power – created a crisis in the meaning of poetry (as
an ideation) that generated debates about how poems (as objects) should

be recognized and read. As Edmund Wilson put it in his 1932 essay "The Literary Class War": "It has now become plain that the economic crisis is to be accompanied by a literary one" (539). Framing this "literary crisis" in terms of an ideological clash between cultural workers associated with the Communist and Popular Front Left and a revanchist Southern agrarian movement perhaps risks reducing the numerous complex debates that played out across the ideological spectrum to a simple left/right binary. And yet conservative discourses about poetics were frequently formulated as reactions to Marxist thought, even if sometimes implicitly. What is more, the disputes between the two sides remain instructive for understanding formations of modern poetry reading.

During the 1930s, the political urgencies attending the widespread economic crisis at home and fascism abroad led to a consolidation of left movements that Michael Denning has influentially described as a "cultural front" that "triggered a deep and lasting transformation of American modernism and mass culture" (xvi). This left front heavily influenced poetic production – in terms of both personal commitments that affected individual compositions and broader movements that shifted networks of publication, circulation, and exchange. While many politically committed artists never officially joined the Communist Party, CPUSA-sponsored institutions like the John Reed Clubs and the *New Masses* gained a wide influence. At a time of "historic conflicts" that necessitated taking sides, poets and critics were urged, in the words of a 1932 John Reed Club statement, to "join with the literary and artistic movement of the working class in forging a new art that shall be a weapon in the battle for a new and superior world." The conception of art as a weapon in the class struggle was echoed in multiple forms across a period that spanned the shifts from the Communists' revolutionary third period of the early 1930s to the Popular Front "people's poetry" of the late 1930s to the "wartime progressive poetry" of the 1940s.[2] This includes Stanley Burnshaw's admonition in his "Notes on Revolutionary Poetry" (1930) that, "if literature is to be a weapon it must not be a thin, shadowy, over-delicate implement but a clear, keen-edged, deep-cutting tool" (22); Joseph Freeman's declaration in the introduction to *Proletarian Literature of the United States* (1935) that "art, as an instrument in the class struggle, must be developed by the proletariat as one of its weapons" (24); and Shaemas O'Sheel's description of the poems collected in the antifascist anthology *Seven Poets in Search of*

---

[2] This schematic is adapted from Wald, *American Night*, 251.

an Answer (1944) as a resumption of "the great tradition of poetry as a sword against evil" (8).

By associating poems with revolutionary weapons, left critics established a set of aesthetic criteria that valued traditional and mass cultural forms as well as poems that could circulate widely, such as traditional folk songs, ballads, and other metrically regular poems that could be easily read aloud or memorized. Such forms were favored by left cultural workers because of their historical roots in workers' traditions, their potential use at meetings and marches, and their presumed accessibility. In terms of reading practice, such criteria also focused on how poems would be received by "everyday readers" rather than on the interpretive protocols used by professional critics or public intellectuals.[3] The composer and folklorist Charles Seeger recalled that, in a 1934 competition for the best May Day song sponsored by the radical Composers Collective, everyone in the Collective "preferred Aaron Copland's setting of [the poet] Alfred Hayes's 'Into the Streets May 1st.'" Seeger's own entry, however, was deemed "much more singable. This was, after all, a marching song, and what worker could carry a piano with him on a march?" (Lieberman 30–32).

Despite the focus on reaching mass audiences, the "Art Is a Class Weapon" slogan effectively disparaged other traditions. For example, Wald notes that the slogan created a "hostile" attitude "toward the poetic achievements of the 1920s" by encouraging "the use of political criteria to judge the quality of literature" (*Revolutionary* 3). Left critics who interpreted the formal innovations of literary modernism as merely "the bankrupt outlook of disoriented middle-class intelligentsia" missed how modernist formal and representational techniques (such as fragmentation, abstraction, genre-mixing, allusiveness, and stream-of-consciousness) could be deployed to reimagine socioeconomic realities and modes of revolutionary praxis (*Revolutionary* 3).[4] In her introduction to the women revolutionary poets collected in the anthology *Writing Red* (1987), Charlotte Nekola points out that the demand for weaponlike poems also excluded women's poetry traditions that were "largely private" and "often domestic" (128). Noting the prevalence of phallic imagery in "poem as

---

[3] On the political significance of "everyday reading" practices, see Mike Chasar, *Everyday Reading: Poetry and Popular Culture in Modern America* (New York: Columbia University Press, 2012).

[4] Ibid., 3. On the place of modernist experimental techniques in the development of anticapitalist poetics, see also Ruth Jennison, *The Zukofsky Era: Modernity, Margins, and the Avant-Garde* (Baltimore, MD: Johns Hopkins University Press, 2012) and Mark Steven, *Red Modernism: American Poetry and the Spirit of Communism* (Baltimore, MD: Johns Hopkins University Press, 2017).

weapon" discourses, Nekola concludes that most 1930s "accounts of revolutionary literary history," no matter the aesthetic bent, "did not find a place for the female revolutionary" (130).

The tensions Wald and Nekola outline are evident in a 1937 *New Masses* debate between the communist critic and anthologist Granville Hicks and left poet and critic Horace Gregory. The debate began when Hicks reviewed negatively Gregory's anthology *New Letters in America* (1937) under the auspicious title, "Those Who Quibble, Bicker, Nag, and Deny." At the center of the Hicks-Gregory dispute is the divide between writers who embraced the tenets of "proletarian poetry" and those who eschewed them, choosing instead to meld the modernist techniques of the 1920s with the demand for revolutionary content during the 1930s. Hicks's review first seems to endorse Earl Browder's statement at the first American Writer's Congress that the Party "had no literary line"; but the review goes on to denigrate the poets in Gregory's volume who write in the tradition of 1920s modernism for belonging to a "pessimist tradition" that did not appeal to a reading public ready for the "good news" of Communism (22–23). Moreover, and important to my arguments, when Gregory responded to Hicks's review, he attacked Hicks for being a "poor reader" who failed to understand that "poetry is reviving under the stimulus of more than one literary tradition" (18). While it is tempting to read Gregory's accusation as allying with later disparagements of 1930s verse cultures – such as Thurston's point that political poems are treated as ipso facto "bad" – his criticism of Hicks does not amount to a defense of ahistorical formalism. Rather, Gregory's reaction is related to the ways left writers attempted to discern relationships between poetic form and political content.[5]

The various methods writers associated with left institutions developed in their efforts to interpret poems in terms of their political function were countered by a conservative wave of critical reception that, while still being developed in the 1930s, would for a time become a dominant way of reading in US academic institutions (Kalaidjian 140). What would eventually be codified as American New Criticism began at Vanderbilt University in Nashville, Tennessee, and included the poets and critics Donald Davidson, John Crowe Ransom, Allen Tate, Robert Penn Warren, and

---

[5] In "Notes on Revolutionary Poetry," for example, Burnshaw argued for art as a revolutionary weapon, but he also cited the practical criticism of I. A. Richards to forward arguments about the inseparability of content and form. Joseph North argues that Richards's "Practical Criticism" was distinct from the US New Criticism in its incorporation of materialist approaches. See North, *Literary Criticism*, 28–43.

Cleanth Brooks. The movement was inaugurated by the first issue of the literary journal *Fugitive* (1922), and the positions of the group were further consolidated in *Fugitives: An Anthology of Verse* (1928) and the essay collection *I'll Take My Stand: The South and the Agrarian Tradition* (1930). As literary historians such as Vincent Leitch have shown, the Southern New Critics' desire to dismiss engaged poetry was far from apolitical in its intent. "Though they endeavored to purify criticism," Leitch writes, "the practice and theory of these American formalists was typically tied to a traditional conservative . . . ideology and value system" (24).

I'll Take My Stand is perhaps the most instructive of these texts for considering the ideological underpinnings of New Critical reading methods. The twelve contributors to the volume, though not identical in their politics, were united in their attempts to establish a distinct Southern identity and literary culture by, paradoxically, forwarding the idea that literary texts should be read apart from their historical, political, and/or biographical contexts (Maxwell 108). Such efforts were clearly formulated in reaction to emerging social movements and were meant to buttress an anticommunist stance that, as Walter Kalaidjian writes, "imbricated class with racial oppression in its broader agenda of promoting cultural squirearchy" (148). Kalaidjian notes that three of the contributors to *I'll Take My Stand* (Andrew Lytle, Allen Tate, and Robert Penn Warren) proposed *A Tract Against Communism* as the original title (133) – a literary fact that's hardly surprising when one considers the volume's introductory "Statement of Principles," which asserts that the authors "look upon the Communist menace . . . as a menace indeed" (Davidson et al. xlv).

As Joseph North suggests, the Southern Agrarians "insistent . . . anti-communism" appeared to "determine much of their position" (37). In *Outside Literary Studies: Black Criticism and the University*, an account of how midcentury Black left critics countered New Critical practices, Andy Hines illuminates the racial dimensions to this anticommunism, showing how "New Critical activity" was "a reactionary and counterrevolutionary response to the political and cultural activities of Black writers" (7). Hines demonstrates how Black writers affiliated with the communist left such as Lorraine Hansberry, Langston Hughes, and Melvin B. Tolson developed critical practices that exposed the racist assumptions of New Criticism while also creating modes of Black left critique in resistance to the university and the US surveillance state.

When *I'll Take My Stand* was first published it was the subject of widespread public criticism, and the negative reaction to the book necessitated a shift from the Southern Agrarian to the New Critical position.[6] This shift, as the historian Angie Maxwell explains, has vexed literary scholars. Drawing on earlier accounts of the development of New Criticism by scholars such as Mark Jankovich, Maxwell outlines the paradoxical means by which Southern Agrarian poets and critics elevated the "art of criticism" and the position of the critic in an effort to "redefine the standards of literary achievement" while shedding the Southern identity politics of *I'll Take My Stand* (149).[7] The term "New Criticism" was used broadly in the United States in 1941 after Ransom published a book by the same name, but New Critical methods garnered acclaim through a number of late 1930s and early 1940s books, including Ransom's *The World's Body* (1938), Tate's *Reactionary Essays on Poetry and Ideas* (1936), and Brooks and Warren's *Understanding Poetry* (1938). Collectively, these texts outlined ideas about literary value and practices for reading poems that, as Gerald Graff argues, fundamentally changed literary criticism.[8] Significant to this story is the establishment of a method of "close reading," whereby a poem is treated as an internally complex object that can be understood through a set of empirical observations and without recourse to historical context or the personal response of the reader.

New Critical protocols for reading, insofar as they assumed that aesthetic concerns transcended social ones, were part of a dismissal of "propaganda" poems and of the literary productions of the socialist and communist left. Such positions were encapsulated in essays such as Brooks's "Metaphysical Poets and Propaganda Art" (1939), which contained a biting critique of Joseph Freeman's *Proletarian Literature of the United States* anthology. For Brooks, left critics valued poetry only as a vehicle for propaganda, and politically committed poetry is "incapable of enduring ironical contemplation." In other words, it does not hold up when subjected to the intricate rules of New Critical close reading. Brooks condemns the protocols for reading developed by left writers, asserting: "The error made by some of the more naïve Marxists, ironically enough, arises from a clumsy and inadequate account of poetry. However revolutionary their economics, the aesthetic theory of such critics is not revolutionary at all. It represents little advance over the Victorians with their 'message-hunting'" (51). Brooks's criticism of revolutionary writers

---

[6] For an account of this, see Maxwell, *Indicted South.*
[7] Maxwell draws on Mark Jankovich, *The Cultural Politics of the New Criticism* (Cambridge: Cambridge University Press, 2006).
[8] The most oft-cited account of New Critical dominance in the academy is Graff, *Professing Literature.*

repeats, with a slight difference, Brooks and Warren's earlier admonishment in *Understanding Poetry* of "message-hunting," the interpretive mis-
take of "looking only for the statement of an idea which the reader thinks
he can apply profitably in his own conduct" (10). While *Understanding
Poetry* described message hunting solely in terms of an abstract morality,
the juxtaposition of Brooks and Warren's pedagogical text with Brooks's
more direct disparagement of left poetry further illuminates the politics
that undergirded New Critical reading methods and that, in turn, redefined the parameters of poetry. For Brooks and Warren, a poem written to
communicate a message is not a poem at all: "The fact that we have just an
idea in itself is not enough to make a poem," they write, "even when the
idea may be a worthy one" (12).

   If for most of the 1930s there was little regard for the New Critical
pronouncement that poetry and politics don't mix, by the end of the decade
the spoils had fallen to those on "the side of the eternal verity of purportedly
apolitical art" (Nelson 67). Following the disillusionments of the 1939
Nazi-Soviet Pact, certain strains of left writing and criticism began to echo
the New Critics' dismissals of "propaganda" as well as their emphases on
form and freedom of expression.[9] By 1939, the Marxist critic Philip Rahv,
who once published in Jack Conroy's worker-writers' magazine *Rebel Poet*,
would argue in the pages of Warren's New Critical *Southern Review* that the
writing formulas promoted by the Communist Party during the 1930s were
"empty of aesthetic principle." Rahv's essay, titled "Proletarian Literature:
A Political Autopsy," forwards that 1930s communist literary criteria served
as a "complex political mechanism" whereby writers were made to believe
that they were allying themselves with the working class when, in effect, they
were surrendering their "independence to the Communist Party" (627).
Rahv writes against the imposition of political doctrine on literary works,
arguing that 1930s proletarian literature mistakes the "literature of a party,"
which only reproduces party ideology, for the "literature of a class," which
allows for "conflict" and "free exchange" and which "constantly strives and
partially succeeds in overcoming its social limitations" (619–621). Rahv
closes the essay by insisting on the superiority of the "media of art" over the
"media of politics" in a way that replicates the art/propaganda distinction
outlined by Brooks.

   [9] On the consolidation of reading methods within a Cold War New Critical hegemony, see Alan
   Wald, *The New York Intellectuals: The Rise and Decline of the Anti-Stalinist Left* (Chapel Hill:
   University of North Carolina Press, 1987). On the relationship between New Critical practice and
   postwar anticapitalist racial liberalism, see Jodi Melamed, *Represent and Destroy: Rationalizing
   Violence in the New Racial Capitalism* (Minneapolis: University of Minnesota Press, 2011).

To be clear, the consolidation of formalist methodologies in relation to the specific political crises of the 1940s grew out of distinct political positions and formalist critics did not produce uniform ideas about the aesthetic or the autonomy of poetry. Nonetheless, the reading practices associated with New Criticism persists – to the point that it at times remains unclear how to read outside of ideas about modernism, poetic expression, and formal mastery that are themselves products of what Gillian White has described as "a diffuse New Critical discourse by now so thoroughly absorbed so as to seem natural" (2). While it would seem that scholars have collectively debunked New Criticism, many New Critical assumptions remain operational, though they might go under different names or function in different ways. As the next section demonstrates, while contemporary poetry scholars have sought to recover and revalue political poems, it remains important also to recover ways of reading poems that were developed in the Depression-era left milieu.

Reading from the Left

The New Critics' offhand dismissals of political poems as "propaganda" is part of a by now familiar story about how the institutionalization of New Critical reading methods acted to repress left poetry traditions. The contestations between New Critical and left literary interpretive practices can be further understood if framed in terms of the juxtaposition between the New Critics' ahistorical formalism and left critics' materialist approaches to poems. Such a juxtaposition usefully shifts focus from evaluative statements to interpretive practice. Particularly illustrative is the contrasting ways that two critics on opposite sides of the ideological spectrum – the Southern Agrarian–turned–New Critic Allen Tate and the communist poet and critic Genevieve Taggard – approached Emily Dickinson in their 1930s literary criticism. (This is particularly illuminating considering that Dickinson's work is often recruited in debates about how to read poems.[10]) Juxtaposing Tate's and Taggard's approaches to Dickinson thus helps to demonstrate how the politics of poetry also resides in the ways a critic chooses to read. What is more, the specific example of

---

[10] The most predominant example is Virginia Jackson, *Dickinson's Misery: A Theory of Lyric Reading.* (Princeton, NJ: Princeton University Press, 2005.)

Taggard bears out Paula Rabinowitz's argument that "reckoning" with the
significance of Depression aesthetics "holds gendered resonances" (33).

Tate's 1936 *Reactionary Essays on Poetry and Ideas* opens with
Dickinson. The first essay, "Four American Poets," begins with a lauda-
tory account of Dickinson's oeuvre that acts as a thinly veiled critique of
materialist reading practices. Dickinson's poetry "is not like any of the
innumerable kinds of verse written today," Tate writes. "It is a poetry of
ideas, and it demands of the reader a point of view – not an opinion of
the New Deal or of the League of Nations" (3). Tate then argues that
Dickinson's poetry has gone unread because it contains a "specific quality
of poetry" that eludes most readers. The present culprit is "Marxian
criticism," what he calls the "latest disguise" of a "heresy" that prevents
a "critical reference point" for reading Dickinson's poems (3-4). In a
performance of New Critical close reading practices that emphasizes
rhythm patterns and precision of image, Tate demonstrates how
Dickinson's "Because I could not stop for death" is "one of the most
perfect poems in English," exemplifying Dickinson's "pure" devotion to
poetry (10).

In his analysis, Tate singles out Taggard's 1930 biographical study, *The
Life and Mind of Emily Dickinson*, a book so popular that it went into a
second printing, as an example of the perils of biographical criticism. While
he calls Taggard's study "excellent," he damns her with faint praise.
"Admiration and affection are pleasant to linger over the tokens of a great
life," Tate avers, "but the solution to the Dickinson enigma is peculiarly
superior to fact" – and, presumably, is to be discerned through ahistorical
close reading (8). Tate's dismissal of Taggard's biographical approach
shares with Brooks's earlier disparagement of Taggard's poems in
"Metaphysical Poetry and Propaganda" as displaying the "vice" of "sentimentality" (51). When considered in the broader historical and political
contexts of New Critical formations, it is clear that Tate's snub of Taggard's
biography is connected to Brooks's more explicit dismissal of political
poetry as well as the ways in which New Critical canons were built as
masculinist traditions. John Crowe Ransom's essay "The Poet as Woman,"
for example, disparages a woman-authored critical biography of Edna St.
Vincent Millay, Elizabeth Atkins's *Edna St. Vincent Millay and Her Times*
(1936), for comparing Millay's achievements as a sonneteer to John
Donne's. Whereas Atkins compares Millay to Donne, Ransom dismisses
Millay's sonnets as "little-girl things" and concludes Millay is not a poet at
all but a woman: "No poet ever registered herself more deliberately in that

light," he writes. "She therefore fascinates the male reviewer but at the same time horrifies him a little too" (76–77).[11]

Any reading of *The Life and Mind of Emily Dickinson* as simply bio-graphical misses the political contexts for, and implications of, Taggard's study. In her own poetic practice, Taggard saw Dickinson as a model for how to generate effective political poems, and she found in Dickinson a complicated reimagining of the relationship between inner and outer existence that she calls a "double reality." Taggard describes this in dialectical terms: "Emily's eye saw a double reality, and she was forever at work to compose that external contradiction into one. It was this troublesome 'double' that compelled her to be a poet" (*Life* xv). The ways this framework translates to interpretation are evident in the notes for Taggard's second planned study of Dickinson, never published and tenta-tively titled, "Emily Dickinson and Other Poets." In her notes, Taggard wrote that Dickinson's "The wind begun to rock the grass" produced the "strange effect" of feeling "as if one were the whole universe and were in everybody." Taggard's understanding of Dickinson's poems, in contrast to Tate's, also anticipates later political readings of Dickinson's work in its insistence that Dickinson's poetry sprang from the political realities of the Civil War. Reading Dickinson's poems this way, Taggard proffers a challenge to the New Critical ideal of poetry as a transcendent art form whereby a "poem" is that which contains "poetry" (Jackson and Prins 161). Taggard's Dickinson is not devoted to "pure poetry"; rather, she "sometimes . . . wrote down what she felt, but she did not call it song" (*Life* 5). *The Life and Mind of Emily Dickinson* may not be explicitly framed as Marxist in its approach – and it may not read any proletarian poets – but it does exemplify a mode of materialist poetry criticism that counters the formalist practices of the New Criticism.

Whose Era?

In 1968, the communist poet Martha Millet submitted a grant application to the Rabinowitz Foundation to support the research and completion of a literary study to be titled, "The Ezra Pound Myth." Millet had been

---

[11] For an account of how Millay's poems were repressed by New Critical traditions, see Melissa Girard, "Forgiving the Sonnet: Modernist Women's Love Poetry and the Problem of Sentimentality," in *A History of Twentieth-Century American Women's Poetry*, ed. Linda Kinnahan (Cambridge: Cambridge University Press, 2016), 307–322.

involved in US left literary organizations since her teenage years: publishing her first political poems in the communist children's magazine *The New Pioneer*, regularly contributing poems to left publications, and teaching poetry workshops at the communist-affiliated Jefferson School of Social Science. In her later career, Millet turned more concertedly to literary and social criticism – and her study of Pound was born from a lifetime commitment to the principles of international Marxism that manifested itself as an urgent need to address the intellectual climate of the Cold War. The resulting manuscript uses biographical and literary analysis to demonstrate how any understanding of Pound's career as a poet is inseparable from the development of his fascist political views. In so doing, Millet indicts the mid-twentieth-century intellectual culture that granted Pound "immunity" by creating a "myth" of poetic achievement that would effectively sever Pound's poetry from his politics. "The dichotomized Pound is not only false," she writes in the final lines of the manuscript's introductory chapter, "but it provides a new theoretical basis and haven for immunity which intellectuals, in this age above all, dare not otherwise claim" ("Pound Myth").

"The Ezra Pound Myth" was never published, but Millet's extant research notes and manuscript drafts, which span the late 1950s to the early 1970s, constitute a remarkable alternate record of a literary era that would, at least for a time, bear Pound's name. Indeed, at the same time that this self-described "working woman, mother, and activist" would summon a lifetime of political commitment for a critical project that condemned the US institutionalization of fascism under the guise of "good poems," Hugh Kenner, fresh out of Yale and newly appointed as an assistant professor at the University of California, Santa Barbara, was deep in work on *The Pound Era*, a hagiography that arguably stakes a claim for the very mythos Millet condemned.

While Millet was likely unaware that Kenner was also at work on a book-length study of Pound, she did engage with aspects of the eventual book when, in 1968, she penned a scathing thirty-six-page letter to the *New York Times Book Review* in response to Kenner's column on Forrest Read's *Pound/Joyce: The Letters of Ezra Pound to James Joyce* (1967). Kenner's depiction of Pound, Millet argued in the unpublished letter, evinced the privileges of a US intellectual elite hell-bent on upholding the myth of Pound's genius ("Letter"). And it was perhaps a prescient critique. Kenner's study established Pound as a synecdoche for a specific version of modernist aesthetics that focuses on Pound's formal innovations without addressing his politics. As Ruth Jennison puts it: the "critical impact" of *The Pound Era* "was just as much about positioning Pound as Anglo-American modernism's central impresario as it was about the advancement of a specific ideology of modernist form under the banner of the poet's individual creative vision" (7).

Both "The Ezra Pound Myth" and *The Pound Era* were conceptualized and written during a crucial moment when the New Critical methods that had predominated mainstream academic and literary institutions during the Cold War would become diffuse. The version of modern US poetry crystallized in Kenner's study – one based in Pound's dictum to "make it new" – was part of a narrative of modernist poetic experimentation that equated revolutions in form with revolutionary content. What is more, and perhaps most important to this essay's arguments, is that at the moment during which Millet and Kenner began their studies, the prestige of the poet-critic archetype was firmly entrenched in the academy (Kindley 9). I thus close with the contrast between Millet and Kenner to emphasize that any consideration of the politics of how to read must also turn to the economic and institutional contexts that condition reading practice. While Millet aimed to produce a short polemical book that could be part of a "bigger game" in the "real world of continuing living importance to real men and women" outside academe, Kenner planned a "great book" in which Pound's career would provide a "central image" of modernist American poetry that persisted in scholarship ("Pound Myth").[12] The distinct ways in which Millet and Kenner are positioned in relation to the academy suggests the necessity of institutional critique.[13] Indeed, as Hines warns, contemporary readers would do well to shift focus from interpretive methods to institutional contexts: "The persistence" of "methodological emphasis," he writes, "stands as one of several indices of the continuation of New Critical practice within literary studies, despite the widespread sense that the method is a practice of the past" (26). By returning to earlier debates and, in particular, the interventions of communist writers like Millet, we might begin to shift away from the question of how to read poetry and focus instead on the historical and political ground that manages our ideas about what poetry is and the work it does.

---

[12] The quotation from Hugh Kenner is from a 1960 letter Kenner penned to then *Poetry* editor Henry Rago, and discussed in Alan Filreis, "Pound as Central Image," 1960 Blog (March 14, 2009).

[13] In addition to Spahr and Hines, see Nowak, *Social Poetics*.

WORKS CITED

Briante, Susan. *The Market Wonders*. Boise, ID: Ahsahta Press, 2016.

Brooks, Cleanth. *Modern Poetry and the Tradition*. New York: Oxford University Press, 1965.

Brooks, Cleanth, and Robert Penn Warren. *Understanding Poetry: An Anthology for College Students*. New York: Henry Holt and Company, 1938.

Burnshaw, Stanley. "Notes on Revolutionary Poetry." *New Masses* 10.8 (February 1934): 22.

Cowley, Malcolm. *Exile's Return: A Literary Odyssey of the 1920s*. New York: Penguin, 1934.

Davidson, Donald, John Gould Fletcher, and Henry Blue Kline, et al. *I'll Take My Stand: The Southern Agrarian Tradition*. Baton Rouge: Louisiana State University Press, 2006.

Denning, Michael. *The Cultural Front: The Laboring of American Culture in the Twentieth Century*. New York: Verso, 1996.

Dowdy, Michael. "Shakeout Poetics: Documentary Poetry from Men of Fact to Data Bodies." *College Literature* 47.1 (Winter 2020): 155–184.

Freeman, Joseph. "Introduction." In *Proletarian Literature of the United States: An Anthology*, ed. Granville Hicks, Michael Gold, Isidor Schneider, Joseph North, Paul Peters, and Alan Calmer. New York: International Publishers, 1935.

Girard, Melissa. "Forgiving the Sonnet: Modernist Women's Love Poetry and the Problem of Sentimentality." In *A History of Twentieth-Century American Women's Poetry*, ed. Linda Kinnahan. Cambridge: Cambridge University Press, 2016: 307–322.

Graff, Gerald. *Professing Literature: An Institutional History*. Chicago: University of Chicago Press, 1987.

Gregory, Horace. "'Good News' in American Literature." *New Masses* (October 12, 1937): 17–19.

Harrington, Joseph. *Poetry and the Public: The Social Form of Modern U.S. Poetics*. Middletown, CT: Wesleyan University Press, 2002.

Hicks, Granville. "Those Who Quibble, Bicker, Nag, and Deny." *New Masses* (September 28, 1937): 22–23.

Hines, Andy. *Outside Literary Studies: Black Criticism and the University*. Chicago: University of Chicago Press, 2022.

Jackson, Virginia, and Yopie Prins, eds. *The Lyric Theory Reader: A Critical Anthology*. Baltimore, MD: Johns Hopkins University Press, 2014.

Jankovich, Mark. *The Cultural Politics of the New Criticism*. Cambridge: Cambridge University Press, 2006.

Jennison, Ruth. *The Zukofsky Era: Modernity, Margins, and the Avant Garde*. Baltimore, MD: Johns Hopkins University Press, 2012.

Kalaidjian, Walter. *The Edge of Modernism: American Poetry and the Traumatic Past*. Baltimore, MD: Johns Hopkins University Press, 2006.

Kindley, Evan. *Poet-Critics and the Administration of Culture.* Cambridge, MA: Harvard University Press, 2017.

Leitch, Vincent. *American Literary Criticism since the 1930s,* 2nd ed. New York: Routledge, 2009.

Lieberman, Robbie. *"My Song Is My Weapon": People's Songs, American Communism, and the Politics of Culture, 1930–50.* Urbana: University of Illinois Press, 1995.

Maxwell, Angie. *The Indicted South: Public Criticism, Southern Inferiority, and the Politics of Whiteness.* Chapel Hill: University of North Carolina Press, 2014.

Millet, Martha. "Letter to editor" (unpublished), *New York Times Book Review,* February 8, 1968. Martha Millet Papers, Kislak Center for Special Collections, Rare Books and Manuscripts, University of Pennsylvania, Philadelphia.

Typescript of "The Ezra Pound Myth," undated. Martha Millet Papers, Kislak Center for Special Collections, Rare Books and Manuscripts, University of Pennsylvania, Philadelphia.

Nekola, Charlotte, and Paula Rabinowitz, eds. *Writing Red: An Anthology of American Women Writers.* New York: Feminist Press, 1987.

Nelson, Cary. *Repression and Recovery: Modern American Poetry and the Politics of Cultural Memory.* Madison: University of Wisconsin Press, 1989.

North, Joseph. *Literary Criticism: A Concise Political History.* Cambridge, MA: Harvard University Press, 2017.

Nowak, Mark. *Social Poetics.* Minneapolis, MN: Coffee House Press, 2020.

O'Sheel, Shaemas. "Introductory Note." In *Seven Poets in Search of an Answer,* ed. Thomas Yoseloff. New York: Bernard Ackerman, 1944.

Rabinowitz, Paula. "Between the Outhouse and the Garbage Dump: Locating Collapse in Depression Literature." *American Literary History* 23.1 (Spring 2011): 33–55.

Rahv, Philip. "Proletarian Literature: A Political Autopsy." *Southern Review* 4.3 (1939): 619–621.

Ransom, John Crowe. *The World's Body.* Baton Rouge: Louisiana State University Press, 1938; 2nd edition, 1968.

Spahr, Juliana. *DuBois's Telegram: Literary Resistance and State Containment.* Cambridge, MA: Harvard University Press, 2018.

Taggard, Genevieve. Annotated typed copies of *The Poems of Emily Dickinson,* ca. 1942. Genevieve Taggard papers, Manuscripts and Archive Division, New York Public Library.

The Life and Mind of Emily Dickinson. New York: Knopf, 1930.

Tate, Allen. *Reactionary Essay on Poetry and Ideas.* New York: Scribner's, 1936.

Thurston, Michael. *Making Something Happen: American Political Poetry between the Wars.* Chapel Hill: University of North Carolina Press, 2001.

Wald, Alan. *American Night: The Literary Left in the Era of the Cold War.* Chapel Hill: University of North Carolina Press, 2012.

The Revolutionary Imagination: The Poetry and Politics of John Wheelwright and Sherry Mangan. Chapel Hill: University of North Carolina Press, 1983.

White, Gillian. *Lyric Shame: The "Lyric" Subject of Contemporary American Poetry.* Cambridge, MA: Harvard University Press, 2014.

Wilson, Edmund. "The Literary Class War." In *The Shores of Light.* New York: Farrar, Strauss, and Young, 1952.

CHAPTER 4

The Politics and Poetics of Revolution

Mark Steven

If poetry is the imperfect approximation of ungovernable forces and feelings, a revolt from within and against the distribution of the sensible, there will have always been something poetic about revolutionary possibility in the United States. And yet American poetry has often understood social revolution as an alien phenomenon, a foreign concept in the most literal sense of that term. When Walt Whitman pressed for "quenchless, indispensable fire" with his "Songs of Insurrection," he only did so with thoughts cast far away from home and to Paris in the year of its Commune. "Then courage!" we read in his 1871 cluster. "European revolter! revoltress!" (632). Before that outwardly political poet could speak the word, Emily Dickinson had already overlaid the American Civil War and the Republican Revolution in France by calling forth a tempestuous image of social transformation:

> Revolution is the Pod
> Systems rattle from
> When the Winds of Will are stirred
> Excellent is Bloom (1082)

Here the poem is conceived as a gust of wind that might liberate the pod of revolution from the inactive stalk of civil society. As it would later do so for Whitman, poetry announces itself as the medium for agitation and incitement, a revolutionary catalyst at work on American soil. Indeed, with the third line's alliteration, prosody is both named and performed as the medium of system-rattling renewal. While that revolution has not arrived, in Dickinson's time or in ours, the causal relationship between poetry and politics cuts both ways. The poem simultaneously resolves and responds to that almost unthinkable break with the way things are. Just as one poem might spread the seeds of revolution, poetry as a totalized if disunited endeavor draws nourishment from the possibility of revolution's future bloom, with each sustaining and energizing the other.

This is as true for literary production now, at a time of heightened political militancy punctuated by riotous action the world over, as it would have been in the aftermath of the American Civil War. It was, however, during the century between then and now that a positive affinity between poetic form and revolutionary politics clarified into a source of specifically left-wing utopianism, giving rise to what this chapter will describe as an antifascist, anti-imperialist, anticapitalist – and socialist if not avowedly communist – poetics. What this chapter documents, then, is the crystallization of a poetry that emerged through what Fredric Jameson has termed the "immense Left force-field" (12) that exerted its own gravitational presence from within the United States all through the twentieth century, integrating what might otherwise be understood as modernist experimentation within both the solidaristic landscapes and the internationalist imaginations of revolution.

The twentieth century would update the revolutionary dyad as it had been given poetic expression by Dickinson and Whitman, wherein the United States had understood its politics in relation to Europe and especially France. After 1917, socially engaged poetry from around the world was affectively charged by the international rivalry between a newly formed socialist republic, in Russia, and the solidifying cultures of late capitalism, which found its economic and ideological powerhouse in the United States. There, opposing the iron laws that would sustain accumulation, we find a rich history of revolutionary verse, in poems that describe if not enact solidarity with the capacity of the working masses to determine their own destiny against the brutalizing juggernaut of industrial capitalism. Alongside a raft of proletarian songbooks and picket rhymes – these were, of course, poetic modes to which the popular front laid claim – the literary left also occupied a variety of institutions and produced poems written across numerous other forms and genres, giving expression to the revolutionary impulse as classed and racialized vernacular (H. H. Lewis and Langston Hughes), as experiments in political symbolism (Lola Ridge and Lorine Niedecker), as intricate social documentation (Tillie Olsen and Gwendolyn Brooks), and even as the totalizing modern epic (Louis Zukofsky).

While these forms and their poets merge literary traditions and technical devices with images and impressions of local or national struggles, with a broad conception of revolutionary thought, and with an emphatically internationalist outlook, we find an exemplarily powerful expression of that confluence with Claude McKay's celebrated sonnet of 1919, which in many ways provides the keynote for subsequent poetry of revolutionary commitment:

> O kinsmen! we must meet the common foe!
> Though far outnumbered let us show us brave,
> And for their thousand blows deal one death-blow!
> What though before us lies the open grave?
> Like men we'll face the murderous, cowardly pack,
> Pressed to the wall, dying, but fighting back! (117)

These lines were written in the middle of the Red Summer of 1919, as a tide of white riots in black neighborhoods surged up from the South and into the northern and western cities where demobilized, white veterans confronted the black migrants drawn out by wartime labor shortages. McKay, a communist radical originally from Jamaica, was working at the time as a waiter in a dining car on the Pennsylvania Railroad and writing poetry while on the job. In this, his most famous poem and the only one he would read aloud to his comrades and coworkers, the Elizabethan sonnet – a form traditionally used for the expression of romantic desire – undergoes political recalibration, being repurposed here as a medium for revolutionary action. While Black militants would appropriate classic, European culture for the critique of race – "I sit with Shakespeare and he winces not," wrote W. E. B. Du Bois in perfect blank verse (76) – here that form is transformed into a weapon. As Jasper Bernes suggests, the "compressive power of poetic form" renders itself explosive in "the thou-sand-to-one concentration of its performative address into the spondaic death-blow of the eleventh line," whereby the sonnet is revealed as having "the form of a piston in a cylinder – the pressure of the encircling mob pressing speaker and addressee together into volatile, collective action that explodes forth in singular, vocative death-blow" (245). Revolutionary action convokes its own mass, the fighting "we," in those final two lines. The affirmative simile, "like men," describes the revolutionary subject, a people reborn from social antagonism, but also the form in which they come to life: the emphatic, masculine rhyme of "pack" and "back," with that final, exclamatorily end-stopped monosyllable fired like a gunshot. Such animating rage is not a purely literary phenomenon, either; while this poem enjoys a long history of being read out by African American revolutionaries and in revolutionary situations, from the prison riot at Attica to the bedside of Assata Shakur, it was during Red Summer that McKay started carrying a pistol – as though to prefigure the armed propaganda of Black Panthers and the Black Liberation Army, two insurgent organizations whose members took inspiration from his work.

Just as McKay harnessed literary tradition in his capacity as a committed revolutionary – an organizer who would eventually join the Industrial Workers of the World (IWW) – his sonnet seems to distill what has always been practically revolutionary about the modern poem as such, namely its post-Romantic attachment to what Ruth Jennison and Julian Murphet describe as "the means for a collective psychotherapy of the alienated urban citizen: a poetics of communal belonging to a way of life crucified and 'repressed' by industrialization and the unchecked profit motive" (4). Though McKay's poem is socially radical but formally conservative – or if not conservative then at least antiquated in its deployment of the sonnet – many other left poets were contemporaneously engaged in a program of aesthetic innovation, producing works not only informed by political commitment and revolutionary imperative but also beholden to the modernist mission of literary reinvention. These poets – writing in their capacitary as labor organizers, as insurrectionary agitators, and as comrades at arms – set out to socialize the means of poetic expression, creating verse that is revolutionary in form no less than content. Their undertaking would be in keeping with revolution's signal thinkers. Social revolution, Marx once said, "cannot take its poetry from the past but only from the future," and this kind of temporal break, he argued, is a matter of form and content. "There," he looked back to previous, failed revolutions, "the phrase went beyond the content – here," looking about Europe in which revolution seemed all but inevitable, "the content goes beyond the phrase" (597). In other words, social revolution and its poetry are both phenomena for which there is not yet any adequate or established forms of narrative expression; the task of the revolutionary poet, therefore, is to simultaneously enact and narrate the process of revolution, to contribute and respond to the real movement to abolish the present state of things.

Perhaps the most striking manifestation of this commitment to revolution in both poetry and politics is in the transformation of the ideology of the subject, via an emphatic swerve away from the sovereign individual with its lyric singularity – the personification of what Gillian Brown terms "domestic individualism" – to embrace a collective sociality, the proletarian agent of revolutionary social transformation. This transformation is best figured historically in the distance between Dickinson's critically cherished lyricism, the apparent inwardness of her poetic thought, and McKay's apostrophic and interpersonal exhortations, which strike out at the reader like a slap to the face. For Vivian Gornick, writing in her memoir of American communism during the 1940s and 1950s, this shifting, metamorphosing, and ultimately contested sociality has been the very core of revolutionary politics in the United States, and its mismanagement by the CPUSA during the 1940s and 1950s was part of their undoing: "The Party's understanding of Marx and of the revolution that we were working for involved – deeply – the tension between the individual and the collective. The Party never understood how vital this tension was, never paid attention to it." All through the twentieth century, however, the same tension would animate many individual poems, each of which set out to enact that multiplication of what the poetic subject can and should be, to create new kinds of collective voice and human community from against the alienation, isolation, and atomization of lives under the rule of capital. Readings of three distinct expressions of this commitment follow, excerpted from the poetry of Muriel Rukeyser, George Oppen, and Diane di Prima, all of whom combine poetic creation with political organization in the hope of giving voice to the experience of revolutionary becoming.

Muriel Rukeyser: We'll Be Everyone

Born in 1913, Muriel Rukeyser lived on the economic and cultural periphery of North America's literary avant-garde. She was not part of any self-defined -ism and she did not benefit from literary patronage. For male and mostly middle-class poets, literary modernism can be defined – in Rachel Blau DuPlessis' formulation – by a multitude of "eros-laden dyads," those well-nigh oedipal relationships of masculine patronage "that have been vital (if sometimes temporary) in their poetic careers, with their intense fluctuations between filiation and affiliation" (7); Rukeyser, as a working-class woman, was largely excluded from this opportunistic network. Like other radical poets during the interwar years and thereafter, Rukeyser divided her energies between poetic composition and political organization. During the early 1930s, she attended Vassar College in New York where she edited the college newspaper and from which she never graduated owing to her family's financial difficulties. Throughout that decade and working as a journalist, she was directly involved, as both witness and participant, in several historical events that would receive literary treatment in her writing and which collectively inspired her political and poetic commitments. These events include the Scottsboro Trial of 1931, in which nine African American teenagers from Alabama were unjustly convicted of raping two white women; the Hawk's Nest

Tunnel disaster, also in 1931, during which 2,000 migrant workers from
West Virginia died of silicosis as a result of criminally perilous working
conditions; and the opening days of the Spanish Civil War in 1936, during
which Rukeyser was stranded with a team of athletes and reporters
attempting to reach the antifascist People's Olympiad in Barcelona. So
she would come to reflect on her time in anarchist Catalonia: "if this was
real," she described a moment of revolutionary fervor and possibility, "it
was because it was nearer the sum of everything that had happened before
it than anything had ever been" (*Savage* 143). Experiences such as these
disposed Rukeyser toward an anticapitalist politics that found poetic
articulation through the political expressions of communism. "These
worlds are straining," she would write of each revolutionary action, "to
make your Soviet" (*Collected Poems* 54).

But communism is more than descriptive citation. Her definition of
poetry represents a medium of interpersonal communication, a sociality
free from economic mediation and the depredations of monetized
exchange, and this – she insists – is why poetry is socially marginal
compared to the other narrative arts:

> A way to allow people to feel the meeting of their consciousness and the
> world, to feel the full value of the meanings of emotions and ideas in their
> relations with each other, and to understand, in the glimpse of a moment,
> the freshness of things and their possibilities.... There is an art which gives
> us that way; and it is, in our society, an outcast art. (*Life of Poetry* x)

While Rukeyser's literary reputation is primarily wagered on the long
poem of 1938, "The Book of the Dead," by the time of its publication
she had already become deeply embroiled in the red-baiting of that decade.
With that came a critical desire to divest aesthetic form from political
commitment, to extricate her literary achievement from her politics, as
though the two are in any way separable. In this sense, Rukeyser is
emblematic of what Cary Nelson has documented as the systemic erasure
of left-wing culture and its poetry from American literary history since the
1870s. This is exemplified nowhere more clearly than in the summary of
Stephen Vincent Benét's 1935 review of Rukeyser's poems, recorded
nowhere less auspicious than in the poet's dedicated FBI file. According
to the file, Rukeyser is "essentially an urban poet," as well as "a left-winger
and a revolutionary, but her poetry contains no direct appeals to the
proletariat and her symbols of revolt are imaginative." While Rukeyser's
best scholars have all engaged her political commitment, here we should

emphasize just how significant that commitment was to catalyzing literary creation. From the earliest stages – in Rukeyser's first collection of poems, *Theory of Flight*, published in 1935 and winner of the Yale Younger Poets Award that year – we can see that a revolutionary imperative supplied the poetry with its affective intensity.

If the poems in *Theory of Flight* sustain thematic unity, if there is a force that consistently mediates between historical content and literary form, then that unifying theme is a preoccupation with communist desire. This phrase, "communist desire," is taken from political scientist Jodi Dean, for whom it has two major, overlapping designations: "first, communist desire designates the subjectification of the gap necessary for politics, the division within the people; second, this subjectification is collective – our desire and our collective desire for us" (179). In other words, communist desire names an affect that divides people, for or against, uniting a group under banners red and in opposition to the standing order of what was then industrial capitalism. Rukeyser mobilizes poetry in precisely this way, as a means of affectively transforming literary bodies into communist subjects that are both opposed to capitalism and affirming of the communist collective. Such desirous affect is given cause to effloresce by the May Day march – annual events that Michael Denning has described as "the visible signs of the Popular Front, the massed forces of the city's people marching under banners of unions, mutual benefit associations, and organized fronts" (54). And it is here that a subjective transformation takes place, as though from within the call-and-response between an orator and their audience:

> Mayday is moment of proof, when recognition
> binds us in protest, binds us under a sun
> of love and subtle thought and the ductile wish.
> Tomorrow's Mayday. – How many are we?
> We'll be everyone. (*Collected Poems* 68)

This is a moment of epiphanic "recognition." Note the grammar and the repetitions within the second and third lines. The anaphora of "binds" overlays the social combinations of protest with the experience of diurnal time, linked too by a conceptual pun between "solar" and "solidarity," lending the march a sense of both futurity and inevitability. That material substance of that binding registers via polysyndeton, so that "love" and "subtle thought" and "the ductile wish" read more like a heightening of consciousness registering its own desires excitedly, one after the other, rather than a simple list of nouns. That the final noun phrase is clarified by the definite article emphasizes its singularity as the motive force behind these lines, so that what is recognized is the transformative force of "the ductile wish." In other words, the energizing presence that breathes life into this poem is a collective desire.

The final two lines make good on that desire with their subtle grammatical disagreement, in a formulation that urges both speaker and reader together from the present and into the future: instead of "we are" the speaker sounds "we'll" or "we will," with a pronoun that just about seems to know itself to be collective but accompanied by a verb that tells us the collective will grow. So much depends on the pronouns. For Rukeyser, the first-person singular has always been coterminous with the multitudinous "we," which here reaches out in hope of embracing the late Joycean "everyone." While there is an argument to be made that – as Dean puts it – skepticism of the first-personal plural "treats collectivity with suspicion and privileges a fantasy of individual singularity and autonomy," by contrast, pronouns like "we" and "us," and adjectives like "our," combine to "enhance a partisan sense of collectivity" (12). Rather than assume the final form of this collectivity, this poem stages it as a grammatical becoming. The subject of revolution is not and cannot be one but it is not yet everyone.

George Oppen: Each to Each Other

After publishing his first book in 1934, a collection of elliptical poems collectively titled *Discrete Series*, George Oppen turned aside from literature to organize with the Communist Party and the Workers Alliance of America. After leaving the CPUSA in 1941, disillusioned with the non-aggression pact between Stalin and Hitler, he enlisted as an infantryman in order to fight fascists in Europe, serving in the Battle of the Bulge where he was wounded by exploding shrapnel. After returning home – and having received the Purple Heart in 1945 – he and his wife, Mary, relocated to Mexico, where he would practice carpentry far from the FBI agents that were increasingly attracted by his political commitments. While Oppen's departure from writing might imply a disengagement between poetry and politics, he would later insist that the two are continuous if nevertheless in constant tension: "FROM DISCRETE SERIES TO THE MARXISM WAS NOT A 'BREAK' ———— BY ANY MEANS ..." (*Selected Letters* 255). When, twenty-five years later in 1968, he finally returned to literature, he would do so with a retrospective poem, originally titled "To Date" but later renamed "Blood from the Stone," which looks back to the decade in which he stopped writing as a time of explosive yet unrealized revolutionary potential:

> The Thirties. And
> A spectre
> In every street,
> In all inexplicable crowds, what they did then
> Is still their lives.
> As thirty in a group –
> To Home Relief – the unemployed –
> Within the city's intricacies
> Are these lives. Belief?
> What do we believe
> To live with? Answer.
> Not invent – just answer – all
> That verse attempts.
> That we can somehow add each to each other?
> – Still our lives. (*New Collected Poems* 31)

These lines give voice to both the familiar language of international communism and the endemic homelessness of the era: the unemployed and immiserated are the animate form of communism made flesh, its "spectre," haunting capital from the urban landscape's "intricacies" and amassed outside the assistance bureau. Following that description, "are these lives" is a syntactical end to the previous line, the grounding of life within economic exigency and the realization of social categories as the stuff of life, but it is also a question, visually articulate with the punctuation at the end of its line: By what standard can we call this, waiting in groups of thirty for home relief, life? In other words, those first nine lines figure a distinction between subsistence and flourishing, survival and some other, more sustainable "relief" that is not the kind of thing that might be rationed out by the hostile state. Unlike Rukeyser's affirmative, booming verse – written in a voice that would have been familiar to Oppen, who had once been dubbed "best of the soap boxers" – this poem assiduously avoids the performance of anything like oratorical force: it stops and starts, it questions itself, with enjambment betraying uncertainty. Where Rukeyser declaims, Oppen stutters. Perhaps this is because, on retrospect looking back three decades but also in the poem's compositional present, revolution is an unsolved mystery: how to mobilize with these "inexplicable crowds" to create the world anew remains the most pressing question of all.

To some extent, then, revolution is always a matter of belief, as the poem wonders – of living without knowing. With this, and moving through the poem's second half, poetry finds a practical purpose for itself, a vocation: not to "invent" a belief system with which to live but to provide an answer to pressing questions, clarifying a vision of what is already there in the social substance of the world. That kind of poetic vocation is granted in the final, unrhymed, uneven, and still questioning couplet. Belief, according to Oppen, might be an interdependent flourishing, in which we all add each to each other. Here, the formulation does more than just morph the alien "other" into a collective "each other"; it also implies a statement for poetic force and political threat: the repeated "each" conjures another communist adage to match the specter, "from each, to each," the abbreviated form of "from each according to his ability, to each according to his needs," a program through which "their lives" become, finally, "our lives," an expression of collective autonomy and self-determination.

The mention of addition ("add to each other") prefigures a whole new poetic project, which would be realized in Oppen's Pulitzer Prize–winning collection of 1968, *Of Being Numerous*. Its title and content provoke a series of questions, which together necessitate critical thought about the conditions of living as well as a communist desire for their transcendence – or, in the words of Rukeyser, both "subtle thought" and "the ductile wish" are at work in this collection. "In what ways," asks Natasha Lennard in a discussion of Oppen, "are we numerous, enumerated, counted, uncounted, dividuated, enmassed, and divided? In what ways have we chosen to live this way, and in what ways is it chosen for us? In whose interests are lives thus organized; which powers does this serve?" Parts six and seven give voice to these questions through descriptive ambiguity. They imply the experience of an actual situation more so than some generalized social condition, but anything like referential description is omitted, so that a narrative fissiparousness takes hold, whereby the poem might at that moment be responding to a protest or a rally or a riot, or to the workplace or pension cue. That the poem can be all these things at once imposes a choice on the reader, clearing a path to the road not taken.

In part six, this resolutely ambiguous setting is the ground upon which political commitment takes hold, giving way to an allusion against which the poem sets its revolutionary compass:

We are pressed, pressed on each other,
We will be told at once
Of anything that happens

And the discovery of fact bursts
In a paroxysm of emotion
Now as always. Crusoe

We say was
"Rescued."
So we have chosen. (*New Collected Poems* 165–66)

The first line crowds. The repeated "pressed" carries with it the echo of the near etymological descendent, "oppressed," but it also visualizes a state of compaction. This overlong line visualizes and gives sonic form to social combination, the material circumstances that enable the existence of a speaking "we are" as opposed to the atomized and individuating "I am," thus occupying space within some truly "inexplicable crowd." More broadly, the opening tercet is animated by a sense of anticipation: "we are" becomes "we will," as the grouped mass awaits notice of some kind of eventful action. The second tercet provides that event in the form of a "fact" that detonates – not as information, to be sure, but as a "paroxysm of emotion," which might transform the staid "we" who remain, as though bound by social entropy, as they were "now and always," as though awaiting the event of an uprising. The reference to Robinson Crusoe is likewise polyvalent and ambiguous. On the one hand, Crusoe is the exemplary individual "rescued" from solitude and returned to collective sociality. Yet he is also an individual who embodied and enacted the laws of capital, whose "rescue" meant returning to a world he never really left because he always carried it within himself. It is in the manner of this ambiguous rescue that "we have chosen," deciding our own fate as together we are "pressed," but the choice itself remains undetermined, as though to invite the questions: What have we chosen and why are we choosing it?

Without providing an answer, part seven announces the conditions on which an answer might be suggested:

Obsessed, bewildered

By the shipwreck
Of the singular

We have chosen the meaning
Of being numerous. (*New Collected Poems* 166)

Unlike Rukeyser, for whom the poem's subject is an all-embracing every-one, here the poem is animated by the "the shipwreck of the singular," which is the potential for real solitude – the kind experienced by the shipwrecked Crusoe – but also solitude's annihilation. This ambivalence lives in the grammar. To be stranded alone on an island is the very definition of "the shipwreck of the singular." But that rescue, however ambiguous and ambivalent, is also singularity's shipwreck: it is the point at which the idolatrous self is forcibly relocated into the social world, into the experience "of being numerous." Like Crusoe, we haven't chosen our numericity – it has been forced upon us – but we can still choose what it means: either entropy or its opposite, revolution; to rebuild or reinte-grate, like Crusoe, within capitalist society, or to choose to work for something else entirely. As with the lines from Rukeyser, this poem assumes nothing but invites everything. What it does, in Margaret Ronda's formulation, is promote a subject that "is the antithesis of the liberal democratic citizen, a figure of negation and sameness rather than singularity amidst diversity" (246), and these are the only grounds on which we choose what to mean: together. If there is revolutionary force in these lines, or at least its potential, then that force belongs to a prevailing sense of numericity, a reckoning with the fact that we are not nor will ever be one, but are many.

Diane di Prima: Endless as the Sea

Diane di Prima lived among the poets. Born in 1934, she went to school and was close friends with Audre Lorde, with whom she would hold seances to try to commune with the specter of John Keats; at age nineteen, she was a correspondent of Ezra Pound; she spent parts of the 1950s and 1960s with the Beat movement in New York and would teach at the Jack Kerouac School of Disembodied Poetics alongside Allen Ginsberg, Anne Waldman, William Burroughs, and Gregory Corso; for two decades she edited a newspaper with Amiri Baraka; and, in 2009, she was made poet laureate of San Francisco. Her poetry belonged in part to these socialities, to the sometimes joyous and sometimes blunt convivi-ality of exchange, and her most celebrated work found its origins in correspondence with Lorde. According to Francesca Wade, this exchange "between friends – poems and greetings shuttling back and forward in the mail – not only charts the evolution of one of di Prima's defining poetic achievements; it forms a template for the Revolutionary Letters, with their conversational style and direct engagement with the reader" (i). The other side to the social life of her poetry, however, is that of a revolutionary organizer. Like Rukeyser and Oppen, di Prima spent much of her life working and agitating within social movements, and this too provides a context for the poems that would become Revolutionary Letters. She began composing the text in 1968, soon after she moved to San Francisco to work with the Diggers, an activist-performance troupe who distributed mutual aid around the Bay Area. Alongside these activities she was engaged in more illicit, militant actions, in particular running ammunition for the Black liberation movement. When the poems discuss fighting and armaments, when they note "there are those who can tell you how to make molotov cocktails, flamethrowers, bombs whatever," cautioning to "define your aim clearly, choose your ammo with that in mind," this is what we should hear: not a belligerent metaphor but the practicalities of insurrection (13). And it is worth knowing, too, that the poems' first audience was rarely the reader of published verse. "Over the coming decades," adds Wade, "di Prima would try out new poems at marches, in coffee shops, at benefits and concerts, on the steps of San Francisco's City Hall, via megaphone from the back of flatbed trucks passing through New York" (ii). While the collection would evolve over the course of di Prima's life, like a yet-more-radical *Leaves of Grass*, the poems sustained thematic if not formal unity around the advocacy of that eponymous revolution, which they would explore from multiple interlocking and sometimes contradictory perspectives. "NO ONE WAY WORKS," we read in letter eight, "it will take all of us shoving a thing from all sides to bring it down" (14).

Poetic community and revolutionary action: these two antecedents inform a poetics that is, as it was for Rukeyser and Oppen, in opposition to the sovereign self. Sophie Lewis describes di Prima's poetic social being as "directly addressing and seeking to conjure a riotous collective subject"; the resulting poems are "full of incitements to riot against whiteness and capitalism and for liberation in all forms, molten desire for the commune, unruly loyalty to imaginative experience, and angry, sacred, utopic, waywardness" (ix). While the first named letter begins with a moment of personal accountability – "I have just realized the stakes are myself," read the opening lines, "I have no other ransom money, nothing to break or barter but my life" – it rapidly takes that self as a means for contribution to some pluralistic, collective, and well-nigh monstrous being, "as we slither over this go board, stepping always (we hope) between the lines" (5). The second letter clarifies the first. It is dedicated to the substance of that "we," the ideological unlearning it requires, and the premodern antecedents it

calls forth. Its two stanzas are the pronouncement of that "riotous collective subject" as a living weapon:

> The value of an individual life a credo they taught us
> to instill fear, and inaction, "you only live once"
> a fog in our eyes, we are
> endless as the sea, not separate, we die
> a million times a day, we are born
> a million times, each breath life and death: get up, put on your shoes, get
> started, someone will finish
>
> Tribe
> an organism, one flesh, breathing joy as the stars
> breathe destiny down on us, get
> going, join hands, see to business, thousands of sons
> will see to it when you fall, you will grow
> a thousand times in the bellies of your sisters (6)

Individualism is acknowledged as an entrenched ideology, an attachment
born from indoctrination, and one that ultimately serves the state by
engendering mass trepidation. The individual, from this perspective, is a
construct that pacifies desire, redirects social antagonism, and maintains
the status quo. This critical perspective is translated into the natural
(and meteorologically San Franciscan) metaphor of "fog in our eyes,"
which is then displaced by the affirmative "we are," as though that fog
burns off in the morning sun, to reveal a vision of oceanic boundlessness.
Subjectivity, in this emergent revolutionary consciousness, is "endless as
the sea," and with that truly sublime form death and life are reinscribed
as one with the absolute, wherein each individual is multiplied by the
power of a million. The voice then shifts from the meditative, reflective,
lyric poet to the revolutionary, urging action right now. Crucially, the
efficacy of that action is sanctioned by the foregoing lines: only because
together we are endless will our start, however modest, be finished by
some potentially anonymous other, either the comrade fighting alongside
us on the street or someone else many years from now. In the second
stanza, that subject is made relative to the premodern social form of the
tribe, the forerunner to what Marx once described as "primitive communism," a society in which there are no social classes but only kinship
relations: "a further extension of the natural division of labour existing in
the family" (151).

While tribalism was outmoded by the development of private property,
and though it contains within itself all kinds of gendered domination, here

it is repurposed and modernized to serve once more as a model for revolutionary reproduction, the organic form through which social transformation becomes permanent, absolute, or truly "endless." When read alongside the first stanza, these lines imagine something like the deep time of our collective subject – a sociality "breathing joy as the stars breath destiny" – and in so doing provide a crucial lesson in revolution. To know that tribalism predates or precludes capitalism is to render the social order of the present as vaporous and dispensable as the fog of individuality. It implies, finally, that any human power can be resisted and changed by human beings, provided they act together. Perhaps this is the kind of "fact" that, for Oppen, gave rise to a "paroxysm of emotion," insofar as it pries open the gates of history to make the world otherwise than it is. From this point, with the collective subject now firmly established, the letters become exceptionally programmatic, combining spiritual and acidhead wisdom, insurrectionary agitation, and the utmost practical advice: "store water," begins the third, "make a point of filling your bathtub at the first news of trouble" (7).

The transformation of the poetic subject from the individual to the collective is one of the hallmarks of American poetry from the twentieth century. It also persists as one of the dominant tropes in revolutionary poetry from the early twenty-first century, in the collapse of liberal-democratic consensus and when the illegitimacy of the state and the depredations of capital have been met with protest, strikes, and riots. An exemplary instance of this revolutionary poetry, much of which has been written under the influence of the poets described here, can be found in the radical press Commune Editions, which is self-described as the result of "friendships formed in struggle," citing as its formative moments the experience of riots and occupations and communes wherein "the people committed to poetry and the people committed to militant political antagonism came to be more and more entangled, turned out to be the same people." For Wendy Trevino, whose *Cruel Fiction* was published by Commune in 2018, experience within social movements necessitates some further clarity on the composition of the collective subject, insofar as the "we" of revolution belongs not to everyone who simply wants to lay claim to an identity but wholly and exclusively to those who fight – anyone else, "even if they are on your side," is a mere bystander, so "just get them out of the way of the fight you came for" (38). Trevino's poem, which is named after di Prima's collection, summarizes its position in a brief coda, using an apostrophic language that convokes a collective subject while simultaneously abjuring false friends:

tl;dr you don't need or want
the people who you know
aren't "with you" to be
with you. really, you don't (38)

WORKS CITED

Benét, Stephen Vincent. "Singing Youngsters." *Time*, December 16, 1935.

Bernes, Jasper. "Poetry and Revolution." In *After Marx: Literature, Theory, and Value*, edited by Colleen Lye and Christopher Nealon. Cambridge, Cambridge University Press, 2022, 240–52.

Blau DuPlessis, Rachel. *Purple Passages: Pound, Eliot, Zukofsky, Olson, Creeley, and the Ends of Patriarchal Poetry*. Iowa City, University of Iowa Press, 2012.

Brown, Gillian. *Domestic Individualism: Imagining Self in Nineteenth-Century America*. Berkeley, University of California Press, 1992.

Dean, Jodi. *The Communist Horizon*. London, Verso, 2012.

Denning, Michael. *The Cultural Front: The Laboring of American Culture in the Twentieth Century*. London, Verso, 1997.

Dickinson, Emily. *The Complete Poems*, edited by Thomas H. Johnson. London, Faber and Faber, 1975.

di Prima, Diane. *Revolutionary Letters*, edited and foreword by Francesca Wade, introduction by Sophie Lewis. London, Silver Press, 2021.

Du Bois, W. E. B. *The Souls of Black Folk*, edited by Brent Hayes Edwards. Oxford, Oxford University Press, 2007.

Gornick, Vivian. *The Romance of American Communism*. London, Verso, 2020. Ebook.

Jameson, Fredric. *The Modernist Papers*. London, Verso, 2007.

Jennison, Ruth, and Julian Murphet, eds. *Communism and Poetry: Writing against Capital*. London, Palgrave, 2019.

Marx, Karl. *The Marx-Engels Reader*. 2nd ed., edited by Robert C. Tucker. London, Norton, 1978.

McKay, Claude. *Complete Poems*, edited by William J. Maxwell. Urbana, University of Illinois Press, 2004.

Nelson, Cary. *Repression and Recovery: Modern American Poetry and the Politics of Cultural Memory*. Madison, University of Wisconsin Press, 1989.

Oppen, George. *New Collected Poems*, edited by Michael Davidson. New York, New Directions Books, 2002.

The Selected Letters of George Oppen, edited by Rachel Blau DuPlessis. Durham, NC, Duke University Press, 1990.

Ronda, Margaret. "'Not/One': The Poetics of Multitude in Great-Recession Era America." In *Class and the Making of American Literature: Created Unequal*, edited by Andrew Lawson. London, Routledge, 2014, 245–62.

Rukeyser, Muriel. *Collected Poems of Muriel Rukeyser*, edited by Janet Kaufman, Anne Herzog, and Jan Heller Lev. Pittsburgh, University of Pittsburgh Press, 2005.

The Life of Poetry, edited by Jane Cooper. Ashfield, Paris Press, 1996. Ebook.

Savage Coast, edited by Rowena Kennedy Epstein. New York: Feminist Press, 2013.

Trevino, Wendy. *Cruel Fiction*. Oakland, CA, Commune Editions, 2018.

Whitman, Walt. *Leaves of Grass: A Textual Variorum of the Printed Poems*, edited by Sculley Bradley, Harold W. Blodgett, Arthur Golden, and William White, vol. 3. New York, New York University Press, 1980.

CHAPTER 5

Wallace Stevens, Stanley Burnshaw, and the Defense of Poetry in an Age of Economic Determinism

Alec Marsh

Writing at the precise moment of the stock market "crash" of 1929, and the onset of the Great Depression, the philosopher and public intellectual, John Dewey declared flatly: "Economic determinism is now a fact, not a theory." Ours is a "money culture," he said (Dewey 119, 9), simply stating as anthropological fact what is our cultural experience. After the crash, economic determinism and therefore economic reform, if not revolution, seemed more than ever the key to the vicissitudes of modernity. It was the crash, critic Edmund Wilson noted, which made him turn to *Das Kapital* (Wilson 495). Kenneth Burke, at the same time, for the same reasons, found himself taking "avid notes on corporate devices whereby business enterprisers had contrived to build up empires by purely financial manipulations" (Burke 214). On the Left, Louis Zukofsky's "Song 27" (1934) explicitly directed readers to *Capital*, Chapter 3, "Money or the Circulation of Commodities," and other passages from Marx (Zukofsky 58–61). On the Right, Ezra Pound included two pages of quotes from *Capital*, Chapter 10, "The Working Day," in Canto XXXIII (33/ 162–163).

There were only two sides to every radical question. "'Are you for or against ...?'" (Filreis 22). Are you for or against Franco, Mussolini, Stalin, the New Deal? Poetry was "politicized." For the Left of the 1930s, "The world, so pleasingly simple, [was] divided according to one groundplan only: We (Left). They (Right) and You (Left, Right or Middle), with the Escapists in Limbo" (Burnshaw, "Wallace Stevens and the Statue" 362). Poets took up frankly economic themes: labor and capital, money, finance, and the corporations. Poetry was to be "socially useful," in service of the political struggle.

Robert Frost satirized the awkward position of intellectuals, including poets, in "To a Thinker" (1936):

> The last step taken found your heft
> Decidedly upon the left.
> One more would throw you on the right.
> Another still – you see your plight.

Reason, Frost claims is not the way out; "don't use your mind too hard, / but trust my instinct – I'm a bard" (325–326). Underneath the sneer is a poet's defense: trust instinct, not reason. Salvation for the artist maybe, but the epitome of social irresponsibility from a Marxist perspective!

And the Left set the agenda; to be useful in the social struggle, art should function as propaganda. In response, Harriet Monroe's essay "Art and Propaganda" in *Poetry* (1934)[1] allows that "all art of all the ages is propaganda" (210); but

> If all art is propaganda, a heroic effort to convert the world, its force comes from the artist's spirit and not from his will – that is, it is a force elusive, intangible and free, not to be directed or confined. Thus the deliberate propagandist rarely achieves art, and the artist, though possessed by a cause, can rarely become a successful propagandist. (211)

Conceding the Left's effort to politicize it, Monroe is arguing against didactic and for expressive poetry. Poetry is of the spirit, not the will. Its origin is instinctive, personal, and, implicitly, apolitical. In a reply[2] *New Masses* reviewer (later a distinguished literary critic) Stanley Burnshaw remarked on the confusion in Monroe's position, but his own position is far from clear. "Marxist criticism," he claimed, "finds bad art to be bad propaganda, good art good propaganda and every creator of a good work of art successful both as artist and propagandist" ("Stanley Burnshaw Protests" 352). This circular statement begs the larger question of Marxist determinations of social value, of what was "good." It certainly was out of touch with Soviet – if not Marxist – realities. To Burnshaw, "good" means "allied with the proletariat" and he claims:

> The poet allied with the proletariat may write about any theme that interests him. Being a normal rounded human being, he will not be excited exclusively by strikers and Stalin, although these are excellent themes. He will see the implications of the class struggle in numberless events and objects ignored by bourgeois poets. Not every one of his poems, obviously, will explicitly call for revolution, but the totality of his work will be a weapon fighting on the side of the revolutionary proletariat. (Burnshaw, "Wallace Stevens and the Statue" 353)

---

[1] *Poetry*, vol. 64. no. 4 (July 1934), pp. 210–215.
[2] *Poetry*, vol. 64, no. 6 (September 1934), pp. 351–354.

Here, "good," "useful," poetry becomes unthinkable except in alliance with the proletariat. It is but a short step from socially good to politically correct. The poem should be an intelligible, moral commentary on life and loses its privileged status as an "instinctive" expression of life itself. Poetry is no longer a foundational language; instead, poetry fulfills a program imposed upon it. Such poetry is indeed a "production," *already made* by historical forces – not true *poesis*, or making. The problem for poets is that "the imposition of individuality as something made in advance always gives evidence of a mannerism," John Dewey thought, "not of a manner." Manner is "something original and creative"; mannerism is mere style (Dewey 169). "Poetry must limit itself in respect to intelligence," the poet Wallace Stevens wrote to a correspondent. "There is a point where intelligence destroys poetry" (*CL* 305); his book of poetry *Ideas of Order* (1935, 1936) is "not a thesis" (*CL* 279).

In an April 1935 issue of *New Masses*, Stanley Burnshaw published "'Middle-Ground' Writers," explaining the "duty of the Marxist critic" like himself. Burnshaw abjured the usual Stalinist "skull-cracking," a mode typical of Marxist criticism, for a softer more inclusive approach (19). "We need every ally who can be enlisted," and allies were to be found in "the ranks of waverers – confused writers who believe themselves to be standing in a supposed middle ground between capital and revolution" (19). A softer, more diplomatic response to their work might draw them leftward. Hitherto seen as "incipient fascists," might these bewildered folks be incipient communists (20)?

For writers and publishers on the Left, Wallace Stevens could be especially interesting in this regard. He had published only a dozen new poems in the previous decade. Known for playful, exhilarating verse, his politics were a cypher.

Searching for the Center: Wallace Stevens

A successful insurance executive and corporate vice president by 1934, Wallace Stevens seems to have fully absorbed the imaginative possibilities inherent in the corporate liberal position, which allowed him, among other things, the luxury of appearing "nonpolitical" in the poems he was about to publish in *Ideas of Order*, while giving him a vantage from which to engage, criticize, and meditate on the alternatives offered by the Left and Right without forcing him to subscribe to particular programs. Despite the hard times, Stevens does not appear to have been much threatened by the Great Depression. But, as Alan Filreis has demonstrated, Stevens was fully engaged with the issues of the day and attended assiduously "to what one reads in the papers" (Filreis xvii–xviii). His poems address issues that lie behind the struggle of the poet to make sense of "things as they are" (Stevens, *CP* 165); that is, the social responsibilities of the poet, and attend to deeper, expressive responsibilities to the poetic self, struggling in an incorporated world of militant mass politics and economic crisis.

In *Modernism from Right to Left: Wallace Stevens, the Thirties and Literary Radicalism* (1994), Alan Filreis shows unequivocally the decisive effect of a review in *New Masses* by young but ubiquitous Stanley Burnshaw on the trajectory of Stevens' poetry. As important, Filreis has discovered that the questions to which Stevens responded in his enormously informative letters to the man who called himself J. Ronald Lane Latimer were "in fact, ghostwritten by a well-connected communist poet who was at the same time a devotee of Stevens' work" (Filreis 12–13). Latimer, whose real name was James Leippert, was the head of Alcestis Press, which published the original edition of *Ideas of Order* in August 1935. Both Latimer and the concealed questioner, Willard Maas, clearly hoped to encourage Stevens to steer his politics leftward.[3] "I hope I am headed left," Stevens conceded to Latimer after admitting the interest and stimulus of Burnshaw's review, "but there are lefts and lefts and certainly I am not headed for the ghastly left of [New] MASSES" (WS to Latimer, October 9, 1935, *CL* 286).

Stevens was already reacting to the harsher politicized poetic climate of the 1930s in the first Alcestis version of *Ideas*; that volume led off with "Sailing after Lunch," which Stevens told Latimer was "an abridgement of a temporary theory of poetry" (*CL* 277). "It's the word *pejorative* that hurts," it begins, "my old boat goes round on a crutch / And doesn't get underway" (*CP* 120). And, as Stevens explains to Latimer, "pejorative" refers to the disgraced "romantic" aesthetic that Stevens preferred. For

> poetry is essentially romantic, only the romantic of poetry must be something constantly new, and therefore, is just the opposite of what is spoken of as romantic. Without this new romantic, one gets nowhere; with it, the most casual things take on transcendence, and the poet rushes brightly.... What one is always doing is keeping the romantic pure: eliminating from it what people speak of as the romantic. (*CL* 277)

Although Stevens professes that this explanation is "perfectly clear," it isn't quite. Stevens' romantic is not identical with the Romantic movement, nor

---

[3] Latimer himself joined the CPUSA in the latter half of 1935 – at just the time he was publishing Stevens' *Ideas of Order* (Filreis 123).

the poetry of Keats and Shelley, nor sentimental mush. Stevens' romantic
is signified by brightness, glamour, and its transitory quality – it is
glimpsed. It should be here, there, and everywhere, but as soon as one
focuses on it, it is gone, for "the romantic must never remain."[4] The
romantic "is least what one ever sees. / It is only the way one feels, to say /
where my spirit is, I am" (*CP* 120). The romantic may be caught in
ordinary language we overlook: "The light wind *worries* the sail.... The
water is *swift* today" (*CP* 121, my emphasis). Clichés? Possibly, but "the
most casual thing can take on transcendence" because the romantic is
romantic in "the way one feels": this feeling is where the poet's spirit is –
it's inspired. Stevens prefers to know he exists by feeling, not by thinking
in Descartes' sense – or Marx's. "Poetry must limit itself in respect to
intelligence," he told Latimer. "There is a point at which intelligence
destroys poetry" (*CL* 305). This is what Stevens meant when he wrote
"Marx has ruined Nature, / For the *moment*," an important caveat, in
"Botanist on an Alp No.1" (*CP* 134, my emphasis). Still, feeling is a kind
of thinking, as Stevens' work constantly shows. For all of its thoughtful,
meditative depth, Stevens' poetry resists reason; it exists to be
misunderstood.

In Burnshaw's *New Masses* review of October 1, 1935, "Turmoil in the
Middle Ground," Stevens is one of his (two) examples of significant
"middle ground poets"[5] (the other is Haniel Long, forgotten today).
These are not mere escapists, but deeply unsettled. "The harmonious
cosmos" of Stevens' early work, Burnshaw observes, "is suddenly screech-
ing with confusion. *Ideas of Order* is the record of a man who, having lost
his footing, now scrambles to stand up and keep his balance" ("Wallace
Stevens and the Statue" 365).

Burnshaw sees Stevens as "skeptical of man's desire" for an achievable
order; he "can speculate on the wisdom of turning inward and a moment
later look upon collective mankind" – that is, the "Sudden mobs of men" –
as "the guilty bungler of a harmonious life, in 'a peanut parody for peanut
people'" ("Wallace Stevens and the Statue" 365, *CP* 143). In a deliberate
ironical echo of a line from *The Waste Land*, Burnshaw remarks how the
poet "pours out in strange confusion his ideas of order" in what he
discretely calls a "long poem," that is, "Decorations in a Nigger

---

[4] The "glimpse" is of great importance to Emerson, William James, and W. C. Williams. See Alec
Marsh, "William Carlos Williams and the Prose of Pure Experience," in *The Cambridge Companion
to William Carlos Williams* (Cambridge: Cambridge University Press 2016), 90.
[5] Frost's "Build Soil" had not yet appeared, but Burnshaw revered Frost and may have exempted him
for criticism of this sort in 1935. Or they were still hoping he might come aboard *New Masses*.

Cemetery" (*CP* 151). As an "acutely conscious [member] of a class menaced by the clashes of capital and labor," Stevens finds himself "in a struggle for philosophical adjustment," Burnshaw concludes ("Wallace Stevens and the Statue" 366).

Immediately after reading the review, Stevens wrote "Mr. Burnshaw and the Statue" in a few weeks. Now, thanks to Filreis' literary detective work, we can discern more of the poet's reaction throughout the Knopf edition of *Ideas of Order* (1936), which contained three new poems, two of them among his very best, "Farewell to Florida," and "A Postcard from the Volcano."

"Farewell to Florida," which now opens the Knopf volume, is a clear, if rueful, renunciation of Stevens' earlier "escapist" *Harmonium* manner and the sensuous Floridian landscape that inspired it; "the snake has shed his skin / upon the floor. Go on through the darkness" to some new, colder, poetic destination. Florida was a Calypso whose "mind had bound me round." The North is a cold, violent Ithaca. In the poem, Stevens imagines himself sailing away from the seductive subtropics, exclaiming, "How content I shall feel I shall be in the North to which I sail / and to feel sure and to forget the bleaching sand . . ." (*CP* 117). Clearly, the poet doth protest too much; he regrets deeply the loss of the sunny clime that fed his romantic imagination. "My North is leafless and lies in wintry slime / Both of men and clouds, a slime of men in crowds" – slimy new masses. Yet this voyage is supposedly a journey to *freedom*! To leave the fecund subtropics to return to the cold, stony, realist Ithaca demanded by Marxist critics is, supposedly,

> to be free again, to return to the violent mind
> That is their mind, these men, that will bind
> Me round, carry me, carry me misty deck, carry me
> to the cold, go on high ship, go on, plunge on. (*CP* 118)

This is irony verging on sarcasm. To be free is to be bound by the masses to "the actual world" and to history. The imagination of the poet is inhibited by the moral criticism of the communist super-ego. Florida, Key West, Cuba were the beloved subtropics of Stevens' imagination, as in this final stanza of "Floral Decorations for Bananas" from *Harmonium* (1923):

> And deck the bananas with leaves
> Plucked from the carib trees
> Fibrous and dangling down,
> Oozing cantankerous gum

> Out of their purple maws,
> Darting out of their purple craws
> Their musky and tingling tongues. (*CP* 54)

This playful, eroticized elaboration of Edward Lear is just the kind of thing that persuaded contemporary critics in the 1920s to "market the thesis of Stevens's aestheticism, his verbal acuteness and emotional lassitude – a thesis that stuck" (Filreis 55; Bates 93–126). Stevens' intent in *Ideas* was to reject all that. Joan Richardson has noticed how "all through the poems of *Ideas of Order*, Stevens echoes lines, stanzas and rhythms of *Harmonium*. The wonderful Hoon of 'Tea in the Palaz of Hoon' reappears in 'Sad Strains of a Gay Waltz'" (*CP* 65, 121). Richardson finds the "rhythm, diction and images of 'The Emperor of Ice Cream' in "Mozart, 1935'" (*CP* 64, 131). She doesn't mention the connection, but "Decorations in a Nigger Cemetery" may well be a purposeful contrast to "Floral Decorations for Bananas." Stevens' "decorative" poetry is now treated as so much trash littering alienated ground (*CP* 152, *CL* 288).[6]

The earlier defense of the misunderstood "romantic" in the first 1935 *Ideas* has become by the second version an attempt to "apply the point of view of a poet to Communism" (*CL* 289). "Confused" from the communist point of view; Stevens is, in fact, an acute critic of the problem the Left posed for poetry.

Furthermore, Stevens' new poems, however, are sufficiently saturated with economic structures and metaphors for Frank Lentricchia to have commented on his "capitalism of mind" (Lentricchia 227). Stevens' habitual use of odd intensifiers – bluest, "most spissantly," "exceeding brightness," "antiquest," "deeplier" (*CP* 133, 137, 119), and so on – suggest and

---

[6] Burnshaw would later insist that the poem's title was a deliberate provocation and affront ("Wallace Stevens and the Statue" 363). Stevens explained to Morton Zabel that the shocking title of this poem "refers to the litter one usually finds in nigger cemeteries and is a phrase used by Judge [Arthur] Powell last winter in Key West" (*CL* 172). This "litter" is anything but, as Robert Farrish Thomson shows in *Flash of the Spirit*: "Nowhere is the Kongo-Angola influence more pronounced, more profound, than in black traditional cemeteries in the South of the United States. The nature of the objects that decorate the graves there reveal a strong continuity" with West African practice, "that might be characterized as a reinstatement of the Kongo notion of the tomb as a charm for the persistence of the spirit ... the surface 'decorations' frequently function as 'medicines' of admonishment and love, and they mark a persistent cultural link between Kongo and the black New World" (132). Thompson notes that "Both Kongo and Kongo-American tombs are frequently covered with the last objects touched or used by the deceased" (134), which provide a tactile link between the worlds of the dead and the living. Such things could be confused with litter by the uninitiated or white southerners like Judge Powell of Georgia, to whom racially segregated cemeteries were just the way things were: natural. See Thompson 132–142. He includes many photos.

may reflect the accumulative propensities of finance capital. In a letter to Latimer, Stevens claimed that there is no secret to the merit of a poem – no more, that is, than there is to the stock market (*CL* 299–300). No more and no less! In any case, Stevens' imaginative "capitalism" is not just some reflexive "collaboration" with the economic structures from which, as an insurance lawyer, he undoubtedly benefited, but a considered response to the imaginative opportunities he recognized in capitalist financial structures and the intractable problem, for the poet, of a social self.

In dust jacket copy, Stevens commented on the Knopf edition of *Ideas* (1936). Note the reliance on the *individual*, the Self, practicing its art, its technique, in opposition to "political and social changes" and "the elimination of established ideas":

> We think of the changes today as economic changes, involving political and social changes. Such changes raise questions of political and social order.

> While it is inevitable that a poet should be concerned with such questions, this book, although it reflects them, is primarily concerned with ideas of order of a different nature, as, for example, *the dependence of the individual, confronting the elimination of established ideas, on the general sense of order created by individual concepts*, as of the poet in "The Idea of Order at Key West": the idea of order arising from the practice of any art . . .

The Alcestis *Ideas* was already full of farewells; in the Knopf introductory remarks we can see that the book is an elegy for much more, in particular, those established ideas scheduled for elimination by the Left and the bourgeois way of life they expressed. Along with "Farewell to Florida," we have "Waving Adieu, Adieu, Adieu" and "Sad Strains of a Gay Waltz," telling us, "There comes a time when the waltz / Is no longer a mode of desire / a mode of revealing desire and is empty of shadows" (*CP* 121). Stevens presents a similar scene in "Mozart, 1935" (*CP* 131–132), a poem, Stevens claimed to Latimer, concerning "the status of the poet in a disturbed society" (*CL* 292). There, Mozart – that is, the poet – is asked to "Play the present, its hoo-hoo-hoo" in onomatopoeic sounds of "the envious cachinnation," mimicking the sounds of 1930s-style big-band jazz. The obstreperous contemporary jazz audience is likely to "throw stones upon the roof" while Mozart practices arpeggios "because they carry down the stairs / A body in rags" – a suggestion of cultural decay, but also a joke on the popular genre of ragtime. "We may return to Mozart," the poem concludes doubtfully, but "The snow is falling / And the streets are full of cries" of the same rowdies who throw stones and distract the artist from his work. The past and Mozart's music are treated as a mere "divertimento," a pleasant, if "lucid," escape from the present when what is wanted by the masses is "That airy dream of the future / The unclouded concerto" promised by the communist millennium. In poem after poem the sun is gone or "Fading" (*CP* 139); the weather "muddy," even spring is "snarling" (*CP* 147); in "Autumn Refrain," undoubtedly written with Keats in mind, Stevens laments the "sorrows of the sun" and "the yellow moon of words about the nightingale / In measureless measures, not a bird for me/ But the name of a bird and the name of a nameless air / I have never – shall never hear" (*CP* 160). Farewell to romance – and Romantics – we live in a world haunted by "the skreaking and skrittering residuum" of gravel-voiced grackles, not the (romantic) evasions of the nightingale (*CP* 160). Finally, the haunting female voice, the voice of poetry itself, that "single artificer of the world" in the title poem, "The Idea of Order at Key West," sings in the past tense: She "sang beyond the genius of the sea" but the singing has ended (*CP* 128–130). Why? Because the free imagination is not only scanted, but repressed by the pressure of external events and actively suppressed by political demands on it – the subject of Stevens' 1942 lecture "The Noble Rider and the Sound of Words." The poet must evade and resist the pressure of these realities (*NA* 1–36). Stevens concludes his dust jacket remarks:

> The book is essentially a book of pure poetry. I believe that, in any society, the poet should be the exponent of the imagination of that society. *Ideas of Order* attempts to illustrate the role of imagination in life, and particularly in life at present. The more realistic life may be, the more it needs the stimulus of the imagination. (*CPP* 997)

Stevens' obsession with "pure poetry," much apparent in his letters as well as his poems, is one of those things that makes him "escapist." But, for him, "pure poetry" is the voice of the imagination responding to contemporary life. In accord with cultural convention, "real life" is the life of the lower, working classes: "I think we all feel that there is a conflict between the rise of a lower class, with all its realities and the indulgences of an upper class," Stevens insists to Latimer. However, contrary to Marx, this class conflict is "temporary," not "essential" (*CL* 291); it merely supplies "tentative ideas for the purposes of poetry" (*CL* 293). If poetry has declined from "oriole to crow" and "Crow is realist," even if "Oriole, also, may be realist," it is the gaudy oriole that flaunts its brighter colors and sweeter song (*CP* 154). Poetry cannot live without illusions; that is to say, without the hope that only the imagination can supply.

"Mr. Burnshaw and the Statue" clearly bothered Stevens and he revised it extensively after its appearance in Alfred Kreymborg's annual, *New Caravan* (1936); it became "The Statue at the World's End" in *The Man with the Blue Guitar* (1945). Burnshaw, "the practical communist" (*CL* 289) has been excised as too topical, or too reminiscent of the tiresome ideological struggles of the 1930s to be interesting in 1945. In the event, *Owl's Clover* of which the section was a part, is cut entirely in *Collected Poems* (1954), reappearing only after Stevens' death in *Opus Posthumous* (1957).[7]

"The general effect of *Owl's Clover* is to emphasize the opposition between things as they are and things imagined; in short, to isolate poetry" from what really is, Stevens wrote on the dust jacket of the Knopf edition (see *CPP* 997). *Owl's Clover* is a series of five long poems focused on a single heroic statue of horses, seen from five different perspectives, of which "Mr. Burnshaw" is the second. ("The Old Woman and the Statue" had appeared earlier.) Luckily, Stevens explicated the allegorical poem in letters to Latimer. In "The Old Woman," the statue stood as a symbol for art, while the old woman allegorized the Depression itself. She is too destitute and fearful to be moved by art (*OP* 44). Taking up the communist point of view in "Mr. Burnshaw," Stevens told Latimer, the statue becomes "a symbol for things as they are" – he almost says "society" (*CL* 290).

"Mr. Burnshaw" begins by telling us, "The thing is dead . . . Everything is dead / Except the future, Always everything / That is is dead except what ought to be." What ought to be is the radiant future promised by the Soviets; what is – the statue – appears to the communist eye as the worthless manifestations of the wrong kind of artist doing the wrong kind of art. "They are not even Russian animals," he complains of the statue, which appears to him as so much dreck (*OP* 46). Pretty clearly this is a caricature of the *New Masses* response to Stevens' own work.

Ironically, the poem proceeds dialectically (in the Hegelian, not Marxist sense) with Section I given over to the pitiless communist perspective on the statue; Section II evokes the "celestial paramours," the muses of the Imagination to transfigure the statue with music and light; Section III gives us the terse inscription on the work that will replace the statue: "'The Mass / Appoints These Marbles of Itself To Be / Itself.' No more than that,

---

[7] Commenting a few years later, in a note to the *Sewanee Review* piece, Burnshaw seems to regret the posthumous appearance of *Owl's Clover* with "his" poem and thus the resurrection of the controversy. See Burnshaw, "Wallace Stevens and the Statue," 366n.

no subterfuge" (*OP* 48). In conjunction with this antirhetorical, "bare and blunt" reality, Section IV again address the muses ("Mesdames"). In the fifth section a solemn voice, possibly that of Stevens' familiar "single artificer," but "*not* Mr. / Burnshaw's," announces "At some gigantic solitary urn, / A trashcan at the end of the world, the dead / Give up dead things and the living turn away" (*OP* 49, my emphasis). There, "buzzards eat the bellies of the rich," while the crows "Sip the wild honey of a poor man's life" amid a junkyard of toppled columns and the beheaded sculptor himself. Nonetheless, out of "the immense detritus of a world / that is completely waste," there are "faint, portentous lustres," intimations "Of rose, or what will once more rise to rose" when newer generations come into their own (*OP* 49). Paraphrasing the poem, Stevens told Hi Simons, "We live constantly in the commingling of two reflections, that of the past and that of the future, whirling apart and wide away" (*CL* 367; see *OP* 50). Imagine a dialectical dance between things imagined (the future) and things as they are (the past), which may be far apart, but still reflect each other. The problem is to adapt to this truth. "It is impossible to be truly reconciled, if one romanticizes the past (ploughmen, peacocks, doves)" – see Section II, *OP* 47–48 – nor to approach the "oncoming future if one enters it with indifference ... What is necessary is to recognize change as constant" (*CL* 367). The future is not a thing, not a destination, but a becoming, an arrival endlessly deferred.

In Section VI, Stevens urges a synthesis on the muses, wherein they are "to live incessantly in change" and accept "a moving chaos that never ends." There is no serene, still point. "Change composes too, and chaos comes / to momentary calm" – even the deceptive stillness of a summer's day conceals signs of "chaos and archaic change." So we need not fear "a drastic community" or the "mighty flight of men" – the masses – preparing what appears to be "an abysmal migration into a possible blue." The dreaded apocalypse of capital and labor may, just possibly, lead to better times (*OP* 50–51).

So, (Section VII) come down ladies! Come down and dance close to earth, barefoot on the grass. Dance like "damsels captured by the sky / Seized by that possible blue"; conceive then, that while you dance the statue (things as they are) falls to pieces, and new marble men – new heroes – "make real the attitudes / Appointed for them." And learn to speak and repeat a new mantra: "*To Be Itself*," until "your feelings are changed to sound, without a change" – that is, into pure poetry – "until the waterish ditherings" (of a poem like this?) "turn to the tense, the maudlin, true meridian that is yourselves" (*OP* 52). By Section VII, the muses become flesh, at one with the breathing earth, yet somehow are transfigured into living fire. Whether this Hegelian move to the sublime allows Stevens to square the dialectical circle remains a question; regardless, it is a move a ruthlessly realistic earthbound Marxist aesthetic cannot risk.

In the same dust-jacket copy to *The Man with the Blue Guitar* mentioned above, Stevens described "The Man with the Blue Guitar" as a series of notes – a suite of short poems – on the subject of pure poetry – or isolated poetry: "This group details with the incessant conjunctions between things as they are and things imagined" (*CPP* 998). A Marxist might have called the "incessant conjunctions" the dialectic, but Stevens is "not a Marxian poet" (*CL* 294). He adds significantly, "Although the blue guitar is a symbol of the imagination, it is used most often simply as *reference to the individuality of the poem*, meaning by the poet any man of imagination" (*CPP* 998, my emphasis). Stevens suggests the imagination is equivalent to individuality. The opposite may also be true; those who have no imaginations have no individuality. The mass man is the unimaginative man, therefore, unfree. Freedom, the ostensible goal of Marxism, is in fact predicated on the individual's freedom to imagine, a contradiction Soviet socialism never overcame.

In "The Man with the Blue Guitar" Stevens poses the individual guitarist/poet against the orchestra of social labor. Living by feeling and instinct – the "tom-tom, c'est moi" of his own heartbeat – the artist lacks, in the communist view, any political relevance. But he finds something else to express, if only his own "timid breathing," for "the blue guitar / And I are one." The expressive act of the imagination in music, which lacks any explicit semantic content, implicitly resists the collective red orchestra with its ominously proletarian image of "shuffling men."

The problem socialism has set for the self, nonetheless, instigates and informs this meditation on the intimate relationship between the poet, his imagination and the poem, symbolized by the guitar, which the poet can "pick up" and which "momentously declares" itself in the sounds the poet elicits through it. Since the music produced is of instrument and poet at once, the question is: Where does the poet begin and end? In other words, where in the psyche does the individual self encounter the political?

In Canto XIX of "Blue Guitar" Stevens hopes to "reduce the monster to / Myself, and then may be myself // in the face of the monster" (*CP* 175). If, as I take it, this monster is Marxist modernity, Stevens wants "to be more than part / Of it"; he wants to "not be / Alone, but reduce the monster and be, // Two things, the two together as one, And play of the monster and of myself" (*CP* 175).

"I believe in social reform," Stevens told Latimer, "and not in social revolution. From the point of view of social revolution IDEAS OF ORDER is a book of the most otiose prettiness . . . quite inadequate from any social point of view. However, I am not a propagandist" (WS to Latimer, March 17, 1936, *CL* 309). Yes, as he explained to Hi Simons later, he wants to do "everything practically possible to improve the condition of the workers" but he doesn't think that communist methods are the answer. "I think this explains my rightism," he adds dryly. What he wants for himself is to find, in fact, Burnshaw's "middle ground." "I wanted to get to the center," he says. He felt "isolated." And he "wanted to share the common life" of others, to engage with the "actual world." "People say that I live in a world of my own," he continues. Instead of seeking therefore for a "relentless contact" with that world, he prefers to "attempt to achieve the normal, the central" (WS to Simons, January 12, 1940, *CL* 351–352). From the center, Stevens believed, with normal, not relentless, contact with reality, he might attain pure poetry without worrying too much about social usefulness. It is from some such a center that the great late meditative poems arise.

Milton Bates says that Burnshaw's "review stimulated [Stevens'] imagination as no other external incident of the thirties had done" (Bates 173). But also it marks what Burnshaw in a late, retrospective talk called the "great divide of taste" in his reception. While many think Stevens' best and most profound work lay in the future, there is another school of thought that wished he had stuck to the playful style of *Harmonium*. For these readers (Yvor Winters, Al Alvarez, even Randall Jarrell), Stevens' philosophical "pure poetry" – especially the long poems – present unreasonable and unreadable enigmas. To these readers, Stevens' philosophizing in verse is too loose to be coherent – too "gaseous," too instinctive perhaps – to grasp (Burnshaw, "Reflections on Wallace Stevens" 123). Ironically, Stevens' slippery meanings – if any! – helped his postwar reputation. Critics were happy to see him as essentially post-ideological, an aesthete when young and a philosopher or "pure poet" when old.

In "The Noble Rider and the Sound of Words" Stevens claimed the poet has no political obligations (*NA* 27). An evasion perhaps; but politics has obligations to poetry that have never been acknowledged or understood, neither in the 1930s nor today. As we know to our sorrow, politics is part of the pervasive system of cultural production; poetry, when it is poetry, cannot be reduced to that. It slips away.

WORKS CITED

Bates, Milton J. *Wallace Stevens: A Mythology of Self.* University of California Press, 1985.

Burke, Kenneth. *Counter-Statement.* 1931. University of California Press, 1985.

Burnshaw, Stanley. "Middle-Ground Writers." *New Masses*, vol. 15, no. 5, 1935, pp. 19–21.

"Reflections on Wallace Stevens." Stevens and Politics, special issue of *The Wallace Stevens Journal*, vol. 13, no. 2, 1989, pp. 122–126.

"Stanley Burnshaw Protests." *Poetry*, vol. 44, no. 6, 1934, pp. 351–354.

"Turmoil in the Middle Ground." *New Masses*, vol. 17, no. 1, 1935, pp. 41–42.

"Wallace Stevens and the Statue." *Sewanee Review*, vol. 69, no. 3, 1961, pp. 355–366.

Dewey, John. *Individualism Old and New.* 1930. Capricorn, 1962.

Filreis, Alan. *Modernism from Right to Left: Wallace Stevens, the Thirties and Literary Radicalism.* Cambridge University Press, 1994.

Frost, Robert. *The Poetry of Robert Frost.* Holt, Rinehart and Winston, 1969.

Lentricchia, Frank. *Criticism and Social Change.* University of Chicago Press, 1985.

Poirier, Richard. *Robert Frost: The Work of Knowing.* Oxford University Press, 1979.

Pound, Ezra. *The Cantos.* 1925. 6th ed. New Directions, 1996.

Richardson, Joan. *Wallace Stevens: A Biography: The Later Years 1923–1955.* William Morrow, 1988.

Stevens, Wallace. *Collected Poems* [*CP*]. 1954. Vintage, 1982.

Collected Letters [*CL*]. Edited by Holly Stevens. University of California Press. 1996.

Collected Poetry & Prose [*CPP*]. Library of America, 1997.

Ideas of Order. Knopf, 1936.

The Necessary Angel [*NA*]. 1951. Vintage.

Opus Posthumous [*OP*]. 1957. Vintage, 1982.

Thomson, Robert Farrish. *Flash of the Spirit: African & Afro-American Art & Philosophy.* Random House, 1983.

Wilson, Edmund. *The Shores of Light: A Literary Chronical of the Twenties and Thirties.* Farrar Straus and Young, 1952.

Zukofsky, Louis. *Complete Short Poetry.* Johns Hopkins University Press, 1991.

CHAPTER 6

The Line of Wit

Stephanie Burt

Critics and poets who talk about wit most often describe the eighteenth century, the decades of Alexander Pope and Jonathan Swift and Oliver Goldsmith, of discursive, pointed, end-stopped couplets. "True wit is nature to advantage dressed; / What oft is thought but ne'er so well expressed," as Pope concluded in "An Essay on Criticism" (1711). Eighteenth-century wit meant a way for superior, well-read equals to speak and write with one another, a means of communication that displayed humor, intelligence, and proportion, even calm; it could also mean indirection, double meanings, humorous ways to say or imply what a poet could not highlight or say outright, from a monarch's indiscretions to the ridiculousness of an entire social system.

Surely modernism and its successors – movements and poets focused on overt innovation, on Romantic versions of strong feeling, on versions of cultural nationalism, or (all else failing) on stand-alone, urn-like poems – would not be likely to follow Pope's lead. Indeed the most common ways to introduce, teach, and summarize modern poetry in America focus on one of those four goals, accounted for elsewhere in this volume. And yet modern poets also extend the line of wit. Take Marianne Moore, insulting a ponderously masculine, literally overbearing figure in the guise of construction equipment in "To a Steamroller" (1917):

> The illustration
> is nothing to you without the application.
> You lack half wit. You crush all the particles down
> into close conformity, and then walk back and forth on them. (17)

Steamrollers were scarcely older than Moore herself: commercial production for the heavy vehicles began in the late 1860s. Her metaphor, like her syllabics, remains modern. Her mode of operation, however, dates back to Pope, as she recognizes near the end of her compact, sting-in-each-tail poem:

> As for butterflies, I can hardly conceive
>   of one's attending upon you, but to question
>   the congruence of the complement is vain, if it exists.

Pope had mocked the effeminate Lord Hervey, then imagined objections to his mockery: "Who breaks a butterfly upon a wheel?" (Hervey had earlier mocked Pope's disability.) Pope's wheel (a torture device) was Pope's wit; the steamroller's wheel, erasing nuance and rolling over opponents, is a kind of anti-wit. It is Moore, not her clumsy opponent, who respects distinctions, who deploys a lepidopteran nuance.

Moore's line of wit continues through her later, longer, more elaborate poems. "He 'Digesteth Harde Yron'" (1941) praises the ostrich's unsolicitous wartime "heroism" and endurance:

> How
>   could he, prized for plumes and eggs and young
> used even as a riding-beast, respect men
>   hiding actor-like in ostrich skins, with the right hand
> making the neck move as if alive
> and from a bag the left hand strewing grain, that ostriches
>
>   might be decoyed and killed! Yes, this is he
> whose plume was anciently
> the plume of justice; he
>   whose comic duckling head on its
> great neck revolves with compass-needle nervousness
> when he stands guard. (151–52)

We stand with the ostrich against the "actor-like" men, who could never fool us: and yet the defiant bird also looks ridiculous, with his "comic duckling head" (as ridiculous, perhaps, as a government in exile; as the Free French). The wit aids the ethical project: one need not look proud, or dignified, to be a hero or do good – in fact, a concern for looks might get in the way.

Rachel Trousdale, in her study of humor in modern poems, finds that Moore's early satirical portraits – "To a Steam Roller" among them – display "her ethical commitment to empathy even when she is most critical of her subject" (69). In Moore's later, longer, more ambitious "The Pangolin," wit and its cognates distinguish humanity from admirable animals: "Humor saves a few steps, it saves years" – "the only difference between humans and animals," Trousdale continues, "which Moore explicitly acknowledges" (89).

Wit, like humor, is more often praised than defined, and no wonder:
the term (as opposed to, say, "tragedy" or "satire") refers to a common-
ality among writers and readers, a sociability inseparable from that other
hard-to-pin-down quality, tone. We can say, however, that literary wit,
like humor, appeals to experience shared between readers and writers.
And yet, as Anna Furlong writes, "wit is not coextensive with humor"
(137). Instead, effects of wit, in verse or prose, require "quickness,"
intellectual agility, and a reader or listener who can revise, reinterpret,
realize that first impressions do not suffice. "The sense of discovery is
crucial," Furlong explains. "It enlists the reader as a participant, even co-
creator" (139).

No wonder, then, that the other preeminent poet of wit in the early
twentieth century drew so much of his technique, and so many of his
subjects, from the familiar environs of his primary imagined readers:
Harlem, New York. As against the very serious import of Langston
Hughes's few most famous poems ("I, too, sing America") we might
consider his immortal end-stopped couplet "Little Lyric (Of Great
Importance)": "I wish the rent / Was heaven-sent" (*Poems* 226).
Hughes's ironic mode uses rhyme to point up inequalities. In "Sister," a
boy asks his older sister why she appears to be dating a "little Negro" who
already has a wife and a child. "Does it ever occur to you, boy / that a
woman does the best she can?" replies his interlocutor. A neighbor adds,
"So does a man" (*Poems* 391).

The vernacular wit of Hughes's poems can rely on situational irony: we
recognize the distance between what would motivate a character in a conventional romantic poem (erotic fulfillment, artistic aspiration) and what
motivates people in real life (money, safety, self-respect). "Shakespeare in
Harlem" remembers that young women might well prefer protection to
romance, as well as a bluesy quatrain to a Shakespearean pentameter:

> Hey ninny neigh!
> And a hey nonny noe!
> Where, oh, where
> Did my sweet mama go?
>
> Hey ninny neigh
> With a tra-la-la-la!
> They say your sweet mama
> Went home to her ma. (*Poems* 260)

Hughes expects readers to recognize the difference between real-life Harlem (where people need money and safety) and the imagined romantic environment of Romeo and Juliet. The joke behind the joke is that Shakespeare's play makes the same point: this "sweet mama" appears so young that she'd be better off with "her ma."

Hughesian wit can arrive through recurring characters: "Jessie B. Semple," in the prose columns Hughes wrote for the Chicago *Defender*, or Madam Alberta K. Johnson, the "assertive, brassy Harlem heroine," "feminine counterpart to ... Semple" (so Hughes's biographer put it), who speaks in jaunty ballad stanzas, as in "Madam and the Phone Bill" (Rampersad 79):

> You say I O.K.ed
> LONG DISTANCE?
> O.K.ed it when?
> My goodness, Central,
> That was *then!*
>
> I'm mad and disgusted
> With that Negro now.
> I don't pay no REVERSED
> CHARGES nohow. (*Poems* 353)

Madam Johnson is a comic rogue, and the poems invite us to take her side.

As far apart as Hughes and Moore may seem in other respects, both poets rely on what Moore's onetime disciple Elizabeth Bishop would later call a "constant sense of readjustment": a set of devices, rhyme among them, that bring implied author and implied reader together, helping us understand – or judge – third parties, and helping us do so (moreover) with a kind of light touch. That resemblance may be the soul of wit, a word that recurs in the postwar poet and World War II veteran Richard Wilbur. The title poem from Wilbur's *Ceremony* (1950) praises an outdoor portrait by the French Impressionist J. F. Bazille, most likely "La robe rose":

> I am for wit and wakefulness
> And love this feigning lady by Bazille.
> What's lightly hid is deepest understood,
> And when with social smile and formal dress
> She teaches leaves to curtsey and quadrille,
> I think there are most tigers in the wood. (210)

Wilbur writes in favor of artifice, game-playing, and formality, and perhaps in defense of the feminine too. Such poems as Wilbur's depend on them, almost as Hughes's poems depend on the flow of vernacular conversation. Without a listener, an exchange, a "social smile," no language game can be played.

Edward Brunner takes Wilbur's style as a means toward democratic accessibility: a Wilbur poem's "clues chart a pathway that can be followed with deepening understanding and pleasure," "an assemblage of useful techniques that guarantee consumer usability" (8). Wilbur might have balked at the term "consumer": he tended to envision his readers instead as democratically collaborative producers, working together to replace war with peace, chaos with order, a discredited sacred realm with a civic and secular one: "What does it say over the door of Heaven," he wrote in "For the New Railway Station in Rome," "but *Homo fecit*," "man-made"? Wilbur may seem – at least acoustically – to follow the lead of Robert Frost. Frost, too, presented himself as playful, as a gracious host, as in the opening poem from *North of Boston* (1914), "The Pasture":

> I'm going out to fetch the little calf
> That's standing by the mother. It's so young,
> It totters when she licks it with her tongue.
> I sha'n't be gone long. – You come too. (1)

But Frost almost never extends invitations to equals: his games become tricks, as in the near-fatal farmhouse prank he describes in "The Code." Frost's last major poem, "Directive," presents the poet not as the reader's peer but as a "guide / Who only has at heart your getting lost," inviting us not (like Wilbur) into a civilized space but rather into an "abandoned cellar-hole," like a grave, with a Lethean chalice "beyond confusion" (377–78).

Wilbur's acoustics may derive from Frost, but his sensibility owes far more to W. H. Auden, who marked his relocation to America with a nearly complete change of style. The era's preeminent reviewer, Randall Jarrell, recognized Auden's long poem "New Year Letter" (1940) as something new to modernity, the sort of thing that might have been predicted by "Pope's ghost": "a didactic epistle of about nine hundred tetrameter couplets" full of "Wit, Learning and Sentiment," "the entirely unexpected feat of making a successful long poem out of a reasonable, objective, and comprehensive discussion" (*Kipling* 55–57).

What "New Year Letter" discussed was hardly reasonable, even if it was predictable: a world war. And yet its goals, its Augustan models, and its insistence on a potential community of intimate equals (starting with Auden's friend Elizabeth Mayer) would set a kind of outer limit – a wittiest, clearest, most Augustan outer bound – for much subsequent American verse. Rather than watching a masterful poet perform feats – or, worse, an orator exhort – Auden's readers might play with language together:

> No longer can we learn our good
> From chances of a neighborhood
> Or class or party, or refuse
> As individuals to choose
> Our loves authorities and friends
> To judge our means and plan our ends;
> For the machine has cried aloud
> And publicised among the crowd
> The secret that was always true
> But known once only to the few,
> Compelling all to the admission,
> Aloneness is man's real condition,
> That each must travel forth alone
> In search of the Essential Stone . . .
>
> Like any Jamesian character,
> [We] Learn to draw the careful line,
> Develop, understand refine. (238–39)

"Aloneness" here refers both to an inescapable human condition and to the malady we can ameliorate by assembling ourselves, not into "crowds" or states but into small, friendly groups. The transatlantic poet would insist later that "if poetry has any ulterior purpose it is to disenchant and disintoxicate" (*Dyer's* 27). He titled one of his most beguiling poems of the 1950s, quoting Shakespeare, "'The Truest Poetry Is the Most Feigning'": these pentameter couplets suggest that the cleverest – and most effective – poetic art speaks from author to reader carefully, playfully, perhaps in code, over the heads of tyrants, establishing a kind of secure community free from steamrollers, composed of those in the know. "Be subtle, various, ornamental, clever," that poem advised. "Good poets have a weakness for bad puns." Under a dictatorship, or in a homophobic society driven by the Red Scare, a poet writing of erotic love might encode their sentiment in friable praise for a tyrant, turning "Goddess of wry-necks and wrens / To Great Reticulator of the Fens" (Mussolini had literally drained Rome's fens).

Auden's praise for code is itself a code: under cover of Cold War support
for dissidents, Auden could hint that he wrote gay love poems. Auden's
identity as a gay man in what he regarded as a marriage to Chester
Kallman – one that lasted from the early 1940s until Auden's death in
1972 – remained an open secret in pre-Stonewall literary America, a
hidden subject in "'The Truest Poetry Is the Most Feigning'" as in his
other love poems. And yet, as Richard Bozorth points out, "the poem's
conclusion ... should challenge the reader who would see here the coded
confession of a gay Auden"; instead, it makes circumspection "a metaphysical condition entailing ... a spiritual duty" (235).

Auden's disarming elaborations of the 1940s and 1950s substitute wit
for oratory, "the bullhorn for the blackboard," as Bonnie Costello put it, or
even the drawing room (132). Perhaps more mandarin than they are
inviting, Auden's frame-breaking choral passages and monologues in his
long poems – in particular the prose poetry of "Caliban to the Audience" –
are for Costello "a way of getting the audience on the stage by proxy,"
turning a potentially passive set of readers and listeners into participants in
an "antimonological monologue" (129, 139). Her critical language here
looks forward to Auden's slightly later, often-admired stand-alone poem
"In Praise of Limestone," with its "antimythological myth": "If it form the
one landscape that we, the inconstant ones, / Are consistently homesick
for, this is chiefly / Because it dissolves in water" (540). For another critic,
Edna Longley, Auden's calcium carbonate "represents the play of our
minds" and "questions fixed boundaries between life or Nature and
civilization or art" – moreover, "it has a politics": meliorist, antirevolu-
tionary, uncynical (177). Auden's long, Latinate, unemphatic lines underscore the flexibility that porous, easy-to-carve limestone must support.

If we see wit as lightness of tone applied to a serious subject, as a way to
share a perspective with an audience marked out as civilized or tolerant or
superior, then the line of wit unites much of Auden's late work, both
sacred and secular, from his elaborate homages to each room of the house
in "Thanksgiving for a Habitat" to his sequence about the Crucifixion,
"Horae Canonicae," which concludes with distant, harmonious birdsong:

> Among the leaves the small birds sing;
> The crow of the cock commands awaking:
> *In solitude, for company.*
>
> Bright shines the sun on creatures mortal;
> Men of their neighbours become sensible:
> *In solitude, for company.* (642)

"Sensible" means "aware," but also something like "reasonable" or "accepting" – an achievement, in Auden's eyes.

Trousdale's study of humor in modern American poems underlines "laughter's role in revealing or creating common ground" (37). Auden, she writes, "only start[ed] to be funny after ... he gained a sense of the possibility of communion with other people"; the transatlantic poet saw in light verse (he edited *The Oxford Book of Light Verse* in 1937) "poets who consider themselves on equal terms with a broad audience" (42, 43). Critics and poets who failed to find that audience in their own day could look back to a time when (in their view of history) it existed. Nicknamed Possum (for his habit of playing dead), T. S. Eliot had, in his essays on Andrew Marvell and John Dryden, imagined an "alternative 'tradition' of minor poets" as a remedy for "both the situation of literary culture in his own time and the situation of his coterie" (Guillory 148). For Eliot minor poets appeal to – while major poets reject, or reshape – an existing order, both among poems and among people. That order, renamed "reasonableness," becomes in Eliot's essay on Marvell a requirement for the particular kind of wit that Marvell (but not Pope, a "great master of hatred") could support (161–62).

While Eliot's heirs among American critics dominated the academy during the 1940s and 1950s, his influence as a poet arrived – and peaked – earlier. With Auden things were otherwise. Aidan Wasley devoted a book to Auden's influence in America, where the English poet – from successive homes in Michigan, Brooklyn, Italy, Austria, and Manhattan – found potential American peers, imagining "his poetry as the site of hopeful exchange between himself and his reader," inviting a conversational "reciprocity" that took in, at the start of their careers, such dissimilar – but white – writers as John Ashbery, Allen Ginsberg, John Hollander, and Sylvia Plath, as well as such not-quite-contemporaries as Jarrell, who devoted a series of lectures at Princeton to Auden's poetic development thus far: "the range and levels of his wit are astonishing" (Wasley 15, 47; Jarrell, *Auden* 71). "Despite Jarrell's mixed feelings about Auden's American career," Wasley continues, "his analysis of Auden's utility for future poets was indeed borne out" (57).

We can hear that utility in Jarrell himself, who got attention first for cutting, accurate reviews, and then for his serious poems about airmen, soldiers, and prisoners in World War II; later in life he wrote sensitively, even romantically, about childhood, and about overlooked or disempowered women. Common takes on his career have it that he put his wit and much of his "genius into his criticism" and his feelingful "talent into his poetry" (Vendler, *Part* 111). And the poems do feel – they open themselves to yearning, and to loneliness, and to tenderness, as no other poet of his era could. But they are, also, models of quiet wit. They reach out to imagined peers, as when a lonely, apparently unemployed man (perhaps he works from home; perhaps he's a writer) sees himself in the neighborhood's outdoor pets:

> We nod to each other sometimes, in humanity,
>
> Or search one another's faces with a yearning
> Remnant of faith that's almost animal . . .
> The gray cat that just sits there: surely it is learning
> To be a man; will find, soon, *some especial*
> *Opening in a good firm for a former cat.* (*Complete Poems* 259)

Who has not wished to be a cat? (Jarrell responded to the bombings of Hiroshima and Nagasaki, in a letter to his editor at the *Nation*, "I feel so rotten about the country's response . . . that I wish I could become a naturalized dog or cat" [130].) A more famous poem, "Next Day," takes the voice of a homemaker who has (it is the title of Jarrell's book of essays) "a sad heart at the supermarket":

> Moving from Cheer to Joy, from Joy to All,
> I take a box
> And add it to my wild rice, my Cornish game hens.
> The slacked or shorted, basketed, identical
> Food-gathering flocks
> Are selves I overlook. Wisdom, said William James
>
> Is learning what to overlook. And I am wise
> If that is wisdom. (279)

The formal intricacies (paired rhymes, for example: box/flocks, all/identical, and so on for ten stanzas) reveal themselves on rereading; so does the despair. First, though, the readers of "Next Day" encounter a voice, the voice of a woman making light of her heavily frustrated life, imagining listeners who (like her) read William James and might smile along with her at the puns on the shelves.

For Costello, Auden's career shows how "poetry as an art not only refers and reflects but also imagines and formulates *potential* community" (13, original italics). Such a community "forms around a conversation as in a friendship or marriage, rather than around the consensus of a tribe" (27). That kind of conversation takes place throughout the later poetry of James Merrill, surely Auden's most vivid and most inventive follower. If Merrill turns wit, always, into wordplay, the wordplay itself, in his strongest work, points to community longed-for, imagined, or finally found, whether in the social group of the living and the dead in his Ouija-board epic *The Changing Light at Sandover* or in the child's fantasy Merrill sketches out in "Days of 1935," where he imagines being kidnapped, like the Lindbergh baby, for ransom:

> I'd hoped I was worth more than crime
> Itself, which never paid, could pay.
> Worth more than my own father's time
> Or mother's negligée
>
> Undone where dim ends barely met,
> This being a Depression year . . .
> I'd hoped, I guess, that they would let
> Floyd and Jean keep me here. (308)

Father time, negligée undone, making ends meet: the "dim ends" of the language itself become the material Merrill stitches together for our amusement, as he recalls his earlier life as a child with too few companions, and too much time in his small hands. (The ballad form, meanwhile, looks back to Auden's late 1930s murder ballads: Merrill, unlike Auden, and very much like a psychoanalyst, hopes to bring us back to the scene of the crime.)

Wit means framing important matters as shared, as the potential subject of in-jokes; it also means treating the most important matters as potentially trivial, and trivia as important – sunset as death, death as sunset, the creation of the world as a book blurb, as in Merrill's late poem "To the Reader":

> Each day, hot off the press from Moon & Son,
> "Knowing of your continued interest,"
> Here's a new book – well, actually the updated
> Edition of their one all-time best seller –
> To find last night's place in, and forge ahead.
> If certain scenes and situations ("work,"
> As the jacket has it, "of a blazingly
> Original voice") make you look up from your page
> – *But this is life, is truth, is me!* – too many
> Smack of self-plagiarism. Terror and trust,
> Vow and verbena, done before, to death,
> In earlier chapters, under different names . . .
> And what about *those* characters? No true
> Creator would just let them fade from view
> Or be snuffed out, like people. (616)

"Like people." Few poets have stated so smoothly, nor so entertainingly, that there is no afterlife and no benevolent God. And yet Merrill never positions himself as a God substitute, a sub-creator; instead, he shares, with us, this topsy-turvy, elaborate, beautiful world, along with his learned ways of regarding it, treating each day as a book – an entertaining, best-selling one – to be opened and read.

That reading recalls the other, more effortful readings that Merrill performs through the Ouija board in *Sandover* (1976–83), itself a massive, even an overbalanced, effort to combine wit with science fiction and both with political doctrine. Ephraim says to Merrill, and to Merrill's boyfriend David Jackson: "Must *everything* be witty? AH MY DEARS / I AM NOT LAUGHING I WILL SIMPLY NOT SHED TEARS" (*Sandover* 17). "Merrill is unusual," writes Helen Vendler, "in that almost every plane of the linguistic, including the pun (a taste he shared with Keats), appeals to him. He possessed an enormous facility in rhyme, but he also enjoyed its simplest games" (*Ocean* 208). Eleanor Cook points to puns as signs of humility as well as ways to participate in the ongoing, shared life of a given tongue: "language so tested and so paronomastic displays its own vitality. Words do have a life of their own" (183). His poems – especially their openings – could go over the top, alerting readers not to take his discoveries too seriously at first, as in "Rhapsody on Czech Themes," Merrill's final travel poem: "A mauve madness has overrun Moravia" (859).

For Gary Saul Morson, wit is not so much an expression of common cause as a verbal victory over nonverbal adversity: "*the successful witticism expresses the triumph of mind and its adequacy to any social situation.* In an instant, the wit masters all the complexities of a set of social circumstances and formulates a perfectly apropos remark" (147). And yet the remark, for effect, must find readers or listeners – and quickly, too. Those listeners may well belong – pace Costello – to an ethnic group, or a "tribe." Wilbur and Frost, in their ways, are writing about, and primarily for, and certainly as, white people, while Hughes wrote primarily for Black Americans (it is the subject of his essay "The Negro Artist and the Racial Mountain"). Epigrammatic address to Black America persisted even through the relative earnestness of the 1970s. Take Alvin Aubert's three-line poem "My Name Is Arrow": "my old man bent down / so long so low / he turned into a bow" (quoted in Thomas 184). The poem invites us to connect its last word to its title, releasing (as it were) the poet himself to soar above what troubled his hardworking father, made strong by a life of unfairly delayed gratification.

To read for wit is to consider an audience; it is, as well, to scramble some of the lines dividing highbrow from middlebrow, so-called poet's poets (such as Moore) from the genuinely popular, such as journalist Don Marquis, famous for conversational free verse supposedly written by a cockroach named Archy, leaping from typewriter key to typewriter key (he could not reach the shift button). "i was once a vers libre bard," Archy's first poem begins,

> but i died and my soul went
> into the body of a cockroach
> it has given me a new outlook upon life
> i see things from the underside now
> thank you for the apple peelings in the wastepaper basket
> the paste is getting stale so i cant eat it
> there is a cat here called mehitabel i wish you would have
> removed she nearly ate me the other night why don't she
> catch rats that is what she is supposed to be for
> there is a rat here she should get without delay (4–5)

Archy understands himself as social, interacting not only with the journalists who read his words but with the other creatures in the office, such as Mehitabel, and a ghost, and a flea, who informs the cockroach-poet

> i am
> going to have dinner off a
> man eating tiger if a vacuum gets
> me I will try and send you word
> before the worst comes to
> the worst some people i told him inhabit
> a vacuum all their lives and
> never know it then he said it don t
> hurt them any no i said it don't but it
> hurts people who have to associate
> with them and with these words
> we parted each feeling
> superior to the other and is not that
> feeling after all one of the great
> delights of social intercourse (108–9)

It is, but so is sharing a joke, or a pun (like Marquis's pun on "vacuum"), or a lighthearted poem.

Marquis rarely figures in discussions of influence. And yet we can find Archy's disarming manner, treating the trivial as profound and vice versa,

and making a style self-consciously and humorously from the physical
limits of the page, recurring in the far more ambitious, critically lauded
poetry of A. R. Ammons, whose first long poem *Tape for the Turn of
the Year* (1965) took its external form and its maximum line length
from the width of adding machine tape – Ammons called it a "long / thin
/ poem/ employing certain / classical considerations" (2). Ammons, too,
takes seriously – if jocularly – the idea that other creatures (baboons,
"birds," cockroaches) can communicate as we do: "we are not singular in
language," he mused in *Garbage* (1988); "have some respect for other
speakers of being and / for god's sake drop all this crap about words, //
singularity and dominion ... I know the entire language of chickens," he
mused, "from rooster crows to biddy cheeps" (50–51). He even described
himself as "another archie":

> I'm merely an old person: whose mother is dead:
>
> whose father is gone ... it was all quite frankly
> to be expected and not looked forward to, even
> old trees, I remember some of them, where they
>
> used to stand: pictures taken by some of them,
> quad dogs with their *hierarchies* (another *archie*) (22–23)

It is, perhaps, the wit of self-deprecation: an "old person" who knows
enough to realize that experience is not wisdom, and who passes that anti-
wisdom along.

William Empson's extended analysis of the word "wit" considers its use in
Pope, where the main sense of "power to make ingenious (and critical)
jokes" subtended other implications having to do with audience, "the smart
milieu that Pope was addressing" (561). In other poets the wit can seem
aspirational: the poem looks out for someone, somewhere, who can work as
the poet's intellectual equal. That kind of yearning, an undertone in Jarrell,
becomes a major driver in the poetry of John Hollander, known during
his lifetime for his scholarship as well as for his many kinds of verse,
some indebted to Jewish religious learning, others to Hollander's own
meticulous study of verse techniques. Hollander often noted his debts to
Auden, mythologized in *Reflections on Espionage* under the pseudonym
"Steampump": "the poem as a whole," Kenneth Gross writes, "is a farewell
to Auden," "the poet of moral wit and decorum and riddle" (260). *Powers of
Thirteen* (1984) shows that Hollander had not left wit and riddle behind. It
comprises 169 sonnet-like poems of thirteen thirteen-syllable lines:

Unanswered, our riddles remain wise and beautiful
In their impossibility of is and is-nots, ones
And manys at once, fluctuating numbers of legs.
The Gordian knot was gorgeous if you stopped to look.
Solving them shoots down the angels of their oddity,
And the prize that thunks down on the hard ground at one's feet
Might as well have been store-bought. (*Selected* 89)

The poet of riddles, conunudrums, puns, and intellectual goose-chases here gestures at their opposite, the romantic challenge, the emotional mystery, that lies at the heart of all life and can never be solved.

Can wit be avant-garde? The quality seems incompatible with any stance that attributes special powers and knowledge to the poet alone. It fits, on the other hand, an "experimental" or hard-to-interpret poetry founded on shared or sharable skepticism about what can be known, a poetry composed in opposition to bourgeois or conventional verities. Rae Armantrout has written poems like that throughout her now half-century-long career, which began (confusingly, for her interpreters) among Bay Area poets as devoted to book-length projects, to ambitious expansion, as Armantrout herself was to small, strange, spiky, stand-alone, sayable things. "My poetry," she asserted in 2000, "involves an equal counterweight of assertion and doubt. It's a Cheshire poetics, one that points two ways then vanishes in the blur of what is seen and what is seeing" (*Prose* 55)

Armantrout derives her wit less from making language easy to share than from showing, sometimes sarcastically, how much of the language we take to be our own comes to us already borrowed, common, compromised. She may start by making fun of a phrase from an advertisement, or a self-help slogan ("can you phrase your demand as a question?"), appealing to our shared sense that we readers of poems know too much to fool ourselves, and then ends by asking whether we even have selves. Consider the opening couplets of "Attention," from *Necromance* (1991):

> Ventriloquy
> is the mother tongue.
>
> Can you colonize rejection
> by phrasing your request,
>   "Me want?" (*Necromance* 39)

Armantrout may not have had, before the 2000s, many readers who overlapped with Merrill's, but the two poets share a devotion to puns and a desire to share their skeptical orientations with a select audience singled out through those puns. If the transatlantically well-traveled Merrill pursues the hot press of sun and moon, the California-based Armantrout finds herself stuck in freeway traffic, "in surplus meaning / quite heavy of late" (27). *Necromance* also makes fun at once of all social life ("a string of favors"), all human desire, and the Catholic rosary:

> A string of favors, one per bead,
> to be asked in sequence.
>
> This hasn't worked for us, but we know
> this is how things work. (44)

"We" know: we have lived too long and seen too much to believe that things will always work out, and if we complain we can at least entertain one another by casting those complaints in terse, sharp verse.

Armantrout bridges the twentieth and the twenty-first century, but her antecedents are modernist: William Carlos Williams, Lorine Niedecker, Emily Dickinson. She has published essays about all three. Other major American poets of wit, in-jokes, sarcasm, and lightness had barely found their styles before that century began, Lucia Perillo, Angie Estes, and Terrance Hayes among them. Perillo enjoyed an outdoor career in the Pacific Northwest with the National Park Service before she began to publish poetry in the late 1980s; soon afterward she was diagnosed with multiple sclerosis, and her twin engagements with nonhuman animals and with her own disability form the backdrop for many of her poems. The foreground can bring in almost anything, from "The Oldest Map with the Name America" (the title poem of her third collection) to the "Inseminator Man" responsible (indirectly) for impregnating cows to the "foley," the creator of sound effects for movies, whose job reminds Perillo in turn of

> my friend who does phone sex
> because it's a job that lets her keep at her typewriter all day,
> tapping out poems. Somehow she can work
> both sides of her brain simultaneously, the poem
> being what's really going on and the sex being what sounds
> like what's going on: the only time she stops typing
> is when she pinches her cheek away from her gums,
> which is supposed to sound like oral sex. (43–44)

The men on these calls agree to deceive themselves – but we belong to the circle of friends who understand what's really happening, who may not be laughing, but will not shed tears. Perillo's wit shows up her distance – and our distance, too – from authority over the body, that odd collocation of bone and meat and nerves that often refuses to do what we wish it could do. Instead we come together and pretend, even though "what's been walking around in my clothes all these years / turns out to have been a swap meet of carbons / and salts" (57).

Perillo speaks from a position not of disavowing power but of never having had much of it. Perillo's American English, her free verse, also keeps its distance from "European" formal effects, such as rhyme and meter. So do the communities in Terrance Hayes's early work, making bleak humor out of historical atrocity and present-day making-do: "'Buy one, get one free,' said the slave trader to cotton heads / when pregnant African girls mounted the auction block. America! / Everything has its price; nearly everything has been bought" (27). Without the elaborate formal armatures that characterize his later work, the Hayes of *Muscular Music* (1999) relies on an audience that will join him in his flights from pathos to sarcasm and then back the other way:

> Who will save the big men of this world?
> Earlier I watched *King Kong* and was sorry again
> for those building-size fuckers we see falling
> from miles away. Those we thought invincible,
> almost permanent like the sun which burns,
> truthfully, only a few hours every day. (51)

"Those building-size fuckers" are us: we can laugh at ourselves, and then try to save our friends.

As for Estes, her links to the European past, to rhyme, to other languages (French and Italian), and to older artistic technique would give her motors for her most original books, beginning with *Chez Nous* (2004). During the 1990s her sonic intricacies were still to come. She had, however, developed the casually accepting, disarming stance before prior art that Auden had encouraged, puncturing authority while admiring technique, deploying wit to let her readers in. On statuary in "The Classical Tradition," Estes wrote in her first book, "The most distinctive feature ... is that the nose / is always the first / to go" (3). Depicting herself as an iron (an ironist but also a clothes iron) she concocts a poem about loving women as wink-filled as Auden's poems about loving men: "I chose instead to give pleasure to pleats / and hung out with darts aimed at all manner / of breasts" (43). And in a poem called "Poems," the young Estes envisions a succession of houseguests, or poems, or readers, or lovers:

> They restock
> the pantry with foods you can't pronounce, renovate
> your appetite and leave crumbs all over the house.

It's just as you imagined, discoveries abound:
poems don't do dishes, but make strudel

you can't live without. One morning they get up and announce
they're moving on. (44)

Conclusion

What have these workers in the line of wit to do with workers and bosses,
with revolutionary aspirations, with attempts on poets' part to alter electoral
politics? Sometimes (as with "New Year Letter") everything: they draw
together, explicitly, communities of imagined friends who face threats from
the state, or from the news. Sometimes the connection seems less sure. And
yet the line of wit persists, even among poets (such as Hayes) who also see
urgent, political, ethical problems: wit lends us (these poets imply) a sense of
community, a sense of perspective, a sense, not of how to fight, but of what
we fight – and negotiate, and organize, and even compromise – for.

WORKS CITED

Ammons, A. R. *Garbage*. New York: Norton, 1988.
  Tape for the Turn of the Year. New York: Norton, 1965.
Armantrout, Rae. *Collected Prose*. San Diego, CA: Singing Horse, 2007.
  Necromance. Los Angeles, CA: Sun & Moon, 1991.
Auden, W. H. *Collected Poems*, ed. Edward Mendelson. New York: Vintage, 1991.
  The Dyer's Hand. New York: Random House, 1962.
Bozorth, Richard. *Auden's Games of Knowledge*. New York: Columbia University Press, 2002.
Brunner, Edward. *Cold War Poetry*. Urbana: University of Illinois Press, 2000.
Cook, Eleanor. *Against Coercion: Games Poets Play*. Stanford, CA: Stanford University Press, 1998.
Costello, Bonnie. *The Plural of Us: Poetry and Community in Auden and Others*. Princeton, NJ: Princeton University Press, 2017.
Eliot, T. S. *Selected Essays*, ed. Frank Kermode. London: Faber and Faber, 1957.
Empson, William. "Wit in the Essay on Criticism." *Hudson Review* 2:4 (1950): 559–77.
Estes, Angie. *The Uses of Passion*. Layton, UT: Gibbs Smith, 1996.
Frost, Robert. *Complete Poems*, ed. Edward Connery Lathem. New York: Henry Holt, 1973.
Furlong, Anna. "The Soul of Wit: A Relevance Theoretic Discussion." *Language and Literature* 20:2 (2011): 134–50.
Gross, Kenneth. "John Hollander's Games of Patience." In Jenn Lewin, ed., *Never Again Would Birds' Song Be the Same*. New Haven, CT: Beineke Library/ Yale University, 2002. 247–67.
Guillory, John. *Cultural Capital*. Chicago: University of Chicago Press, 1993.

Haughton, Hugh. "Poetry and Good Humor: Marianne Moore and Elizabeth Bishop." In Rachel Trousdale, ed., *Humor in Modern American Poetry*. New York: Bloomsbury, 2018. 97–120.

Hayes, Terrance. *Muscular Music*. Pittsburgh, PA: Carnegie-Mellon University Press, 2006 (1999).

Hollander, John. Interview. *Auden Society Newsletter* 21 (2001). https://audensociety.org/21newsletter.html#P21_13047.

Selected Poetry. New York: Knopf, 1991.

Hughes, Langston. *The Collected Poems*, ed. Arnold Rampersad and David Roessel. New York: Vintage, 1994.

The Langston Hughes Reader. New York: Georges Braziller, 1958.

Jarrell, Randall. *The Complete Poems*. New York: Farrar, Straus and Giroux, 1969.

Kipling, Auden, & Co. New York: Farrar, Straus and Giroux, 1980.

The Letters of Randall Jarrell, 2nd ed., ed. Mary von Schrader Jarrell. Charlottesville: University Press of Virginia, 2002.

Randall Jarrell on W. H. Auden, ed. Stephanie Burt with Hannah Brooks-Motl. New York: Columbia University Press, 2006.

Longley, Edna. *Poetry and Posterity*. Newcastle-upon-Tyne: Bloodaxe, 2000.

Marquis, Don. *The Annotated Archy and Mehitabel*, ed. Michael Sims. New York: Penguin, 2006.

Mendelson, Edward. *Later Auden*. New York: Farrar, Straus and Giroux, 1999.

Merrill, James. *Collected Poems*, ed. J. D. McClatchy and Stephen Yenser. New York: Knopf, 2001.

The Changing Light at Sandover. New York: Knopf, 1982.

Moore, Marianne. *New Collected Poems*, ed. Heather Cass White. New York: Farrar, Straus and Giroux, 2017.

Morson, Gary Saul. "Contingency, Games and Wit." *New Literary History* 40:1 (2009): 131–57.

Perelman, Bob. *The Trouble with Genius*. Berkeley: University of California Press, 1994.

Perillo, Lucia. *Time Will Clean the Carcass Bones: Selected and New Poems*. Port Townsend, WA: Copper Canyon, 2016.

Rampersad, Arnold. *The Life of Langston Hughes, vol. 2: I Dream a World*. New York: Oxford University Press, 1988.

Thomas, Lorenzo. *Extraordinary Measures: Afrocentric Modernism and 20th Century Poetry*. Tuscaloosa: University of Alabama Press, 2000.

Trousdale, Rachel. *Humor, Empathy and Community in 20th Century American Poetry*. New York: Oxford University Press, 2021.

Vendler, Helen. *The Ocean, the Bird and the Scholar: Essays on Poets and Poetry*. Cambridge, MA: Harvard University Press, 2015.

Part of Nature, Part of Us: Modern American Poets. Cambridge, MA: Harvard University Press, 1980.

Wasley, Aidan. *The Age of Auden: Postwar Poetry and the American Scene*. Princeton, NJ: Princeton University Press, 2011.

Wilbur, Richard. *Collected Poems 1943–2004*. New York: Harcourt, 2006.

CHAPTER 7

US Poets on War and Peace

From the Spanish-American War to Afghanistan

Mark W. Van Wienen

In April 1917, Woodrow Wilson's call for a declaration of war – "The world must be made safe for democracy" – enshrined liberal-democratic nation-building as central to the US military mission, conceivably extended to every nation on earth (Tooze 9). Such sentiments might be credited with inspiring the most voluminous outpouring of *pro*war poetry in American literary history. Yet under the idealistic veneer Wilson's aim was no less than US hegemony in a world capitalist system, in which "political liberty" would promote an open global marketplace that the United States could dominate (Dayton 15). This contradiction between Wilsonian ideal and reality catalyzed, in turn, a body of trenchant antiwar poetry. Broadly speaking, this minority report has become the pattern for most American poetry of war and peace written ever since, which has sought to debunk the recurring fantasy that, in American hands, war might become an instrument of peace and liberation. Yet this largely antiwar trajectory has remained largely at the cultural margins, only under exceptional circumstances speaking for the political mainstream.

I

The Wilsonian doctrine of war-making was not altogether novel. Its underlying aims of national aggrandizement had been implicit in the Manifest Destiny undergirding 300 years of intermittent genocidal warfare against Indigenous Americans. Moreover, a version of Wilson's claim that the United States was fighting "for the rights of nations great and small" had already been trotted out for the Spanish-American War, which had freed Cuba from Spanish colonization but, in brazen hypocrisy, colonized Puerto Rico and the Philippines for the United States.

As Robert Walker's *The Poet and the Gilded Age* (1963) reveals, Cuban freedom fighters had been so constantly championed by American versifiers that the latter "played a role in encouraging [their] country to come to the aid of the beleaguered Isle" (193–94). Madison Cawein is one of these poets who today has some name recognition; there were scores of others now practically unremembered, including women poets Harriet Leighton and Nellie Slingerland. When, however, the United States proceeded to seize the Philippines, the majority of poets responded with fury (Walker 201). The best-known poem to emerge from the Spanish-American War, William Vaughn Moody's "An Ode in Time of Hesitation," was first published in 1900, when the author expressed uncertainty about US policy. But when the United States initiated a military campaign to destroy the Filipino independence movement, Moody's further response, "On a Soldier Fallen in the Philippines" (1901), was unequivocal in its condemnation. While Moody made allowance for the patriotism of the soldier, the poem's devastating closing couplet excoriated the country that used him as a tool of imperialist conquest: "Let him never dream that his bullet's scream went wide of its island mark, / Home to the heart of his darling land where she stumbled and sinned in the dark" (25).

The war and peace poetry of Moody's generation is notable not only for an anti-imperialist critique that runs through later American war poems but also for its convictions about the public role of the poet. Tim Dayton, author of *American Poetry and the First World War* (2018), has located over 400 volumes by American authors with one or more poems about the war (1). Although the overwhelming majority ultimately supported the war mobilization, the diversity of US poetry, especially prior to 1917, is significant. Henry van Dyke's 1914 offering, "A Scrap of Paper," echoed the British case for joining war against Germany, while Percy MacKaye's "Return of August," published in 1915, offered a temporizing attitude more in line with the neutrality of the Wilson administration (Van Wienen 76, 105–7). Meanwhile, America's best-known soldier-poet to emerge from the war, Alan Seeger, favored Wilson's chief rival, Theodore Roosevelt. Seeger's "Message to America" sought to boost Roosevelt's prospects in the presidential election of 1916, hailing the former president as "A prophet that once in generations / Is given to point to erring nations" (qtd. in Dayton 50). Later, Seeger's "I Have a Rendezvous with Death" would add his posthumous endorsement to the value of a life well lived *because* of its being cut short on the battlefield.

Meanwhile, poets criticizing state power and military force were also active. Leading the way were women poets, often speaking as and for mothers. Their stark alternative to militarism was articulated already in August 1914, when Edith M. Thomas's "The Woman's Cry" responded to a newspaper report of the docile way that Russian men complied with the call to arms, demanding as an alternative that women's dissent in Russia and all nations be heard. The poem culminates in an exhortation to men of all nations to resist the draft (Van Wienen 57). That this perspective proved widely popular is evidenced by the best-selling American song in early 1915, "I Didn't Raise My Boy to Be a Soldier," which proclaimed that "There'd be no war today, / If mothers all would say, / 'I didn't raise my boy to be a soldier'" (87).

Poets on the Left mounted a critique of the economic and political interests that ultimately propelled the United States into the war. Representative pieces by a relatively mainstream poet were Carl Sandburg's "Ready to Kill," which lambastes public monuments idolizing American military heroes, and "Buttons," which satirizes sensational war reportage obscuring the human cost (Van Wienen 58, 91–92). More radical perspectives – sustained right through the US crackdown on dissent in 1917–20 – were articulated by members of the Industrial Workers of the World (IWW), a revolutionary union that since 1905 had functioned as the industrial branch of the Socialist Party of America but had been expelled by the party for refusing to condemn industrial sabotage. Ralph Chaplin offered a labor alternative to Woodrow Wilson's "Preparedness" campaign of 1916, opining that the only real enemy of the workers was capitalism on the home front: "Resist the foe, we shall! from sea to sea / The lewd invaders battle-line is thrown; / Here is our enemy and here alone – / The parasite of world-wide industry" (135). IWW poetry remained defiant even as an anti-sedition legal dragnet closed around the organization in 1917, with the leading example being Arturo Giovannitti's "When the Cock Crows," a tribute to Frank Little, an IWW organizer lynched in Butte, Montana, for draft opposition (179–83).

Particularly observant about the geopolitical ambitions of the United States – and its roots in deeply entrenched racism – were Black poets and their allies. Pointed criticism of home-front racism was offered by the soldier-poet Lucian B. Watkins, a veteran of the US counterinsurgency warfare in the Philippines as well as of the Great War. His poem "The Negro Soldiers of America: What We Are Fighting For" (1918) expressed readiness "To brave whatever hells there be" in France but also cites recent incidents of lynching that belie Wilsonian commitment to democracy, for in the United States, evidently, "Wrong is Might / With Hate and Horror on the throne, / Where GOD'S DEMOCRACY of LIGHT / AND LOVE, it seems, has never shown" (Van Wienen 221–22). Criticism of US global ambitions in the postwar settlement was articulated in Claude McKay's "The Little Peoples," which mocked the Versailles

Treaty–making process for its backing of "The little nations that are weak and white" whereas colonized people of color throughout the world "to the ancient gods of greed and lust / Must still be offered up as sacrifice" (262).

Although peace advocates were marginalized when the United States intervened in Europe in 1917, Michael Kazin's *War against War* (2017) observes that pacifism came to define majority opinion after the war. But it was not a very robust movement. As the United States had found in 1914–16, nations arming for war made good business partners. So it happened that the United States embraced trade with Nazi Germany and fascist Italy but prohibited material assistance to Republican Spain engulfed in civil war against insurgents backed by Germany and Italy (Kazin 281). Ironically, it was the radial Left – the American political faction that had been the most implacably opposed to US intervention in the First World War – that stepped into the breach.

The Spanish Civil War was an opportunity for Left activists to put their political convictions into action. World War I had been an imperialist war; in contrast, the Spanish Loyalist cause was a battle for the democratic masses, backed by the USSR, and progressives volunteered by the thousands to fight in the International Brigades defending the Spanish Republic. Left poets formed a virtual international chorus, explains Cary Nelson, publishing in "literally dozens of journals in Britain, France, Spain, Latin American, and the United States" (197). Among the early responders was Langston Hughes, some of whose poems adopt the persona of a Black volunteer from Alabama, "Johnny," and indeed Black Americans were among the volunteers in the International Brigades. In "Letter from Spain," Johnny reports an encounter with a dying Moorish soldier "just as dark as me" that leads not only to the realization that this man, drafted to fight for the Fascists, is as much a victim of the war as anyone, but also to the observation that England may be remaining neutral to protect their own colonial possessions: "Cause they got slaves in Africa – / And they don't want 'em to be free" (Hughes 1:253).

The "premature antifascism" of the Left in Spain was, in fact, soon vindicated, for by 1941 the United States and USSR were fighting together against fascist Germany and Italy. Retrospective poems emerging from the fight for Republican Spain often played upon this bitter irony. Edwin Rolfe, one of the American volunteers comprising the Abraham Lincoln Brigade, could write already in the fall of 1939: "To say *We were right* is not boastful, / Nor *We saw, when all others were blind* /Nor *We acted, while others ignored or uselessly wept*" (qtd. in Nelson 118). In 1941 Genevieve

Taggard's "To the Veterans of the Abraham Lincoln Brigade" could present the verdict of history as unambiguously vindicating those veterans:

> When the eminent, the great, the easy, the old,
> And the men on the make
> Were busy bickering and selling,
> Betraying, conniving, transacting, splitting hairs,
> Writing bad articles, signing bad papers,
> Passing bad bills,
> Bribing, blackmailing,
> Whimpering, meaching, garroting, – they
> Knew and acted
>   Understood and died.
> Or if they did not die came home to peace
> That is not peace. (Goldensohn 180)

Counterpointing the heroism of the volunteers with the inaction of politicians and capitalists, Taggard grasps the thread of national self-interest that explains the flip-flop from neutrality to armed intervention characterizing both Woodrow Wilson's and Franklin D. Roosevelt's responses to global conflict. However idealistic US aims were in both world wars – and in the second war, particularly, the ethical case for involvement was strong – the United States did not intervene in either until national sovereignty was directly threatened, and both war efforts were prosecuted only on terms that would promote long-term US global influence.

II

By the end of World War II, the United States would largely achieve the Wilsonian project of global hegemony. The fact that US economic supremacy coincided with the moral good of vanquishing authoritarian regimes both in the West and in the East buttressed the popular impression that World War II was America's "good war." Meanwhile, however, US poetry culture had changed substantially between the world wars, and postwar disillusionment with US participation in World War I had contributed, especially given the degree to which traditional literary culture had affiliated itself closely with Wilson's war policies (Dayton 246–47). The result was a split between American popular culture, generally in sync with the US government, and American poetry-writing culture, increasingly professionalized, working in Modernist styles largely incomprehensible to average readers, and often expressing dissenting political views. Traditional closed-form poetry continued to be written, but this verse had largely left the field of political debate by World War II. A telling index of the shift might be found in the poem-of-the-day appearing on the *New York Times* editorial page throughout this era. In April 1917, when the United States entered World War I, the editorial-page poem was about the war on twenty-seven out of thirty days. In a comparable thirty-day period in 1941, December 8, 1941, through January 7, 1942, just seven war poems appeared. All, as in 1917, were supportive of the national mobilization, but it is the contrast between the two sets of poems that most stands out: in April 1917 it was unequiv-ocally the responsibility of the poet to rally to the colors; in the month after Pearl Harbor, the poet's duty seemed to lie in largely avoiding war and politics, as a typical poem reflects on nature and the change of seasons.

A number of distinguished poets supported US involvement in World War II, joining the posters, newsreels, and movies that became the government's preferred media for political messaging. In fact, the most ambitious efforts of American poets to act politically in response to fascism employed the new medium of radio to amplify their message. Archibald MacLeish's *The Fall of the City*, broadcast nationally in 1937, had warned against fascist regimes, while a second radio verse-drama airing the next year, *Air Raid*, depicted the Nazi bombing of Guernica, Spain (Schweik 70–73). Edna St. Vincent Millay likewise turned her hand to verse-drama for radio. Her *Murder of Lidice*, performed on radio in 1942, depicted the elimination of an entire town in Czechoslovakia because residents were suspected of sheltering the Czech-resistance assassins of the Nazi SS General Reinhard Heydrich (61).

Yet many other poets were deeply troubled by the war. To begin with, home-front racism raised doubts about how different the United States was from its enemies. Already in 1943 Langston Hughes's "From Beaumont to Detroit" pulled no punches in excoriating the white mobs that had rioted and killed Blacks in the Texas and Michigan cities named in Hughes's title: "You tell me mussolini's / Got an evil heart. / Well, it mus-a been in Beaumont / That he got his start – " (Hughes 2:245–46). Gwendolyn Brooks's war writing also carried on the Black critique we have seen in Watkins and McKay. Brooks's sonnet sequence *Gay Chaps at the Bar*, published in 1945, charts how Black men in arms had proved – once again – their heroism and humanity, but its final poem evokes the long-term effects of combat trauma and finds that little has changed in the social order at home:

But inward grows a soberness, an awe,
A fear, a deepening hollow through the cold.
For even if we come out standing up
How shall we smile, congratulate: and how
Settle in chairs? Listen, listen. The step
Of iron feet again. And again wild. (Brooks 29)

The United States cast itself as the defender of democratic liberty during World War II. American poets including combatant-poets, however, testified as to how unfree and disempowered US citizens had become through the war. That, from an Allied perspective, the war had a compelling justification seems only to have given sanction to its unrestricted destructiveness. James Dickey, a bomber pilot in the Pacific theater, describes an "'anti-morale' raid" in his poem "The Firebombing." However far below the cities of Japan might be, Dickey cannot shake off his all-too-immediate perception of the horror his bombs had caused. The veteran's comfortable postwar life serves only to amplify his guilt, as American neighbors at his front door evoke the specters of Japanese residents of Beppu vaporized by his incendiary bombs: "I can imagine / At the threshold nothing / With its ears crackling off / Like powdery leaves" (Goldensohn 232). The dehumanization of America's citizen-soldiers, meanwhile, is captured succinctly in the most famous of all American poems of the war, "The Death of the Ball Turret Gunner" by US Air Force veteran Randall Jarrell. Both macro and microcosmic levels are suggested:

From my mother's sleep I fell into the State,
And I hunched in its belly till my wet fur froze.
Six miles from earth, loosed from its dream of life,
I woke to black flak and the nightmare fighters.
When I died they washed me out of the turret with a hose. (Goldensohn 209)

Here the American birthright is to be at the disposal of state power. Jarrell's "State" that the gunner "fell into," like Brooks's ambiguous and disquieting "step / Of iron feet again," raises the central issue of what the United States, now standing at the apex of its economic supremacy, backed by military power, might do next.

As Philip Metres argues in *Behind the Lines*, citing Paul Virilio, "we live in a state of Pure War, in which the real war is not the battle itself ... but the endless preparation for war" (9). Such endless war calls for individual citizens to be continually targeted for ideological formation by the nation-state and for the state's war machine to remain in constant readiness – to be deployed whenever and wherever a "national interest" might dictate. In this, which was the situation throughout the Cold War, the various hot wars blur together; their underlying issues remain relatively constant, and the permanence of the military-industrial complex enables the swift deployment of military force anywhere in the world. Hence, in "Remembering That Island" by World War II veteran Thomas McGrath, the war in the Pacific is effectively repeated in the Korean War a decade later:

> I see the vast stinking Pacific suddenly awash
> Once more with bodies, landings on all beaches,
> The bodies of dead and living gone back to appointed places,
>
> A ten year old resurrection,
> And myself once more in scourging wind, waiting, waiting.
>
> While the rich oratory and the lying famous corrupt
> Senators mine our lives for another war. (Goldensohn 215)

Building a bridge, in turn, from the Korean War to Vietnam is William Childress, one of the combatant poets of the 1950–53 conflict featured in the anthology *Retrieving Bones* (1999). Childress was a nineteen-year-old enlisted man serving in Korea by 1952, but began writing and publishing poetry in the 1960s (Ehrhart and Jason xxxv–xxxvi). In "The Long March" Childress counterpoints the callousness of "leaders whose careers / hung on victory" with the war's devastation as manifested in the starved Korean children whose bodies the common soldiers collect, "retrieving bones in thin sacks" (167). In the end, the poem also contrasts the fate of the GIs with that of "the General": "Any victory will be his. / For us, there is only / the long march to Vietnam" (167).

The connection between US ideology and its always-ready war machine is front and center in the work of Keith Wilson, who served as a naval officer in the Korean War and – in what we have seen as a common pattern – began writing antiwar poetry only when recognizing his war experience being repeated in the *next* war (Ehrhart and Jason xxxix–xl). Wilson's "December, 1952," published in 1969, presents an immediate awareness of the civilian casualties caused when a battleship targets a village onshore and, at the same time, a critical ear for the rhetoric justifying such a mission – "United Nations," "a new dream," "One World," "Peace." Such ideals are merely "The old bangles, dangled / once more, always working, / buying allegiances" (200). The juxtaposition leads Wilson to insist in the poem's closing stanza:

> Casualties are statistics
> for a rising New York Stock Market –
> its ticket tapes hail the darkeyed
> survivors, and cash registers
> click, all over the nation, these men
> deceive themselves. War is for. The Dead. (201)

Although Wilson hopes that readers will become wise to the "lies, tricks /
that blind the eyes of the young," his indictment suggests that war-making
is not only a product of American ideological formations but a producer of
national wealth. Hence American citizens might have powerful material as
well as psychological incentives *not* to be undeceived in Korea or
Vietnam – or for that matter in Iraq or Afghanistan.

III

While the wars that launched America's imperial course in the twentieth
century – the Spanish-American War and World War I – might be
counted as the major conflicts in which American poets assisted in
bringing the United States into war, the Vietnam War is the one conflict
in which poets substantively contributed to ending US war participation,
working in concert with a burgeoning civilian opposition movement. The
intensity and speed of the antiwar response might be judged by the
number of poetry collections appearing, including *A Poetry Reading
against the Vietnam War* (1966), *Where Is Vietnam?* (1967), *Poems of
War Resistance* (1968), *Out of the Shadow* (1968), *Campfires of the
Resistance* (1971), and *Winning Hearts and Minds* (1972) (Metres 97).
Other than *Winning Hearts and Minds*, these were books primarily by
civilian poets.

   A common theme was that the war was waged as much on the home
front as on the battlefields of Southeast Asia. Allen Ginsberg's *Wichita
Vortex Sutra* (1966) presents the Middle American city of its title as the
very vortex from which the destructive energies of the war emanate, given
the political complaisance of its residents and its rail hub transporting war
materiel. If only the common people of Wichita can be won over to peace-
making, Ginsberg suggests – no small task when the airwaves and print
journalism serve up patriotic cant – then the war will be over. Similar
themes run through Robert Bly's similarly long and complex poem,
The Teeth Mother Naked at Last (1970), which features several montages
of the US President spouting absurd lies as an expression of a culture
that, beneath promises of democracy and prosperity, is fundamentally

committed to death and demagoguery. Bly, too, asserts the relationship of American wealth with Vietnam's depredation: "It's because tax-payers move to the suburbs that we transfer populations. / The Marines use cigarette lighters to light the thatched roofs of huts / because so many Americans own their own homes" (15).

Perhaps the most widespread theme in the anti–Vietnam War campaign of American poets was empathy with the Vietnamese people. It is central in the work of Denise Levertov, for example. In her "Fragrance of Life, Odor of Death," with a place-time stamp of "Hanoi-Boston-Maine, November 1972," Levertov writes that in the "rubble" of North Vietnam she finds a "good smell / of life," whereas

> It's in America
> where no bombs ever
> have screamed down smashing
> the buildings, shredding the people's bodies,
> tossing the fields of Kansas or Vermont or Maryland into the air
> to land wrong way up, a gash of earth-guts . . .
> it's in America, everywhere, a faint seepage,
> I smell death. (Lauter 3215)

The poem seeks not only to humanize the Vietnamese people but to challenge American readers to imagine themselves in their place. Empathetic concern with Vietnamese war victims is key to combatant poets, as well. Jan Barry, one of the editors of *Winning Hearts and Minds*, offers in a poem of his own, "Memorial for Man in Black Pajamas," essentially his older Vietnamese counterpart: "Trinh Vo Man was a poet / in his own land a scholar / to his own people . . . an hospitable man to all" (Rottman, Barry, and Pasquet 94). But through the lens of American racism he is transmogrified, for this "venerable / and wise old man" is viewed by "the blue-eyed visitors" who kill him as "just a slope, a dink, a gook."

As Barry's poem suggests, racism pitted Americans against Vietnamese. As with previous wars, racism also pitted Americans against Americans, and again poets of color testified to this. In Black veteran Yusef Komunyakaa's 1988 collection, *Dien Cai Dau*, the poem "To Do Street" offers a glimmer of hope that racial and cultural gaps might be bridged. After all, US servicemen who patronize Saigon brothels have just "fought / the brothers of these women / we now run to hold in our arms" (Goldensohn 320). By the same means, seemingly intractable racial antagonisms between white and Black American soldiers are challenged:

>There's more than a nation
>inside us, as black & white
>soldiers touch the same lovers
>minutes apart, tasting
>each other's breath,
>without knowing these rooms
>run into each other like tunnels
>leading to the underworld.

Yet there is as much that disturbs here as affirms. With ties between white and Black, American and Vietnamese, negotiated through the bodies of exploited Vietnamese women, and connections between races and nations running through hell itself, this poem raises anew the problem of war as a means of achieving justice or peace.

Komunyakaa's somber vision may be shaped by an awareness of how limited were the progressive gains emerging from the antiwar and countercultural movements of the 1960s and 1970s. But poetry did contribute significantly to the antiwar protest of civilians and soldiers, not least in connecting with young people who resisted the draft, and this movement, coupled with battlefield stalemate, prompted the United States to withdraw from Vietnam without achieving either its military or its political objectives. Small wonder, then, that antiwar poetry of the Vietnam era has provided a template for responses to America's ongoing military-industrial complex and world-hegemonic economic aspirations in the decades since.

That the vast military power of the United States posed not merely an occasional but a constant threat had been the testimony of a number of poets before Vietnam. For William Stafford, a conscientious objector in World War II, the threat had been evident throughout the Cold War, even as the possibility of global nuclear annihilation made his dissent seem dangerous. "'Forget your faith; / be ready for whatever it takes to win: we face / annihilation unless all citizens get in line'" are the admonitions attributed to "The Pentagon" in Stafford's poem "Objector" (Stafford 94). But after Vietnam, protests proliferated against the huge US arsenal of nuclear weapons and the country's willingness to employ them in the bombings of Hiroshima and Nagasaki. In 1982, Galway Kinnell, a participant in the anti–Vietnam War protests, organized a Poets against the End of the World reading in New York City. *Atomic Ghost: Poets Respond to the Nuclear Age* (1995), edited by John Bradley, indicates that the 1980s movement opposing nuclear weapons had definite precedents, including poems by Gary Snyder, Gregory Corso, William Stafford, and a few others published between 1959 and 1977. Yet the overwhelming number of antinuclear poems collected by Bradley are from the 1980s and 1990s, including a who's who of US poets across multiple generations: John Balaban, William Dickey, Carolyn Forché, Linda Hogan, June Jordan, Adrian C. Louis, Naomi Shihab Nye, Richard Wilbur.

Meanwhile, for practically every subsequent war, American poets have followed the formula that ultimately succeeded in response to the Vietnam War, staging antiwar poetry readings and publishing one or more multi-author anthologies. In response to the First Persian Gulf War (1990–91) there was Jay Meek and F. D. Reeve's compilation *After the Storm* (1992). In response to the Second Gulf War, four collections came out in swift succession in 2003 – *100 Poets against the War, Poets against the War, Enough,* and *101 Poems against War* (2003) (Metres 222) – and another, *D.C. Poets against the War,* appeared in 2004. Not only did Hamill's *Poets against the War* feature 262 original antiwar poems authored by both obscure versifiers and some of the biggest names in US letters, but it was preceded by some 200 poetry readings across the country orchestrated by Hamill and an e-text consisting of 13,000 original poems by 11,000 American poets delivered to Congress (xviii–xix).

Whether in the Persian Gulf and Iraq, the Balkans, or Afghanistan, US armed forces have been committed to goals of regime change and reconstruction, always with the ultimate aim of fostering a global political-economic environment conducive to US interests. This, in short, is the Wilsonian hegemonic project, still going strong after 100 years. At the same time, the resistance of US poets to US nationalism and hegemony has also become institutionalized – part of the cultural DNA of many of the most renowned American poets in the postmodern era.

One might hope that this long-running contest might result in something like a standoff, except that the power wielded by the military-industrial-ideological complex remains overwhelming. Indeed, the chief concerns of recent antiwar poetry place dismay over the immense power of the US military alongside emphatic identification with fellow human beings throughout the world who suffer under this power. Both themes are evident in Adrienne Rich's "The School among the Ruins," included in *Poets against the War,* whose epigraph mentions several cities throughout the world that suffer from US military or diplomatic misadventures and, at the same time, suggests the protection of US cities gained by American global hegemony: "Beirut. Baghdad. Sarajevo. Bethlehem. Kabul. Not of course here" (Hamill 190). Rich's poem begins with a glimpse of normality – an ordinary day at school that could be taking place in many different communities around the world – which is shattered by sudden war. As depicted by Rich, geopolitics fundamentally corrodes human relationships so fully that schoolteachers can no longer answer the most straightforward questions of their pupils:

> One: I don't know where your mother
> is Two: I don't know
> why they are trying to hurt us
> Three: or the latitude and longitude
> of their hatred Four: I don't know if we
> hate them as much I think there's more toilet paper
> in the supply closet I'm going to break it open (192)

Of course, Rich's approach encompassing multiple war zones risks flattening out the political specificities of different wars and various communities devastated by war. Indeed, for the war in Bosnia, the complaint of some poets actually echoes the Spanish Republican partisanship of leftist poets of the 1930s, with the United States being faulted for being dilatory in its military intervention. Joseph Brodsky's "Bosnia Tune" alludes to US policies that permitted the stronger states of the former Yugoslav confederation to wage genocidal war against weaker states. Yet whether criticism centers on sins of commission or omission, the common thread is that US geopolitics is constantly oriented to the maintenance of US global power, which is conditioned by indifference toward other citizens of the world. As Brodsky puts it, "In small places you don't know / of, yet big for having no / chance to scream or say goodbye, / people die" (Goldensohn 341). In Dale Jacobson's "Night Vision of the Gulf War," responding to the bombardment of Iraqi Army troops in 1991 when the United States "released the power of seven / Hiroshima bombs, 88,500 tons," the complacency of the United States is essentially the same: "Some 200,000 buried alive – no one / cared to keep count, or could" (Goldensohn 345). After the 9/11 attacks, the new sense of imminent threat to US citizens – much commented on as opening a new era in American culture – resulted merely in the hardening of long-standing American solipsism.

The post-9/11 war "against terrorism" has been novel only insofar as it prompted a fuller rollout of new, post-Vietnam military doctrines that diminished opportunities for empathy. Consequently, "The million-dollar missiles [that] rose over the sea, and the swift jets," referenced by Jacobson, have been supplemented by newer "smart bombs [that] are thinking their way / into Baghdad, on video grids, in primary colors," as described by Wendy Battin in "Mondrian's Forest" (Goldensohn 347). Such sophisticated weaponry delivers ever greater devastation while decreasing casualties among US service members and diminishing their exposure to the killing in which they participate. The upward spiral in technological sophistication has also made smaller armed forces feasible, hence facilitating the continuation of the post-Vietnam recruit-only armed forces. Whether or not by intention, the end of the draft greatly diminished the chances for re-creating the coalition between civilian antiwar activists and draft-age individuals that came together in the Vietnam era, as is evidenced in the longevity of the US campaigns in Iraq, from March 2003 to December 2011, and in Afghanistan, from October 2001 to August 2021.

Just as with Vietnam and other conflicts, antiwar voices have emerged from the ranks of combatants in the post-9/11 wars. Yet in much of this contemporary work the ethical compass gyrates wildly, perhaps because so much of the poetry is concerned with the ambiguous responsibilities of nation-building and military occupation. In *Here, Bullet* (2005) by Brian Turner, the most widely recognized of the post-9/11 soldier-poets, the poem "What Every Soldier Must Know" captures the uncertainties of the mission, as the poem randomly juxtaposes advice meant to win Iraqi hearts and minds with paranoid cautions about deadly roadside hazards. The poem's tight, ironic conclusion seems certain only that there will be no solution to the conundrum of attempting friendship while guarding against ambush:

> Small children will play with you,
> old men with their talk, women who offer chai –
>
> and any one of them
> may dance over your body tomorrow. (10)

With danger to the soldier so immediate, the poem cannot locate any reason for *why* the seemingly friendly Iraqis might celebrate the death of their occupiers.

"Observation Post," in *The Stick Soldiers* (2013) by Iraq War veteran Hugh Martin, recognizes the harm done by as well as to US soldiers, depicting the assassination of a translator who collaborates with the Americans but receives inadequate protection from them. The poem also depicts US alliance with Kurdish fighters whose methods of interrogation are inhumane, as "they drag suspects / to the police station, / where they'll take turns / with the rifle butting" (46). But in Martin's poem, too, responsibility for the mayhem is touched upon lightly as a component in the general absurdity of war. A stronger stand is taken by a poet who continues both Black and women's antiwar traditions, Iraq War veteran

Nicole Goodwin. "Unsaid (Confession)," in her collection *Warcries* (2016), describes a scene in which it is the American soldiers who are responsible for inhumane treatment of Iraqi prisoners of war. Goodwin shows that Black as well as white soldiers engage in this shameful behavior, and the indictment extends to herself:

> Of one black man enslaving another.
> Of this sin I have barely spoken.
> Confession – I became accomplice to
> This action.

We need more poems like this. "Unsaid (Confession)" both extends Komunyakaa's picture of violent collaboration between Black and white GIs and exposes the neocolonialism implicit in the US global-hegemonic project.

In *The War Makes Everyone Lonely* (2019), combatant poet Graham Barnhart describes many of the same issues in the Afghanistan War. "Augury," for instance, explores the vagaries of attempting to locate roadside bombs (57–58), much like Turner's "What Every Soldier Must Know." "How to Transition a Province" is as self-aware as any poem about the efficacy and ethics of military occupation. The only substantial accomplishment of the soldiers in their nation-building mission lies in their systematically destroying their encampment:

> We named the region self-sustaining
> and ended an eight-month occupation
>
> frightening children from the burn pit,
> petitioning elders not to send them
>
> after imagined valuables in our refuse. (75)

In asserting the soldiers' awareness that they have left nothing of genuine value, the poem essentially predicts the rapid reconversion of Afghanistan's provinces to Taliban control as the US military withdrew in summer 2021. The poem also offers a glimpse into a utopian alternative, imagining a scenario in which the United States actually *could* withdraw its military power from Afghanistan or other countries and have done no harm.

Yet the capriciousness of the US military adventure – coming and going seemingly according to whim, with material resources to burn – suggests the flat, inhumane unresponsiveness of a distant and higher power that acts according to its own inscrutable plans. The world-hegemonic power of the United States can be relatively benign in its results, particularly when US policy is implemented on the ground by military personnel as humane as Goodwin and Barnhart. Nonetheless, the godlike power assumed by the government of the United States, coupled with the immense destructive capacity of its military-industrial complex and the relative marginality of the antiwar positions of most civilian and combatant poets, provides a definite augury that their critiques of US military power and geopolitics will be pertinent and necessary for decades to come.

WORKS CITED

Barnhart, Graham. *The War Makes Everyone Lonely.* University of Chicago Press, 2019.

Bradley, John, ed. *Atomic Ghost: Poets Respond to the Nuclear Age.* Coffee House, 1995.

Brooks, Gwendolyn. *Selected Poems.* Harper and Row, 1963.

Dayton, Tim. *American Poetry and the First World War.* Cambridge University Press, 2018.

Ehrhart, W. D., and Philip K. Jason, eds. *Retrieving Bones: Stories and Poems of the Korean War.* Rutgers University Press, 1999.

Goldensohn, Lorrie, ed. *American War Poetry: An Anthology.* Columbia University Press, 2006.

Goodwin, Nicole S. *Warcries.* CreateSpace, 2016. E-book.

Hamill, Sam, et al., eds. *Poets against the War.* Thunder's Mouth/Nation Books, 2003.

Hughes, Langston. *The Collected Works of Langston Hughes.* 3 vols. Ed. Arnold Rampersad. University of Missouri Press, 2001.

Kazin, Michael. *War against War: The American Fight for Peace, 1914–1918.* Simon and Schuster, 1917.

Lauter, Paul, et al., eds. *The Heath Anthology of American Literature.* 7th ed. Volume E. Cengage Learning, 2014.

Martin, Hugh. *The Stick Soldiers.* BOA Editions, 2013.

Metres, Philip. *Behind the Lines: War Resistance Poetry on the American Homefront since 1941.* University of Iowa Press, 2007.

Moody, William Vaughn. *Poems.* Houghton, Mifflin, 1901.

Nelson, Cary. *Revolutionary Memory: Recovering the Poetry of the American Left.* Routledge, 2001.

Rottman, Larry, Jan Barry, and Basil T. Paquet, eds. *Winning Hearts and Minds: War Poems by Vietnam Veterans.* McGraw-Hill, 1970.

Schweik, Susan. *A Gulf So Deeply Cut: American Women Poets and the Second World War.* University of Wisconsin Press, 1991.

Stafford, William. *Every War Has Two Losers: William Stafford on Peace and War.* Ed. Kim Stafford. Milkweed, 2003.

Tooze, Adam. *The Deluge: The Great War, America and the Remaking of the Global Order, 1916–1931.* Penguin, 2014.

Turner, Brian. *Here, Bullet.* Alice James Books, 2005.
Van Wienen, Mark W. *Rendezvous with Death: American Poems of the Great War.*
     University of Illinois Press, 2002.
Walker, Robert H. *The Poet and the Gilded Age: Social Themes in Late 19th
     Century American Verse.* University of Pennsylvania Press, 1963.

CHAPTER 8

Institutions of American Poetry
From the Pound Era to the Program Era

Loren Glass

Most poetry pays poorly, and so most of the institutions that have developed to facilitate its production and distribution in the United States have served as patrons, insulating poets from the need to earn money directly from the publication of their poems. In the first third of the twentieth century this patronage was largely private, as wealthy individuals such as John Quinn and Scofield Thayer subsidized modernist poets such as T. S. Eliot and Ezra Pound, for both prestige and, ultimately, profit in the form of limited and signed editions that would in turn enable the emergence of a collector's market. Inherited wealth also formed the basis of modernist publishing, as the "new breed" of American publishers such as Horace Liveright and James Laughlin used family funds to finance their ventures, again frequently producing limited editions that would ultimately accrue value in the collector's market even as they functioned as prestigious loss leaders in the mainstream literary marketplace.

Patronage was necessary because the audience for modernism, at least initially, was small, and therefore insufficient to provide an income for the poets who produced it. Indeed, the rise of modernism in the first half of the twentieth century generated a widespread and persistent assumption that poetry was becoming too obscure and difficult for mainstream audiences, resulting in recurring laments of its death and disappearance. However, these jeremiads either ignored or decried the continuing popularity of more traditional verse forms in the everyday life of Americans. In the pages of daily newspapers and elementary school primers, in scrapbooks and popular anthologies, the fireside poets and their modern progeny persisted, providing spiritual and emotional succor for readers and reciters, and reliable profits for publishers. As Joan Shelley Rubin has documented in her important study *Songs of Ourselves: The Uses of Poetry in America* (2007), reading and writing rhyming verse informed the entire life cycle of many if not most Americans over the first half of the twentieth century, gradually fading over the course of the second half when rote memorization declined as a pedagogical practice and popular poetry vanished from periodicals.

By the second half of the twentieth century the patronage of modernist poets and poetry had shifted from private wealth to well-endowed public institutions such as the Rockefeller and Ford Foundations and, ultimately and spectacularly, American colleges and universities, which essentially absorbed the entire field of professional poetry by the end of the century. Thus, as popular poetry faded from the elementary and high school curriculum, modern lyric poetry came to constitute the core collegiate curriculum, first as something to be studied and then as something to be written. And the lyric reigned supreme since, like its prose companion the short story, it fit so snugly into the space and time of both the classroom and the semester. It would become the ideal object for the workshop method, which mandates that the class have time to discuss at least one poem per student, and for the workshop ideology of expressive individualism, which consecrates the lyric poem as the product of the poetic subject's gift.

The process whereby such poetry was absorbed into college and university English departments began with visiting poets such as Robert Frost, who famously coined the term "education by presence" to describe the pedagogical function of his charismatic appearances on college campuses across the country. Visiting gigs would continue for the more temperamental type of late modernist poet, such as Robert Lowell and John Berryman, who were too unreliable and unstable to be permanent professors. On the other hand, a more administrative-minded generation of scholar-poets such as John Crowe Ransom and Archibald MacLeish found institutional careers both appealing and remunerative, establishing a crucial role for poets in the rapidly exfoliating and expanding bureaucracies of governments, foundations, and universities during the postwar boom. By the end of the century the Master of Fine Arts (MFA) reigned supreme and now almost every American poet has some relationship with at least one creative writing program, as either student or teacher or both.

Finally, during this period poets themselves became institutions, generating an elaborate star system that determined the value, both aesthetic and economic, of modern poetry. Starting with high modernists such as Pound and Eliot, expanding out into midcentury "schools" such as the Beats and Black Mountain with their charismatic avatars, and then becoming securely institutionalized in the MFA system with poet-professors such as Jorie Graham and Rita Dove, the institution of celebrity has secured popular prestige and economic profitability for poets and poetry, as well as the organizations that support them, across the entirety of the twentieth century. If poetic style and form has varied widely and wildly over the course of the century, the *figure* of the poet as charismatic bearer of talent and inspiration has been persistent and consistent, sustaining the integrity of the entire field and cementing the idea of the "poet" as a gifted figure and their poetry as bearer of symbolic value irreducible to economic exchange.

If any American poet became an institution it was surely Ezra Pound, who almost single-handedly curated the canon of American modernism in the first half of the twentieth century by promoting the publication of those in whom he saw the potential to put American poetry on the world literary map. To do this he needed a venue and he felt that he had found one in *Poetry* magazine. Thus, on August 18, 1912, he wrote to Harriet Monroe to express his strong enthusiasm for her plan to launch an American magazine devoted entirely to contemporary poetry. Pound was excited by the prospect, and he hoped that *Poetry* would become a platform to disseminate his and his cohort's poetry, and prose about poetry, to an American audience. A few paragraphs in he asks Monroe, "Are you for American poetry or for poetry? The latter is more important, but it is important that America should boost the former, provided it don't mean a blindness to the art. The glory of any nation is to produce art that can be exported without disgrace to its origin." And Pound was confident that, with his assistance, this glory would be achieved, as he affirms in his postscript: "Any agonizing that tends to hurry what I believe in the end to be inevitable, our American Risorgimento, is dear to me. That awakening will make the Italian Renaissance look like a tempest in a teapot!"[1]

At the time, Pound was developing this idea of an "American Risorgimento" in a book-length essay titled *Patria Mia* that he would complete in 1913 but that would not be published until 1950, since it was lost and then found by accident many years later by its publisher, the Chicago-based artist and illustrator Ralph Fletcher Seymour. Here Pound is somewhat more circumspect than he is in his postscript to Monroe, stating his thesis that "America has a chance for Renaissance."[2] The two-part essay that follows lays out what will need to happen for that chance to be realized and, crucially, how it will be subsidized. If the Italian Renaissance was paid for by the aristocratic Medici, then the American

---

[1] Ezra Pound to Harriett Monroe, August 18, 1912, in D. D. Paige, ed., *The Letters of Ezra Pound: 1907–1941* (New York: Harcourt Brace, 1950), 9–10.
[2] Ezra Pound, *Patria Mia* (Chicago: Ralph Fletcher Seymore, 1950), 24.

one will have to be paid for by capitalist millionaires. As Pound bluntly affirms, "In fostering and hastening a renaissance the millionaire may be, often, very useful. It is his function as it is the function of any aristocrat to die and leave gifts. Die he must, and he may as well leave gifts, lest people spit upon his tomb and remember him solely for his iniquities" (70). Patronage, in this formulation, is a reputational investment in posthumous honor. In a sense, the wealthy patron is purchasing a portion of the acclaim that redounds to the artist. As Cary Wolfe affirms, Pound suggests that "the gifts of the patron might be thought of as a sort of investment, but in a different kind of economy."[3]

This is especially true if the artist is young and only shows potential, in which case the patron is in essence enabling a career that might not succeed without this crucial early subsidy. As Pound proudly affirms, "in advocating subsidy I am more unashamed than shameless. The artist's work goes ultimately to the public and it is the public who should pay. The sincere artist wants leisure for his work. At the beginning of his course he wants little or nothing beyond this. He does not obey or concede to the laws of commerce, to the law of supply and demand" (94). If the United States is to achieve a cultural Risorgimento it will have to liberate an elite cadre of young artists from the very capitalist wage-labor system that has enabled its great wealth. As Pound boldly concludes, "there should be a class of artist-workers free from necessity" (97).

Pound would be the matchmaker in this scheme, linking wealthy patrons to promising young writers in order to curate this class of American artist-workers into being. One patron on whom he would come to rely was John Quinn, the wealthy American lawyer and art collector best known for defending Margaret Anderson and Jane Heap against obscenity charges for publishing chapters of *Ulysses* in their *Little Review*. On March 8, 1915, Pound wrote a lengthy letter to Quinn, in response to Quinn's request for advice on acquiring some work by the French sculptor Henri Gaudier-Brzeska. In extolling the value of patronage to a potential patron, Pound tactically altered his philosophy of posthumous honor: "My whole drive," Pound wrote, "is that if a patron buys from an artist who needs money (needs money to buy tools, time and food), the patron then makes himself equal to the artist: he is building art into the world; he creates."[4]

[3] Cary Wolfe, "Ezra Pound and the Politics of Patronage," *American Literature* 63:1 (March 1991), 32.
[4] Ezra Pound to John Quinn, March 8, 1915, in *The Letters of Ezra Pound*, 53.

According to his biographer, this vision "became part of Quinn's notion of himself and his ideal modes of behavior."[5] Over the ensuing decades, Quinn would continue to take art collecting advice from Pound, the finder's fees from which Pound would use to finance his own literary ventures. Pound in turn defended Quinn against all criticism. Thus when Margaret Anderson questioned Quinn's dedication to their cause in the case against the *Little Review*, Pound admonished her: "Tis he who hath bought the pictures; tis he who both getteth me an American publisher and smacketh the same with rods; tis he who sendeth me the Spondos Oligos, which is by interpretation the small tribute or spondooliks where-with I do pay my contributors, wherefore is my heart softened toward the said J.Q., and he in mine eyes can commit nothing heinous."[6] Pound was careful not to bite the hand that fed him and his acolytes.

Quinn in turn was central to the American publication of T. S. Eliot's *The Waste Land* in book form, an event that would loudly signal, as Lawrence Rainey affirms in his seminal study *Institutions of Modernism: Literary Elites and Public Culture*, "the crucial moment in the transition of modernism from a minority culture to one supported by an important institutional and financial apparatus."[7] The contract was in fact signed in Quinn's New York office, and Eliot was so gratified by his facilitation that he gave him the original manuscript with comments by both Pound and Vivienne Eliot. This detail is oddly left out of Rainey's otherwise meticulous account of *The Waste Land*'s complicated publica-tion history, though it emphatically illustrates his thesis that literary modernism was enabled by a "circuit of patronage, collecting, speculation, and investment" (3).

The publication of *The Waste Land* also signaled to the emerging modernist literary field that the lyric was not enough; it is by definition a minor and modest aesthetic object, suitable for apprenticeship and graduate school, but if one aspires to be a major poet one must produce a modern epic, a poem including history. And the ensuing history of twentieth-century American poetry is strewn with the wreckage from the many attempts at matching Eliot's achievement, the most spectacular of which is surely Pound's interminable and unfinished *Cantos*, which casts its formidable fragmentary shadow over all poets working in its wake.

---

[5] B. L. Reid, *The Man from New York: John Quinn and His Friends* (New York: Oxford University Press, 1968) 199.

[6] Ezra Pound to Margaret Anderson, January 1918, in *The Letters of Ezra Pound*, 129.

[7] Lawrence Rainey, *Institutions of Modernism: Literary Elites and Public Culture* (New Haven, CT: Yale University Press, 1998), 91.

Modern American poetry has its own version of the dialectic of minimalism and maximalism that Mark McGurl has so compellingly anatomized in modern American prose, and with a similar aesthetic logic: the lyric poem and the short story are minimalist exercises in the control of craft, while the epic poem or novel is maximalist evidence of literary mastery.

The other person in Quinn's office on that day was Horace Liveright, the maverick publisher and courageous defender of literary modernism in the 1920s. Liveright was one of those cultural entrepreneurs, so crucial to the success of modernism, who went into publishing not to make money but to spend it, in this case his wife's inherited fortune. Like most of the "new breed" of publishers, Liveright was wealthy but nevertheless locked out of high society by the genteel anti-Semitism that saturated the cultural elite of the era. Publishing and defending daring and experimental work, including prose and poetry by Ezra Pound, that the more staid and established houses would not touch became a strategy for earning the kinds of cultural prestige that simply possessing wealth could not provide. As with Monroe and Quinn, Pound recognized an ally and acolyte, squiring Liveright around Paris in early 1922, introducing him to Joyce and Eliot, and ultimately arranging to be the European scout for Boni and Liveright for a fee of $500 per year. An alcoholic, womanizer, and a spendthrift, Liveright would die penniless at the age of forty-nine, but not before he brought both *The Waste Land* and Hart Crane's *The Bridge* to American audiences. He blazed the trail for publishing modern poetry as a loss leader in a battle for cultural prestige and reputation, a strategy that would be adopted more successfully for James Laughlin's New Directions, which would become Pound's most consequential conduit for bringing modernism and its critical advocates to American readers.

Ultimately Pound determined that millionaires weren't enough, and it was Eliot's difficulties making a living in the turbulent economy of postwar Europe that led him to this conclusion. He was deeply troubled by Eliot's nervous breakdown, which he interpreted as caused at least partly by financial stress, and in the very year of *The Waste Land*'s publication he launched a fundraising venture he called "Bel Esprit," to provide financial support to Eliot and impecunious poets like him. Arguing that "millionaires are tapped too frequently," Pound hoped that he could form a sort of cooperative to which his friends and acquaintances would contribute, which would in turn give starving artists the "leisure to work in."[8] He promptly proceeded to send requests out to a range of potential donors,

---

[8] Ezra Pound to William Carlos Williams, March 18, 1922, in *The Letters of Ezra Pound*, 172–73.

from William Carlos Williams to H. L. Mencken to John Quinn, who promised to purchase six shares at $50 a piece. As he wrote to Wyndham Lewis, "if there aren't 30 or 50 people interested in literature, there is no civilization and we may as well regard our work as a private luxury."[9] The plan turned out to be unnecessary. Eliot didn't really mind working at Lloyd's bank, where he had been employed as a clerk since 1917, and when he left Lloyd's a few years later to become an editor at Faber and Faber he was pretty much set for life, both financially and reputationally, as he became the model of the poet-critic for generations of American authors, winning the Nobel Prize in 1948. American modernist poetry had arrived.

Eliot's career trajectory establishes that, while poets may not have been particularly proficient at making money, they did occasionally possess administrative skills, and could help spend the money that was amassing in the United States. Pound was correct that millionaires would leave gifts, and when these gifts grew into foundations, poets were available to help them decide how to spend their money. This is the story Evan Kindley tells in his important recent study, *Poet-Critics and the Administration of Culture* (2017). As Kindley explains, the Depression depleted the funds of the private patrons modernists had relied on, but in their place emerged "a set of interlinked bureaucratic institutions: the federal government, philanthropic foundations, and universities."[10] And this development provided the opportunity for a handful of poet-critics to become poet-administrators, providing the aesthetic judgment and cultural savvy whereby large foundations and government bureaucracies could determine how to distribute their funds.

The key figure here is Archibald MacLeish, who, as Kindley affirms, "exemplifies the administrative role that the nation-state called on poet-critics to play" (14). Wealthy and privileged, a Hotchkiss graduate with a BA in English from Yale and a JD from Harvard, MacLeish was impeccably credentialed, well connected to America's political elite and a close confidante of, and speechwriter for, President Roosevelt, who appointed him first as Librarian of Congress and then as Director of the War Department's Office of Facts and Figures during World War II. He was also a well-respected and widely published award-winning modernist poet, a friend of Hemingway, and fellow traveler of the lost generation in Paris

---

[9] Ezra Pound to Wyndham Lewis, April 5, 1922, in *The Letters of Ezra Pound*, 176.
[10] Evan Kindley, *Poet-Critics and the Administration of Culture* (Cambridge, MA: Harvard University Press, 2017), 5.

in the 1920s. Thus, he was a rare figure able to straddle America's political and cultural elites during the epochal shift from individual to institutional patronage of American poetry. He would complete his government career representing the United States at the UN for the creation of UNESCO (whose inaugural directorship he declined), after which he would spend the remainder of his professional career as the Boylston Professor of Rhetoric and Oratory at Harvard University, a chair now occupied by Jorie Graham. MacLeish's career arc, then, parallels the passage of modernism from an outsider art of radical experimentation and cultural dissent to an insider art at the heart of American higher education and liberal ideology.

If Pound as a poet *was* an institution, MacLeish was a poet who worked *for* institutions, and Pound correlatively casts a far longer shadow over the Program Era, which he in fact envisioned in *Patria Mia*, published in 1950, by which point many of Pound's prophecies had been realized. American millionaires had subsidized modernist poets, both directly as patrons and indirectly as owners of publishing houses and establishers of foundations. And most of those poets had been beneficiaries of Pound's relentless promotion. The Risorgimento he envisioned had occurred. But how would it be sustained and maintained? Who or what would serve his role in the future? Pound had a vision for this as well, one that was underway at the time of *Patria Mia*'s publication. Here is how he puts it:

I. To drive the actual artist upon the university seminar . . .
II. To drive the theses and the seminary upon the Press
III. The super-college.

When he wrote these words Pound anticipated skepticism given the state of American academia at the time, where philological methods reigned supreme and modernism was anathema. As he concludes, "Of these, the first two may seem mad and the third, as I state it, probably incomprehensible, but have patience. I may be in one of my lucid intervals" (84). When *Patria Mia* finally came out a version of this vision was coming into being at the University of Iowa under the energetic directorship of Paul Engle, and in the ensuing years, the "Iowa Model" of the Writers' Workshop would exfoliate out into American academia. Pound had envisioned this transition from the Pound Era to the Program Era, but he himself was no longer lucid, at least in official terms. Arrested for treason after spouting anti-Semitic pro-fascist screeds on Italian radio during World War II, he had been deemed unfit to stand trial and was confined to the Chestnut Ward at St. Elizabeth's Psychiatric Hospital in Washington, DC. Pound never taught in an MFA program, but he did end up in an institution to which it would frequently be compared, and many who did teach and take creative writing would sit at his feet in this twilight of his life.

It was at this point that James Laughlin, in league with T. S. Eliot, decided to publish *The Pisan Cantos* and submit them for consideration for the inaugural Bollingen Award, funded by the Mellon Foundation and conferred by the Library of Congress. Allen Tate, appointed by MacLeish as consultant in poetry to the Library of Congress in 1943, in turn appointed the board that would make the decision, and it included Robert Penn Warren, Louise Bogan, Karl Shapiro, Robert Lowell, Conrad Aiken, W. H. Auden, and T. S. Eliot. They were, for the most part, New Critics, postwar canonizers of literary modernism, and it was ultimately their authority and hegemony that was at stake. The "Bollingen Controversy," as it came to be called, was a turning point in American literary history, and in retrospect, it can be understood to have been a necessary accommodation in the transition from the Pound Era to the Program Era. Pound never taught in an American university, but he was a father figure to all the poets who did, straddling establishment and countercultural poetries in his influence. It would be necessary to redeem and domesticate him before the integrity and authority of American modernist poetry could carry forward into the postwar era.

One of the more comprehensive accounts of the lengthy and complex affair can be found in Jed Rasula's polemical study, *The American Poetry Wax Museum: Reality Effects, 1940–1990* (1996). As Rasula puts it, "the simple mechanics of conceptual travel required a layover at Pound Central."[11] The controversy arose when Robert Hillyer loudly dissented from the award in the pages of the *Saturday Review*, in two widely read articles provocatively entitled "Treason's Strange Fruit" and "Poetry's New Priesthood," in which he warned that the prize committee, and by extension the New Critics, represented "the mystical and cultural preparation for a new authoritarianism" in American literature.[12] Debate over the appropriateness of the prize, the sanity of its recipient, the obscurity of his project, and the bloody crossroads of poetry and politics raged for a

---

[11] Jed Rasula, *The American Poetry Wax Museum: Reality Effects, 1940–1990* (Urbana, IL: National Council on Teachers, 1996), 99.

[12] Quoted in William McGuire, *Poetry's Catbird Seat: The Consultantship in Poetry in the English Language at the Library of Congress, 1937–1987* (Washington, DC: Library of Congress, 1988), 118.

number of years in the pages of both literary journals and popular periodicals, and when the dust settled, the path was clear for the triumph of the New Criticism, which Rasula tendentiously calls "the administrative security system that had assumed custodial control of poetry" (114). The affair marked the wholesale redemption of Pound's vision of an American Risorgimento stably sustained by the country's rapidly expanding and magnificently well-endowed system of higher education, with Pound himself as a charismatic if problematic founding figure. Indeed, ten years later William Van O'Connor and Edward Stone published a *Casebook on Ezra Pound* explicitly designed to be the basis for college term papers in English classes. The controversy wasn't so much resolved as it was contained by the classroom. By that time, MacLeish had secured Pound's release from St. Elizabeth's.

At midcentury the poetry world was divided in terms that would be set by the so-called anthology wars and named by Robert Lowell as the "raw" and the "cooked" in his acceptance speech for the National Book Award in 1960. As Lowell's brief but trenchant speech indicated, the division opposed the seminar room to the city streets, indicating that the "raw" poetry of the Beats and their brethren was hostile to academia, and for a decade or two it was. The Beats, along with the New York School, the San Francisco Renaissance, and the "open-field" poets who gathered briefly at Black Mountain, positioned themselves in principled avant-garde opposition to the academic establishment, now dominated by poet-critics in the Eliotic mode. The establishment was formalist and individualist, focusing on carefully crafted lyric poems that required close reading to be understood; the new avant-garde poetries experimented with open forms and were far more communal and collective in their aesthetic and political orientations.

But it didn't take long for the so-called opposing poetries to be incorporated into the expanding classrooms of the American university system. Indeed, that is where they all started: most of the poets in Donald Allen's groundbreaking anthology *The New American Poetry* (1960) had been students at the prestigious universities that housed and hosted most of the poets in Donald Hall et al.'s *New Poets of England and America* (1957), and most of the poets in both books could trace their lineage back through Ezra Pound by one path or another. Formalism and the New Critical focus on craft got poetry into the halls of academia as something that could be studied and taught, as a profession that could be credentialed and practiced, but once the door was open other more dissident poets rushed in, tempted by the opportunity to profess to an eager crowd of young acolytes.

This incorporation was first achieved by the reading circuit, which blossomed along with the rapid expansion of enrollments at American universities, at both the graduate and undergraduate levels. These young Americans were in fact the target audience for the new American poets, and Ginsberg in particular was enormously popular on American campuses, drawing crowds of students and faculty to every reading he gave in every college town he visited in the 1960s. The Beats and their fellow travelers perfected and then imported the coffeehouse style and structure of poetry reading into the auditoria of academia. This circuit, in turn, would become the bread and butter, as well as the social and professional nexus, of many poetic careers in the second half of the twentieth century. Since then, poets have been expected to perform as well as write and teach, thus supplementing their pedagogy and publications with a kind of theatrical demonstration of how to "be" a poet in the Program Era.

This wholesale incorporation of the poetry network into the university system was further facilitated by a parallel development in the publishing world that would come to be called the Quality Paperback Revolution. The more widespread and extensive Paperback Revolution that kicked in after the war was mostly a matter of prose, both fiction and nonfiction, with a small smattering of plays and poetry anthologies, usually centered on earlier eras and accessible material long out of copyright. These were paperbacks for the drugstore and train station, "good reading for the millions" as the New American Library proudly trumpeted. Modernist prose, from Faulkner to Joyce, was popularized by this format, but modernist poetry, generally speaking, could not break even at this scale of production, and loss leaders were not part of the economic logic of the paperback marketplace.

The company that bucked this trend was, not surprisingly, built on inherited wealth. James Laughlin, heir of a Pittsburgh Steel magnate, had hoped to be a poet himself, but Ezra Pound, whom he had deliberately sought out in Rapallo in the 1930s, dismissed his attempts and suggested that he instead "do something useful" and get into publishing, which Laughlin promptly did.[13] New Directions would become the principal outlet for Pound and his stateside affiliate William Carlos Williams, alongside a canon of poets, both ancient and modern, both European and American, all based on Pound's advice and connections. Once Emil Lustig came on board to design the covers, New Directions had a stable

[13] Linda Kuehl, "Talk with James Laughlin: New and Old Directions," *New York Times Book Review* (February 25, 1973), 355.

and a look that was immediately identifiable and resolutely modernist. These were "quality" or "trade paperbacks," as they were called to differentiate them from their more ephemeral mass market cousins, and they found a reliable market in the classrooms and college bookstores of university towns across the country after the war. These books were affordable but also durable and aesthetically pleasing in and of themselves as objects to treasure. Along with Lawrence Ferlinghetti's City Lights and Barney Rosset's Grove Press, New Directions would pioneer this format as the platform whereby contemporary and classic poetry was delivered to its growing audience of college students, many of whom were aspiring poets themselves.

The final piece of this institutional puzzle is prizes, which James English has affirmed are "of fundamental importance to the *institutional* machinery of cultural legitimacy and authority."[14] Prizes are particularly important for poetry, which lacks the popular legitimacy of other genres such as novels and films. Most Americans neither read nor like modernist poetry, and thus its value needs to be continually confirmed by the cultural apparatus in which it circulates. Prestige in poetry is measured by prizes, and, starting with the Yale Series of Younger Poets, the acquisition of awards has become a necessary component of any successful career in poetry. As English affirms, such prizes "have become an integral and indispensable feature of the contemporary American poetry scene" (140). Given the essentially insular world of modern and contemporary poetry, the system of awarding prizes has tended to be an incestuous and nepotistic affair, as illustrated most spectacularly by W. H. Auden's legendary tenure as judge for the Yale prize from 1947 to 1959, and then, more embarrassingly, by the notorious "Jorie Graham Rule" forbidding judges from selecting their students for awards.

Patria Mia opens with the following declaration: "America, my country, is almost a continent and hardly yet a nation, for no nation can be considered historically as such until it has achieved within itself a city to which all roads lead, and from which there goes out an authority" (21). Pound couldn't have expected that this city would be a small college town in the middle of Iowa. And yet Paul Engle, who directed the Iowa Writers' Workshop from 1941 to 1965, understood and shared Pound's understanding of American cultural geography, and for him Iowa City was the ideal place to build a "community of writers" to and from which literary authority

---

[14] James English, *The Economy of Prestige: Prizes, Awards, and the Circulation of Cultural Value* (Cambridge, MA: Harvard University Press, 2005), 37.

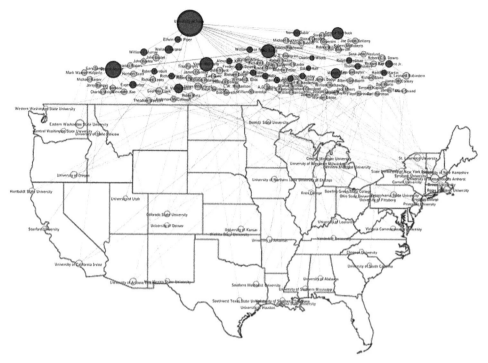

Figure 8.1   Creative writing programs launched by Iowa Workshop graduates.
Visualization by Nicholas Kelly.

would flow. Thus in 1963 he wrote to University of Iowa President Virgil Hancher boldly announcing his plan to "run the future of American literature, and a great deal of European and Asian, through" Iowa City.[15] As he states in his introduction to *Midland: Twenty-Five Years of Fiction and Poetry, Selected from the Writing Workshops of the State University of Iowa* (1961), which came out in the midst of the anthology wars, "in a country with so ranging a landscape, with its concentrations of culture so widely diffused, the problem of where a young writer is to feel at home becomes far more urgent than in England, where London is in easy reach. There must be an alternative between Hollywood and New York, between those places psychically as well as geographically."[16] In those twenty-five years Engle built up the workshop from an obscure experiment to a hegemonic

---

[15] Paul Engle to Virgil Hancher, October 31, 1963, UI Special Collections Library.
[16] Paul Engle, *Midland: Twenty-Five Years of Fiction and Poetry, Selected from the Writing Workshops of the State University of Iowa* (New York: Random House, 1961), xxv.

institutional formation. Donald Justice, originally Engle's student and then his heir as reigning poet of the program, called it a "pyramid scheme," as he watched his students spread out across the country launching programs as they went, all based on the workshop model developed at Iowa.[17] The pattern would be retrospectively and empirically mapped out by Stephen Wilbers in his thesis and then book, *The Iowa Writers' Workshop: Origins, Emergence, and Growth* (1980), the Appendix to which lists "Writing Programs Founded or Directed by Iowa Workshop Graduates."[18] His list includes some twenty-five programs across the country that were launched by Iowa graduates between 1960 and 1980. These programs in turn would lay the groundwork for the apotheosis of creative writing as an academic discipline in the 1980s and 1990s. By the turn of the new millennium, the entire poetry world had essentially been absorbed by the American university system, and creative writing has shifted from an adjunct enterprise to a staple of English department curricula. (See Figure 8.1.)

The system has arguably been a victim of its own success, and there are few poets sanguine enough to celebrate it. Rather, the lifeworld of Program Era poetry and poetics is constituted by an ethos of cranky dissatisfaction as a kind of structure of feeling. Much of the critical dissent has come from poet-critics loosely or directly affiliated with Language Poetry, which over the course of the 1970s and 1980s established itself in principled resistance to what Charles Bernstein dubbed the "official verse culture" of the academy, still based in New Critical paradigms of formal complexity and in romantic attachments to the idea of poetry as personal expression and poets as exceptionally gifted individuals. Language Poetry dissented from the legacy of the new criticism on political grounds, allying itself with the rise of theory in English departments and basing itself in the original avant-gardes of the earlier twentieth century, who positioned themselves against the high modernism of Pound and Eliot.

With the rise of theory as a dominant paradigm in literary study, creative writing programs came to be seen as hopelessly conservative ideologically, and initially creative writing was at a disadvantage in what became a series of turf wars over the course of the later twentieth century. This was at heart an institutional issue: academic programs are almost always supplemental or ancillary to academic departments, and in the middle of the century English departments were at the peak of their power

[17] Quoted in D. G. Myers, *The Elephants Teach: Creative Writing since 1880* (Chicago: University of Chicago Press, 2006), 164.
[18] Stephen Wilbers, *The Iowa Writers' Workshop* (Iowa City: University of Iowa Press, 1980), 137–39.

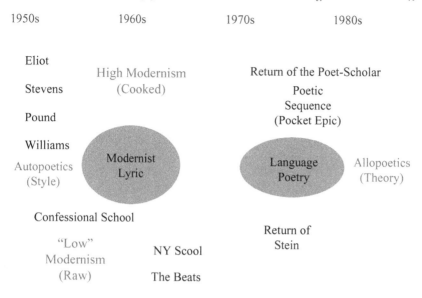

Figure 8.2   Program Era poetics. Illustration by Loren Glass.

in the American system of liberal arts education. English professors, with PhDs and research agendas, controlled decisions about policy and funding, about hiring and promoting, about curriculum and pedagogy, while creative writers struggled to adapt to a bureaucratic system that they frequently resented as a necessary evil. Thus, in the later twentieth century the institutional battle lines were loosely drawn between "anti-intellectual" creative writers who naively believed in things like inspiration and beauty and "soul-crushing" theorists who saw only power and ideology. It was a war more of skirmishes than of extensive engagements, and one in which both sides tended to deny or obscure their shared dependence on the larger institution that made their careers possible in the first place.

Indeed, it was not entirely clear that a war was going on until Mark McGurl attempted to end it with his magisterial *The Program Era: Postwar Fiction and the Rise of Creative Writing* (2009), which begins by disavowing any concern for judging literary value and then concludes by adopting a "strategic triumphalism" regarding the aesthetic achievements of Program Era fiction.[19] No comparable effort has been made to account for Program

---

[19] Mark McGurl, *The Program Era: Postwar Fiction and the Rise of Creative Writing* (Cambridge, MA: Harvard University Press, 2009), 409.

Era poetry, though it is surely the "purer" example of an institutionally patronized artistic practice. The closest we have is Jed Rasula's *American Poetry Wax Museum*, which has a much more tendentious parti pris in the developments it chronicles. Rasula is candid about this; as he states in his "Polemical Preface," he sees the current state of poetry circa 1996 as "a groundswell of verbal toxic waste" in which "the lyric voice has contributed to a mode of subjectivity as distinctly American as self-help primers, television game shows, and video arcades" (3). And the "museum" in which this voice is sacralized is simply a metonym for institutionality itself, which is Rasula's real adversary. As he ambitiously proclaims, "all the small times and micronarratives fade in the presence of the grand time of the institution, the federated array" (22).

Tendentious as it is on the grand scale, *The American Poetry Wax Museum* provides a number of useful micronarratives that illustrate the history of American poetry over the course of what Rasula himself never names as the Program Era, and its principled dissent provides an ironic hindsight on the current popularity of literary theory among American poets today, when it has waned as a methodology for literary analysis, replaced at least partly by institutional approaches to literary history and practice. In his conclusion, Rasula sees American poetry as having spread out into four zones: (1) the Associated Writing Programs, (2) the New Formalism, (3) language poetry, and (4) various coalitions of interest-oriented or community-based poets (440). He concedes that, when viewed in terms of actual poetic practice, these four "easily resolve into two: formalism, and open form poetry," and that these two in turn can be "resolved into a split or fractious One inasmuch as they represent a dispute over the legacy of early twentieth century modernism" (440).

As with fiction, Program Era poetry can be most broadly understood as the gradual institutionalization of modernist paradigms, starting with the high modernism of Pound and Eliot, that was so amenable to New Critical consecration and analysis, but then incorporating its dialectical opposite in the avant-garde (see Figure 8.2). This process begins with the various "raw" poetries of the literary underground and then achieves a kind of philosophical authority and principled dissent with the academic incorporation of Language Poetry in its alliance with literary theory and its lineage running back through Gertrude Stein instead of Eliot or Pound. This undertheorized alliance reveals the degree to which the larger story here is in fact the story of the American English department, the institutional space in which this history has played out. New Criticism facilitated the rise of creative writing as a discipline focusing on the formally crafted lyric poem, and then literary theory facilitated the incorporation of Language Poetry that established and incorporated a sustained avant-garde resistance to these New Critical paradigms and practices. By the end of the twentieth century, American English departments had, in essence, absorbed their objects of study, usually as subordinate programs within their larger departmental provenance.

But that provenance has been shrinking for some time, and it is unclear what the fate of Program Era American poetry will be as the department that housed it loses its institutional power in the American university. Ironically, creative writing has become the bread and butter of English departments, and MFAs are beginning to outpace PhDs as a result. But poetry in this most recent formation is the poor stepsister of the genres, far less popular than Young Adult fiction and screenwriting, which cater more effectively to a digital culture in which content is king. But this is a story for another century.

CHAPTER 9

African American Political Poetries

Matthew Calihman

Because most African American poetry imagines social pasts, presents, and futures, most of this verse can be described as political poetry. What Cary Nelson says of political poets in general applies to many African American poets in particular: "historical contingency," the mutability of society, "is the very marrow of their work" (5). From the beginning of the twentieth century to the 1960s, African American political poetry was often engaged with the southern Jim Crow regime that rose after the end of Reconstruction and with this regime's northern counterpart, some features of which survive today in ostensibly race-neutral law and institutional practice. With the rise of Jim Crow came new Black institutions, among them literary magazines (e.g., *The Colored American Magazine, The Voice of the Negro, The Horizon,* and *The Crisis*) and literary societies (e.g., the Bethel Literary and Historical Association and the Boston Literary and Historical Association), and many of the new Black cultural institutions opened spaces where Black intellectuals could resist Jim Crow.

In the forefront of this group was W. E. B. Du Bois, who brashly challenged the prevailing accommodationist ideology of Black racial progress and interracial relations, according to which both literary writing and politics were unaffordable luxuries for a people one generation out of slavery. In a 1910 issue of his *Horizon,* he asked of Black writers, "How long, O Lord, how long shall we bow tongue-tied or double-tongued before our enemies?" ("Literature" 4). Du Bois's "A Litany at Atlanta" (1906), first published in the *Independent* and collected in *Darkwater* (1920), adapted a liturgical form to call down judgment upon the Jim Crow regime and the racial violence on which it relied. The event that occasioned Du Bois's poem was the September 1906 race massacre in Atlanta, where Du Bois then lived. Spurred by months of race-baiting gubernatorial campaign rhetoric and by lurid newspaper reports about a series of alleged rapes of white women by Black men, whites brutalized and killed Black citizens and destroyed Black-owned property. During the preceding year, Du Bois had cofounded the Niagara Movement, which pressed African Americans to defy racial subordination in every arena of American life and urged whites to claim the legacy of abolition by joining the new struggle for interracial democracy. "A Litany" expressed the anguish of this struggle. When Robert Kerlin included the poem in *Negro Poets and Their Poems* (1923), he featured it as an example of recent work in such vanguard forms as "free-verse, rhythmic strophes, [and] polyphonic prose" (Kerlin 196), but the poem's form is also traditional. Like many other litanies, this one alternates between sections spoken by a leader and responses voiced by a congregation. Together representing the entire Black population, the leader and congregation implore a "Silent God" to intervene on their behalf (line 1).

Du Bois had begun in the 1900s to embrace socialism, and, in "A Litany," he describes Jim Crow and anti-Black terror as the racial politics of a US capitalism that will not do without an isolated Black subproletariat. "[A]ll this," the leader says in the language of biblical parable, "was to / sate the greed of greedy men who hide behind the veil of vengeance!" (lines 41–42). The ultimate cause of the massacre was white capital's need to keep Atlanta's Black workers in virtual slavery. Complicit in the real crimes against Black Atlantans, the poem further suggests, were the brokers of the decade-old "Atlanta Compromise," the symbolic accord in which Booker T. Washington withdrew African Americans' claims on full citizenship and political power in exchange for assurances that the white South would fully involve the Black tradesperson and farmer in the region's economic life. Now Du Bois's Black faithful see what this compromise has wrought:

> Behold this maimed and broken thing; dear God it was an humble black man who toiled and sweat to save a bit from the pittance paid him. They told him: *Work and Rise.* He worked. Did this man sin? Nay, but some one told how some one said another did – one whom he had never seen nor known. Yet for that man's crime this man lieth maimed and murdered, his wife naked to shame, his children, to poverty and evil.
>
> *Hear us, O heavenly Father!* (lines 49–56)

The supplicants conclude that, far from protecting Black southerners, Washington made them more vulnerable by advising them to limit their sphere of social action to labor – manual labor – alone.

With the image of "this maimed and broken thing," Du Bois contributed to the new subgenre of lynching poetry, a body of political writing that includes the work of his contemporaries and near-contemporaries – for example, Paul Laurence Dunbar's "The Haunted Oak" (1901), Angelina

Weld Grimké's "Beware Lest He Awakes" (1902), and Carrie Williams Clifford's "Little Mother" (1922) – as well as poems by later generations of writers. Near the end of "A Litany," Du Bois's Black souls wonder if even God identifies with the moral abomination of Jim Crow whiteness and so abides anti-Black racial violence: "Surely Thou too art not white, O Lord, a / pale, bloodless, heartless thing?" (lines 71–72). The congregation reminds God of his promises to the righteous, simultaneously suggesting the difficulty of Black Christian faith: "*Vengeance is mine; I will repay, saith the Lord!*" (line 91). Their queries, plaints, and provocations go unanswered. But, through them, the poem bears witness to Black life in a violent white supremacist social order.

Finally, however, "A Litany" begins to imagine Black Americans moving to destroy this order. Carolivia Herron writes that, in "Beware," Grimké took up "the usually disallowed subject of revenge on whites" (114), and Du Bois here violates the same taboo. His leader describes the Black millions' barely suppressed desire for vengeance: there is "a red and / awful shape" "clamoring and clawing" within them (Du Bois, "A Litany" lines 87–88). If God will not "*repay*," then they will make their own justice. "Lord, we have done these pleading, wavering words," the leader warns, weary of the ritual of accommodation (line 94). At the same time, the sections become shorter, the poem resolving into a portentous silence. The litany form, along with the social forms to which it corresponds, cannot much longer contain the "red and / awful shape" of Black social grief.

The struggle against Jim Crow was also the unifying political project of the Harlem/New Negro Renaissance of the late 1910s, 1920s, and 1930s. Among the Renaissance's various institutional foundations were civil rights organizations and their house organs (the National Association for the Advancement of Colored People, the National Urban League, and, respectively, *The Crisis* and *Opportunity*); literary collectives and magazines affiliated with the Communist Party (e.g., the John Reed Club, *The Liberator*, and *The New Masses*); other Left journals and unaffiliated little magazines (e.g., *The Messenger*, *Modern Quarterly*, and *Fire!!*); Marcus Garvey's Black nationalist and pan-Africanist *Negro World*; mainstream magazines, downtown publishers, public facilities and programs (e.g., the New York Public Library and the Federal Writers' Project); and philanthropic organizations. A short list of Harlem Renaissance poets might include Gwendolyn Bennett, Arna Bontemps, Sterling Brown, Countee Cullen, Langston Hughes, Georgia Douglas Johnson, Claude McKay, and Jean Toomer, as well as older writers like Du Bois, Grimké, Fenton

Johnson, and James Weldon Johnson. These poets were proponents of various kinds of integrationism, Black nationalism, cultural pluralism, pan-Africanism, Marxism, and feminism and worked in aesthetic traditions as diverse as romanticism, modernism, and the blues. Because the Renaissance was not a centralized and doctrinaire movement, generalizing about even its approaches to the problem of Jim Crow is difficult. But in Langston Hughes's work of the 1920s and 1930s we can see several characteristic approaches to this problem.

Hughes's "Mulatto" (1927), first published in *The Saturday Review* and collected in *Fine Clothes to the Jew* (1927), challenges the racial taxonomy on which Jim Crow was predicated. Though not long, "Mulatto" might be called a "lyric-epic," to borrow James E. Miller's term for Walt Whitman's synthesis of the personal lyric and the national epic. The poem is a Black modernist lyric-epic of the making and unmaking of Jim Crow. This narrative emerges from a cubist assemblage of voices, those of a white father, his white children, his unacknowledged multiracial son, and a third-person narrator. The first utterance is the multiracial son's declaration, "I am your son, white man!" (line 1), a statement that becomes a refrain and functions not merely as family genealogy but as regional and national history. The father rejects this assertion, replying, "You are my son! / Like hell!," and one of the white children later protests, twice, "N———s ain't my brother" (lines 5–6). Yet by claiming kinship with the white father, the multiracial son has struck the edifice of Jim Crow society. "One of the pillars of the temple fell," intones the narrator (line 4), alluding to the two columns that are said to have flanked the entrance to the First Temple and to have perished when the building was destroyed. Binary "race" will not survive the social reconstruction that the poem augurs.

"Mulatto" strikes another blow at Jim Crow racialism in a long strophe about the history of southern white men's sexual violence against Black women. Initiating another refrain, the narrator gazes upon "The Southern night / Full of stars, / Great big yellow stars" (lines 8–10). The southern sky mirrors a social world full of multiracial people – "little yellow bastard boys," as Hughes describes them in yet another refrain (line 35). Following the ancient epics, the poem recognizes its hero's world-historical significance by establishing his connection to the celestial realm. And the poem's proliferation of refrains further suggests the multiracial subject's ubiquity; his presence resounds everywhere. But if "Mulatto" discovers the male multiracial subject, the poem also discovers his Black mother and the circumstances of his conception. The white father inwardly recalls a scene of

> Juicy bodies
> Of n——— wenches
> Blue black
> Against black fences. (lines 11–14)

Here the color line is the site where race is made, where white men violently impose race on Black women, and where it is unmade, where this same violence gives the lie to race.

In other poems, Hughes resisted Jim Crow not by directly challenging racialization itself but by confronting the racist notion, widely accepted until the 1960s, that African Americans lack a history and a culture. Hughes had grown up admiring Du Bois and shared his conviction that Black people have a "message for the world" (Du Bois, *Souls* 4). "The Negro Speaks of Rivers" (1921), first published in Du Bois's *Crisis* and collected in *The Weary Blues* (1926), traces Black culture back to the very beginning of human civilization. Hughes's first lyric-epic (and indeed his first published adult verse), the poem places its speaker in epochs evoked metonymically by "the Euphrates," "the Congo," "the Nile," and "the Mississippi" (lines 6, 8, 10, 12). With this inventory, with the speaker's expansive "I," and with the poem's long lines and anaphora, "The Negro Speaks" also recalls Whitman, the avant-garde populist with whom Hughes would remain engaged, usually sympathetically, throughout his career. Similar to the "I" of "Song of Myself" (1855), who comprises every American type that Whitman could imagine, Hughes's Black speaker comprises all of the civilization-builders of the past. Among them are the enslaved people who glimpsed a reconstructed America as they watched the Mississippi's "muddy bosom turn all / golden in the sunset" (lines 14–15). The poem's "I" is civilization's Black "soul," a pan-African sensibility "ancient as the world / and older than the flow of human blood / in human veins" (lines 5, 2–4). With the poem's evocations of the Congo and the Nile, it entered a tradition of Africa lyrics that includes Du Bois's "Day in Africa" (1908), McKay's "Africa" (1921), Bennett's "Heritage" (1923), Cullen's "Heritage" (1925), Bontemps's "The Return" (1927), and many later poems.

Hughes remained an internationalist throughout his career. In much of his work of the 1930s and 1940s, when he was closely identified with the Communist movement, he portrayed the struggle against Jim Crow as part of a transnational, interracial, multiethnic struggle against capitalism and imperialism. Similarly, in the poems that he published during the movement's Popular Front period (1935–39) and during World War II, the struggle against Jim Crow is often part of, or analogous to, the fight against fascism, which the Communist Left then regarded as a threat to the USSR, international working-class radicalism, ethnic minorities, and, ultimately, all of humankind. Among the many writers with Hughes on the literary Left (at one time or another, and with various kinds of commitment) were Renaissance poets Bennett, Bontemps, Brown, Cullen, and McKay, as well as such younger poets as Gwendolyn Brooks, Robert Hayden, Melvin Tolson, and Margaret Walker. Although Hughes continued to publish in a wide variety of venues, his poems often appeared in Left magazines and under the imprints of Left publishers.

Like his earlier writing, Hughes's work from this period is both ideologically and formally radical. "Let America Be America Again" (1936), first published in *Esquire*, is another important example of the poet's experimentation with multiple voices. Also, like "A Litany," "Let America" plays with the prayer form – in this case, such patriotic devotions as Samuel Francis Smith's "America" (1831), with its appeals to "let" America's glory be heard. The first voice, which dominates the speech at the beginning of the poem, longs to return to a national golden age, a bygone era of true republicanism and limitless economic opportunity. In response to these pleas, a second speaker utters the refrain "(America never was America to me)" (line 5), each iteration of it standing alone as a single-sentence strophe, its parentheses suggesting that these words barely get in edgewise. This second voice, which soon prevails over the first, is really many: the nation's Popular Front chorus of African Americans, poor whites, Indigenous people, immigrants, farmers, industrial workers, and young people. Here we have another expansive Whitmanian "I," along with catalogues, long lines, and anaphora, but this "I" encompasses a multiracial, multiethnic American people determined to "make America again" – to realize its noblest ideals – by "redeem[ing]" "The land, the mines, the [industrial] plants, the rivers / The mountains and the endless plain" (lines 83–85). "Let America" is thus a lyric-epic of the refounding of America as an antiracist, cultural pluralist workers' society. The poem's radical vision and capacious conception of American nationality made apt its inclusion in Hughes's *A New Song* (1938), which was published by the International Workers Order, a Communist-led federation of ethnically and linguistically identified fraternal societies that took part in various Popular Front political struggles and cultural projects.

For Hughes, however, the emergence of a multiracial, multiethnic Left by no means signified the end of racial oppression, an account of which had to be part of the Popular Front's story of the nation. In "Let America,"

Hughes's capsule history of post-Columbian settlement contrasts
Europeans' deciding to leave their native lands with Africans' being forced
to leave theirs, and only a tortuous syntax can make a single narrative of
these histories in just one sentence:

> O, I'm the man who sailed those early seas
> In search of what I meant to be my home –
> For I'm the one who left dark Ireland's shore,
> And Poland's plain, and England's grassy lea,
> And torn from Black Africa's strand I came
> To build a "homeland of the free." (lines 45–50)

Linking past to present, the speaker proclaims in another strophe, "I am
the Negro bearing slavery's scars" (line 20). We are also reminded of
Jim Crow: "I am the farmer, bondsman to the soil. / I am the worker
sold to the machine. / I am the Negro, servant to you all" (lines 31–33).
Returning to the dialogic mode, naming and addressing this "you" within
his "I," Hughes refuses to write racial inequality and conflict out of his
Popular Front national epic.

Margaret Walker took a similar stance, making vividly present the Black
Americans whom the Communist movement hoped to organize and even
making special claims for them. Raised in the South by Talented Tenth
parents, she moved to Chicago in 1932 to attend Northwestern and
remained in the North for about a decade. Walker worked for the
Federal Writers' Project, moved in Left circles (e.g., the South Side
Writers' Group, the League of American Writers, and the Communist
Party itself), completed a master's at the Iowa Writers' Workshop, and saw
her thesis, *For My People* (1942), published in the Yale Younger Poets
series. Throughout these years, she remained engaged with Black people's
struggles under US racial capitalism but also with African American
vernacular culture, and she later praised Hughes's blues poetry for revealing this tradition as a resource for Black poets.[1] Her "For My People"
(1937), first published in *Poetry*, is an ode to Black America. The poem is
also an epic: like "Let America" and "Song of Myself," "For My People" is
a lyric-epic whose individual-collective subject is still becoming. And like
"Let America" and "A Litany," "For My People" is a prayer. The first nine
of its ten free-verse strophes together form a very long and complex
dependent clause portraying the Black Americans for whom the speaker
appeals and suggesting the duration of their suffering. The second strophe,

---

1 See, e.g., Margaret Walker, "New Poets," *Phylon*, vol. 11, no. 4, 1950, p. 351.

for example, pictures Black people's work lives, representing them as a long oblivion of estranged labor:

> For my people lending their strength to the years: to the gone years and the now years and the maybe years, washing ironing cooking scrubbing sewing mending hoeing plowing digging planting pruning patching dragging along never gaining never reaping never knowing and never understanding; ...
> (lines 6–11)

Later, the speaker envisions Black workers rising as one in struggle. The seven independent clauses in the final strophe, each beginning with a prophetic "Let," petition for Black Americans' material and spiritual redemption in social revolution (lines 51–58). To be sure, the new world that the poem dreams is one that "will hold all the / people all the faces all the adams and eves and their / countless generations" (lines 48–50). But these phrases constitute the poem's only possible reference to a larger working-class movement. Whereas "Let America" encompasses "the people," drawing some pointed distinctions among its constituent groups, "For My People" is resolutely focused on Black Americans. The first strophe hails the poem's dedicatees as descendants of enslaved people and as traditional practitioners of African American vernacular culture, which has long sustained them:

> For my people everywhere singing their slave songs repeatedly: their dirges and their ditties and their blues and jubilees, praying their prayers nightly to an unknown god, bending their knees humbly to an unseen power; ...
> (lines 1–5)

Walker makes clear, though, that this living heritage is no compensation for Black people's exclusion from full citizenship or for their material deprivation. In a strophe describing the new Black urban communities formed by mass migration to the nation's cities, the migrants appear as a

> ... lost disinherited dispossessed and HAPPY
> people filling the cabarets and taverns and other people's
> pockets needing bread and shoes and milk and land and
> money and Something – Something all our own; ... (lines 30–33)

Walker thus acknowledges both the plenitude of Black vernacular culture and African Americans' persistent social need, including their need for "Something all our own," a vital Black subsociety, within even a reconstructed America of the future.

Many of the poets who were identified with the Black Arts Movement (BAM) of the late 1960s and early 1970s shared these commitments to the vernacular tradition and institution building – thanks in part to Walker herself. During the Civil Rights Movement, "For My People" had been read aloud to jailed activists to strengthen their resolve (Walker and Campbell 97), and the BAM later claimed Walker as a literary ancestor. (Hughes and Brooks were also notable forebears.) Although most BAM writers were cultural nationalists and did not share Walker's faith in Left interracialism, they, too, were engaged in writing vernacular Blackness and a Black revolutionary consciousness from the inside, even proposing that African Americans' identification with their culture was the motive force behind their future liberation. Addison Gayle's *The Black Aesthetic* (1971), an anthology of BAM manifestos and some of their early twentieth-century antecedents, begins with an epigraph from "For My People": "*Let the martial songs be written, let the dirges disappear. Let a race of men now rise and take control*" (vii). Writing at the end of the BAM era, Eugene Redmond pronounced that "[t]here are few volumes of poetry published since *For My People* that can be considered any *blacker*." "Rich in cultural folk references, black phonology, and social history," the collection "brilliantly illuminate[d] the hope, humor, pathos, rage, stamina, and iron dignity of the race" (269, 151). Amiri Baraka invoked "For My People" in the same breath in which he recalled Malcolm X's teachings. Arguing that Black communities needed to nationalize all of the white-owned "properties and resources" within their geographical boundaries, Baraka wrote that "[a]s Margaret Walker said in her poem 'For My People': *A race of men must rise, and take control*" [sic] ("Legacy" 249). This massive redistribution was not accomplished, but BAM intellectuals devoted much energy to building African American cultural institutions: journals and magazines (e.g., *Black Dialogue*, *The Journal of Black Poetry*, *Liberator*, *Negro Digest/ Black World*, and *Soulbook*), publishers (e.g., Broadside Press and Third World Press), theater and dance companies, museums, and so on. Among the dozens of poets who were identified with these institutions and who appeared in movement anthologies were Baraka, Jayne Cortez, Etheridge Knight, Audre Lorde, Haki Madhubuti, Larry Neal, Sonia Sanchez, Gil Scott-Heron, and Lorenzo Thomas, as well as older writers like Brooks and Walker.

Jayne Cortez was one of the many BAM writers who, like Walker, took solace in the Black vernacular heritage but also pressed for the establishment of new Black cultural institutions. Among Cortez's inspirations were "For My People," Hughes's experiments with oral forms, Brown's blues poems, and the work of Négritude poets Aimé Césaire and Léon Damas (Cortez and Melham 44). A veteran of labor struggles in Los Angeles and of the southern Civil Rights Movement, she cofounded the Watts Repertory Theatre Company (1964) and the Bola Press (1972), the latter of which put out several of her books as well as recordings of her collaborations with the jazz group the Firespitters. Her "How Long Has Trane Been Gone" (1969), first published in *Black Dialogue,* collected in *Pisstained Stairs and the Monkey Man's Wares* (1969), and performed on a 1974 recording with bassist Richard Davis, is one of the movement's many elegies for John Coltrane. The saxophonist, who had died young in 1967, was cherished as both a conservator of the vernacular tradition and a vanguardist. In his work could be heard the dialectic of tradition and innovation – what Baraka famously called "the changing same" ("The Changing Same" 203). Like much of the vernacular tradition, Cortez's poem is polyphonic. A first voice pleads, "tell me about the good things," and a second answers, "I'm tellin you about / John Coltrane" (lines 64–66). This second speaker laments not only the musician's death but also the demise of Black radio programming that, like Coltrane's performances, kept the past and the present in conversation:

> There was a time
> when KGFJ played all black music
> from Bird to Johnny Ace
> on show after show ... (lines 44–47)

By segmenting the tradition into separate, reified styles and marketing each to a particular generation of Black people, the culture industry has severed Black youth from jazz and the blues. The record companies and radio stations have "divided black music / doubled the money / and left us split again" (lines 50–52), and Black people have not yet built the institutions that would restore the community and make it less vulnerable to such violence. At the end of the poem is an image of exile, of Black people cut off from tradition and one another. In one of Cortez's surrealist conjunctions, Coltrane is "gone," "Riding in a portable radio" (lines 96–97). Next to the radio is "your son" (line 98), but he may not hear Coltrane's sound, which may be playing on another frequency. The son "walks into nothing / No City No State No Home No Nothing" (lines 99–100). Only a dual commitment to a changing Black vernacular tradition and a Black institutional infrastructure, the poem affirms, can keep the Black community intact.

BAM writing and institutions were also sites of conflict concerning the true identity of the Black vernacular subject. Audre Lorde identified with the BAM, publishing two books with Broadside and contributing to

movement magazines and anthologies, but she understood herself as a
Black lesbian feminist, and she contended with sexism and homophobia
within the BAM at the same time that she confronted racism, sexism, and
homophobia outside it. Years later, she spoke of the "Black Lesbian-
bashing" that took place within the BAM (Rowell and Lorde 63). She
also remembered that Broadside's editor, Dudley Randall, persuaded her
to omit her homoerotic "Love Poem" from the manuscript of *From a Land
Where Other People Live* (1973) (Lorde and Rich 727–28). For Lorde,
though, there could be no effective political organizing without the energies created by the recognition and acceptance of difference. Furthermore,
for Lorde, the erotic was an indispensable form of knowledge, especially
for women – the means by which they come to know what they have a
right to expect from the world.

Published in *Cables to Rage* (1970), at a time when the Black Power
Movement and the BAM were in full swing, Lorde's long poem "Martha"
disclosed her lesbian identity to the reading public and claimed for women
a new personal autonomy, including the prerogative to love women. The
poem's titular subject is Martha Einson, a white Jewish woman whom
Lorde had known since high school and with whom she had had a long
sexual-romantic relationship. This affair may have coincided partly or
wholly with Martha's marriage and with Lorde's own, which was troubled
from the outset and ended in divorce in 1975. In 1968, following a car
accident, Martha was in a coma for nearly two months, during which time
Lorde visited her daily (De Veaux 66, 69, 101). "Martha" is a polyphonic
composition, an imaginative record of these vigils and of the women's
shared past. Lorde proclaims her love for Martha, recollects their intimacy,
and imagines that Martha's hospital room is not only a "deathplace" but
also a "womb" from which she might be reborn into a new freedom (lines
16, 92). Reflecting, it seems, on her marriage, Martha once asked, *"How
long must I wander here / In this final house of my father?"* (lines 46–47), and
Lorde, in a sentence that could serve as an answer, tells her that

> ... the gods who honor hard work
> will keep this second coming
> free from that lack of choice
> which hindered your first journey
> to this Tarot house. (lines 24–28)

By Lorde's reckoning, Martha has long prepared to bring an end to her
marital exile, and surely much of what Lorde says to Martha spoke also to
the poet's own situation as a lesbian married to a man. Indeed, the poem

implicitly compares such a predicament to a problem of racial identity. The first two lines announce, "Martha this is a catalog of days / passing before you looked again," the enjambment heightening anticipation of the word "passing." Later, in one of this verb's several returns, we find the hospital room abuzz with medical staff endlessly "testing whoever passes for Martha" (line 249). With this repeated invocation of passing, Lorde employs a familiar language of racial imposture to delegitimate the exile ordered by a heterosexist, patriarchal society.

Making the same ethical claims for the acceptance of women's autonomy and of queerness that the BAM made for the acceptance of Blackness, Lorde took part in an opening of African American poetry in the 1970s. Since that decade, many Black writers have sought to broaden definitions of Blackness and Black freedom. Still, BAM legacies can be seen nearly everywhere in contemporary African American poetry. Among them are commitments to representing the subjective content of oppression and struggle, recovering Black collective pasts and envisioning collective futures, engaging Black vernacular culture without essentializing it, and building literary institutions that support writers of color. At no previous time have there been as many nationally prominent Black poets as there are today (it is no longer possible to venture a short list of major living Black poets), and this unprecedented achievement and recognition has been made possible, in part, by such institutions as *Callaloo*, the Dark Room Collective, the Cave Canem Foundation, the Before Columbus Foundation, the Hurston/Wright Foundation, the Nuyorican Poets Café, and the Furious Flower Poetry Center. It is difficult, however, to see this success as a plotline in a larger social progress narrative concerning Black Americans and work, housing, education, health care, women's and LGBTQ rights, voting, police, and prisons.

African American poets have long written about Black people's experiences in the nation's criminal justice system. But this subject has demanded greater attention in recent decades, which have seen the rise of a new regime of racialized mass criminalization and mass incarceration (established under the banners of "law and order," "the war on drugs," etc.) as well as the rise of new decarceration and prison abolition movements and the Black Lives Matter Movement. Much of poet Reginald Dwayne Betts's memoir *A Question of Freedom* (2009) is an attempt to explain how, as a college-bound sixteen-year-old in 1996, the author came to rob and carjack a white man at gunpoint (taking the man's car without also abducting him) and how Betts then came to be certified as an adult and to spend eight years behind bars. Throughout this always recursive reckoning, Betts recognizes both his personal agency and powerful social forces, ones operating at the levels of law and entrenched institutional practice. In "The Sound of My Mother Crying," from *Shahid Reads His Own Palm* (2010), he also recognizes economic forces behind the law: deindustrialization and disinvestment. At the time of the speaker's crime, "[p]arole / had been dumped for truth in sentencing & GM / had laid off half the people in a city I've never visited" (lines 7–9). Several of the memoir's sentences land heavily on the phrase "my crime," but Betts also sees that "[j]udges learned to read [Black male teens'] complexions, crimes, and communities as reasons why we needed the bars of a jail" (Betts, *A Question* 10, 16). Prison is a place full of "young boys," mainly boys of color, "hurting from what they did and from what others did to them" (153). So epochal is their experience that it might be added to the Black lyric-epic of Hughes's "The Negro Speaks." "They have known cells like rivers," Betts says of these young men in "Bastards of the Reagan Era," a poem from a collection by the same name (2015) (line 344).

Now also a lawyer, Betts has emerged as a prominent decarceration advocate. In "House of Unending" (2019), first published in *Poetry* and collected in *Felon* (2019), he fashions a crown of sonnets to represent incarceration and life after prison as deadly repetition. He joins a tradition of African American political sonneteers that includes McKay, Cullen, Hughes, Tolson, Walker, and Brooks, along with such contemporary poets as Wanda Coleman, Rita Dove, Terrance Hayes, Marilyn Nelson, Patricia Smith, and Natasha Trethewey. Repetition is both theme and form in "House." Among the formal conventions that Betts follows is repeating each poem's final line at the beginning of the next poem in the sequence. Evoked within and by such forms are the speaker's exercise regimen, his subjection to the prison's "count-time & chow-call logic," his recollection of his crime and of "unspoken larcenies," his sense of isolation even after his release, and his discovery and rediscovery that the nation's prisons are always "holding on to those lives, / Holding on, ensuring that nothing survives" (lines 23, 82, 41–42).

But "House" also thwarts its own repetitions. Like many African American practitioners of the sonnet, Betts breaks the form. His lines are not reliably iambic, and most are not decasyllabic. Some hold out until the end only to defy metrical convention with polysyllables like "chromo-some" and "stereotype," flouting the determinisms evoked by these words (lines 20, 68). Betts likewise troubles rhyme at many points throughout the sequence. The first sonnet, for example, proposes to end-rhyme "push-ups" and "upset," thus upsetting the rhyme scheme, just as the same poem's pairing of "daughters" and "fractured" fractures the prescribed pattern (lines 9, 11, 10, 12). Betts furthermore violates the convention of beginning and ending the crown with precisely the same line. In the first and second lines of the first poem, prison is figured as a "house of shredded & torn / Dear John letters" (lines 1–2). But this phrase returns transformed: the crown's final words are "house, shredded & torn" (line 98). Now it is the prison itself – the "House of Unending" – that is "shredded & torn," just as this sonnet sequence is. Severing the crown's circular form, Betts casts doubt on the prediction that Black people will end up in prison. In "Tell This to the People You Love," a poem from *Shahid Reads*, the speaker observes that "prison cells drive men to practice / history" (lines 7–8). But, for Betts, this practice is not prophecy. Like the work of all the other writers discussed here, his is a poetry of historical contingency.

WORKS CITED

Baraka, Amiri. "The Changing Same (R&B and New Black Music)." In *Black Music*. Morrow, 1968, pp. 180–211.
  "The Legacy of Malcolm X, and the Coming of the Black Nation." In *Home: Social Essays*. Morrow, 1966, pp. 238–50.
Betts, Reginald Dwayne. "Bastards of the Reagan Era." In *Bastards of the Reagan Era*. Four Way, 2015, pp. 15–30.
  "House of Unending." *Poetry*, vol. 214, no. 1, 2019, pp. 32–35.
  A Question of Freedom: A Memoir of Learning, Survival, and Coming of Age in Prison. Penguin, 2009.
  "The Sound of My Mother Crying." In *Shahid Reads His Own Palm*. Alice James Books, 2010, p. 41.
  "Tell This to the People You Love." In *Shahid Reads His Own Palm*, pp. 26–27.
Cortez, Jayne. "How Long Has Trane Been Gone." *Black Dialogue*, vol. 4, no. 1, 1969, pp. 28–30.
Cortez, Jayne, and D. H. Melhem. "Interview with Jayne Cortez." *The Greenfield Review*, vol. 11, nos. 1–2, 1983, pp. 31–47.
De Veaux, Alexis. *Warrior Poet: A Biography of Audre Lorde*. Norton, 2004.
Du Bois, W. E. B. "A Litany of Atlanta." *The Independent*, October 11, 1906, pp. 856–58.
  "Literature." *The Horizon*, vol. 5, no. 3, 1910, p. 4.
  The Souls of Black Folk. McClurg, 1903.
Gayle, Addison, Jr., ed. *The Black Aesthetic*. Doubleday, 1971.
Herron, Carolivia, ed. *Selected Works of Angelina Weld Grimké*. Oxford University Press, 1991.
Hughes, Langston. "Let America Be America Again." In *A New Song*. International Workers Order, 1938, pp. 9–11.

"Mulatto." *The Saturday Review of Literature*, January 1927, p. 547.

"The Negro Speaks of Rivers." *The Crisis*, June 1921, p. 71.

Kerlin, Robert T. *Negro Poets and Their Poems*. Associated Publishers, 1923.

Lorde, Audre. "Martha." In *Cables to Rage*. Breman, 1970, pp. 10–16.

Lorde, Audre, and Adrienne Rich. "An Interview with Audre Lorde." *Signs*, vol. 6, no. 4, 1981, pp. 713–36.

Miller, James E., Jr. *Leaves of Grass: America's Lyric-Epic of Self and Democracy*. Twayne, 1992.

Nelson, Cary. *Revolutionary Memory: Recovering the Poetry of the American Left*. Routledge, 2001.

Redmond, Eugene B. *Drumvoices: The Mission of Afro-American Poetry*. Doubleday, 1976.

Rowell, Charles H., and Audre Lorde. "Above the Wind: An Interview with Audre Lorde." *Callaloo*, vol. 23, no. 1, 2000, pp. 52–63.

Walker, Margaret. "For My People." *Poetry*, vol. 51, no. 2, 1937, pp. 81–83.

Walker, Margaret, and Ruth Campbell. "Interview with Margaret Walker." In *Conversations with Margaret Walker*, edited by Maryemma Graham. University Press of Mississippi, 2002, pp. 92–97.

CHAPTER 10

Our Terribly Excluded Blue
Gwendolyn Brooks and the Politics of Poetic Framing

J. Peter Moore

One of the most immediate ways to query the political stakes of poetry is to consider the context in which one encounters a poem. Take for instance Abel Meeropol's antilynching poem "Strange Fruit." In the 1937 issue of the Marxist labor magazine *New Masses* the work is an article of working-class allyship and protest, whereas the more popular musical rendition, recorded by Billie Holiday in 1939, underscores the elegiac quality of the work, emphasizing a connection between jazz and Black folk traditions of social mourning. In certain instances, poems use extraliterary markers to indicate the circumstantial conditions out of which they arise; these are commonly referred to as framing devices. In his succinct comment on "The Literary Frame," John Frow defines the frame as the material and immaterial border that "surrounds a text and defines its specific [literary] status and the kinds of use to which it can be put" (26). The frame includes the material boundaries of the books' two covers, the blank space encircling the text and even the silence that marks the start and conclusion of a public reading. But it also includes the immaterial boundaries that communicate the generic and historical particularity of a given work, thus generating what Hans Robert Jauss has called our horizons of expectation. These horizons are cued by such seemingly extra-literary elements as the poem's date of composition (occasionally stamped at the bottom of the page), the author's name, the work's title, the publishing house, as well as the dedicatory material. Taken together these inscriptive settings carry major implications for how we derive meaning. Yet we often overlook them in our rush to privilege content. When accepted uncritically, the frame fulfills its principle duty, to present the separation of literature from everyday life as uncontested and natural. Like any border concept – silence, for instance – when we pay attention to the frame, the ideological biases constructing the border come into view. Each framing occasion provides the receiver with the opportunity to consider the occluded relationships of production and exchange that underpin the creation and reception of a poem. Attending to the frame acknowledges the poem as an ongoing series of events, with each iteration carrying the potential to reroute its meaning. It is for this reason that practitioners of socially attuned innovative poetries have made it a perennial habit to call attention to the frame in order to relax its authority.

Few writers in the twentieth century present a more thorough consideration of the expressive potential of framing than Gwendolyn Brooks. Given her consistent creed to be "a Watchful Eye; a Tuned Ear; a Super-Reporter," Brooks's poetry makes a consistent effort to use titles and dedicatory frames to index her work in relationship to the contextual "whirlwind" of history (Melham 157). This is evident in her intimate portraits of Black urban life in the wake of the Great Migration, her eulogies to fallen heroes of Black America from Medgar Evers to Malcolm X, and her pointed responses to headline atrocities, as in the case of her two-poem sequence on the murder of Emmett Till. Extending her tendency to thematize the frame, Brooks gives voice in many of her early collections to her lived experience as a domestic worker, being dispatched by an agency to labor for an affluent family, the Burns-Coopers of the world. Through such characters as Hattie Scott, Sallie Smith, and Maude Martha, Brooks speaks to the condition of being an aberrant element within the claustrophobic frame of a well-behaved brand of white supremacy. After becoming the first Black author to win a Pulitzer Prize, Brooks soon became a local institution in her own right, receiving consistent requests to pen commemorative poems for public events, leading to such works as "The Chicago Picasso," which addresses the unveiling of the sculpture in Daley Plaza. One could even consider Brooks's long-standing interest in architecture, culminating in her long poem "In the Mecca," as a sublimated meditation on the literary frame.

But the clearest evidence of her concern with framing comes in the form of her own extensive efforts to frame her career into two parts, evident in her choice to divide her relatively short memoirs into two volumes: *Report from Part One* and *Report from Part Two*. Brooks describes her early work in terms of an adherence to Eurocentric ideas of aesthetic formalism, which she ultimately aligns with a political faith in the project of integration. Arguing for a clear break after aligning herself with the movement for Black nationalism in the late 1960s, she insisted that she would steer her work toward a more racially attuned brand of literary populism. In a well-cited passage, she explains that her intention would be to "develop a style that will appeal to black people in taverns, black people in gutters, schools offices, factories, prisons, the consulate; ... in pulpits, black people in mines, on farms, on thrones" ("My People" 56). Critics continue to debate to what extent her career falls into two neatly delimited periods. In the years closely following her self-described "conversion," readers such as D. H. Melham, Norris Clark, and Chicago's Third World Press publisher Haki R. Madhubuti himself lend support to the narrative, referring to it as a shift from "an egocentric orientation to an ethnocentric one," which they argue is evident at the level of form through her departure from the normative values of European literary tradition (Clark 83). However, more recent readers have resisted the notion that her work undergoes a radical transformation, calling attention to the ways in which she bends European verse models like the sonnet to her own discrepant purpose in such early work as her series "Gay Chaps at the Bar." Add to this a retinue of scholars who remain convinced that her work from the very beginning concerns itself with the condition of Black social life in Chicago, in a manner that demonstrates the influence of Popular Front leftist politics.

One might contest Brooks's narrative as overly simplifying, but one cannot ignore the steps she took to instrumentalize her awareness that frames bear political implications through their capacity to structure reception. The late work may or may not represent a significant shift in her style, but it does bear an unmistakably distinctive frame. Marking her commitment to the radical struggle for Black liberation, Brooks amicably severs ties with her mainstream publisher, Harper and Row, in order to publish all of her subsequent work with small, politically active, Black-owned presses, such as Dudley Randall's Broadside Press and Third World Press. The latter of the two was organized by three writers – Haki Madhubuti, Johari Amini, and Carolyn Rodger – whom Brooks mentored through informal workshops that she hosted in conjunction with the Blackstone Rangers, a large fugitive social organization, classified as a street gang. This framing gesture suggests that Brooks was keenly aware of the ways in which distribution and material production affect not only the reception of one's work but also the content of one's message. In her words, the first critically acclaimed books – *A Street in Bronzeville, Annie Allen, Maud Martha,* and *The Bean Eaters* – "did a lot of poetic, dramatic, and fictional whining ... addressed to white people" (Untitled 8). For Brooks, working with a predominantly white publishing outfit meant publishing for a predominantly white audience, thus perpetuating an asymmetrical relationship in which white expectations structure the representation of Black experience. More than a matter of symbolic capital, the shifting of presses enabled her to circumvent the disempowering cycle of complaint and gradual mollification, as a new framework meant a new audience, which in turn meant the prospect of a new utterance.

To return to the opening claim of this chapter, I will spend the rest of the chapter considering the context in which one encounters a single poem. In what follows I address an extraordinary instance from Brooks's career, one that has yet to be discussed by the extensive body of criticism surrounding her highly regarded career. In it the poet uses the technology of the literary frame to mark a defiant turn from one audience to another, as a means of theorizing alternatives to the exclusionary frame of normative citizenship.

Between April 30 and May 4, 1965, the United States Civil War Centennial Commission organized a five-day ceremony in Springfield, Illinois, to observe the anniversary of the death of Abraham Lincoln. For the final gala, which culminated five years of commemorations in cities across the nation, the committee invited Brooks to deliver an original ode to Lincoln at the event. This decision, along with the poem Brooks produced, both reflect the fraught circumstances of the event, conceived as an attempt to promote national solidarity at a time of geopolitical tension. Leaning into their charge, the committee prohibited any discussion of slavery, the institution that was central to the historical conflict, as issues of race, reparations, and the contemporary struggle for civil rights were regarded as divisive subjects that would threaten the patriotic zeal of the event. The title of Brooks's poem, "In the Time of Detachment, in the Time of Cold," takes this framing context into consideration as she situates Lincoln in relation to both the global Cold War and the rising tide of segregative violence. And yet the poem adheres to the propagandistic priorities of the committee by refusing to explicitly name the crisis at hand. Rather than call attention to low employment opportunities, crumbling social services, and police brutality – all of which would figure prominently in the presidential report on urban race riots produced three years later by one of the attendees at the gala, Illinois Governor Otto Kerner Jr. – Brooks describes the threat in abstract terms, as "vivid heathen," "affectionate evil," "grave legalities of hate," and "the gray / Jubilees of our demondom." This stands in contrast to the poem's treatment of Lincoln, whom Brooks describes as the "still enhancer, renouncer" – the "good man" who can "put hand in hand land over." If Brooks's mere presence at the event foregrounded the discordant matter of race in America, her poem made the issue palatable for the predominantly white audience, as she omitted details and saluted the seemingly incorruptible symbol of the Great Emancipator.

Although Brooks suppressed overt references to race relations in the poem, she would years later turn suppression into a subversive strategy by rerouting essentially the same poem toward a different audience with a different set of political imperatives. Aside from the broadside that the committee printed for the occasion, Brooks published the poem only once, in *A Portion of That Field* (1967), a slim limited volume of materials from the celebratory weekend produced by the University of Illinois Press. Never does it appear in any of her other single volumes nor her collected poems. As if refusing to claim the poem was not suppression enough, twenty years later, she further distances herself from the entire event by repurposing the poem with one astounding difference: she removes all references to Lincoln. In the 1987 volume *Near-Johannesburg Boy*, Brooks includes a virtually identical copy of the poem, under the new title "The Good Man." Aside from minor changes in capitalization and punctuation, the poem preserves all of the language of the original, except the references to Lincoln. "Coherent/Counsel! Good man! Good Lincoln! Abraham! – " becomes simply "Coherent/Counsel! Good man" (510). Furthermore, the poem is no longer dedicated to Lincoln but rather to her friend and former student, the Black poet, social organizer, and publisher Haki Madhubuti, bearing the inscription "For Haki / In the time of detachment, / in the time of cold." While scholars have made passing comments about both versions of this poem, none has discussed the strange circumstances in which Brooks, late in her career, reappropriates a discarded ode to a slain president in order to praise a poet who championed Black political and cultural revolution.

Brooks uses the two versions to theorize two different conceptions of community. In the first, the poem establishes a community wherein the collective provides a context for legitimizing the politics of the citizen subject. This is the community that serves to protect the rights of property holders and extends legible autonomy to its rightful participants. The second poem, however, presents a community in accord with Robert Esposito's conception of *communitas*, a body that emerges out of material lack. In this form, community is not the consortium of property owners seeking mutual protection, but a radical acknowledgment of the inadequacy of the normative citizenship model to accommodate those people who it had historically excluded on the grounds of race, gender, class, and sexuality. In one sense, the Lincoln/Madhubuti affair adds to a growing canon of works that use poetry as a means of imagining new structures of social relation. Presently I will examine the ways in which Brooks shifts between two Janus-faced visions of communal life. I then look at the way in which the two poems when read together frame a generative interstitial space that exists between both versions, which I associate with the unrepresentable power of radical sociality. What transpires between the two poems is Brooks's firsthand experience with the unpredictable expressivity of social collectives. To this point, the 1965 Lincoln centenary event in Springfield should be read in conversation with another event, the 1967 Second Black Writers' Conference at Fisk University in Nashville. Inspired by the student movements toward Black Consciousness, in the weeks following the conference, she begins working actively with a number of organizations, agitating for social justice within the immediate context of her neighborhood in the Chicago South Side. In the context of the latter, she meets the young poet who would eventually replace Lincoln as the titular good man in her rededicated poem.

***

When laid side by side, "In the Time of Detachment, in the Time of Cold" and "The Good Man" point to both the power and limits of the literary frame, as they enable generative confusion over the status of the work as at once singular (one lyric repurposed) and plural (two distinct lyrical engagements). This confusion bears out in terms of form and content as the poem stages a dialectical tension between exceptionalism and collectivity. Tweaking the dedicatee poses a paradigm shift at the level of what Jonathan Culler calls, in his work on the theory of lyric utterance, the enunciative apparatus. Here the apparatus is in part the expressive body that the poem calls into being through the speaking on behalf of a collective personal pronoun, but it also includes the object of the collective appeal, the exceptional leader. The fungibility of the leader points to the dialogic reciprocity that exists between a community and its leaders. The reframing of the work asks us to ponder if it is the new leader who calls into being a new community, or if it is the underlying social forces that introduce real change that the leader merely embodies. What validates the frame and thus the distinctiveness of the two works is the apparent disparity between the two figures, as readers bring to the two works different expectations about the kinds of collectives that might salute Lincoln as opposed to Madhubuti. Brooks is not only rerouting her praise; she is repurposing her poem in order to speak from two different communities, effectively making the overall message of the second poem unique, thereby precluding any easy conclusion that the works are one and the same. And yet, given their obvious points of extensive overlap, it is impossible to see them as completely separate. The meaning of the first in isolation reads as incomplete without considering the way in which Brooks cancels it with the second. Similarly, the depiction of Madhubuti carries the spectral trace of Lincoln – less as stand-in than as strategic alternative. Without its corollary, the second poem loses its denunciative force. The clearest sign of their redundancy lies in Brooks's efforts to suppress the first version by including only the second one in her collected poems, signaling an awareness that they appear to be the same work, an apparent instance of self-plagiarism. The assertive, if compromised, frame invites the receiver to engage both works as one might a community, attending to what each piece says in and through its antiphonal associate.

When compared to the second version, "In the Time of Detachment, in the Time of Cold" represents a clear integrationist's anthem. Though abstract, the titular claim to detachment suggests the severe threat that segregation poses to the nation's "prime registered" promise of a "more perfect union." Brooks writes the poem months before President Lyndon B. Johnson signs into law the Voting Rights Act, a context that pervades the poem as its collective voice expresses hope for an actualized representative democracy. In deploying Lincoln, Brooks advocates for reform and not revolution, evident in her description of the president as the only one capable of saving the nation, by "constrain[ing]," "reprov[ing]," "reinforc [ing]," and "renew[ing]." The collective voice speaks on behalf of a model of liberal citizenship that the poem defends, as she compels Lincoln to fulfill the integrationist's mission and "require of us our terribly excluded blue." Brooks's personal pronoun is comprised of citizens, the legally protected members of a nation. The poem then dramatizes what Esposito regards as normative conditions of community life, in which the commons provides the stage upon which participants practice mutual recognition as whole, self-authoring agents of autonomous will.

However, when the two versions are read together, one finds reason to read against the patriotic grain of the original. In the year leading up to the ceremonial reading, Brooks expressed critical reservations about Lincoln's legacy. "We remember not only the Lincoln steadiness but also the totterings and peregrination. We remember that he did not endorse black-and-white equality in political power; that he did endorse schemes for colonial settlement of Negroes in Africa and entreated Negro leaders to cooperate" (Angle 36). From this perspective, the poem does not simply empower a symbol of democracy; it demands civil rights that have been withheld. The appeal to Lincoln is at once an appeal to Johnson, as the poem speaks from a recognition of the long history of political gradualism and vacillation on the race question.

As much as Brooks succeeded in suppressing the first poem through expurgation and reappropriation, the second poem, once brought into conversation with the first, is far from a seamless reclamation. There are extant lines in the second version that do not apply to Madhubuti. The phrase "our prime registered reproach and seal," which clearly works as a description of Lincoln and his iconic representation on monuments and official imprimatur, does not take into account the distinctiveness of Madhubuti, whose likeness may be recognizable but is not the stuff of listed insignia. This failure is a telling one, as it lends credence to the distinctiveness of the commons the second poem means to enact. The fit is askew because Madhubuti does not fit the precedent set by national leaders of state, just as the commons he represents does not reiterate national models of subject citizenship. Where the first poem speaks on the behalf of an imagined community, strangers who believe that their nationality binds them to a shared collective identity, the second invokes a particular formation of Black communal context. It is dedicated not to an abstract historical hero of Black liberation, but to a situated contemporary friend of the poet. Brooks meets Madhubuti through the writing workshops she helped coordinate with the Blackstone Rangers, which offered community education programs on the South Side of Chicago. His presence in the poem once again points back to the previous version, and its endorsement of racial integration. Reflecting on his impact on her ideas of national politics, Brooks writes in her biography, "I know that the black-and-white integration concept, which in the mind of some beaming early saint was a dainty spinning dream, has wound down to farce, to unsavory and mumbling farce." She then quotes a poem by Madhubuti: "I / seek / integration / of / negroes / with / black people" ("Contemporary" 45). Through replacing Lincoln with Madhubuti, the second iteration replaces one community with another. The geopolitical nation becomes the commons of Black culture, which Brooks figures in terms of a regionalist formation that – keeping in mind Madhubuti's Third World Press – has diasporic scope.

The second poem, then, is not simply posing one community as the replacement of another. It is, rather, an errand in reconceptualizing the conditions of communal life. In making Madhubuti the dedicatee, Brooks essentially makes an entire poem out of a single line from the first version. In the first she speaks of the "terribly excluded blue" as one who can promote the extension of the rights of citizenship from within to previously excluded groups. In the second version, the collective voice speaks from this condition of racialized exclusion, gesturing to Amiri Baraka's formulation of Black Americans as *Blues People*. Where "In the Time of Detachment, in the Time of Cold" presents the margins as the object of incorporation in pursuit of a more complete national body, "The Good Man" presents the margins as something to be defended. The excluded possess a privileged relationship to the relinquishment of exceptionalism as imagined through the functions of state government, representing, in the language of the poem, coherent counsels on the logic of exclusion and its "abler droughts." This collective invalidates the idea of the commons as what Esposito calls "a mode of being, [responsible for] a 'making' of the individual subject." "It isn't," in his words, "the subject's expansion or multiplication but its exposure to what interrupts the closing and turns it inside out" (7). The "rhyme" that the community in the Madhubuti poem "rouse[s]" takes place outside the voting booth and the belief in the state as a valid adjudicator of civil rights. The defiant tenor of the second poem depends on the existence of the previous text, which makes the second version at best a fragment, bound to its oppositional other half. So too, the vision of the commons it brings into being acknowledges the commons as that space constituted by members who have negated that which has been withheld from them, the prospect of equal standing as a legitimate citizen subject within the purview of the legal establishment. The terribly excluded eschew the prospect of community as the project of sovereign individuals. The terribly excluded enact marronage, as they are never fully redressed, never fully settled, never completely empowered and thus carry on an incomplete practice of open and imperfect participation.

In trying to define the gestalt effect of the two works, I have treated them as if they are two panels constituting a larger diptych. The first is the suppressed premonition of the second, which makes the latter a revisionary extension of the former. One can make an argument, as I have, that the second version, in its incongruous application of the nationalist anthem to a counternationalist figure, demonstrates a slippage in the representational agenda of the first poem, which allows a reader to see in it a sloughing-off of the vestments of normative individualism. And yet, as much as Brooks overturns the integrationist politics in the former with the latter, she is nevertheless using the symbolic capital of the iconic, paternal leader in a recuperative gesture. The second iteration remains invested to some degree in the power of a mythic individual. The poet in both poems is an extension of the same dynamic. Speaking on behalf of a collective voice, Brooks reduces the social to a substrate that can be represented by the individual poet in the closed frame of the isolated lyric. The poem then speaks to an inherent limitation in the form. Even in instances when poets strain against the valorization of subjectivity and coherent personhood, poems circulate within contexts that privilege authorship and aesthetic finitude as foundational conditions for reception.

The diptych metaphor, then, reaps additional benefits. Let's imagine that the two panels are connected by a hinge. The hinge for Brooks is her encounter with new philosophies of Black social life in the years directly following her participation in the 1965 ceremony. By dedicating the poem to Madhubuti the poet points to the contexts that led her to suppress the original lyric and then subsequently reprise its language. One way of reading the two poems is to imagine Brooks as taking ownership of her tokenized participation in the Lincoln ceremony, by asserting her own will over the direction and reception of her words. And yet, if we read the entire reclamation as a function of the hinge, then the two works and the space between them point to the power of insurgent modes of collective organizing to both drive authorial shifts and undermine the assumed positive values of representation. The hinge as conceived is a communal space of interruption, to borrow Esposito's language, possessive of a socially constitute expressive force that exceeds the representational capacity of any singularly authored poem. If we attend to the hinge and not the panels, a new conception of the relationship of community to poetic utterance comes into view. It is no longer a body that desires conventional markers of legibility, be they the inclusion of marginalized people within the dominant model of representative democracy or the inclusion of the collective as an expressible element in the symbolic form of the poem. It figures instead as an ongoing transitional process that proves disruptive to the narratives of national belonging and the discretionary power of authorial intention, as it undermines Brooks's initial agenda.

In response to an interviewer's question in 1971 – "How did you, a Pulitzer prizewinner, get turned on to the black revolution?" – Brooks replies that the watershed moment came in 1967 when she attended the Second Black Writers' Conference at Fisk University ("My People" 54). Reflecting on the conference in her autobiography, Brooks narrates the bewildering scene in terms that harken back to her description of the anonymous Black pedestrian. "First, I was aware of a general energy, an electricity, in look, walk, speech, gesture of the young blackness I saw all about me" (84). She describes a scene in which historian Lerone Bennett was "taken to task, by irate members of a no-nonsense young audience, for affiliating himself with *Ebony Magazine*, considered at that time a traitor for allowing skin-bleach advertisements in its pages, and for over-featuring light-skinned women." Aligning herself at the outset with "another Old Girl," the poet Margaret Danner Cunningham, the two received in

Brooks's account "cold Respect" from the crowd, who relegated them politely to the class of "has-been." Admitting that she was immediately given to a state of shock, Brooks recounts the disruptive force of the students as they hijacked the conference.

> In 1967's Nashville ... I was in some inscrutable and uncomfortable wonderland. I don't know what to make of what surrounded me, of what with hot sureness began almost immediately to invade me. *I had never been, before, in the general presence of such insouciance, such live firmness, such confident vigor, such determination to mold or carve something* DEFINITE. (85)

Here is the hinge. When confronted with what she describes as the "new black today," Brooks finds herself undergoing a radical reconceptualization of her relationship to the communities that had populated her verse. As much as Brooks is impressed by the message put forward by the young attendees, it is the social reality of them as a crowd that Brooks finds particularly compelling. Mobilization becomes more than a means of enabling new modes of study; the fact of the gathering, its palpable force, issues a call to reformulate the very meaning of intellectual endeavor. Suddenly the crowd is not something outside her, something she could pinpoint with the right phrase and deploy in a poem at will. It is an intellectualism of social aid that invades her, rendering her subject to the informal sway of an insurrectionary calling to concretize utopia.

The effects of her time in Nashville bear implications for the social work Brooks takes up after returning to Chicago. Months after Fisk, she reaches out to the singer and songwriter Oscar Brown Jr., who had produced a recorded musical revue, *Opportunity Please Knock*, with young members of the Blackstone Rangers gang, expressing interest in coordinating a similar program for aspiring writers in the group. He puts her in touch with Walter Bradford, a college student with close connections to the organization, who eventually becomes the primary organizer of the writing group that Brooks proposes. "Eagerly and meticulously," she writes, "he developed a class of about twenty no-nonsense young fellows who, with an eager meticulousness of their own, arranged chairs, maintained order, and afforded him their strict attention" (Brooks, *Report* 194). The group consisted primarily of young people in their early twenties – including Don L. Lee, "who had already published *Think Black*," and Carolyn Rodgers. Their impact on Brooks mirrored that of the Fisk group:

> With the arrival of these people my neatly-paced life altered almost with a jerk. Never did they tell me to change my hair to "natural." But eventually

> I did. Never did they tell me to look about me, to open my eyes. But soon
> I did. Never did they tell me to find them sane, serious, substantial,
> superseding. But soon I did.

Here she emphasizes the disruption posed by being among a vibrant
community that surpasses any confined sense of political consciousness.
With the change in hairstyle, Brooks becomes the pedestrian she describes
in her early *Phylon* statement, to the degree that she becomes aware of her
own appearance as an aesthetic performance, capable of expressing group
solidarity. The eye-opening force of the social field leads her to reconceptualize the hierarchical assumptions inherent in the idea of teaching a
workshop:

> I "taught" nothing. I told them, almost timidly, what I knew, what I had
> learned from European models (well, Langston Hughes too!). And they told
> me without telling me that the European "thing" was not what they were
> about. "Iambic pentameter," they twittered.

In these scenes, Brooks forfeits her status as the public figure, vested with
authority to speak among political dignitaries at an extravagant celebration
for a fallen national icon, taking on instead the rank of pupil, "qualified to
enter at least the kindergarten of new consciousness now" (86).

   In her description of the events, Brooks shows how the goal of the
workshop was not the creation of stand-alone poems, or even collective
anthologies, but rather the advancement of new social imperatives. The
group's willingness to transgress poetic convention carries overt political
implications. "What are the clichés, what are the offenses against standards? What are the standards? Who decides? Are the rulers of *other*
nations to decide? ... In a new nation, what *are* the 'mistakes'"? (194).
In part this new social imperative manifests in the horizontal organization
of the group, as participants challenge Brooks on her own assumptions
about poetic form: "'Iambic pentameter,' they twittered. 'Hmmmm. Oh
yes, iambic pentameter. Well, now ...'" (195). The social imperative also
extends to the goals they set for their poetry. Rather than write beautiful
lyrics that attest to inner depth and intense feeling, they compose poems in
order to change the linguistic fabric of the communities in which they
lived. "Many of these black writers," writes Brooks, "are now involved in
an exciting labor, a challenging labor; admitting that it is not likely all
blacks will immediately convert to Swahili, they are blackening English.
Some of the results are effective and stirring." In these passages, Brooks
makes clear that the group was generating content as a secondary result
through questioning the received frameworks of literary production, here

signaled in the move to validate a range of multiple Englishes, converging with concurrent work in the field of sociolinguistics, as figures like William Labov would argue for the inherent logic of purportedly nonstandard English. As if speaking directly to Laura Harris's theoretical inquiry into the merger of aesthetics and sociality, Brooks describes the indifference of the group to the "detachment" of aesthetics from social life. "These black writers do not care," she explains, "if you call their product Art or Peanuts. Artistic survival, appointment to Glory, appointment to Glory among the anointed elders, is neither their crevice nor creed." As Brooks specifies, the group sees art not as a work, finite and complete, framed and dispensable, but rather as labor, the process of constituting the means of their own production as a revolutionary collective.

While Brooks makes several attempts throughout her career to articulate the impact of Fisk and the Blackstone Rangers Workshop on her writing, none of these efforts more accurately demonstrate the significance of the rupture than the unspoken hinge that exists between the two companion poems. Aside from the reference to Madhubuti, the "Good Man" makes no explicit mention of this history, but the absented context nevertheless presides as the impetus behind Brooks's decision to suppress the original only to subsequently use it to document her turn away from integrationist ideology. Although both poems make an effort to describe a vision of community, it is the space in between, the space of social organizing and bewildering contact, where a force that exceeds the charge of any single leader or poet takes hold.

WORKS CITED

Angle, Paul. "Where We Stand: Lincoln Scholarship." In *A Portion of That Field*, ed. Civil War Centennial Commission. University of Illinois Press, 1967.

Beach, Christopher. *Poetic Culture: Contemporary American Poetry between Community and Institution.* Northwestern University Press, 1999.

Brooks, Gwendolyn. "Contemporary Literature Interview." Interview by George Stavros. In *Report from Part One*. Broadside Press, 1971.

"The Good Man." In *Blacks: The Collected Poems of Gwendolyn Brooks*. Third World Press, 1987.

"In the Time of Detachment, in the Time of Cold." In *A Portion of That Field*, ed. Civil War Centennial Commission. University of Illinois Press, 1967.

"My People Are Black People." Interview by Ida Lewis. In *Conversations with Gwendolyn Brooks*, ed. Gloria Wade Gayles. University of Mississippi Press, 2003.

"Poets Who Are Negros." *Phylon* 11 (4th Qtr., 1950).

Report from Part One. Broadside Press, 1971.

Untitled contribution to *A Capsule Course in Black Poetry Writing*, ed. Dudley
    Randall. Broadside Press, 1975.
Clark, Norris B. "Gwendolyn Brooks and a Black Aesthetic." In *A Life Distilled:
    Gwendolyn Brooks, Her Poetry and Fiction*, ed. Maria K. Moorty and Gary
    Smith. University of Illinois Press, 1987.
Cobb, Jelani, ed. *The Essential Kerner Commission Report: The Landmark Study on
    Race, Inequality, and Police Violence.* Liveright, 2021.
Culler, Jonathan. *Theory of the Lyric.* Harvard University Press, 2015.
Damon, Maria. *The Dark End of the Street: Margins in American Vanguard Poetry.*
    University of Minnesota Press, 1993.
Esposito, Roberto. *Communitas: The Origin and Destiny of Community.* Stanford
    University Press, 2010.
"Gwendolyn Brooks: A Poet's Work in Community." The Morgan Library &
    Museum, February 28, 2022, www.themorgan.org/exhibitions/gwendolyn-
    brooks.
Harris, Laura, *Experiments in Exile: C. L. R. James, Hélio Oiticica and the Aesthetic
    Sociality of Blackness.* Fordham University Press, 2018.
Jameson, Frederic. *Marxism and Form.* Princeton University Press, 1971.
Lee, Don L. "Gwendolyn Brooks: Beyond the Wordmaker: The Making of an
    African Poet." In Gwendolyn Brooks, *Report from Part One.* Broadside Press,
    1972.
Leonard, Keith. *Fettered Genius: The African American Bardic Poet from Slavery to
    Civil Rights.* University of Virginia Press, 2006.
Melham, D. H. *Gwendolyn Brooks: Poetry and the Heroic Voice.* University of
    Kentucky Press, 1987.
Mullen, Bill. *Popular Fronts: Chicago and African-American Cultural Politics,
    1935–46.* University of Illinois Press, 1999.
Smethurst, James. *The New Red Negro: The Literary Left and African American
    Poetry, 1920–1946.* Oxford University Press, 1999.
Spahr, Juliana. *Everybody's Autonomy: Connective Reading and Collective Identity.*
    University of Alabama Press, 2001.
Washington, Mary Helen. *The Other Blacklist: The African American Literary and
    Cultural Left of the 1950s.* Columbia University Press, 2014.

CHAPTER II

Poetry and the Prison Industrial Complex

Michael S. Collins

American politics has long been shaped by a desire to make the nation a sort of rock-ribbed utopia. In the twentieth century this desire became a "jurismania" – a compulsion to catch every tremor of social life in a net of legal "rationality" – that criminalized so much of life that unprecedented levels of incarceration, particularly of minorities, were the result (Campos vii, 98). A critical moment in the rise of mass incarceration came in 1986, when President Ronald Reagan demanded that the country which "divine providence" itself had established be saved from the threat to it posed by drug abuse ("Address to the Nation"). Invoking a comic-strip version of the nation's history that glossed over slavery, Jim Crow, and the negative impacts on the poor of his own efforts to dismantle "big government," Reagan averred that "[w]e Americans have never been morally neutral against any form of tyranny" (Gray 110). Reagan's rock-ribbed prose is a reminder of the value of the prismatic language of poets – especially those who have been caught up in the legislation written for comic-strip reality rather than the real thing.

This essay explores the contrast between mind-closing comic-strip poetics and the mind-opening practices of actual poets by examining, in chronological order, works by Bob Kaufman, Etheridge Knight, and Reginald Dwayne Betts. All three experienced incarceration, and as African American males all three are members of the community most devastated by anti-drug "jurismania" and its precursors in the US justice system.

Bob Kaufman

First, Bob Kaufman: During the 1940s-through-1960s' prehistory of mass incarceration, he was shadowed by the FBI, beaten by police, jailed, and subjected to involuntary electroshock treatments.

Born in New Orleans in April 1925 to a Pullman porter father and a schoolteacher mother (Damon 33), Kaufman graduated from a segregated high school in 1942 and joined the merchant marine that same year. In 1943, he became active in the National Maritime Union, a powerful organization cofounded by a Jamaican immigrant and Communist Party member at a time when the Party was one of the only organizations that championed racial integration (Horne vii–xi). In 1947, with the National Maritime Union increasingly enveloped in Red Scare paranoia, Kaufman published a letter in the Union's *Pilot* newspaper denouncing the "present hysterical campaign against the Communist party" being led by the House Un-American Activities Committee (Kaufman xxix–xxxi, Horne 195–198). By 1950, Kaufman was tagged as a Communist and closely monitored by the FBI.

To see why such Red Scare phenomena are a precursor of mass incarceration, one need only consider the extent to which they criminalized ordinary activity and thought. The same year Kaufman wrote his letter to the *Pilot*, FBI Director J. Edgar Hoover defied the bedrock American principle of presumption of innocence and challenged the House Un-American Activities Committee and the public to not be fooled by the mere appearance of innocence among "[f]ellow travelers and sympathizers" of Communists. Such people, even if they denied party membership, "have played into the Communist hands thus furthering the Communist cause," Hoover said (Schrecker and Deery 102–103).

In the atmosphere fueled by Hoover and set ablaze a few years later by Joseph McCarthy, a "pseudo-conservativism" willing to save the American system by destroying such central features of it as freedom of association became an indispensable psychological garment for many (Hofstadter 44).

As the subject of a Communist Index Card, Kaufman was part of a comprehensive FBI list of potentially dangerous persons. Although he had committed no crime, it was a strike against Kaufman that permitted him to be closely surveilled. A second strike was averted when the FBI learned that, in 1951, Kaufman had been "expelled from the CP for degeneracy" after admitting that he participated "in the drug traffic" and "took the needle" himself ("Bob Kaufman FBI File"). Nevertheless, Kaufman's ability to earn a livelihood on the high seas was destroyed by a US Coast Guard declaration that he was a poor security risk. He thus became part of a massive purging of Black and Puerto Rican sailors (Horne 195).

The FBI afterward closed its file on Kaufman, concluding that he had become a drifter not worth the expense of tracking. By 1953, Kaufman was in San Francisco, "ranging through North Beach with the fury of a marauding tiger – bellowing his poetry on street corners, carousing with

Jack Kerouac and Neal Cassidy, holding court for drink-buying tourists and scribbling verse on cocktail napkins," according to Tom Moran (3).

Kaufman was also writing and publishing his poetry at a feverish pace. Yoking the American A-bomb and "Communist Manifesto" in his punning title, Kaufman got some revenge on Red Scare paranoia in his "Abomunist Manifesto," published as a broadside by Lawrence Ferlinghetti in 1959. A carnivalesque mixture of free verse, prose poetry, gags, couplets, and satirical letters, "Abomunist Manifesto" takes on the criminalization of persons like Kaufman by the House Committee on Un-American Activities in particular and the Red Scare in general:

> When attacked, Abomunists think positive, repeating over and under:
>
> "If I were a crime, I'd want to be committed . . .
>
>   No! . . . Wait!"

Here Kaufman articulates a major need of members of oppressed populations: to resist accepting the characterization of them imposed by a hostile society (Alexander and Klein 16–21). On the one hand, the statement "If I were a crime, I'd want to be committed" is defiant and self-affirming. On the other hand, accepting the definition of oneself as a crime is self-defeating. Hence Kaufman's abrupt, "No! . . . Wait!"

Kaufman goes on to mock middle-class conformity, Red Scare loyalty tests, and the opiates of conspicuous consumption:

> Civilian Defense Headquarters unveils new bomb shelter with two-car garage, complete with indoor patio and barbecue unit that operates on radioactivity, comes in decorator colors, no down payment for vets, to be sold only to those willing to sign loyalty oath . . .

The bomb shelter barbecue unit that runs on radioactivity and turns even the prospect of Armageddon into a shopping opportunity is of course antithetical to Kaufman's Abomunist (anti-A-bomb-unist) world view. Therefore, the poem concludes with an advertisement for the "Abomunist" alternative:

> Foregoing sponsored by your friendly neighborhood Abomunist . . . Tune in next world.

If no one tunes in, of course, the next world might be the one created by atomic radiation or by an iron conformism that tolerates no Kaufmans. So, like someone firing off a flare, Kaufman elaborated on the alternative in an addendum to the Manifesto published in 1960:

> We shall demand that ex-communists be allowed to
>   cheer at Army-Navy games.
> We shall demand that Mississippi be granted statehood
>   In some other country.
>   . . .
> We shall fly stoned in jet planes and drop poetry on
>   South Dakota. (176–177)
>   . . .

Unfortunately for Kaufman as a prophet of Abomunism – condemning Mississippi racist brutality and advocating for poems instead of bombs as mind-blowing substances – he continued to receive the unwanted attentions of the American justice system (Seymour, "No Gods").

Eileen Singe, whom Kaufman met and married in San Francisco, reported that the police "had their sights out" for him as someone not afraid to mock them to their faces and defy America's racial rules with his marriage to her, a white woman (Seymour, "Don't Forget"). They "got so mad at Bob they would stop elevators between floors and beat him up," she recalled (David Henderson, "Introduction").

Kaufman comments on this brutality in "Abomunist Manifesto":

> I am writing this in my cell. I was framed. How can they give the death sentence on charges of disorderly conduct and having public readings without a permit? . . . Maybe that lawyer Judas is getting me can swing it. If he can't, God help me.

The suggestion that in insisting on Abomunism he was leaving himself open to a kind of martyrdom via death sentence is expanded upon in "Jail Poems," a thirty-five-part sequence written, according to a Kaufman note at the end of the work, in Cell 3 of the San Francisco Jail, in 1959. In the sonnet that opens the sequence, Kaufman writes:

> I am sitting in a cell with a view of evil parallels,
> Waiting thunder to splinter me into a thousand ME's.
> It is not enough to be in one cage with one self;
> I want to sit opposite every prisoner in every hole.

This opening quatrain has Kaufman modeling one of the cures for what later became mass incarceration: empathy – "to sit opposite every prisoner in every hole" (in solitary confinement) is to end each prisoners' isolation. The visionary second line delivers the message that, for the sake of such empathetic imagining, it is worth being splintered into countless "me's."

Reflecting on this poem in 2002, in "For Kaufman, as for Artaud," Jeffrey Falla writes, the dissolution of self is not a self-destruction but a freeing from the socioculturally influenced sense of self that imprisons everyone as social subjects through internalized images of normative identity (be it racial, gender, sexual, national, or psychological) and, indeed, internalized images of self-inferiority ... (187)

The middle lines of Kaufman's sonnet elaborate further on the fruits of empathy:

> Noises of pain seeping through steel walls crashing
> Reach my own hurt. I become part of someone forever.

Openness to others pays dividends for those who (like the version of Kaufman memorialized in these lines) risk it, because the pain of other lives sometimes rhymes comfortingly with the pain of one's own life, allowing the existence of the solidarity of souls "forever."

The conclusion of the poem introduces perhaps the best-known of all prisoners:

> Wild accents of criminals are sweeter to me than hum of cops,
> Busy battening down hatches of human souls; cargo
> Destined for ports of accusations, harbors of guilt.
> What do policemen eat, Socrates, still prisoner, old one?

The evocation of Socrates, who was sentenced to death for supposedly corrupting Athens' youth and defying its gods, is a telling one for a poet who himself was expelled from the Communist Party, barred from his profession, and, in 1963 (after being arrested for walking on the grass in a New York park and then found to be "a behavioral problem"), subjected to forced electroshock treatments from which he never fully recovered (Woodberry).

Indeed, this entire opening sonnet and the rest of "Jail Poems" are Kaufman's version of the *Apology*, where Socrates admits that he himself was "almost carried away" (4–5) by the eloquence of his accusers, but then insists that he has done nothing but harangue Athenians to make their chief concern not their bodies or possessions but the "welfare of [their] souls" (16).

Kaufman must have recognized his own attacks on consumerism in passages like this one. And where the maltreatment of the soul is concerned, Socrates also haunts Kaufman's castigation of cops "battening down hatches of human souls" for shipment to Red Scare–style "ports of accusations, harbors of guilt." In the rest of "Jail Poems," Kaufman evokes the scent of sacrificed men ("All night the stink of rotting people, / Fumes rising from pyres of live men"); gives glimpses of the day when the jail, "a huge hollow metal cube / Hanging from the moon by a silver chain," will be chopped down by Johnny Appleseed (perhaps one of the "thousand me's" Kaufman writes of in line 2 of the sonnet); exposes his own vulnerability and the protective function his poetry serves ("I sit here writing, not daring to stop, / For fear of seeing what's outside my head"); and ends with a final bit of mockery of the sort of anticommunist and racist overkill that led to the denial of his mariner's card and his hopes of returning to the sea: "Come, help flatten a raindrop."

From Penal Welfarism to Mass Incarceration

The 1959–1969 period during which Kaufman did most of his time behind bars can seem, if one does not look too closely, like a golden age preceding the era of mass incarceration. It is not inconceivable that, under three-strikes-you're-out regimes established later, someone with as many arrests as Kaufman, and someone who, like him, used drugs and alcohol for self-medication and poetic inspiration, would have been handed a life sentence and made to serve it in brutal conditions. But Kaufman's run-ins with the law took place during the era of "penal welfarism," which, the scholar David Garland explains, has as its "basic axiom" the idea that criminal justice should focus on "rehabilitative interventions rather than negative, retributive punishments" and should emphasize

> indeterminate sentences linked to early release and parole supervision; . . . individualization of treatment based upon expert assessment and classification . . . social work with offenders and their families; and custodial regimes that stressed re-educative purposes of imprisonment . . . (34–35)

Now in 2022, when the idea of prison as counterproductive has reemerged from the wreckage of the lives of many nonviolent offenders warehoused during the era of mass incarceration, it is natural to ask: Why was penal-welfarism abandoned? Kaufman-like experiences with electroshock "therapy" and with beatings and jailings as an antimiscegenation measure are part of the answer.

Such brutality was widespread enough that influential voices from the left attacked penal welfarism for its "willingness to impose 'treatment' in punitive settings, with or without the consent of offenders," Garland explains. Penal welfarism was attacked also for assuming that "violations of criminal law are symptomatic of individual pathology and that the customs of the white middle classes are synonymous with the norms of social health" (56). Kaufman is a paradigmatic example of the sort of person a too-rigid penal welfarism could not fathom, but only damage.

Indeed, young criminologists of the 1970s critiqued their elders, Garland explains, in part because of a sensitivity to racial injustice that grew out of experience in the civil rights movement. All this climaxed in events like the trial and 1972 acquittal of the Communist philosopher-activist Angela Davis on potentially capital charges, and in volumes like the one edited by Davis in jail, where she links her cause to that of W. E. B. DuBois when he was brought up in 1951 on Red Scare charges and acquitted. Davis quotes prose by Du Bois that might have been written by Kaufman: "God only knows how many who were as innocent as I and my colleagues are today in hell" (33).

But 1970s penal welfarism was also savaged from the right. Aided by increasing and sensationalized crime rates, together with sensationalized urban and prison uprisings, the right enjoyed regular electoral success between the late 1960s and the 1990s, and gradually seized control of the entire debate. One of the most prominent conservatives, James Q. Wilson, argued that society did not really know how to rehabilitate offenders or how to tell when they *had* been rehabilitated, and so should admit that all it knew how to do was deter with tough, inflexible sentences (193–194). In due course, inflexible sentences became a feature of War on Drugs legislation (Alexander, 87–88). Incarceration rates spiked in the next decades, but more as an index of increased criminal-ization of minorities than an index of increased crime, which by the 1990s was falling even as imprisonments continued to rise (Hinton 175; Simon, 46, 164).

Etheridge Knight

In 1960, half a country away from Kaufman's San Francisco, Etheridge Knight was sent to the Indiana State Prison to serve a ten- to twenty-five-year sentence. Knight arguably – and ironically – came to exemplify the upside of penal welfarism, as he took full advantage of the prison library, wrote for prison publications, turned himself from a teller of ribald "toasts" to a literary poet, and connected with the Black arts and Black publishing movement that burst into flower during the 1960–1968 term he served before being paroled. At the same time, Knight became one of the acutest critics of the cracks in the veneer of penal welfarism – cracks in which men like Kaufman, and some whom Knight himself knew, were tortured.

In the preface to his 1970 edited volume, *Black Voices from Prison*, Knight took the carceral system to task, suggesting that it was a continuation by other means of "the 'Christian' slaveship" and declaring that "the whole experience of the black man in America can be summed up in one word: prison."

To support his point, Knight quoted from the 1967 *Report of the President's Commission on Law Enforcement and Administration of Justice*, which declares that crime is a social problem interwoven with "almost every aspect of American life" and that "controlling [crime] involves changing the way the schools are run ... the way cities are planned ... the way businesses are managed and workers hired."

Knight's poem "Hard Rock Returns to Prison from the Hospital for the Criminal Insane" illustrates the need to utterly change the way prisons do their business. The "Hard Rock" of the title is a kind of prison superman "known not to take shit / From nobody" and, according to legend, to have poisoned one guard with syphilitic spit. The prison's response is to lobotomize him. Inmates who drew strength from him are devastated:

> He had been our Destroyer, the doer of things
> We dreamed of doing but could not bring ourselves to do,
> The fears of years, like a biting whip,
> Had cut deep bloody grooves
> Across our backs.

If one believes, as Knight and many others did, that the criminal justice system is polluted with injustice and racism, a period of incarceration starts to look less like just punishment that one has earned because of one's crime and more like a standard hostage situation where bending to the will of the captors in order to survive means falling prey to a species of "Stockholm syndrome" – where one clings to one's captors' vision of oneself and the world. The composite character named Hard Rock by Knight is the ultimate example of resistance to Stockholm syndrome, and other inmates resist vicariously through him, even as they remain scarred and stunted – *Stockholmed* – by "fears of years."

From the point of view of the authorities, the lobotomization of Hard Rock and the cowing of the other prisoners is a mission accomplished. It destroys the kernel of an inmate culture that might foster wider resistance. Knowing this, Knight adopted a strategy different from Hard Rock's. Rather than taking "no shit from nobody," Knight read, thought, wrote, published inside and outside the prison, and opened lines of communication to authorities (such as his mentors Gwendolyn Brooks and Dudley Randall) outside the carceral system.

But he questioned his own strategy in poems like "On the Yard," where a "young fascist / fresh from the Hole," asks him, "Man, / why ain't you / *doing* something?" (14). Knight writes:

> I sat up
> All night wrote 5,000 words
> explaining how
> I
> *was* doing something
>
> but the slim cat –
> beautiful fascist
> didn't buy
> it – nor
> did I
> completely.

Because he wrote for the prison newspaper, Knight was something of a voice for the other inmates, but it is clear that the "beautiful young fascist" – whose unbowed emergence from solitary confinement in "the hole" suggests that he may have chosen the Hard Rock approach to resisting Stockholm syndrome – believes he is not using his voice effectively. Nevertheless, Knight kept his militancy coded, afraid of sharing Hard Rock's fate (Collins, *Understanding Etheridge Knight* 63).

The great flaw of penal welfarism, then, was the Stockholm syndrome normalization it sometimes pressed with more ferocity the more its version of normality was resisted by someone like Hard Rock – or Kaufman (whose Abomunist resistance once went so far, according to one legend, that he peed on a policeman).

Knight was paroled in 1968, a year of transition away from penal welfarism because it was the year of the election of one of the early architects of mass incarceration – Richard Nixon. In 1970, the Nixon administration backed a Washington, DC, law that unleashed "no-knock" police raids, incarceration of "narcotics addicts," preventive detention, and trial as adults of minors charged with intended or actual burglary, armed robbery, rape, or murder.

Much of the content of this law spread nationwide as Nixon had intended. He had help in this regard from Ronald Reagan, who became president in 1980 and, in the midst of a media-driven panic over crack cocaine, signed the draconian Anti-Drug Abuse Act of 1986. Parole in the federal prison system had already been eliminated in 1984. But in Reagan's last year in office, the Omnibus Anti-Drug Abuse Act of 1988 slapped "a 5-year mandatory minimum sentence and a 20-year maximum sentence" on those possessing five or more grams of crack cocaine (Conyers 382). Possession of pricier powder cocaine, used more by whites than minorities, brought much less severe penalties – in part because in the United States white skin is a store of credit, credibility and, ultimately, a presumption of innocence (Ogletree 75–76). The result in minority communities was mass incarceration as a species of penal welfarism run amok – since it is a penal welfarism designed to eliminate the drug danger and rehabilitate the divinely ordained political utopia Reagan saw himself as protecting. Black and Latino young men were vacuumed out of their communities in a way that diminished the communities' political clout, because conviction meant loss of the right to vote (Alexander 193).

In the end such measures were so costly and produced results so contrary to their stated goals that law professor Paul Campos concluded that it would make more sense for a president to perform a ritual dance to drive off bad drug spirits than to sign a new law against illegal drugs. "Jurismania" can seize society like a mental illness (Campos 124).

Reginald Dwayne Betts

The feeling of being caught in a society's mental illness has been memorably chronicled by a successor to Kaufman and Knight: Reginald Dwayne Betts, a 2021 MacArthur Award winner who in 1997, aged sixteen, was tried as a "certified" adult for a carjacking carried out in a Springfield, Virginia, parking lot (Betts, *A Question of Freedom*, 5). Betts opens the first chapter of his 2009 memoir by using an allusion to an Etheridge Knight poem to capture his own extreme vulnerability as a sixteen-year-old entering adult prison: "Sixteen years hadn't even done a good job on my voice."

The Knight poem, "For Freckle-Faced Gerald," is about an inmate who, though "[s]ixteen years hadn't even done / a good job on his voice," is thrown to prison wolves who rape him so often that he collapses into emotional catatonia. Alluding to this, Betts reflects on what might have become of *him* as a sixteen-year-old in an adult penitentiary. But the memoir itself includes no account of Betts being raped. Instead, it documents Betts' Knight-like ascent into self-making despite long stretches in solitary confinement and a stay in a racially hostile, "supermax" facility.

Like Knight, Betts began publishing poetry while he was still incarcerated. He also became something of a jailhouse lawyer and helped another inmate reduce his sentence (Betts, *A Question of Freedom*, 226). After his release, Betts earned a JD and became a juvenile justice advocate.

By that time, he had mastered both the poetic tradition and poetic form, combining in his work everything from African American Vernacular English (AAVE) to the sort of Anglo Saxon accentual rhythms that Ezra Pound revived in his translation of "The Seafarer." In "Elegy with a City in It," from *Bastards of the Reagan Era*, his second collection, Betts condemns both drug war violence carried out with fashionable Glock handguns and the legislative violence of Reagan's "War on Drugs," and does so with a unique combination of AAVE and the accentual:

> Men gone to the grave: men awed
> by blood . . . Red
> the gift of Glocks, red
> sometimes a dark and awful
> omen the best couldn't read.
> Death reinvented when red
> was the curse of men born black
> and lost in a drama Reagan read
> as war.. . . Steel
> in hands, and a god-awful
> law aimed at stilling the red.

Toward the end of the poem, Betts introduces one of his major themes – the failure to escape the peculiar Stockholm syndrome of internalized racism that sometimes causes promising youths like himself (an honor student at the time he carjacked a man asleep in his vehicle) to wear a stereotype like blackface: "Reagan's curse might be real, / might be what has niggas black- / mailing themselves, dancing in black- / face . . ."

Further mythologizing his own incarceration in the fifteen-page title poem, "Bastard of the Reagan Era," Betts takes, as his Virgil-like guide, Derek Walcott's poem 'The Schooner Flight." "The Schooner Flight" is the monologue of an outcast West Indian nicknamed Shabine who seeks to comprehend his own life and his region by using the one thing the Caribbean's former colonial masters have left behind: words.

Seeking comprehension of his own life and country, the Betts-like speaker in "Bastards" sets up ironic parallels between his and fellow prisoners' journeys from prison to prison and Shabine's journeys from island to island: "we half dozen . . . on another / Schooner bound for some Sing Sing, for some / Angola, Folsom, Attica."

Part of the point of the Walcott allusions is the bitter contrast between Shabine – skimming in a schooner from one injured but gorgeous island to the next – and the "Bastards" protagonist's journeying from one humiliating confinement to the next. But Betts' speaker also like Walcott's protagonist – travels from one leaping imaginative escape to the next. "I have / Braved, for want of wild beasts, steel cages," he says.

There are other parallels. In "The Schooner Flight," the Caribbean's young nations are misruled by a corrupt class, one of whom Shabine has heard is his grandfather but who, asked about Shabine's grandmother, a black cook, hawked and spat in a manner "worth any number of words." This moment in "The Schooner Flight" is probably the core purpose of the allusions to Walcott. For the equivalent of Shabine's spitting progenitor in "Bastards" is Reagan himself – albeit not only him, since New York governor Nelson Rockefeller preceded him in demanding crushing drug sentences, and, in the 1980s, Black leaders too were panicked by the crack epidemic and demanded harsh laws. Betts' speaker, who sold crack in civilian life, concludes, "Rockefeller and Reagan, the NAACP / All wanted us away from corners, dead / or jail but gone."

Commenting further, on reports that the CIA itself seeded black neighborhoods with crack cocaine in order to pay for a war against the Nicaraguan government, the narrator quips, "Scarface ain't from Compton." Worse, in the battle against the Panthers, "Hoover won" and Panther heroes like Huey Newton lost, mainly because of Hoover's destructive powers, but partly because of their own tragic flaws. (Newton was murdered near a crack house, and the poem's speaker remarks, if that was a hero's fate, "what chance did we ... have"?)

One of Betts' gifts is to balance the structural and the personal – the speaker's personal journey and the structure that connects his journey to Newton's. Betts reflects on both in his memoir: "There were times when I knew that if I was a young white boy I wouldn't even have been in that jail. But part of me knew that it was the gun in my hand and that man sleeping in his car that made my mother sad" (15).

In "Parking Lot, Too" a poem about this incident from his third book, *Felon*, Betts traces the way American stereotypes discrediting blackness wrapped around his psyche, impairing but not extinguishing his free will. As the poem proceeds, Betts descends ever more deeply into the language of African American criminalization – passing on the way some of the counter-language crafted by hip-hop artists:

... A confession began when I walked
Out of that parking lot a Negro. A confession begins when
That nigga walked into the parking lot. A confession begins
When that nigga & the pistol he carries like a dick walked
Into that parking lot....

"Nigga," a prominent term in the hip-hop lexicon, can mean "friend,"
"other black man," "member of my inner circle." But it is also a persona
that can be worn like a refusal to "rest / from being hard," in the words of a
line from another Betts poem, "Elegy Where a City Burns."

"Parking Lot, Too" next descends into colorism, internalized racism,
and the troubles of someone whose father is absent from his life:

...A confession begins when
My mother laid up with a man the complexion of that nigga's
Daddy. A confession begins when my mother births a child
In a city close enough to make me & that nigga almost related.
A confession begins when the police perceive us as one. We must
Be one. He could not have walked in & driven out & I walked
In & walked out on the same night & whatever gaps in the story
& slight differences in the features of our faces was just
More evidence that niggers will lie....
... A confession begins, my confession
Began, with a woman stitching stars & stripes into a flag. (56)

Reaching back centuries to the sewing of the symbol of national freedom
in an economy built on slavery, this poem becomes, among other things, a
ghost story – a story about the haunting of a person, and the shaping of
one of his most consequential actions, by nothing less than internalized
American racial history. This is why the confession "begins" with Betsy
Ross' flag symbolizing the impossibility of disentangling the creation of the
country from the dehumanization of Africans and African Americans. This
is also why there is a split in the poem between "me" and "that nigga,"
between the voice of the Betts-like persona and the self he keeps in the
third person ("that nigga"), because the latter was and remains a
doppelgänger that took hold of him on the night he committed his crime.
This is the reason, finally, for the reference to the presumed impropriety of
the mother's laying "up with a man the complexion of that nigga's /
Daddy," and for the poem's one instance of the word "niggers" – placed
in the mouths of authorities who use the word to dehumanize the speaker.

The poem is, ultimately, a monument to the ways in which history
haunts our language and, through that language, impacts our thinking and
shapes our decisions – if we let it (Collins, "Komunyakaa" 627–630;

Knight, *Black Voices*, 9–10). Through language, dragging connotations like a tangle of fishhooks, history also haunts public policy by structuring its categories, and its legitimate and illegitimate citizens – bastards of Reagan's and other eras. Part of the advantage of nuance-crowded lines like Betts', Knight's, and Kaufman's is that they allow us to pass history and legislation through phrases like prisms that let us see just what colors are contained by the white light of "the way things are" and by cartoon-simple, War on Drugs–style remedies for the way things are. Seeing the colors makes it easier to understand how conditions became what they are, and how, perhaps, to conjure less maniacal laws.

WORKS CITED

Alexander, David A., and Susan Klein. "Kidnapping and Hostage-Taking: A Review of Effects, Coping and Resilience." *Journal of the Royal Society of Medicine*, vol. 102, no. 1, 2009, pp. 16–21.

Alexander, Michelle. *The New Jim Crow: Mass Incarceration in the Age of Colorblindness*. New Press, 2012.

Betts, Reginald Dwayne. "Parking Lot, Too." In *Felon*. W. W. Norton, 2020.
  A Question of Freedom: A Memoir of Learning, Survival, and Coming of Age in Prison. Avery, 2010.

"Bob Kaufman FBI File." Federal Bureau of Investigation, Department of Justice. ark:/13960/t45q97g65,   https://archive.org/details/BobKaufmanFBIFile/mode/2up.

Campos, Paul F. *Jurismania: The Madness of American Law*. Oxford University Press, 1998.

Collins, Michael. "Komunyakaa, Collaboration, and the Wishbone: An Interview," *Callaloo*, vol. 28, no. 3, 2005, pp. 627–630.
  Understanding Etheridge Knight. University of South Carolina Press, 2012.

Conyers, John, Jr. "The Incarceration Explosion." *Yale Law & Policy Review*, vol. 31, no. 2, 2013, pp. 377–387.

Damon, Maria. *The Dark End of the Street: Margins in Vanguard Poetry*. University of Minnesota Press, 1993.

Davis, Angela Y. "Political Prisoners, Prisons and Black Liberation." In *If They Come in the Morning: Voices of Resistance*. Verso, 2016.

Falla, Jeffrey. "Bob Kaufman and the (In)visible Double." *Callaloo*, vol. 25, no. 1, 2002, pp. 183–189.

Garland, David. *The Culture of Control: Crime and Social Order in Contemporary Society*. University of Chicago Press, 2001.

Gray, Mike. *Drug Crazy: How We Got into This Mess and How We Can Get Out*. Routledge, 2000.

Henderson, David. "Introduction." In Bob Kaufman, *Cranal Guitar: Selected Poems of Bob Kaufman*. Coffee House Press, 1996.

Hinton, Elizabeth. *From the War on Poverty to the War on Crime: The Making of Mass Incarceration in America.* Harvard University Press, 2017.

Hofstadter, Richard. "The Pseudo-Conservative Revolt – 1954." In *The Paranoid Style in American Politics and Other Essays.* University of Chicago Press, 1965.

Horne, Gerald. *Red Seas: Ferdinand Smith and Radical Black Sailors in the United States and Jamaica.* New York University Press, 2005.

Kaufman, Bob. *Collected Poems of Bob Kaufman,* edited by Neeli Cherkovski, Raymond Foye, and Tate Swindell. City Lights Books, 2019.

Knight, Etheridge. *Black Voices from Prison.* Pathfinder Press, 1970.

"On the Yard." In *The Essential Etheridge Knight.* University of Pittsburgh Press, 1986.

Moran, Tom. "The Reemergence of a Streetside Survivor from the Bay Beatnik Era." *Los Angeles Times: West View,* October 4, 1981, p. 3.

Ogletree, Charles. *The Presumption of Guilt: The Arrest of Henry Louis Gates and Race, Class and Crime in America.* Palgrave Macmillan, 2010.

Plato. "Socrates' Defense (Apology)." In *The Collected Dialogues of Plato, Including the Letters,* edited by Edith Hamilton and Huntington Cairns. Princeton University Press, 1982, pp. 3–26.

Reagan, Ronald. "Campaign against Drug Use." September 14, 1986, www.pbs .org/wgbh/americanexperience/features/reagan-drug-campaign/.

Reagan, Ronald, and Nancy Reagan. "Address to the Nation on the Campaign against Drug Abuse." Ronald Reagan Presidential Library & Museum, www .reaganlibrary.gov/archives/speech/address-nation-campaign-against-drug-abuse.

Schrecker, Ellen, and Phillip Deery, eds. *The Age of McCarthyism: A Brief History with Documents,* 3rd ed. Bedford/St. Martin's, 2017.

Seymour, Tony. "Don't Forget Bob Kaufman." *San Francisco Examiner,* April 25, 1976.

"No Gods to Guide, No Herds to Follow." 1975, 1976, 1986, Bob Kaufman Collection no. 1037, Box 1, Folder 2. Howard Gotlieb Archival Research Center, Boston University, Boston.

Simon, Jonathan. *Mass Incarceration on Trial: A Remarkable Court Decision and the Future of Prisons in America.* New Press, 2014.

Woodberry, Billy. *And When I Die, I Won't Stay Dead.* Grasshopper Film, 2017.

Wilson, James Q. *Thinking about Crime.* Vintage, 1977.

CHAPTER 12

"Oh Say Can You See"
Seeing and the Unseen in *Citizen: An American Lyric*

Kathy Lou Schultz

Claudia Rankine's fifth book, *Citizen: An American Lyric* (2014), a volume of poetry and also a *New York Times* bestseller in the nonfiction category, represents her evolving use of form from lyric toward multiple genres and media. Her first book, *Nothing in Nature Is Private* (1992), utilizes the individual, lyric poem; thereafter, *The End of the Alphabet* (1998) expands into lyric sequences. *PLOT* (2001) employs multiple genres, including fragment, lyric, dialogue, prose, and boxes of text. The first of her "American Lyric" pairing, *Don't Let Me Be Lonely: An American Lyric* (2004), is also the first volume to include a wide variety of visual images, employing parataxis as a mode to activate meaning in the "gaps" between individual elements. While her previous books explore individual identities within the context of the social, with *Citizen*, Rankine sought to more explicitly take poetry into public conversations, shaping discussion of racial inequality. Indeed, *Citizen* has held a spot on the public stage since its release.

A striking example, college student Johari Osayi Idusuyi was seen on television reading *Citizen* at a Trump campaign rally in Springfield, Illinois, in 2015. When she saw Trump supporters attacking protesters, while the rest of the crowd – and Trump himself – cheered them on, she turned to her book instead (Brown). Idusuyi's act of reading *Citizen* at the rally drew the attention of national media outlets including *Jezebel*, MSNBC's Rachel Maddow, and *The Huffington Post*'s Claire Fallon, who writes: "Openly reading a book at an event is a highly underutilized form of protest" (Fallon). Reading *Citizen* on a public stage, Idusuyi challenged the Trump campaign's attempts to obscure the racist underpinnings of an "America first" message.

Idusuyi and her friends were situated so that they would appear on TV seated behind the candidate as part of a carefully orchestrated visual presentation of a multiracial group of supposed Trump supporters. With his back to the group, Trump does not address them; he is framed by them. Yet Idusuyi disrupts the rally organizers' attempted visual messaging, which relies heavily on their exploitation of the image of her Black body, by superimposing an image of her own choosing into the cynical photo op: the cover of *Citizen*, which features a stark black-and-white reproduction of David Hammons's sculpture, "In the Hood," made from athletic sweatshirt and wire. While the image now resonates painfully with the memory of George Zimmerman's vigilante murder of young Trayvon Martin in 2012, the piece was completed in 1993. The "hood"/"hoodie" message is conveyed not only through the title (youths from the "hood" assumed to be criminals because of their race and apparel) but by the hood's violent severance from the original sweatshirt. The allusion to grisly images of Black bodies torn asunder by lynching is unmistakable. Thus, by covering her own face with the book, Idusuyi not only rejects the exploitation of her own image; she replaces it with a reverberating image of the violence done to Black bodies by white supremacy.

Like the cover image, the whole of *Citizen* emphasizes the visual, reporting what is seen in everyday life, if one takes the time to look closely, across images, including photographs, screenshots from YouTube and television news, and full-color reproductions of contemporary art that are interspersed within the text. The paratactic arrangement of text and image, along with Rankine's focus on seeing and embodied experience, connects *Citizen* to a lineage of documentary poems by women, including Muriel Rukeyser's "Book of the Dead" from *U.S. 1* (1938), that employs multiple genres and visuals to expose social injustice. Reading Rankine alongside historical social documentaries usefully complicates how the combination of text and image can bring to bear differing relations between the reader/viewer and the subjects being documented. Understanding these relationships is necessary to social documentary's purported purpose of conveying meaning that causes the reader to "feel": "feeling the fact may move the audience to wish to change it" (Stott 26). Rankine expands on this long poem tradition that allows multiple genres to coexist, creating what Rukeyser calls a "third" meaning that is greater than either word or image.

Rukeyser had originally intended for Nancy Naumberg's photographs documenting the plight of miners in West Virginia to be included in "The Book of the Dead." Naumberg, "a lifelong friend and member of the Film and Photo League whose presence was to become an important focal point for the authorial perspective of the poem," accompanied Rukeyser on the trip from New York to West Virginia to document the deaths of miners in Gauley Bridge (Davidson 143). Rukeyser also worked on developing the book into a script, "in hopes of making a documentary film" (Lobo 78), further illustrating the importance of both written and visual forms as the documentary poem and the documentary film were developing and gaining significance in the 1930s. Significantly, Rankine was able to complete both additional steps that Rukeyser had hoped for, with the inclusion of a variety of images, from photographs to reproductions of fine art, throughout the book and the making of video poems based on the text. Section VI of *Citizen* includes eight scripts for the "Situation" video poems on which Rankine and her husband, photographer and filmmaker John Lucas, collaborate.

These interacting elements depict individual bodies, as well as representations of a social body ruptured by everyday acts of racism that occur in interpersonal encounters. Rankine explains: "I wanted to create the field of the encounter; what happens when one body comes up against another and race enters into the moment of intimacy between two people" (Westervelt). Throughout, *Citizen* links the embodied experiences of race and gender with the necessity of looking closely. "Each moment is like this – before it can be known, categorized as similar to another thing and dismissed, it has to be experienced, it has to be seen" (*Citizen* 9). This focus on seeing reveals that regimes of race held in place by the structures of white supremacy render Blackness hypervisible, while paradoxically causing Black people as individuals to be invisible. For example, a white man cuts in front of a Black woman waiting in line because she is invisible to him – "Oh my God, I didn't see you. / You must be in a hurry, you offer. / No, no, no. I really didn't see you" (77). *Citizen* shows that while such interactions may *seem* astonishing (how is it possible not to see a person standing in front of you?) in fact they are common. The "American Lyric" demands that these truths be seen collectively by an audience addressed as "you," reforming a social body accustomed to replicating social inequalities.

Defining the relationship between the individual and the social, individual identity is named the "self-self" in *Citizen*, while the historically weighted body is the "historical-self" (*Citizen* 14), also described as "the histories of you and you" (140). Fractures of the social body, when "race enters" everyday encounters, occur in the space between these two selves. "A friend argues that Americans battle between the 'historical self' and the 'self-self.' By this she means you mostly interact as friends with mutual interest and, for the most part, compatible personalities; however, sometimes your historical selves, her white self and your black self, or your white self and her black self, arrive with the full force of your American positioning" (14). The intimate attachments of the "self-self" become "fragile, tenuous" when transgressed within the social body made up of historical selves (14). While the "self-self" may be friend, poet, or other – identities that one chooses to engage – the "historical self" is located in the preexisting meanings and stereotypes attached to the physical body. Those meanings are transmitted through cultural practices and social institutions. Film, photographs, art, and literature, as well as historical events, laws, education, commerce, and other institutions, augment one's body with historically weighted meaning in physical space.

Careening through time, these historical meanings reappear to explode contemporary life. A therapist who "specializes in trauma counseling" when seeing a Black client for the first time "yells at the top of her lungs, Get away from my house! What are you doing in my yard?," viciously attacking the person who has come for help. Seeing only her misperceptions of Blackness results in the therapist's failure to comprehend the individual person standing in front of her (*Citizen* 18). The collision of "historical selves" also multiplies the meanings of encounters one presumes will be ordinary and unremarkable. Whether intentionally or unintentionally, the white person inflicts harm on the Black or brown person, and the relationship is forever damaged. "And when the woman with the multiple degrees says, I didn't know black women could get cancer, instinctively you take two steps back though all urgency leaves the possibility of any kind of relationship as you realize nowhere is where you will get from here" (45). A supposedly well-educated white woman fails to see that Black women inhabit the same human bodies as white women, and thus are subject to the same diseases. The white woman participates in extending an American history begun in chattel slavery that separates people of African descent from their humanity.

Contemporary art brings this dehumanization sharply into view. Kate Clark uses taxidermy to create sculptures that merge animal and human forms, creating pieces of art that are not only difficult to look at, but also hard to turn away from. Clark's "Little Girl" (2008) features a Black girl's face on a deer-like body constructed of "infant caribou hide, foam, clay, pins, thread [and] rubber eyes" (*Citizen* 163), invoking Rankine's memory "that [her] historical body on this continent began as property no different from an animal" (Rankine, Interview). "Little Girl" is placed opposite the testimony about the therapist, who is described as "a wounded Doberman pinscher or a German shepherd," clarifying who behaved like an animal (*Citizen* 18).

A full-color reproduction of Kenyan-born artist Wangechi Mutu's "Sleeping Heads" is placed in Section VII across from text, which states,

in part, "The worst injury is feeling you don't belong so much / to you – "
(*Citizen* 146). Enacting experiences of alienation born from colonialism,
Mutu's mixed media collage assembles images of human body parts and
discarded objects (including motorcycle parts) into something resembling
a human head, neck, and shoulders (147). Part of a large wall installation
of multiple pieces, all of the bodies in "Sleeping Heads" are prone (not
vertical as the one reproduced in *Citizen*) and thus in this vulnerable
position, described as "sleeping." In the image reproduced in *Citizen*, a
hand is placed across the neck so as to appear to be choking it and a small,
flexed arm blocks the mouth, which appears to be biting into it (147).
Who, the viewer wonders, is eating whom in this grotesque, yet familiar
pastiche of the social body? Assuming agency to remake the female form,
Mutu's work enacts disassemblage and reassemblage to interrogate the
postcolonial positioning of modern Africans.

Emphasizing the importance of social identity, Rankine employs the
second-person "you." "The start of you, each day, a presence already — /
Hey you —" (*Citizen* 140). Being addressed as "you" involves, connects,
even incriminates readers. "And always, who is this you?" the poem asks,
prompting the reader to question their position in the social order (104).
To address someone as "you" can also deny them their individuality:
"Rankine hints at the power that the white 'I' has over the diminished
'you' – since to refer to another person simply as 'you' is a demeaning form
of address: a way of emotionally displacing someone from the security of
their own body" (Chan 140).

> And still this life parts your lids, you see
> you seeing your extending hand
>
> as a falling wave –
> I they he she we you turn
> only to discover
> the encounter
>
> to be alien to this place.
> Wait. (*Citizen* 139–140)

The hand that extends and then falls illustrates fractures in the social body.
The action of the wave cannot be completed and the wave is not recognized, rendering the encounter "alien." In fact, the hand itself is alien,
disconnected from "you" as you watch it extending ("you see / you")
falling as if watching a foreign appendage.

The pronoun "you" also rotates, sometimes "facing inward and sometimes outward"; Erica Hunt argues, "These uses of 'you' compass multiple points of reference, at times denoting an internal 'you' – the 'you' of self-talk and admonition – and at other times, the performing 'you,' as if spoken by a stage director guiding an enactment of the social self" (Hunt). The performing "you" becomes explicit in the version of *Citizen* adapted for the stage by Stephen Sachs. Moreover, because "you" can also be plural, rather than only singular, in modifying the first-person "I" of the lyric form through incorporating the second-person point of view, Rankine switches from lyric individuality to collective relationality. Thus, she matches the form with the content that encourages readers to consider themselves within the context of the social, rather than just as individuals. *Citizen*'s dual-genre status (the way it is received by readers as both poetry and nonfiction) thus requires a seemingly incongruous crossing of the categories of the lyric "I" and its putatively subjective, private feeling with objective reports of what is seen in social interactions.

These alienating encounters, what the poem calls "The opening, between you and you," are already "zoned" by the unseen borders created by the historical weight carried by individual identities, as well as by visible physical barriers created by the history of segregation:

> The opening, between you and you, occupied,
> zoned for an encounter,
>
> given the histories of you and you –
> And always, who is this you? (*Citizen*, 140)

When the "opening" is occupied by preexisting biases and structural racism, the "zone" is already determined. Unacknowledged racism is deeply ingrained, perhaps even unconscious, until blurted out and made visible. "Your neighbor tells you he is standing at his window watching a menacing black guy casing both your homes. The guy is walking back and forth talking to himself and seems disturbed. You tell your neighbor that your friend, who he has met, is babysitting. He says, no it's not him. He's met your friend and this isn't that nice young man" (*Citizen* 15). This encounter illustrates both invisibility and hypervisibility. A friend whom the neighbor has previously met ceases to be a person and instead becomes a hypervisible stereotype, "a menacing black guy" (15). Racist language, *Citizen* tells us, renders Black people "hypervisible in the face of such language acts" (49).

Conversations not meant to be overheard are also recorded: "Standing outside the conference room, unseen by the two men waiting for the others to arrive, you hear one say to the other that being around black people is like watching a foreign film without translation" (*Citizen* 50). Because the majority of Americans form close relationships primarily with those of their own race, "being around black people" appears to be unusual enough that it is remarked on by those who are not Black. Moreover, Black people are not only "foreign" to the two men; they are unreal – seen only on screen ("like watching a foreign film without translation," *Citizen* 50). Separated from their individual humanity, Black people become a caricatured group projected onto the screen of the white imagination. *Citizen* encourages readers to connect such so-called small or micro acts of racism with widespread violence inflicted on Black bodies. Thus, individual actions are expressly shown to be symptoms of systemic dehumanization.

Segregation is also expressed in the built environment. One such physical barrier is the highway in Glynn County, Georgia, that separates a predominantly Black neighborhood from the predominantly white and more affluent area of Satilla Shores where three white men in trucks, one emblazoned with a Confederate flag license plate, chased Black jogger Ahmaud Arbery and shot him with a shotgun. Crossing a neighborhood border, an unarmed Black man going for a run is imagined to be a criminal. The white men also deemed Arbery animalistic ("We cornered him like a rat," one states on a video recorded after the shooting). *Citizen* reveals the links between the injury forged by daily racism, "the lack of recognition of the black body as a body," and large-scale injury and death (Rankine, Interview), including the horrific repetition of shootings of unarmed Black people. Memorialized by a wall of remembrance for the victims in the form of a list in the final pages of the book, the "wall" is updated with new names in each edition, documenting these deaths so that readers will see the people's names. Arbery's name was added to the twenty-second printing (June 2020).

"Defense is sight; widen the lens and see"

Citizen's precursor in documentary poetics, "The Book of the Dead," contains myriad references to glass, windows, lenses, and their relation to seeing and to photographs.[1] The images of reflective glass can appear benign, "eyes over the beerglass" (Rukeyser, *Collected* 78), or even as

---

1 The section heading is from Muriel Rukeyser.

beautiful reflections of the natural world: "the moon blows glassy over our native river" (94). The multiple images of glass also include windows, apertures for viewing. However, the poem reveals that "glass" is also silica dust: "the mouth of the tunnel that opened wider / precious in the rock the white glass showed" (78). The "dust that is blown from off the field of glass" (96) is deadly to the miners breathing it in as they drill the tunnel dry and without protective equipment for the New Kanawha Power Company: "hundreds breathed in value, filled their lungs full of glass" (79). Without knowing why, the men, most of whom were African American, die of silicosis while Union Carbide (the same company later responsible for "more than 600,000 people being exposed to [a] deadly gas cloud" in Bhopal, India, in 1984 and the parent company of the New Kanawha Power Company) profited handsomely from the valuable silica (Taylor).

Finally, glass refers to the lens of the camera and the importance of the photograph in documentary poetry – "The man on the street and the camera eye" (Rukeyser, *Collected* 78) – and to the power of the documentary image: "Defense is sight; widen the lens and see" (110). Yet the poem also contains a warning about such photographs: "until we walk to windows, seeing America / lie in a photograph of power" (107). If one refuses to walk to the window and look out, they cannot comprehend the truth of America, nor can they see America as a "lie." The meaning of the documentary photograph may seem self-evident, but photographs too are framed. Thus, "defense is sight" only if the viewer dares to "widen the lens and see" what may be left out of the frame, or see that a frame exists at all. Does the camera eye capture the man on the street, or do viewers encounter only the "photograph of power"? And, by extension, can the documentary poem defend the powerless, give voice to people rendered voiceless?

In her documentary poetics, Rukeyser understood that the meaning of the photograph is not self-evident. Her multiple allusions to the "transparency" of glass are a metacommentary on the investigative modes needed to uncover, and intervene in, Union Carbide and the New Kanawha Power Company's carefully controlled rhetoric intended to obscure the human and environmental trauma inflicted in Gauley Bridge. By incorporating interviews with survivors alongside official congressional testimony, Rukeyser records different registers of documented speech that can counter the companies' claims, and by including an image of Union Carbide's stock ticker, Rukeyser reveals that the companies hid the truth and the men's bodies to deflect from their merciless accumulation of wealth. Rankine's variety of collected, colloquial speech achieves a similar aim. The reports given by *Citizen*'s multiple "yous" also act as testimony, entering the documentary record and making the truths of daily racism visible.

"or she never actually saw you sitting there"

In *The Life of Poetry* (1949) Rukeyser stresses that, in the combination of images and words, "there are separables: the meaning of the image, the meaning of the words, and a third, the meaning of the two in combination.[2] The words are not used to describe the picture, but to extend its meaning" (*Life* 137). This "third meaning" created when words extend rather than describe is already laid out in "The Book of the Dead": "to photograph and to extend the voice, / to speak this meaning" (Rukeyser, *Collected* 110). The first photograph in *Citizen*, combined with the text above it, enacts Rukeyser's "third meaning." Though taken in color, the photograph emphasizes the contrast of black and white: big white houses with black shutters, a white car with black tires. All is very ordinary, even bland, in this suburban landscape, except for the name of the street on the sign in the foreground: "JIM CROW RD" (Rankine, *Citizen* 6). Despite the brutal segregationist policies in the Jim Crow era and the grotesque blackface minstrel character from which the name derives, there is more than one location in the United States that has had a street bearing this name, including Flowery Branch, Georgia, where this photo was taken.

The juxtaposition of text and photo creates the "third meaning" greater than either element individually, as the "interruption," the pause between them, creates the opportunity for opening perception: in a country where municipalities fail to see a problem with giving a street a name synonymous with the degradation of its Black citizens, Black women will remain unseen. The photograph is placed in Section I with an account concerning two twelve-year-old girls in Catholic school, showing that African Americans' experiences of erasure and hypervisibility begin in childhood: "the girl sitting behind you asks you to lean to the right during exams so she can copy what you have written" (Rankine, *Citizen* 5). The reader learns: "You never really speak except for the time she makes her request and later when she tells you you smell good and have features more like a

---

2 The section heading is from Rankine, *Citizen* 6.

white person. You assume she thinks she is thanking you for letting her cheat and feels better cheating from an almost white person" (5). The Black girl is invisible to the white girl as an individual: the white girl can apply only white standards of beauty to judge her as both looking and smelling "white," in a supposed complement that degrades the black child.

Above the photo of Jim Crow Road, the vignette about the two schoolgirls concludes: "Sister Evelyn never figures out your arrangement perhaps because you never turn around to copy Mary Catherine's answer. Sister Evelyn must think these two girls think a lot alike or she cares less about cheating and more about humiliation or she never actually saw you sitting there" (Rankine, *Citizen* 6). Sister Evelyn, like "Mary Catherine," who cheats off the Black girl's paper, like the man who cuts in line at the store, like the people who sat Idusuyi on stage behind Trump, fails to see Black girls and women as individuals, or fails to see them at all (5). This paratactical arrangement of text and image – the seemingly unconnected photograph and the conclusion of the vignette on the same page – continues the form of documentary poetry seen in Rukeyser's "Book of the Dead" and other long poems from the 1930s. Meaning is made in the "gaps."

Making present the humanity of individual people of color, Rankine presents a searing description of how the wounds of racism can feel: "Certain moments send adrenaline to the heart, dry out the tongue, and clog the lungs. Like thunder they drown you in sound, no, like lightning they strike you across the larynx" (Rankine, *Citizen* 7). Moreover, Rankine demonstrates that these experiences of daily aggression and structural racism are not fleeting but are "stored" in the body: "The world is wrong. You can't put the past behind you. It's buried in you; it's turned your flesh into its own cupboard. Not everything remembered is useful but it all comes from the world to be stored in you" (63). The "storing" of trauma in the physical body is not only metaphor. Scientific research in the field of epigenetic inheritance shows that experiences of trauma may in fact alter the way one's genetic code is deployed, and this altered deployment can be passed on through least a few generations: "a parent's *experiences*, in the form of epigenetic tags, can be passed down to future generations" ("Epigenetics & Inheritance," emphasis added). These embodied experiences remained stored in the flesh's "cupboard" but can be accessed, *Citizen* demonstrates, through writing. Moving the violence out of the "cupboard" allows it to be seen. The video poems take this process a step further, making the unseen visible on the screen.

"Close looking"

"Situation 1," a video poem based on the poem script, "October 10, 2006/
World Cup" in *Citizen* (120–129), begins at the crossing of Zinedine
Zidane's "historical self" (his parents immigrated from a village in the
Berber-speaking region of Kabylie in northern Algeria before the outbreak
of the Algerian war) and his "self-self," captain of the French national
football (soccer) team. As a professional athlete, "race enters" Zidane's
everyday life on a public stage, in view of the live and television-viewing
audience, recording an infamous nine seconds of his life: Italian player
Marco Materazzi mocks Zidane (a former teammate) several times before
Zidane turns and headbutts Materazzi in the chest, knocking him to the
ground. A national hero, Zidane was born in France. Yet, "For all that he is,"
the video poem warns, "people will say, that he remains for us, an Arab. 'You
can't get away from nature' Frantz Fanon" (Rankine, *Citizen* 124–125).

The original video from the 2006 FIFA World Cup Final match – a
game won by Italy through a penalty kick shootout with France in extra
time – is slowed down in "Situation 1," allowing for moment-by-moment
"close looking" that, combined with the poem voice-over, creates an
interplay between text and moving image that multiplies the meanings
of both. In the book, the moment-by-moment progression is represented
visually by individual frames from the video that are printed horizontally
across the left-hand pages, capturing the action frame-by-frame as if on
strips of film, emphasizing the visual activity of the page and putting the
elements into motion as in the historical documentary poem (Rankine,
Citizen 122, 124, 126, 128).

In addition to Fanon, quoted above, the poem script collages quotes
from eight authors, including James Baldwin, Maurice Blanchot, and
William Shakespeare, as well as quotes from Zidane himself printed in
bold, all of which frame the examination of Zidane's historical identity.
The insults documented in the poem script are "Accounts of lip readers
responding to the video of the World Cup" (Rankine, *Citizen* 127). When
quoted material is wedded to Rankine's own prose, it is made evident in
the book with the quotations appearing on the left-hand page, with the
name of the author listed across from it on the right-hand page. However,
in the video poem, a list of cited writers does not appear until the very end,
perhaps evoking surprise that a collage method was used, for the video
poem voice-over is seamless. The viewer may review the video to consider
what these authors signify, and when – and why – the quotes appear,
creating viewer interactivity.

Materazzi's insults were possibly directed toward Zidane's mother or sister (though Materazzi claims otherwise) and likely contain derogatory language concerning Zidane's race and ethnicity. "Every day I think about where I came from and I am still proud to be who I am," states Zidane. "What he said 'touched the deepest part of me'" (Rankine, *Citizen* 122, 128). This was Zidane's last game as a professional athlete; he retired after France's elimination from the World Cup. European sports commentators at the time described Zidane as "crazily headbutting" Materazzi and having "a moment of madness," concluding that "his professional career ended in shameful circumstances" (Stevenson). Another accused Zidane of not "thinking logically" and of behaving "beyond the bounds of normality" (Wilson). In the United States, the *New York Times* reported that Zidane "committed an astonishing act of impudence" and that he was "impertinent" and "insolent" (Longman). From such reports, Zidane's actions can only be understood as insanity, a failure of logic to dominate emotion, or the behavior of a rude child. Zidane is both infantilized and labeled as deviant. The same language is used to vilify tennis superstar Serena Williams, who, after enduring years of racist aggression and questionable calls by umpires and line judges, finally responds in justified anger.

The historical self is suddenly thrown open for both Williams and the reader: "Every look, every comment, every bad call blossoms out of history, through her, onto you" (*Citizen* 32). Williams's frustrations are zoned by a system that renders "the erasure of self as systemic, as ordinary" (32) for a Black female athlete. Yet to reveal this truth is to be labeled "insane." "Perhaps this is how racism feels no matter the context – randomly the rules everyone else gets to play by no longer apply to you, and to call this out by calling out 'I swear to God!' is to be called insane, crass, crazy. Bad sportsmanship" (30). Even in joy, after her "three-second celebratory dance on center court at the All England Club," American media commentators accuse Williams of being "immature and classless" (33) and call her victory dance a "Crip Walk, a gangster dance" (34). In a similar manner, when Zidane, one of the greatest soccer stars of the prior twenty years, responds in justified anger, he is suddenly no longer a rational man – but Rankine and Lucas demand that we look more closely.

"Do you think two minutes from the end of the World Cup final, two minutes from the end of my career, I wanted to do that?" Zidane asks (Rankine, *Citizen* 124). Showing "Something is there before us that is neither the living person himself nor any sort of reality," the video poem exposes France's 132-year colonial occupation of Algeria, and the concomitant penetration of racist attitudes about Algerians, Muslims, and Arabs into French public discourse. Despite Zidane's superstar status, "Situation 1" reveals that some still consider him an outsider for reasons including his Arab heritage, religion, and financially impoverished childhood in Marseille's infamous "La Castellane" suburban housing estate. "The Algerian men for their part are a target of criticism for their European comrades. Arise directly to the level of tragedy" (Lucas). This view is embedded in colonial logic, for example, an 1838 report of the French expedition to Constantine written by Lucien Baudens, then the French army's foremost surgeon and a professor of medicine.

Baudens's "description of the Arabs and Kabyles painted a derogatory picture of the former, stressing their cupidity, cruelty, and fanaticism and [ends] with the statement that there was nothing to compete with the ugliness of Arab traits or their lack of personal cleanliness" (Lorcin). Presented as "objective" medical research and ethnology, these judgments "contributed to the formation of a negative stereotype of the Muslim in Algeria that would eventually be contrasted with the positive image of French culture and civilization" (663). The remarkable similarity of the insults directed toward Zidane in 2006 with the derogatory colonial French descriptions of Algerians in the surgeon's 1838 report ("lack of personal cleanliness," "cruel," "fanatic") shows the reach of these stereo- types across three centuries, rendering Zidane racially other, a "dirty terrorist," "big Algerian shit," and that most hateful racist slur, "nigger" (Lucas). "This kind of racial prejudice can be multiplied indefinitely" as a racist insult used to belittle people of African descent in the United States is also employed in Europe to denigrate Arabs in France.

In the book, the phrase "BLACK-BLANC-BEUR" is printed in gray across each set of left- and right-hand pages (Rankine, *Citizen* 120–129). This technique, overlaying one image with another in the same frame – called superimposition in the language of film – highlights the visual language of the poem scripts themselves, putting the elements on the page into motion in the same manner as historical documentary poems. Always in conversation with the video poems, the poem scripts heighten the spectatorial experience through movement beyond a static, singular set of words on a page. The phrase is familiar to fans of the French national team, indicating a sentimental feeling "that a multicultural team of 'black, blanc, beur' (Black, white, or Arab) players had united under the cause of the French national team" (Downing). Yet, others point out that this media-invented phrase creates a false sense that France had solved its problems with racism and intolerance. "Beur" is also French slang for European-born persons whose parents or grandparents immigrated from

Northern Africa, and "anti-Beur racism is such that, while they make up 40 percent of the foreign population in France, they are the victims of 90 percent of the hate crimes" (Elia 47), revealing the enduring effects of colonialist attitudes.

Looking closely at how race enters everyday life creates opportunities to radically reimagine and revise these power dynamics structurally and interpersonally. As Lauren Berlant articulates, "writing can allow us to amplify overwhelming scenes of ordinary violence while interrupting the sense of a fated stuckness" (Rankine, Interview). Underscoring the importance of both documentation and social connection as remedies for social injustice, "The Book of the Dead" asks and answers: "What three things can never be done? / Forget. Keep silent. Stand alone" (Rukeyser, *Collected* 107). The documentary poem itself creates a new sociality that connects readers and subjects across continents and across time. Utilizing text, image, and video, *Citizen* engages the eye to see "you," disentangling the historical self from the individual, creating a pause in which it is possible to really see the person standing in front of you.

WORKS CITED

Brown, Kara. "A Conversation with Johari Osayi Idusuyi, the Hero Who Read through a Trump Rally." The Slot, November 12, 2015, https://theslot.jezebel.com/a-conversation-with-johari-osayi-idusuyi-the-hero-who-1742082010.

Chan, Mary-Jean. "Towards a Poetics of Racial Trauma: Lyric Hybridity in Claudia Rankine's *Citizen*." *Journal of American Studies*, vol. 52, no. 1, 2018, pp. 137–63.

Davidson, Michael. *Ghostlier Demarcations: Modern Poetry and the Material Word.* University of California Press, 1997.

Downing, Joseph. "Success of French Football Team Masks Underlying Tensions over Race and Class." The Conversation, July 13, 2018, http://theconversation.com/success-of-french-football-team-masks-underlying-tensions-over-race-and-class-99781.

Elia, Nada. "In the Making: Beur Fiction and Identity Construction." *World Literature Today*, vol. 71, no. 1, 1997, pp. 47–54.

"Epigenetics & Inheritance." Learn.Genetics, 2015, https://learn.genetics.utah.edu/content/epigenetics/inheritance/.

Fallon, Claire. "Woman Reading a Book at a Trump Rally Should Inspire a Movement." HuffPost, January 18, 2017, www.huffpost.com/entry/trump-rally-woman-reading_n_56436212e4b060377347248d.

Hunt, Erica. "All About You." *Los Angeles Review of Books*, December 8, 2014, https://lareviewofbooks.org/article/all-about-you/.

Lobo, Julius. "From 'The Book of the Dead' to 'Gauley Bridge': Muriel Rukeyser's Documentary Poetics and Film at the Crossroads of the

Popular Front." *Journal of Modern Literature*, vol. 35, no. 3, 2012, pp. 77–102.

Longman, Jere. "Italy Defeats France in Penalty-Kick Shootout." *New York Times*, July 9, 2006, www.nytimes.com/2006/07/09/sports/soccer/10cupcnd.html.

Lorcin, Patricia M. E. "Imperialism, Colonial Identity, and Race in Algeria, 1830–1870: The Role of the French Medical Corps." *Isis*, vol. 90, no. 4, 1999, pp. 653–679.

Lucas, John. "Situation 1." 2015. Vimeo, https://vimeo.com/129006280.

macfound. "Poet Claudia Rankine | 2016 MacArthur Fellow." 2016. YouTube, www.youtube.com/watch?v=_y6QT2XZRPA.

Rankine, Claudia. *Citizen: An American Lyric*. Graywolf Press, 2014.

"Claudia Rankine by Lauren Berlant." Interview. *BOMB Magazine*, October 1, 2014, https://bombmagazine.org/articles/claudia-rankine/.

Rukeyser, Muriel. *The Collected Poems of Muriel Rukeyser*. Edited by Janet E. Kaufman et al. University of Pittsburgh Press, 2005.

The Life of Poetry. Paris Press, 1996.

Stevenson, Jonathan. "Italy Beat France 5-3 in a Penalty Shoot-Out to Win the World Cup after an Absorbing 1-1 Draw in Berlin." News.bbc.co.uk, July 9, 2006, http://news.bbc.co.uk/sport2/hi/football/world_cup_2006/4991652.stm.

Stott, William. *Documentary Expression and Thirties America*. University of Chicago Press, 1986.

Taylor, Alan. "Bhopal: The World's Worst Industrial Disaster, 30 Years Later." *The Atlantic*, www.theatlantic.com/photo/2014/12/bhopal-the-worlds-worst-industrial-disaster-30-years-later/100864/ (accessed November 12, 2021).

Westervelt, Eric. "In 'Citizen,' Poet Strips Bare the Realities of Everyday Racism." NPR.org, January 3, 2015, www.npr.org/2015/01/03/374574142/in-citizen-poet-strips-bare-the-realities-of-everyday-racism.

Wilson, Jonathan. "Zidane's World Cup Final Headbutt, 10 Years Later." *Sports Illustrated*, July 8, 2016, www.si.com/soccer/2016/07/08/zinedine-zidane-headbutt-materazzi-world-cup-france-italy-2006.

CHAPTER 13

The Political Resonances of Hip Hop and Spoken Word

Dallas Donnell

Introduction

Spoken word refers to poetic performance that relies on or emphasizes the aspects of its construction that must be heard, rather than read, to be fully experienced and appreciated. Factors like intonation, volume, and audience participation are aesthetic elements that might be of some consequence on the page, but they are central to the construction and performance of spoken word. Any discussion about hip hop's aesthetic qualities and sociopolitical weight requires substantive engagement with Black spoken word and performance poetry. What follows is an exploration of the political resonances that emerge from interactions – both historical and into the present day – between hip-hop music and Black spoken word performance.

Spoken word is a radical means of Black self-expression, reflected in its often politically charged content and the transgressiveness of its very mode of articulation. Spoken word is also a site of political contestation, reflecting the various competing ideologies vying for dominance in Black politics at any given time, including issues related to gender, sexuality, class, and the meaning of Blackness itself. Hip hop engages with spoken word as a forebear of the genre that resonates as a signifier for honesty, authenticity, and confrontation, while also grappling with its association with Black nationalist politics that too often devolve into unproductive expressions of sexism, homophobia, and essentialism. Finally, a brief analysis of two of the most influential albums of the twenty-first century – namely, Beyoncé's *Lemonade* and Kenrick Lamar's *To Pimp a Butterfly* – demonstrates how spoken word remains a lasting presence in and relevant to Black popular music and culture.

Formative Influence of Spoken Word on Rap Music

Technically, the practice of spoken word goes back centuries. In the context of Black creative expression, a distinctly Black tradition of oral performance dates back to the shores of Africa, in which griots adopted particular patterns of rhyme and storytelling tropes to maintain and share knowledge across generations. From these traditions come the signifying monkey and other oral folklore traditions (Gates) that were direct influences on the practice of emceeing in hip hop. These include the vocal performances of pastors in Black churches, practices like the dozens, and even the comedy routines of actor and comedian Rudy Ray Moore, whose Dolemite character is often cited as a formative influence for many rap artists of the 1980s and 1990s (Chadwick). Jamaican toasting – the practice of talking, chanting, and boasting over beats played by DJs on massive sound systems – was a wildly popular practice in the 1970s that was brought to New York City by Caribbean immigrants and directly influenced hip hop (Chang). All of these practices include rhyming, call-and-response techniques, and improvisation as key elements. Although distinct from one another, collectively they blur the boundaries necessary to delineate "spoken word" as a practice distinct from these traditions.

However, when one hears the term "spoken word" in relation to hip-hop music and culture, the performance poetry stylings of Black nationalist performers and recording artists like Gil Scott-Heron and the Last Poets inevitably come to mind.[1,2] These artists are among the most significant precursors and influences on hip-hop music and culture, and they are the spoken word artists most widely associated with the genre. Like doo wop and hip hop, spoken word is an egalitarian artform, where simply one's voice and imagination are enough. Its power lies in the accessibility of its performance and the directness of its content. Unlike soul or jazz vocalizing, spoken word – and, later, rapping – allows practitioners to literally say more than they would otherwise be able to in a traditionally melodic song structure.

The roots of the relationship between Black popular music and spoken word run deep. In the 1920s, poets of the Harlem Renaissance like Langston Hughes pioneered jazz poetry, a style of poetry directly influenced by the syncopation and repetition endemic to jazz music, to develop a distinctly Black literary tradition in both style and substance. Jazz poetry would be stripped of its Black politics and adopted by 1950s Beat generation writers like Jack Kerouac – who often performed his work to jazz

---

[1] Rebecca Bengal, "The Last Poets: The Hip-Hop Forefathers Who Gave Black America Its Voice," *Guardian*, May 18, 2018, www.theguardian.com/music/2018/may/18/the-last-poets-the-hip-hop-forefathers-who-gave-black-america-its-voice.

[2] NPR Staff, "Founding Father of Rap, Gil Scott-Heron, Dead," NPR, May 28, 2011, www.npr.org/2011/05/28/136742737/founding-father-of-rap-gil-scott-heron-dead.

accompaniment – to articulate an anti-establishment ethos of improvisation and autonomy.

It took writers, intellectuals, and activists like Larry Neal and LeRoi Jones, later known as Amiri Baraka, to pioneer the reunification of jazz poetry with Black radical politics in the 1960s. Baraka's brand of Black cultural nationalism is foundational to the Black Arts Movement, a movement that championed Black artistic production that centers Black experiences, perspectives, self-determination, and pride. It is out of this historical moment that the spoken word recordings of Gil Scott-Heron and the Last Poets would find a rapt audience of Black youth and help plant the seeds of rap music at the dawn of the 1970s. Gil Scott-Heron and the Last Poets were renowned and controversial for the frank and incendiary content of their works, inhabiting and enacting a form of surrogacy that spoke directly to the concerns of Black communities in the aftermath of the 1960s, as civil rights and black power organizations were either under attack or decimated under COINTELPRO, an official CIA program of surveillance and disruption that targeted radical Black leaders and organizations like Stokely Carmichael, Angela Davis, and the Black Panther Party

Like other elements of hip hop, the appeal of emceeing is in part the unnecessity of formal training, and the ability to perform it anywhere, without equipment or permission. In response to the deindustrial siphoning of jobs from urban Black and brown communities during the 1970s, egalitarian modes of self-expression like rapping were radical acts of individual and collective resistance to structural violence. Spoken word is a critical forebear – both stylistically and politically – as a means of self-expression radical both in its content and in the very mode of its expression.

Gender and Sexuality

In the post–Civil Rights era, Black spoken word was a contested site regarding notions of respectability, critical of the complacency of the Black bourgeois political elite, while also adhering to ideological shortcuts central to the perpetuation of white supremacist hegemony. Spoken word challenged and adhered to at times controversial ideas and postures rooted in the Black nationalist ideologies of the 1960s. Some elements of this ideology – unity, self-determination, and pride – hold real value and imbue spoken word with a palpable sense of honesty and authenticity.

However, spoken word can inherit elements of Black nationalist thought that are rife with the misogynist, patriarchal values constitutive to white supremacist hegemony that cripple Black liberation movements, and do immeasurable damage to Black men's lives. bell hooks explains in *We Real Cool,* "Today it should be obvious to any thinker and writer speaking about black males that the primary genocidal threat, the force that endangers black male life, is patriarchal masculinity" (hooks, xii). Patriarchy keeps Black men confined by a value system that serves the interests of a status quo that oppresses them and keeps them "psychologically locked down, locked out" (xi). It is a necessity that Black men, and Black communities broadly, challenge patriarchy, toxic masculinity, and homophobia for a truly radical movement to thrive.

Many artists of the 1960s and beyond have done just that by developing a Black aesthetic that disidentifies with Black nationalism. Coined by Jose Esteban Munoz, *disidentification* is a process by which queer people of color can identify with race or queerness despite problematic ideas or perspectives in both spaces. Rather than identifying or counter-identifying with an ideology, queer people of color disidentify, working both on and against the ideology to change the structure from within. For many Black women and queer artists, Black Nationalism's inattentiveness to and rejection of the heterogeneity of the Black community makes a Black aesthetic that celebrates difference an artistic and cultural necessity.

Much has been written about the notion of a Black aesthetic. In his seminal essay "The Negro Artist and the Racial Mountain," Langston Hughes rebukes Black artists and audiences that either ignore or deride art that speaks to the unique experiences of African Americans. Hughes urges Black artists to free themselves from a misguided need for affirmation from white audiences and critics by whitewashing their work. The Black Arts Movement reignited Hughes's call for a Black aesthetic. Baraka and Neal wrote extensively about developing radical art that is grounded in the needs and experiences of Black people. The problem with their efforts is the assumption that there is a homogenous "Black people" to write about. Black nationalist art too often eschews complexity in the interest of a homogenous, patriarchal, and homophobic vision of Black liberation. It is this aesthetic to which spoken word artists like Gil Scott-Heron and the Last Poets adhered, and which Black women and queer artists of the post–Civil Rights era would contest.

Gil Scott-Heron was arguably the most iconic practitioner of spoken word of the twentieth century. And while his work spoke truth to power and implored Black people to embrace Black nationalist principles like self-determination, pride, and resistance to white supremacy, the patriarchal, homophobic elements in his work are notorious. Gil Scott-Heron applied a heterosexist and phallocentric approach in his social observations that made the most critical challenges facing Black communities seem interchangeable with the strength and clarity of Black masculinity in America.

His debut album, 1970's *Small Talk on 125th and Lennox*, is a landmark recording, featuring the incendiary classics "The Revolution Will Not Be Televised" and "Whitey on the Moon." History has not been as kind to track six, "The Subject Was Faggots," a three-minute diatribe detailing Heron's encounter with a gay bar, or as he puts it, "faggot ball." In its final moments, the poem makes a clear parallel between gay culture and whiteness:

> But sitting on the corner, digging all that I did
> As I did
> Long, long, black limousines
> And long, flowing evening gowns
> Had there been no sign on the door saying
> "Faggot ball"
> I might have entered
> And God only knows just what would have happened
> The subject was faggots
> I'm glad you made it, Charlie, I'm glad you made it.

Echoing the sentiments of such luminaries of the Black nationalist era as Eldridge Cleaver[3] and Amiri Baraka,[4] Scott-Heron suggests homosexuality is both counterrevolutionary and a detriment to the health and unity of Black communities. In Heron's "the subject was faggots," being Black and queer is tantamount to being a race traitor by consorting with the enemy, or partying with "Charlie."[5]

In contrast to these sentiments, a defining quality of spoken word – and Black art, broadly – in the post–Civil Rights era are the intervening voices of women and queer people of color who harness it in ways that

---

[3] Cleaver's *Soul on Ice* is infamous for its homophobic attack on queer writer and intellectual James Baldwin.

[4] See the first paragraph of Baraka's "America's Sexual Reference: Black Male," from his collection *Home: Social Essays* (1966).

[5] "Charlie" is a pejorative term used in Black communities to refer to a domineering white male figure, such as a boss or overseer.

disidentify with Black nationalist ideology. GerShun Avilez, in *Radical Aesthetics and Modern Black Nationalism*, calls this *aesthetic radicalism*, a theoretical framework for analyzing Black artistic works that value Black nationalist demands to reimagine the social world and Black identity, while also calling out how it falls short in terms of gender and sexual norms. These performances acknowledge and assert the value of Black nationalist principles while maintaining a critical stance toward its homophobic and toxic masculinist elements. In the hip-hop era, spoken word became a site of political contestation, in which its aesthetic value as a practice signifying notions of purity, authenticity, and self-critique is both honored and destabilized by marginalized voices who harness it to critique the Black nationalist delusion of a homogeneous Black community.

This turn is unsurprising in the larger discursive context of Black politics in the Civil Rights and post–Civil Rights eras. Black women challenged the male-centric lens of Civil Rights organizations throughout the 1960s.[6] By the 1970s, Black feminists and queer voices began to rise above the deafening force of masculinist Black liberation ideas and programs. Black woman writers like Nikki Giovanni,[7] Toni Cade Bambara,[8] and Ntozake Shange[9] crafted works that reflect the necessity that antiracist and white women–led feminist movements engage the unique experiences of Black women under the intersecting forces of race, gender, sexual, and class oppression. Nikki Giovanni's groundbreaking work is of note, specifically her own collection of spoken word albums released during the 1970s. Featuring accompaniment by the New York Community Choir, Giovanni's albums – including *Truth Is On the Way* (1971) and *Like a Ripple on a Pond* (1973) – offer a fascinating marriage of Black gospel music with the candid introspection and incendiary Black radical politics that were the hallmarks of the world-making art of the Black Arts Movement. However, Giovanni departed from her male and phallocentric peers by centering Black womanhood. In "Woman Poem" she details the particular kind of sorrow Black women experience in the double crosshairs of both race and gender oppression:

---

[6] See Springer for a book-length exploration of Black feminist activism during the 1960s and 1970s.
[7] *Black Feeling, Black Talk/Black Judgment* (1970).
[8] *The Black Woman* (1970), *Gorilla, My Love* (1972), *The Salt Eaters* (1980).
[9] *For Colored Girls Who Have Considered Suicide/When the Rainbow Is Enuf* (1976).

it's having a job
they won't let you work
or no work at all
castrating me
(yes it happens to women too)

it's a sex object if you're pretty
and no love
or love and no sex if you're fat
get back fat black woman be a mother
grandmother strong thing but not woman
gameswoman romantic woman love needer
man seeker dick eater sweat getter
fuck needing love seeking woman

Songs like "Woman Poem" are testimonials of the hardships unique to Black women under the intersecting yokes of racism and misogyny. Renowned around the world for her unforgettable collections of poetry, Giovanni is woefully underrated as a recording artist.

Black feminism is highly influential on the queer liberation movement, particularly the necessity of an intersectional politics. Black queer artists in the 1980s and 1990s utilized spoken word to intervene on Black nationalist politics with works that critique homogenized notions of Black identity. The films of Marlon Riggs are groundbreaking in part for how they seamlessly weave spoken word into radical Black queer art. The seminal 1989 film *Tongues Untied* and 1995's *Black Is, Black Ain't* are among his most famous works and are prime examples of the incorporation of spoken word into a Black aesthetic that offers a heterogeneous vision of Blackness.

The 1991 music video *Anthem* is his most direct attempt to marry spoken word and hip hop in a larger critique of the homophobia of the Black nationalist movement and hip-hop culture. Released during the AIDS crisis, the music video features prominent use of the "Silence = Death" slogan pioneered by the queer activist organization ACT UP. However, in one scene, the group's triangle symbol features a picture of the African continent, as well as the Pan-Africanist colors of red, black, and green. This and other moments in the video reflect a demand for queer inclusion in movements for Black liberation, as well the necessity of making the experiences of people of color central to AIDS activism in particular, and the gay liberation movement at large. The film features passionate spoken word performances from a group of legendary Black queer writers, including Essex Hemphill, Steve Langley, Colin Robinson,

Reginald Jackson, and Donald Woods. Critically, Riggs utilizes hip hop–
inspired breakbeats as the film's sonic backdrop, reflecting a desire to
forge a new Black aesthetic that can bridge radicalized Black gay culture
and the political resonance and insurgent force of hip hop for revolutionary ends. This union of spoken word, hip hop, and radical politics
serves as a vision for Black liberation that celebrates rather than down-
plays difference.

***

While the radical spoken word artists of the Black nationalist era were
always an ingredient in the sociocultural stew that birthed hip hop, their
influence would not be overt until Public Enemy took the music world by
storm in the late 1980s. Like no rap group before them, Public Enemy
broke new ground by explicitly marrying the sound and aesthetic of hip
hop to the hard funk of James Brown and the righteous radicalism of Black
Nationalism. However, Public Enemy also doubled down on Black
nationalism's sexism and homophobia, often reaffirming a patriarchal
Black liberation agenda, and skirting with homophobia on tracks like
"Meet the G Who Killed Me" and "A Letter to the New York Post."

    In contrast, neo-soul foremother Meshell Ndegeocello emerged hot on
Public Enemy's heels with a unique mixture of jazz, funk, soul, and hip
hop that effortlessly integrated spoken word into the mix while also
turning Black nationalist politics on its head. Ndegeocello's work disidentifies with Black nationalist ideology through the adoption of the
performance poetry aesthetic. Like Public Enemy, Ndegeocello is clearly
influenced by the revolutionary tomes of Scott-Heron and the Last
Poets, but she works both on and against their works by asserting
Black feminist and queer identity as central to any viable and substantive
movement for Black liberation. A particularly arresting example of this
occurs on her 1996 album, *Peace beyond Passion*, where she challenges
the role of religion in perpetuating homophobic belief systems that both
harm queer people of color and perpetuate white supremacy. The
album's centerpiece "Leviticus: Faggot" explores the homophobia, den-
igration, and shame that silences, excludes, and kills Black queer people.
Over an ironically upbeat, funky sonic backdrop, she tells the harrowing
story of a Black gay youth rejected by his family, and the dire consequences that result:

Go to church boy
Faggot you're just a prisoner of your own perverted world

No picket fence acting like a bitch that's all he sees ain't that what faggot means
No love dreams
Only the favors sweet Michael performed for money to eat

'Cause the man kicked the faggot out the house at 16
Amen mother let it be
Before long he was crowned queen for all the world to see bloody body face down
The wages of sin are surely death that's what mama used to say
So there was no sympathy.

Religion was certainly an object of critique during the Black nationalist movement of the 1960s. In fact, Malcolm X called for the deemphasis of religious differences in the interest of racial solidarity in his Black Nationalist primer speech, "The Ballot or the Bullet" in 1964. Ndegeocello shares this spirit of critique but departs from that tradition by addressing the homophobia that at best went unchecked, and at worst was fueled by misguided conceptions of homosexuality as a counterrevolutionary force in Black America. While her work embraces a Black aesthetic that grounds itself in the needs and experiences of Black people, Ndegeocello departs from Black nationalist iterations with an impassioned plea for intrarracial understanding and acceptance across difference that is literally a matter of life and death for Black queer people.

Spoken Word as Signifier of Authenticity and Integrity

Even as hip hop moved far beyond its origins in the 1970s spatially, culturally, and economically, spoken word as a particular vocal practice different from traditional rapping continued to assert itself in the works of artists both within and adjacent to hip-hop music as a contested site —both as a manifestation of antiquated Black nationalist politics and as a signifier of authenticity and integrity necessary to purify an increasingly commercialized Black cultural landscape. For many members of the hip-hop generation, spoken word functioned to critique hip hop itself as it moved increasingly toward mainstream success and corporate control, reasserting itself when hip hop's essence as a radical means of Black creative resistance seemed compromised by corporate interests. However, with the eventual success of the television show *Def Poetry Jam*, as well as the incorporation of spoken word into the works of neo-soul artists like The Roots and Jill Scott,[10] spoken word became a commercial force on a level not seen since

---

[10] Some great examples include The Roots' "The Return to Innocence Lost," featuring Philadelphia-based spoken word artist Ursula Rucker, and Jill Scott's "Watching Me" and "Love Rain" from her debut album, *Who Is Jill Scott?: Words and Sounds Vol. 1.*

the Black Arts Movement by functioning as a lucrative alternative to the supposed vapidity of mainstream hip hop.

The corporate influence on hip-hop music and culture started early. With the mid-1980s successes of artists like Run DMC and LL Cool J, rap music was maximized as an accessible and packageable commodity that could serve the needs of capitalist rather than communal interests. In this context, it makes sense that spoken word poetry, an egalitarian and street-level art form adjacent and formative to hip hop at its inception, would be harnessed and gain resonance as a means of creative resistance to corporate influence on Black cultural expression itself.

The 1990s was a fraught time for Black America on multiple fronts, and in ways that would inform both hip hop specifically and its relationship with the artistic practice of spoken word. The post–Civil Rights era saw the emergence of a Black political elite that was active in the Civil Rights and Black Power movements before going on to take elected office and move firmly into mainstream electoral politics. In *From #BlackLivesMatter to Black Liberation*, Keeanga-Yamahtta Taylor describes how this Black political elite – in ways intentional and unintentional – asserted a politics of exceptionalism and respectability that would only strengthen destructive narratives of Black pathology, the misguided ideological constructs of upward mobility and individual responsibility, and destructive government austerity measures that hurt communities of color.

In this context, hip hop became a major focal point and lightning rod for debates concerning these harmful myths and narratives, which often played out in the media. As Robin Kelley asserts in *Yo Mama's Disfunktional!: Fighting the Culture Wars in Urban America*, Black low-income communities were smeared as lazy, violent, and to blame for their own misfortune by both conservatives and Black elites. Such rhetoric only served to exacerbate class division, inflame the crack epidemic, and reinforce bipartisan "tough on crime" politics that shattered Black communities.

It is in this larger context that spoken word would reemerge as a vital ingredient of Black artistic expression. Prior to the late 1990s, many media representations of Black spoken word and performance poetry were caricatures, depicting spoken word artists in a stereotypical light, complete with parodic signifiers like afros and dashikis, archaic Black nationalist rhetoric, and unfocused rage. Spoken word was associated with a retrograde, out-of-touch, and overly militant Black politics of the past. Examples of this abound in some of the era's most popular Black films and sitcoms. Landmark sketch comedy show *In Living Color* featured the recurring character Ice Poe, a hack who caricatured the archetypal angry, radical Black male spoken word poet in order to hustle money from people in the street. An episode of *The Fresh Prince of Bel Air* featured Will Smith's character taking on the pen name Raphael de la Ghetto to draft funny, faux-profound poems. Later, family butler Jeffrey reveals he was a righteous Black nationalist poet during the 1960s, and performs a satirical poem in an afro and dashiki for an audience of astounded and impressed white people. And in *Don't Be a Menace to South Central While Drinking Your Juice in the Hood* (1996) – a filmic parody of the many so-called hood films released during the 1990s – the character Dashiki is a Black female poet who pens absurdly angry and violent poems about Black men, lampooning Janet Jackson's poet character in John Singleton's *Poetic Justice* (1993).

However, alternative rap (OutKast, Mos Def, The Roots), the neo-soul movement (Erykah Badu, Jill Scott), and films like *Love Jones* (1997) and *Slam* (1998) also presented spoken word as part of an emerging, hip hop–influenced Black bohemian culture that was both artistically rich and culturally relevant. By the end of the 1990s spoken word was widely recognized as a smart, politically astute, and cutting-edge practice of Black cultural surrogacy vital to the contemporary moment. In the midst of a booming Black culture industry, spoken word influenced music and film works that offered an accessible alternative to an increasingly commercialized and sanitized Black cultural landscape.

A key factor in the rise in popularity of spoken word in the 1990s is the success of slam poetry. The brainchild of writer Marc Smith, the first poetry slams were held in the 1980s in Chicago. Slams are spoken word open mics in the form of competition, in which poets battle as competitors and their performances are scored by judges chosen from the audience (Banales). The competitiveness of slam poetry is reminiscent of hip hop, where battles – between emcees, DJs, and break-dancers – is foundational to the culture. Thus, slam poetry would appeal to hip-hop fans, and bring a healthy dose of hip-hop culture to the world of poetry, a sphere of artistic expression widely associated with a far more conservative community. The fast-paced and highly performative nature of the poetry slam greatly influenced the nature of this form of poetic expression. Like the art of emceeing, slam poetry is often performed with considerable vigor to seize control of public space, and with keen awareness of how it will be received by an audience on first listen. Additionally, slam poems are often politically charged, tackling issues related to race, gender, sexuality, class, identity, authenticity, and the capitalist exploitation of artistic expression itself, especially the commercialization of hip hop.

Slam poetry spread like wildfire throughout the 1990s. The movement would directly influence the zenith of spoken word's popularity, *Def Poetry Jam*. Produced by hip-hop impresario Russell Simmons and hosted by alternative rap hero Mos Def, *Def Poetry Jam* premiered on HBO in 2002 as a weekly half-hour showcase for spoken word poetry's finest young practitioners, mostly of color – including Black Ice, Georgia Me, Stacey-Ann Chin, and Suheir Hammad – as well as hip-hop artists like Erykah Badu, Kanye West, and DMX. Before a live audience, *Def Poetry* brought the spoken word movement to the masses by overtly connecting it with hip-hop music and culture at the very moment that the genre was fully saturating American popular culture. The show ran for six seasons, generated great ratings for HBO, and spurred a published collection (Medina and Rivera) and a Tony Award–winning live stage production.[11]

Def Poetry Jam marks the peak of spoken word's popularity, of its cachet as a vital ingredient in the larger gumbo of hip-hop music and culture, and as a lucrative commodity fit for corporate exploitation. While corporate influence always threatens to appropriate and sanitize Black cultural expression, *Def* poets offered a welcome dose of radical politics that challenged dehumanizing representations of Black communities, rampant post-9/11 Islamophobia, and the neoconservative policies of the Bush administration. And although the commercialization of spoken word – like the commercialization of Black cultural products broadly – is a double-edged sword, serving the needs of capital, and thus strengthening the racial capitalist system that inherently perpetuates the antiblack structures of our world, it also served to amplify the voices and incendiary politics of people of color on a mass scale, and inspired a generation of Black youth to pick up a pen and a microphone.

In fact, slam poetry continues to be at the center of a youth-driven movement around spoken word. For example, Young Chicago Authors is an organization renowned for creative writing and performance poetry programs that reach young people of diverse backgrounds in and around the Chicago area.[12] The organization's annual poetry festival, Louder Than a Bomb, is "the largest youth poetry festival in the world," according to its website. The festival stages the slam poetry experience on a mass scale, featuring poetry tournaments and workshops led by young people that encourage them to use art to share their stories, dreams, and values with other youth. Perhaps the most politically significant quality of spoken

---

[11] "The Winners," https://archive.nytimes.com/www.nytimes.com/ref/arts/theater/12TONY-LIST.html.

[12] "Programs," Young Chicago Authors, https://youngchicagoauthors.org/.

word in the twenty-first century is that it continues to inspire young people to think critically about the world around them and to raise their voices and tell their stories in an environment where they can both affirm others and be affirmed themselves. In an increasingly corporatized, policed, and mediated world, it doesn't get more radical than that.

The Enduring Influence of Spoken Word

Spoken word continues to be a key influence and creative ingredient for works by some of the most forward-thinking and influential Black artists of today. Beyoncé and Kendrick Lamar are two key figures in twenty-first-century Black popular music who have harnessed spoken word prominently in works lauded for their substantive engagement with the socio-political concerns of Black people.

Lamar's *To Pimp a Butterfly* (2015) is one of the most critically acclaimed albums of the twenty-first century, a kaleidoscopic journey across the spectrum of Black musical expression. The album is extremely dense, jam-packed with ideas, clever significations, and radical politics. Considering this ambition, it is no surprise that the spoken word stylings of the Last Poets and Gil Scott-Heron make their way into Lamar's sonic world. "For Free" is a fast-paced free jazz freakout in which Lamar adopts the cadence of a 1960s Black nationalist poet, slipping and sliding in, out, and across rapid-fire accusations and admonishments toward America and its continued exploitation, or "pimping," of Black bodies – hence the refrain, "This dick ain't free!" Lamar channels the spoken word aesthetic to levy a critique that – although perhaps specific to the machinations and manipulations of the recording industry – addresses the timelessness of structural antiblackness by way of the timeless tradition of Black performance poetry.

In fact, Lamar harnesses spoken word to provide the scaffolding for the entire *To Pimp a Butterfly* album. Through its recitation during the album's many interludes, Lamar builds a spoken word piece that reaches its full realization on the album's final track, "Mortal Man," as a rumination on the responsibility Lamar feels to assume a leadership role for young Black men, and the fear, insecurity, and guilt that arise from the pressures of that position. With the completion of the poem, the listener finally has a full picture of the psychological, spiritual, and political dilemma at the heart of *Butterfly* – how do young Black men navigate the treacherous, white supremacist terrain of American capitalism without being compromised and corrupted by it? And what will it take to break that oppressive system entirely? Again, it is unfortunately a timeless conundrum, and one that Lamar tackles with clarity and cohesion on *Butterfly*.

While Lamar's *Butterfly* breathlessly reinterprets the spoken word aesthetic of the 1960s and 1970s, it does not depart from that aesthetic conceptually. In fact, its phallocentrism is a direct outgrowth of that era's laser focus on the crisis of Black manhood as the central concern of the project of Black liberation. It is Beyoncé's masterpiece, *Lemonade*, released a year later, that harnesses the spoken word aesthetic in a way that actually expands our understanding of its aesthetic value by weaving performance poetry into the fabric of a project that explores and celebrates the heterogeneity of Blackness at the intersection of race, gender, and sexuality.

Beyoncé's second album, *Lemonade* – accompanied on its release by a film on HBO of the same title – is her most ambitious project to date. An exploration of her experience dealing with her partner's infidelity – addressed on both personal and political terms – the album's fascinating visuals are held together by Beyoncé's spoken word–styled performance of the poetry of Somali British poet Warsan Shire. According to Janell Hobson, Shire's poetry is the glue that holds *Lemonade* together as a cohesive cinematic experience, grounding the film as a Black feminist testimonial to the abuse and betrayal experienced by women of color historically and into the present day, and as a testimonial to the will to persist and thrive in the face of racist and misogynist violence or, as the title suggests, to "turn lemons into lemonade."

As with many Black artists before her in the post–Civil Rights era, Beyoncé harnesses the practice of spoken word to explore questions of identity and power but does so in a way that disidentifies with the Black nationalist aesthetic of a homogenized, patriarchal iteration of Blackness. The film features gorgeous images of Black women across a range of colors and body types, as well as visual expressions of Black queer identity and love, all accompanied by expertly crafted pop music that reaches across the spectrum of genre and style to reflect the vastness of Black creative expression – all at the artistic fingertips of a prodigiously talented woman of color. Spoken word completes *Lemonade* by threading together its striking visuals and dynamic songwriting. The result is a stunning exploration of the complexity of Black womanhood, and one of the most important albums of the twenty-first century.

Lemonade typifies a redefined Black aesthetic for a new generation of Black youth engaged in some of the fieriest, most radical, and sustained organizing work since the 1960s. Black Lives Matter, as a movement and mantra, has revolutionized not just Black politics, but American political discourse by asserting unapologetic Blackness that celebrates complexity and difference. The marriage of Black radicalism and capitalism is always problematic; *Lemonade* attempts the impossible task of straddling the line between commercial product and rebel manifesto. Yet, even in that fraught position, the album harnesses spoken word to maximize the radical possibilities of Black popular culture – modeling a critical posture toward the hegemonic status quo, while also functioning itself as a rich site for critique and contestation.

WORKS CITED

Avilez, GerShun. *Radical Aesthetics and Modern Black Nationalism.* Urbana: University of Illinois Press, 2016.

Banales, M. "Slam Poetry." *Encyclopedia Britannica*, April 6, 2018. www .britannica.com/art/slam-poetry.

Chang, Jeff. *Can't Stop, Won't Stop: A History of the Hip-Hop Generation.* New York: St. Martin's Press, 2005.

Chadwick, Alex. "Comic 'Dolemite' Leaves Mark on Hip-Hop." NPR, October 21, 2008, www.npr.org/templates/story/story.php?storyId=95935377.

Cleaver, Eldridge. *Soul On Ice.* New York: Dell, 1968.

Gates, Henry Louis, Jr. *The Signifying Monkey: A Theory of African-American Literary Criticism.* New York: Oxford University Press, 1989.

Hobson, Janell. *Venus in the Dark: Blackness and Beauty in Popular Culture.* New York: Routledge, 2018.

hooks, bell. *We Real Cool: Black Men and Masculinity.* New York: Routledge, 2004.

Hughes, Langston. "The Negro Artist and the Racial Mountain." In *Within the Circle: An Anthology of African American Literary Criticism from the Harlem Renaissance to the Present*, edited by Angelyn Mitchell. Durham, NC: Duke University Press, 1994, pp. 55–59.

Jones, Leroi. *Home: Social Essays.* New York: William Morrow, 1966.

Kelley, Robin D. G. *Yo' Mama's Disfunktional!: Fighting the Culture Wars in Urban America.* Boston: Beacon Press, 1997.

Medina, Tony, and Louis Reyes Rivera. *Bum Rush the Page: A Def Poetry Jam.* New York: Three Rivers Press, 2001.

Muñoz, José Esteban. *Disidentifications: Queers of Color and the Performance of Politics.* Minneapolis: University of Minnesota Press, 1999.

Springer, Kimberly. *Living for the Revolution: Black Feminist Organizations, 1968–1980.* Durham, NC: Duke University Press, 2005.

Taylor, Keeanga-Yamahtta. *From #BlackLivesMatter to Black Liberation.* Chicago: Haymarket Books, 2016.

X, Malcolm. *Malcolm X: The Ballot or the Bullet.* North Hollywood, CA: Pacifica Foundation, 1965.

CHAPTER 14

Language as Politics in Twentieth- and Twenty-First-Century American Poetry

Tyrone Williams

During the 1970s a new mode of avant-garde practice, language writing, emerged as a reaction to what was perceived as the "cookie-cutter" workshop poem propagated in MFA programs. Though generally characterized by antiexpressionist values (e.g., nonlinear syntax, agrammatical structures, and the demotion of semantic coherence), language writing was initially a loose coalition of writers practicing outside the MFA workshop models prevalent in academia. However, as language writing began to crystallize around social formations (the high school and college friendships among the key language writers Barrett Watten, Ron Silliman, Lyn Hejinian, and Carla Harryman), political values (the expansion of antiwar protests against the Vietnam conflict into Marxist critiques of capitalist imperialism and colonialism), and militant aesthetics (the "turn to language"), the movement was criticized by different camps of poets and critics. Representing both "mainstream" poetics associated with academia and "marginal" poetics associated with racial, ethnic, and sexual minorities, these poets and critics viewed the "turn to language," on the one hand, as a turning away from traditional poetic values and, on the other hand, as an abandonment of social and cultural crises whose urgency seemed to demand the most transparent, direct, and accessible language. While the poetics (and to a lesser extent, the politics) of San Francisco poets like Allen Ginsberg, Kenneth Rexroth, and Robin Blaser set important precedents for the language writers, the latter understood their practice as something more than just a return to, and extension of, the 1950s and 1960s Cold War anarchist politics of the Beat writers. The turn also represented a reconception of the relationship between politics and poetics at the height of the Vietnam conflict, which for many of the language writers represented another stage of the Cold War. Theorizing that anarchism tended to dovetail with American individualism, as evident in the "do your own thing" philosophy of hippie gurus like Timothy Leary, Watten and Silliman, in particular, widely considered the cofounders of language writing, reached beyond the Beats in order to rehabilitate the experimental writings and Marxist politics of, among others, the Objectivist poets, who had started writing and publishing in the 1930s. Louis Zukofsky's and George Oppen's combination of innovative writing and social critique made them especially significant to Watten and Silliman. Thus the more linear narrative forms deployed by Objectivists such as Carl Rakosi, Charles Reznikoff, Muriel Rukeyser, and Lorine Niedecker led to their relative neglect by Watten and Silliman despite their avowal of leftist politics. And while the Objectivists interrogated their alienation from mainstream America as a function, in part, of covert (when not overt) anti-Semitism, the language writers, by and large, ignored or marginalized this aspect of their precursors' experiences, blind spots replicated in relationship to the racial, gender, and sexual orientation upheavals of the 1970s and 1980s.

Thus, as we will see, the language writers' indifference or blindness to other poetries being written in the early and mid-twentieth century set the foundation for the later charges of sexism and racism against them. This separation of particular individuals from earlier poetry movements points less to a certain narrowness of language poetics than to a recognition (conscious or not) that the Objectivists were no more a coterie than those initially associated with language writing. In other words, the language poets initially gravitated toward specific poets, not general movements. Only later, as they began to theorize their poetics in formal essays, did the movements to which specific poets belonged, or were assigned, became more significant. However, it would be misleading to see this particular relationship as a microcosm of poetry movements in general. Some poetry movements, like the Objectivists and language writing, are self-consciously organized as social formations around which related – but not homogenous – aesthetics coalesce. Others are belatedly assigned by critics and academics to manage and give coherence to a body of writing, a process that necessarily will exclude or demote poets writing in the same period and, often, with similar aesthetics. Thus, modernism, as a general category referring to writers reacting to modernity (industrialism, nationalism, and the rise of democratic and autocratic states), is parsed out into eugenicist-inspired categories: lowbrow, middlebrow, and highbrow modernisms (see below).

In many respects the elliptical serialism of Zukofsky and Oppen (both their "early" and "late" works) corresponds to the "high" modernism of Ezra Pound, T. S. Eliot, and Wallace Stevens, while the more straightforward "witnessing" that informs the poetics of Rakosi, Reznikoff, and

Rukeyser corresponds to the "low" modernism of Carl Sandburg, Langston Hughes, and Sterling Brown. However convenient as a mode of academic categorization, this way of thinking about early twentieth-century American poetry neglects the many differences within discrete poetic movements. While academic critics and poets are generally familiar with the poetic and political differences between Pound, Eliot, and Stevens, they are, perhaps, less familiar with the differences among the language writers. In this regard, it is important to recall that the anthology that introduced the language writers to most American poets and critics, *In the Language Tree*, was edited by one person, Ron Silliman. It is also important to recall that the anthology was published in 1986, a decade and half after the first issue of the journal devoted to language writing, *This*, edited by Barrett Watten, appeared. Thus, as Silliman's introductory essay makes clear, the anthology is a rearguard defense of the poetics of language writing, a defense that proceeds by tracing the "origins" of the movement to many past and contemporary movements (e.g., concrete poetry) and individual poets (e.g., Susan Howe and Michael Palmer) working outside the traditional lyric and narrative traditions. For Silliman at least, the effect of the anthology and his essay is canonical: a case is being made for why language writing should not be regarded as an aggregate of outliers but as an important movement "within" the history of twentieth-century American poetry and poetics.

The dissolution of the movement near the beginning of the twenty-first century can be attributed to internal differences and external forces, the latter cause due to the appearance of other movements (new narrative, performance poetry/spoken word, post-avant, flarf, conceptual writing, etc.). Still, the rise and fall of language writing offers an object lesson for those today who have taken up the struggle to wield poetics and poetry as political weapons against mainstream and academic institutions of poetry (i.e., the poetry business or, more acerbically, the po' biz).

The title of Silliman's anthology, *In the Language Tree*, was taken from a Kit Robinson poem that rewrites William Carlos Williams' important book on the origins of the American character, *In the American Grain*. Whereas Williams traces the "grain" of American character back through its Puritan "stem" to its roots in Christian missionaries and political/economic colonization in nine chapters of prose, Robinson compresses this history into fifteen tercets, a series of sardonic observations that begin by alluding to Eliot's world-weary "Gerontion": "A bitter wind taxes the will / causing dry syllables / to rise from the throat" (viii). Robinson's poem is meant to be paradigmatic of the anthology's dismissal of

modernist regret and conservative nostalgia. At the same time its traditional formal features (those fifteen tercets) serve as a reminder that as late
as 1986 language writing still included a poet like Robinson whose work,
then and today, draws on traditional prosodic tools. Robinson's writing is a
reminder that while language writing often deployed agrammatical and/or
antisyntactical structures as motivating forces, it merely demoted (not
erased) expressionist features in favor of impressionist and surrealist values.
Inasmuch as Robinson's work draws from both canonical and noncano-
nical, expressionist and objectivist, poetries and values, his poetry represented a sector of a broad range of practices under the rubric of language
writing as Silliman imagined it in 1986.

The range of procedures and values in the anthology is evident in the
writings of the main core of language writers. Concrete poetics appear in
Michael Gottlieb's "Fourteen Poems," whose "tone" is visually indicated
by alternating Anglo-Saxon/"English," upper- and lowercases:

> FOCKE-WULFS
> callow
> HELLING
> screed
> HEAD-
> WOUNDS
> swab. (377)

In "Wintry," Robert Grenier uses a laconic lexicon to evoke claustrophobic
Nazi ideology:

> oh veil I, oh well, I
> well I don't know
> oh, veil, I don't know
>
> Ah yah
> ah, yah
> ja
> a sod hut
> snow
> blue
> eyes . . . (5–6)

Both Barrett Watten and Lyn Hejinian draw on surrealist parataxis in their
work. Watten's "Plasma" begins this way: "A paradox is eaten by the space
around it // I'll repeat what I said. // To make a city into a season is to wear
sunglasses inside a volcano" (26). And in her bestselling *My Life*, Hejinian
draws attention to the ways that nonlinear structures of memory and

observation can confound rhetorical logics: "The traffic drones, where drones is a noun. Whereas, the cheerful pessimist suits himself in a bad world, which is however the inevitable world, impossible of improvement" (*In the American Tree* 51). All of this work is drawn from *In the American Tree* and suggests the range of writings outside the academic and poetry institutions dominant at the time.

In large part, the poets that became associated with language writing were white, straight, and middle-class (though Silliman is from the working class). Most important, not all the writers included in Silliman's *In the American Tree* would come to be associated with language writing as a self-conscious movement. Forty-plus writers appear in the 1986 Silliman anthology. By 2006 when Barrett Watten published the first edition of the ten-volume *The Grand Piano*, subtitled "an experiment in collective autobiography," only ten writers were represented. This is not merely an indication of attrition or, more pugnaciously, "desertion" from the ranks. Aside from egalitarian differences of opinion, outright and sometimes volatile disagreements about what "language writing" means, as well as the desire on the part of some writers to not be pigeonholed, the reduced number of writers recalling what language writing was also indicates the dispersion and dissemination of language poetics across the general field of American poetry (and beyond). For example, Watten's two major studies in the first two decades of the twenty-first century, *The Constructivist Moment* (2003) and *Questions of Poetics* (2016), respectively situate language writing within the broader international field of *poesis* (especially art and music) and trace the influence of language writing within contemporary poetics. On the other hand, Silliman's anthology is, as he clearly explains in his introduction, a survey of experimentation across the landscape of American poetry. Thus, Silliman's anthology is organized according to large swaths of geography (West and East), concluding with a kind of collective *ars poetics* called Second Front.

However, what is missing, geographically, from Silliman's anthology is the Midwest, precisely what the Chicago Renaissance, for example, had covered not only in the early twentieth century but also, arguably, in the 1960s and 1970s as an important locus of the Black Arts Movement. Given language writing's early animus against the kind of narrative and lyric poetry and poetics that dominated (and continues to dominate) academic creative writing programs and is still promulgated in journals like *Prairie Schooner*, *The Kenyon Review*, and *American Poetry Review*, one might charitably view Silliman's exclusion of Midwestern poets and poetics as less a prejudice against, or elitist snub of, "flyover" territory than a strategic refusal to endorse an already dominant narrative and lyric tradition. That this tradition had been adopted by black, brown, and working-class white poets (to say nothing of other poets who belonged to other ethnic and/or sexual groups) meant that the Marxist poetics of several of the language writers found itself in direct, or sometimes indirect, conflict with the leftist poetics of feminist, working-class, and "people of color" (POC) poets. It is not surprising, then, that language writing was attacked by both mainstream academic poets as well as insurgent POC, queer, and feminist poets.

One approach to the question of the relationship between language and politics in twentieth- and twenty-first-century American poetry is to specify the categories of "low," "middle," and "high" modernism. This simplification is useful despite the problematics of categorization within American culture industries that regularly mix and blend cultural products from all three "classes." In that sense, the terms refer less to actual cultural products than their perceived functions as reflections of social and economic classes. Despite its pretensions of a democratic ethos that suffuses all spheres of life, the United States has always been a culture riven by class anxieties. Consequently, these terms – high, middle, and low – serve as heuristic guideposts here and can help us understand why the Objectivists, who might be viewed as "high" modernists from the perspective of our present, tended to view themselves as "low" modernists, not because of the economic or social status (most were middle-class) but because of ethnicity (most were Jewish) and politics (as noted above, almost all were leftists). And while language writers like Watten, Harryman, and Hejinian rightly regarded themselves as middle-class modernists (Silliman was born into a working-class family), today they all, including Silliman, are probably regarded as high modernists because of their avant-garde aesthetics.

Before turning to the Objectivists who were so influential on several (but not all) language writers, we need to go back to what is often cited as the "origin" of modernist poetry, Imagism, which flourished between 1909 and 1917. Reacting to what they regarded as the linguistic and emotional excesses of Romantic and Victorian poetry, the Imagists – T. E. Hulme, Ezra Pound, Amy Lowell, and others – emphasized economy of language, clarity of expression, and brevity of presentation. Because many of these aesthetic values became the foundation for some of the "high" modernist poets – in addition to Pound, Eliot, and Stevens – Imagism itself has often been regarded as the beginning of aesthetic elitism in modern poetry. For a long time, it had been a critical commonplace that Amy Lowell "stole" the movement from Ezra Pound, but recent scholarship has taken a more complex and nuanced view of the competition between the two poets. Scholar Paul Ballew notes that though Lowell came from an aristocratic background, she was a great popularizer of poetry. As an editor of important anthologies, she gave poets equal space and allowed them to design the layout of their poems. According to Ballew, Pound was the opposite. He wielded absolute control over the first Imagist anthology, *Des Imagistes*; selected the poets and poems; and designed the layout. More telling, all the original Imagist poets – Richard Aldington, H.D., D. H. Lawrence, and others – preferred working with Lowell rather than Pound. Finally, as proof of her popularizing ethos, Lowell's anthologies outsold Pound's. In brief, the "lowbrow" Lowell was better known and better liked than the "highbrow" Pound.

In many respects the problem of modern poetry and politics begins with this rivalry between Lowell and Pound. On the one hand, Lowell's enthusiasm for popularizing poetry, by which is meant her expanding both its readership and its practitioners, reflected a democratic ethos – the more the better – largely silent about cultural and social tensions. On the other, Pound's enthusiasm for difficult poetry presupposed the creation of a cultural elite patronized and supported by neo-aristocrats. However poor his understanding of premodern Chinese and Japanese literary and dramatic traditions, Pound drew a direct connection between imperial politics and literary excellence. For Pound and, to a lesser extent, Eliot, the lyrical sincerity of the English Romantics and Victorians was merely a reflection of, not engagement with, modernity (i.e., industrialism, capitalism, nationalism, and democratic movements). A new poetry had to be reconstituted from the "ruins" upon which industrialism, democracy, and secularism had built their institutions. Collage, in both its imagist and epic forms (e.g., *The Cantos* and *The Waste Land*), thus had the effect of shifting the function of the poet from reporter of the internal and external worlds to assembler of those worlds. In brief, Pound and Eliot could not embrace the modern world as it was; for them the poet had to change the world and do so by revisiting and revising the past as passed down through parallel and overlapping histories. This understanding of the poet's stance in relation to the external world can be seen not only in Pound's and Eliot's major works but also in H.D.'s *Helen in Egypt* and Stevens' "Thirteen Ways of Looking at a Blackbird."

The Objectivists, especially Williams, Oppen, Zukofsky, Reznikoff, and Rakosi, responded to Pound and Eliot by, to varying degrees, separating the anti-Semitic and racist politics of Pound, Eliot, and Stevens from their aesthetic achievements as poets. Pound was, in fact, a mentor and supporter of almost all the Objectivists and he introduced several of them to one another. Politically, the Objectivists all had left-wing tendencies, and three – Zukofsky, Oppen, and Reznikoff – were Marxists. Moreover, their ethnicities – Williams was half Puerto Rican and the others were Jewish – made them all, to varying degrees, apposite vis-à-vis mainstream American culture and politics. More provocatively, the Objectivists insisted on "sincerity" as an ethos, but their general understanding of this term should not be confused with its Romanticist meaning. Whereas Romantic sincerity in the works of John Keats, William Wordsworth, John Clare, and others was, to varying degrees, a sign of the desire to "report" and "express" common concerns in a common language (again, depending on the particular poet), the Objectivist sense of sincerity tended to focus on the desire to define the objects in the world within social, cultural, and political contexts. In brief, if the measure of Romantic sincerity is its expressiveness in the common language of ordinary people, the measure of Objectivist sincerity is the rendering of an object's impression upon the poet. Given their status as ethnic "others" in a largely white, Protestant culture, the Objectivists could not, by and large, presume a 'commons' in the way the Romantics, or Stevens, Eliot, and Pound, had. Still, from a formal and aesthetic perspective, the first-generation modernists had an important influence on the Objectivists, one that would later show up in certain Beat aesthetics as well as in the political and aesthetic concerns of the language poets. Pound's and Eliot's assembly of the epical poem as a collection of paratactic fragments or parts would influence the formal properties of Zukofsky's *A*, Reznikoff's *Testimony*, Williams' *Paterson*, and H.D.'s *Helen in Egypt*.

However, the high modernists are not the only story of early twentieth-century American poetry. The "low" modernism of Carl Sandburg and Langston Hughes, celebrating the ordinary pleasures and disappointments of life in a readily accessible language, to say nothing of the "middlebrow" modernism of Robert Frost, would come to represent most Americans' idea of what poetry is, or should be, consigning Stevens, Pound, and Eliot to the insular chambers of literary academia. Yet, in regard to aesthetic influences, it was the second-generation "high" modernist Objectivist revisions of the first generation (Pound, Eliot, and Stevens) that inspired the formal achievements and, to a certain extent, political orientation, of the language writers. In other words, given the largely leftist orientation of the language writers, why did they, for the most part, eschew the working-class aesthetics that permeated the writings of the Chicago and Harlem Renaissance poets? Race (white) and class (middle) cannot account for this exclusion, since many white, middle-class, young people and college students were drawn to, listened to, read, and supported the experimental work of the Harlem Renaissance and, later, the Beat Poets and the Black Arts Movement. Aside from the question of poetics, the social and cultural criticism directed at the language writers might be related to this blind spot in their work.

Still, we should not overstate the case. Not every up-and-coming poet or movement expressed hostility toward language writing. Given that a few of the language writers had acquired academic positions by the end of the twentieth century (Lyn Hejinian at UC Berkeley, Barrett Watten at Wayne State University, Rachel du Plessis at Temple, Bob Perelman and Charles Bernstein at the University of Pennsylvania), it is not surprising that some of their students were more appreciative of language writing even as some of them moved on to become part of what is sometimes referred to as post-avant writing. Unlike the specific privileging of parataxis and leftist politics underpinning much of language writing, post-avant poetics are broad and varied; "post-avant" simply means after language writing, the hyphen suggesting a writing and politics influenced by, yet independent of, the language poets. Some of the post-avant poets (e.g., Juliana Spahr) have been very critical of what they regard as the hetero-normative and masculinist values underwriting language writing, while others (e.g., Kristen Prevallet) have situated these patriarchal tendencies within a broader cultural context, indicated by the stance of the journals Spahr and Prevallet cofounded, *Chain* and *Apex of the M*, respectively,

Post-avant writing had not, of course, been the first nonacademic movement to challenge some of the precepts of language writing. Its straight male hegemony had already been implicitly challenged by New Narrative writing, which arose alongside language writing in the 1970s in the East Bay. New Narrative, started by Bruce Boone and Bob Gluck, adopted many of the aesthetic strategies of language writing (parataxis, found materials, etc.) to focus on gay, lesbian, and queer prose writing. Unlike most language writing, however, New Narrative is explicit in its leftist and, above all, sexual liberationist politics. And while Gary Indiana, Gail Scott, Dennis Cooper, and Kathy Acker may be its most "famous" practitioners, New Narrative has had a long and lasting influence on American fiction and poetry through second-generation writers such as Kevin Killian, Dodie Bellamy, Camille Roy, and Rob Halpern. Finally, because it came into existence as a complement and response to language writing, New Narrative cannot be situated as one of the post-avant movements that began emerging during the 1990s.

Post-avant poetry can be understood as largely a generational phenomenon, inclusive of all those poets influenced by, but not members of, language writing. In general, post-avant poets are not part of the mainstream narrative and lyric traditions noted above. Their work is often innovative, sometimes reworking older traditional poetic forms like the villanelle, sonnet, palindrome, and sestina, and sometimes creating nonce forms. Parataxis within individual lines is sometimes employed, but more often these poets juxtapose large sections or stanzas not connected by linear narrative. This juxtaposition points to another feature of post-avant poetry: a preference for long, if not serial, forms, thus eschewing the traditional lyric or ballad. However, as the term "post-avant" might also suggest, these innovations in form and writing do not presuppose a political orientation. For that reason, it might be easy to assume that the use of nonce and torqued forms, to say nothing of nonlinear syntax, is merely a hipster's game or a mode of pure aestheticism. However, as I noted above regarding the work of post-avant poets such as Juliana Spahr and Kristin Prevallet, an ethical imperative drives a great deal of this writing, one reason its practitioners tend to be from marginalized ethnic, racial, or sexual groups in American society. The late Reginald Shepherd constructed his own partial list of first- and second-generation post-avant writers in his essay, "Who You Callin' 'Post-Avant'?" In truth, these two lists include writers working in traditional lyric and narrative modes (e.g., Lucia Brock-Broido, Carolyn Forché, Alice Fulton, Jorie Graham, Joseph Lease, Donald Revell) even if some, by no means all, of them may be understood as reworking them. On the other hand, it certainly is the case that those with an explicit political agenda (excepting avowed Marxists like Jeff Clark, Joshua Clover, and Jasper Bernes) are mostly absent from his lists. Insofar as it seems almost encyclopedic in its breadth, it might be said that Shepherd's understanding of post-avant poetry is the new mainstream.

Unlike my list below, Shepherd's list includes only two poets of color, and no black women poets (never mind other women of color), though in 2007–8 (when Shepherd composed his essay), Erica Hunt and Harryette Mullen, for example, were well-established experimental poets. For this reason and more, I will define post-avant poetry as post–language writing that adopts any number of pre-language poetics (from New American poetics via Robert Duncan to feminist lyricism per Denise Levertov) as well as some language writing strategies (e.g., parataxis) to interrogate both micropolitics (including identity politics) and macropolitics (e.g., ecopoetics). From Shepherd's list the poets I would identify as post-avant would include, along with Spahr and Prevallet, Julie Carr, Christine Hume, Laura

Mullen, Timothy Liu, Brenda Iijima, and Elizabeth Willis. And aside from Hunt and Mullen, I would also add, per women poets of color, Wendy Trevino, Dawn Lundy Martin, Duriel Harris, Hoa Nguyen, and others. Some of these poets (Carr, Martin, Nguyen) are more lyrical than others; some (Trevino, Iijima) are more explicitly political than others. Despite the swath of poetics Shepherd and others assign to the category of post-avant poetics, their general political orientation (critiquing misogyny, environmental crises, racism, homophobia, etc.) distinguish them from two other movements that owe their legacy more directly to language writing.

Flarf and conceptual poetry, two important early twenty-first-century movements, can be understood as, respectively, parodic and ironic variations on the language school. Both movements bracket political issues and foreground their formal properties in order to mock (flarf) and demonstrate, by reductio ad absurdum (conceptual poetry), the malleability of quotation, a primary strategy of language writing. Moreover, like at least one proponent of language writing, individuals from both schools have found themselves in hot water over perceived insensitivity to racial and ethnic issues. For this reason, however unfairly, both flarf and conceptual writing have been attacked as regressive movements out of touch with the social, cultural and racial politics of the twenty-first century. However, from the point of view of traditional literary aesthetics, both movements have been criticized by academic and nonacademic critics for different, if related, reasons.

Flarf was "created" by New York poet Gary Sullivan in 2000 when he submitted an intentionally bad poem to a poetry contest. Apparently, Sullivan wanted to demonstrate the absurdity of poetry competitions (from NEA grants to first book contests) in general. Encouraging some of his other New York–based friends (and K. Silem Mohammed, based on the West Coast) to do the same, Sullivan, along with Sharon Mesmer, Drew Gardner, Nada Gordon, and others soon formalized their collective writings into a movement (the term "flarf" was taken from a Sullivan poem). Their method of creating poems by using internet search engines to compile random word lists that are then organized into poems was not as novel as it initially seemed, since deploying chance and constraint procedures to generate poetry can be traced back to the work of multimedia artists like John Cage and Jackson MacLow, the French-based Oulipo movement, and, before them, the early Surrealists and Dadaists. And since these chance operations are, in flarf, generated by specific term searches, flarf also bears a striking resemblance to the language operations of some

language writers. For example, in the emphasis on recording daily perceptions in parts of Silliman's *The Alphabet* or Lyn Hejinian's *My Life*, chance
resides in the unpredictability of random thoughts, objects, events, and
people within specified constraints (e.g., the sentence, the paragraph). For
flarf poets, the search term generates a linguistic frame or constraint, but
"creativity" is still present in how the poet organizes the prefabricated
materials. However, in deliberately creating "bad" poetry from random
internet searches, flarf poets thumb their noses at not only mainstream
poetry traditions but also emerging and experimental modes (including
much language writing) that position themselves as "serious" engagements
with social, cultural, and political issues. And so, as Sullivan notes, flarf is
playful, "corrosive," "un-P.C.," and so forth. For example, when flarf poet
Michael Magee used Asian stereotypes mined from the internet in one of
his poems in his book, *Mainstream*, he was called out by emerging poet
Craig Santos Perez. That Magee's poem was, in fact, an attempt to mine
racist and stereotypical language from the internet in order to neutralize it
was not lost on Perez, but Magee's "success" at doing so was, for Perez, a
matter of debate.

Unconventional though its aesthetic may be, flarf resembles other
American poetry movements in terms of its social and public dissemination. Not only have individual flarf poets published socially and culturally
important books (Michael Magee, Sharon Mesmer, Jordan Davis, Nada
Gordon, Ron Smith, and Drew Gardner, in particular), but its members
have also published an anthology of flarf poetry, organized reading series
throughout the country, and, with Gardner at the helm, dove into performance poetry via the Drew Gardner Flarf Orchestra, which has recorded a
CD. Once a New York–based phenomenon, flarf has become a permanent
presence throughout North America, influencing new generations of
young writers, not via academia so much as through the growing promi-
nence of small presses and reading series.

Much more controversial than flarf, conceptual writing, or conceptual
poetry, owes as much to language writing as it does to conceptualism in art
history. Conceptual art emphasizes the idea rather than the object, creating
what is sometimes termed nonretinal art, a direct reference to Marcel
Duchamp's readymades, which sought to neutralize the traditional visual
appeal of art. Conceptual art after Duchamp evolved in two primary
directions: one track emphasizes verbal descriptions of art objects, present
or absent, while the other track emphasizes appropriation of popular
cultural artifacts (e.g., Jeff Koons) or of classical masterpieces (e.g.,
Sherrie Levine). Conceptual poetry thus far has tended to focus on the

techniques of constraint (e.g., Christian Bok) and appropriation (Kenneth Goldsmith). The major practitioners of conceptual poetry include Kenneth Goldsmith, Craig Dworkin, Christian Bok, Vanessa Place, and Rob Fitterman. Because some conceptual poets mine the internet for source materials, the movement has affinities with flarf, and members of both groups have been mutually supportive. And as with previous movements, the differences among practitioners are often as interesting as their similarities. For example, Goldsmith has published entire books of a newspaper edition (*Day*), baseball game broadcasts (*Sports*), and urban traffic (*Traffic*), and weather reports (*The Weather*). In Bok's *Eunoia*, every chapter is dedicated to a single vowel while Place's *Statement of Facts* repurposes legalese verbatim from court trials and legal documents. Dworkin's most recent book, *The Pine-Woods Notebook*, draws on literary history and botany to investigate the very concept of "nature." Finally, like other poetry movements, the conceptual poets have organized reading series and events and published an anthology, *Against Expression: An Anthology of Conceptual Writing*, edited by Dworkin and Goldsmith.

As the title of the anthology makes clear, the conceptual poets, like the flarf and language writers, position themselves in opposition to the mainstream lyric and narrative traditions that still dominate American poetry. As noted above, a great number of emerging, heretofore marginalized, poets write within these traditions. Consequently, like language writing and flarf, conceptual poetry finds itself at odds – aesthetically and culturally, if not necessarily politically – with these emerging poetries. This opposition is all the more inflected by race, ethnicity, and sexuality when one notices that language, flarf, and conceptual writings are dominated by straight, white men and, to a lesser extent, women. Thus, it is not surprising that just as language and flarf poets have found themselves embroiled in racial and ethnic controversies, so too conceptual poets. Kenneth Goldsmith and Vanessa Place found themselves at the center of controversies within a couple of months of each other in early 2015. In March of that year Goldsmith participated in a conference at Brown University where he presented "The Body of Michael Brown," a remixing of the autopsy report on the young black man killed by a white policeman in Ferguson, Missouri, in August 2014. Although meant as a tribute to the death and after-death of Brown (hence the focus on the autopsy report), the performance was widely condemned as insensitive at best and racist at worst, and Goldsmith wound up donating his stipend to the Brown family. Two months later in May 2015 Vanessa Place was attacked for her tweets quoting the most racist passages in Margaret Mitchell's novel, *Gone with the Wind*. Like Goldsmith, Place wanted to underscore the racism of both the novel and author (she'd actually been quoting from the novel since 2009). Like Goldsmith, Place was criticized for being racially insensitive, if not outright racist, leading to cancellations of several events to which she had been invited. Still, even before these 2015 controversies, conceptual poetry had been criticized by experimental poets/critics as well as a coalition of post-avant poets, known collectively as the Mongrel Coalition against Gringpo. As Judith Goldman has argued, criticisms of language writing, flarf, and conceptual writing are not exclusively political or cultural in nature. All three movements have been attacked on aesthetic grounds as well, with critics from a number of quarters insisting that language, flarf, and conceptual writings are not really "poetry." Thus, academic defenders of the lyric and narrative traditions find themselves aligned with post-avant poets, including members of the anti-academic Mongrel Coalition, against the avant-garde. Their aesthetic differences notwithstanding, the post-avant poets, as a whole, have as their common denominator the lyric and narrative traditions that informed the poetics of some members of the feminist, brown, and Black Arts Movements during the 1960s and 1970s. In short, it remains an open question whether the micropolitics (sometimes called, disparagingly, identity politics) of one sector of post-avant poetics represents "progress" vis-à-vis the Marxism of the historical avant-garde or the macropolitics (predominantly ecopoetics) of that other sector of post-avant poetics.

Not all poets and critics view the politics (micro or macro) of post-avant poetics as more effective than the explicit Marxist critiques of the past. In her excellent analysis of the rumored death of the avant-garde, "Fuck the Avant-Garde," Rachel Greenwald Smith analyzes the contemporary poetry scenes in terms of what she calls compromise aesthetics. Greenwald reads this mode of compromise aesthetics as a political betrayal of the historical avant-garde's "uncompromising ethos of radical oppositionality." For her, the reduction of poetic and linguistic strategies associated with the historical avant-garde's mission to overturn the values of bourgeois culture to mere aesthetic techniques is an index of the impoverishment of political thought among certain poets.

None of this should obscure the fact that post-avant poets are motivated less by aesthetic concerns than political and cultural ones. Hence one of the fields that has enjoyed a resurgence is ecopoetics. Unlike nature poetry, which tends to concern discrete natural phenomena, ecological poetry focuses on systems, which helps explain why ecopoets tend to be anti-industrialist and anticapitalist. Although the history of ecopoetics can be traced back to individuals like Jack Collom, who began publishing in the 1970s, the permanent crises around climate change have elevated the profile of younger ecopoets like Jennifer Scappettone, Brenda Iijima, Forrest Gander, Evelyn Reilly, and Marcella Durand. As this list suggests, women poets, whose work links feminist concerns to the environment, dominate the field. At the same time, in the midst of a resurgence of state violence against black people, poets across the aesthetic spectrum have taken up critiques against the police and white privilege. These criticisms are often wedded to a critique of heteronormativity as more and more LBGTQIA poets enter the public domain of post-avant poetics. A partial list of poets combining both antiracist and sexual liberationist poetics includes Dawn Lundy Martin, Duriel Harris, Ronaldo Wilson, John Keene, Rob Halpern, Cassandra Troyan, Jennifer Tamayo, and Jen Hofer.

In this context language writing as a movement may be over, but individual practitioners have adapted themselves to the charged, political context in which late twentieth- and early twenty-first-century poetry is often embroiled. Carla Harryman, for example, has ventured into film-making and sound recordings inspired by the late Detroit/Los Angeles black poet and playwright Ron Allen, while Steve Benson has recently released a collaborative recording with the San Francisco–based avant-garde jazz band Splatter Trio. Still, the language writing experiment during the latter half of the twentieth century can be understood as a fulcrum that attempted to radicalize, politically and aesthetically, the work of margin-alized modernist movements by excluding or ignoring several postmod-ernist movements. And while it set the stage for the development of early twenty-first-century movements like flarf and conceptual poetry, it also served as a convenient target for its alleged indifference to post-avant, queer, eco-, and second-language/immigrant poetries that regularly appear in traditional journals like *Poetry* and *American Poetry Review*. Language writing was thus an important, if flawed, intervention into twentieth-century mainstream American poetry.

WORKS CITED

Basnet, Ankit, and James Jashoon Lee. "A Network Analysis of Postwar American Poetry in the Age of Digital Audio Archives." *Post45*, no. 7, April 21, 2021, https://post45.org/2021/04/a-network-analysis-of-postwar-american-poetry-in-the-age-of-digital-audio-archives/.

Bernstein, Charles. "Objectivist Blues: Scoring Speech in Second-Wave Modernist Poetry and Lyrics." *American Literary History*, vol. 20, nos. 1–2, spring/summer 2008, pp. 346–68.

Greenwald Smith, Rachel. "Fuck the Avant-Garde." *Post 45*, no. 2, June 13, 2019, https://post45.org/2019/05/fuck-the-avant-garde/.

Goldman, Judith. "Re-Thinking 'Non-Retinal Literature': Citation, 'Radical Mimesis,' and Phenomenologies of Reading in Conceptual Writing." *Postmodern Culture*, vol. 22, no. 1, 2011.

Gottlieb, Michael. "Fourteen Poems." In Ron Silliman, ed., *In the American Tree*. Orono: National Poetry Foundation, University of Maine, 1986, 377.

Grenier, Robert. "Wintry." In Ron Silliman, ed., *In the American Tree*. Orono: National Poetry Foundation, University of Maine, 1986, 5–6.

Heijinian, Lyn. *My Life*. Los Angeles, CA: Sun & Moon Press, 1987.

Pluecker, John. "The Mongrel Coalition against Gringpo." JD Pluecker, February 3, 2015, https://jdpluecker.com/blog/2015/02/our-targets-are-flag-drapers-whitmanian.html.

Pound, Ezra, ed. *Des Imagistes: An Anthology*. New York: Albert and Charles Boni, 1914.

Robinson, Kit. "In the American Tree." In Ron Silliman, ed., *In the American Tree*. Orono: National Poetry Foundation, University of Maine, 1986, xiii–xiv.

Shepherd, Reginald. "Who You Callin' 'Post-Avant'?" Poetry Foundation, www.poetryfoundation.org/harriet-books/2008/02/who-you-callin-post-avant.

Silliman, Ron, ed. *In the American Tree*. Orono: National Poetry Foundation, University of Maine, 1986.

Watten, Barrett. *The Constructivist Moment: From Material Text to Cultural Poetics*. Middletown, CT: Wesleyan University Press, 2003.

——— ed. *The Grand Piano, Part 1: An Experiment in Collective Autobiography: 1975–1980*. Detroit, MI: Mode A., 2006.

——— "Plasma." In Ron Silliman, ed., *In the American Tree*. Orono: National Poetry Foundation, University of Maine, 1986, 26.

——— *Questions of Poetics: Language, Writing and Consequences*. Iowa City: University of Iowa Press, 2016.

Watten, Barrett, with Robert Grenier, eds. *This*, no. 1 (Winter 1971).

Williams, William Carlos. *In the American Grain*. New York: New Directions, 1925.

Young, Thom. "Home Field Advantage: A Conversation with Kit Robinson." *Cold Mountain Review*, spring/summer 2020, www.coldmountainreview.org/issues/spring-summer-2020/home-field-advantage-a-conversation-with-kit-robinson-by-thom-young.

CHAPTER 15

Renovating the Open Field
Innovative Women Poets Reclaiming an Erasure History

Wanda O'Connor

Florence Howe's 1993 revised and expanded poetry anthology *No More Masks!: An Anthology of Twentieth-Century American Women Poets* continues the work of the first edition, with poet Muriel Rukeyser's *The Poem as Mask* providing the "vision" for the collection, as Howe notes the "fragments and the invisibility that control women's lives [to], at last, come to wholeness and vision" (F. Howe xxix). Howe's new edition responded to "new differences [that] now divide women's poetic consciousness" and considered that "to be a woman poet is to encompass," after Adrienne Rich, "the difficult world" (xxix, xxxi). The volume illustrates the collection's purpose with Rukeyser's starting poem where she identifies a mask worn by women that once concealed the individual, the self "unable to speak, in exile from myself" (xxvii). *The Poem as Mask* – focusing on the mythology of Orpheus – calls for "No more masks! No more mythologies!" to put an end to the masking through myths imposed on women writers and to signal a move toward new mythologies that emerge from the women's self, an identity once split that finds its oneness.

In the volume's preface, Howe recognizes the importance of giving space for women's experiences to welcome a "vision of wholeness" – inspired by Rukeyser – given the difficulty of locating work by women poets: "in the early seventies, it was still possible to use a card catalog under the word 'women' and find 'poets,' though we could not have known then that many poets had slipped away, out of that net into invisibility" (xiii). The goal of the anthology was in part to make new introductions and to restore publication absences of twentieth-century women writers. Howe communicates this erasure as evidenced in the silences of others who "lived as closet poets or whose poetic lives ceased after the twenties or the thirties, [which] are painful to enumerate" (xxxv).

Kathleen Fraser, writing in her collected essays of her observations and experiences as a poet writing in the 1970s–1990s, recognizes this same absence of women's publications in literary journals and anthologies. She acknowledges "canon formation with its vagaries of erasure," and she sought to contribute her own work to the "seemingly untouchable world of the already claimed" with an aim to move beyond the "inhibiting field of established precedent" (Fraser, *Translating* 1). Along with other women poets in the 1970s and 1980s, Fraser was seeking new models of language writing to combat the older "received structures of inherited language," and poets looked to theoretical writing that explored more female experiences (135). The pursuit for new models was shared by other contemporaries of Fraser, including poets Rachel Blau DuPlessis and Susan Howe.

The inheritance of erasure in women's poetry provided Fraser and others a renewed focus to invent a map beyond dominant discourse where renovated language and form could give space for female interiority and where, as DuPlessis writes, one could begin "to invent a body of facts – my facts" ("Psyche," 96). As Fraser moved to establish efforts where the "significant body of work being produced by contemporary experimentalist women poets" could become a "two-way street between poets and scholars" (*Translating* 3), she founded a new forum for women's voices and publishing in poetry. This forum provided women the opportunity to "locate a poetics on our own terms" (31) and offered a shared space for contemporary poets interested in innovative poetic practice and emerging from a modernist aesthetic. The pivotal women's poetry journal *HOW(ever): A Journal of Feminist Experimental Writing* appeared in 1983 and published innovative women's poetry and poetics, providing a place that also fostered critical exchange. *HOW(ever)* was to become a site, Fraser writes, where "issues could be aired and some new choices put forward in women's poetry – asserted and selected by women" (35).

Contributors to *HOW(ever)* – including founding editor Fraser, poets Susan Howe, Rachel Blau DuPlessis, and others – began exploring and (re)inventing innovative writing practices involving "expanded" or "extended" forms, through long poems, serial poems, and fragmented and "open form" poems. Fraser looked to identify those women poets experimenting with form whose writing was "expanding onto the FULL PAGE" that took as an initial starting point Charles Olson's influential midcentury manifesto *Projective Verse* (*Translating* 175). Of the work, DuPlessis notes how the term "projective," first appearing in Olson's essay, "suggest[ed] a world-vast space to claim and enter" (DuPlessis, *Blue Studios* 85). Fraser too claims Olson's field, as she notes his poetics was an "immense, permission-giving moment" for women considering "the *visualized* topos of interior speech and thought" that presented the page as a site for possibility (*Translating* 175). This practice was helpful for women in particular to provide "an urgency toward naming, bringing voice to off-the-record thought and experience," and Olson's manifesto provided a "clear concept of PAGE as canvas or screen on which to project flux." This unrest determined a move for women poets to a poetry resistant to "any *fixed* rhetoric ... implied or intoned" and toward that which "in some cases drastically reconceived" the initial contributions of Olson (175–77).

As these poets welcomed new forms of expressiveness to involve the complexity of women's experience, Olson's ideas of form helped give shape to women's own open-ended and innovative forms. It may be helpful to note where Olson's influence landed women poets, according to Fraser, who "enter[ed] literature after 1960 [and] gained access to a more expansive page through Olson's own visual enactment of 'field poetics,' as mapped out in his major exploratory work, *The Maximus Poems*" (175–76). It is here where evidence of expanding and investing in the material of the past (through the epic figure of Maximus) is noteworthy to Fraser. She continues:

> [Looking at] *The Maximus Poems*, one can begin to grasp Olson's graphic intervention in the field of the regularized page. Reviewing, then, a selection of pages from the dozens of spatially innovative texts published by women during the years since the arrival of Maximus, one may read their alterations and detours. (178)

Fraser suggests that the landscape of Olson's new open page, one with "spatial, historical and ethical margins," did help American poets – such as Susan Howe – to not only engage with openness in writing but to begin to explore and in some cases take up new modalities within a renovated sense of the page. This adopted, and adapted, page space transitioned into a strategy of placement: "I don't believe that a single woman poet who entered this 'field' knew, ahead of time, precisely how or what she would project into/onto its emptiness, nor how that field would assist in producing these works" (177). Of such "alterations and detours" that Fraser notes (178), Quartermain suggests that Susan Howe's work sets itself apart from field poetics while also acknowledging it, her "radical assessment of canonical notions of history and language ... her poetics, rejecting the possibility of definitive statement ... [and] the great energy of Howe's writing aris[ing] from a series of tensions" (Peter Quartermain 71). Howe herself discovered this mutable field through *The Maximus Poems*. She tells Cole Swensen in an interview that she "felt an immediate shock of recognition" in the work of "blustering, chopped nervousness" (Howe and Swensen 381). Howe identifies Olson's activity as one she found familiar, with a need to "gather 'facts,' to find something, a quotation, a place name, a date, some documentary evidence in regard to a place" and where connections were not always necessary (381). *Projective Verse* provided women poets with the impetus to move into the "open field" and to explore such blurring of boundaries on the page. Examples of this practice took shape in the plurality or difference of the line, in collage-based fragments, and in palimpsest and supplementary gestures within the textual-visual body. The shaping of plural forms and contexts often instructed unfixed narratives and encouraged further impulses toward openness. Poets exploring these arrangements – as Sharon Doubiago notes in a roundtable discussion in 1997 at the University of Toronto – recognized the importance of writing in extended forms: "open, large expansive forms are feminine and female, very freeing and liberating, and those were the poems I read when I first began [writing]" (Brennan et al. 520).

Olson's projective project provided a space for a new discourse to emerge, where one might move against what was inherited – "tenses," "syntax," "grammar" – in order for these categories to be "kicked around anew" so that the poem's "space-tensions" would be "immediate" (Olson, *Collected* 244). DuPlessis positions *The Maximus Poems* as representative of these tensions. She quotes from Olson directly that "the long poem creates its own situation" and how, despite being bound in book form, the work "is not bounded" (DuPlessis, "Olson" 135). The unbounded nature of the expanded poem can, as DuPlessis writes, "avoid conventions of closure deliberately" (136). We are witness to an "impulsive, unsettled" long poem that amasses materials and where we might wonder if his gathering of "making lists, abbreviating ideas, clustering half-completed associations, sketching, combining, and lumping materials" is, according to DuPlessis, "almost not writing at all," and even as open-ended as our daily experiences (136). Ben Friedlander describes Olson's long poem project as the accumulation of "unexamined source texts" that contributed to a vast archive. Considering that accumulated materials can make up a poem's archive, contours of an archival practice in an expanded form can offer a method where creative process is prone to continual shaping. It is with Olson that such shaping is first given recognition and where poetry's relationship to the full and open page becomes one of renovation, the activity of the field setting in place "a whole series of new recognitions" where "the shaping takes place, each moment of the going" (Olson, *Collected* 240, 242).

These open, expanded forms offered poets unique visual access to the page, providing space for women to contribute "historically focused collage poems to formally intricate lyric sequences to massive works of epic breadth and comprehensiveness" (Brennan et al. 507). The open form practices were used by poets like Susan Howe, who Fraser suggests was a "kind of major force, and also before her [Charles] Olson, in making us very aware of . . . an alternative way of thinking about poetic language and constructing experience" (535). Fraser tells the panel that when she first started working in an expanded sense she was making "an exploration" through a "succession of small scenarios," and she notes the benefit of these exploratory methods in the "possibility of not having to come to a quick closure" (507). Fraser, in thinking through Irigaray and Kristeva, acknowledges interruption as a regular occurrence for women, where "fragmentation wasn't body, but it was time," and that this "living with interruption" is "something that happens to women that you cannot escape." As a teacher she sought a "formal acknowledgment of interruption . . . that could lead to various kinds of what you might call 'female forms,'" where exploration of "new formal arrangements" could help to "capture that temporal interruption" (524). We see the energy of these arrangements in Fraser's page explorations. In her poem sequence "Etruscan Pages," written after an "unsettling visit to the Etruscan ruins" where she "feels the site-specific presence of a vanished people," Fraser writes in such "small scenarios" to evoke the fragments of the site (Hogue). Through illustrative representations, small groupings of text, fragmented yet implicit collections of found interiorities and materials, lines isolated on the page, and interruptions breaking concentrated language and imagery, Fraser makes and unmakes Etruscan life and loss:

> Was A
>   where
> you made and
>   unmade your mind . . .
>
> first hesitation
>
>   when you doubted
> what you
>   thought you
>   were
> looking for? (Fraser, "Etruscan Pages" 106)

In seeking to identify what is left behind – and where Fraser looks to activate the tensions of page space, "stopping. struggle. squeeze of light. sling. slate. shut. / scrutiny. S" (107), these Etruscan subjects are shaped by Fraser in her re-creation of them, whether by fact or fiction – and are as expanding acts in an archival field.

Entering into the expanded, archival-rich field of open form writing positioned women poets writing against closure and welcoming a practice of excess. These poets used materials from their own lives and from historical sources to (re)construct individual identities, and everywhere the shaping of form and content shared the effects of an archival practice, as explorations flooded the page alongside awareness of the "absent history of women and other marginalized groups" (Brennan et al. 509). Texts dwelling in the archival field are situated, and equally fragmented, by voices – in expressions of rediscovered memory – unexpected imagery and rearticulation of events by way of what is left out, left over, or reabsorbed from heterogeneous artifacts. The expanded field encounters objects as well as their absence – which are equally affected – and holds to Sarah Nuttall's instruction that "the archive itself bears testimony to excisions and is itself marked by them" (Nuttall 295). Considering the relationship between women's poetry and excess, Karen Jackson Ford suggests that "excess is, above all, a refusal of silence" (Ford 47), and we bear witness to the movement of women poets claiming that refusal to move beyond an erasure history.

Susan Howe and Rachel Blau DuPlessis make the activity of an archival field explicit in their poetry through both isolated and expanded narratives in open-form arrangements. The archive as a site of excess reliably takes us to unexpected places in our engagements with unexpected materials. It behaves like a heterotopia in its fundamental soliciting of the reinterpretation of place. Formed by an accumulation of material, poetries of excess can be the result of contributing several histories – personal, fictional, and documentary in nature – to the page. Ford suggests that a poetics of excess can "contradict, revise, and affirm existing meanings . . . [and] also generate new ones" (27). In Howe's own practice she writes that "the content is the process, and so it changes" (S. Howe, "Talisman Interview" 165), and her work is said to inhabit "a kind of hybridization of writing practices" (Schultz 145). We see her poems and sequences engaging in disjointed revealing by juxtapositions of fragmented histories. Howe writes of such difference as contributing to the way she begins a project:

> I start in a place with fragments, lines and marks, stops and gaps, and then I have more ordered sections, and then things break up again.... I think a lot of my work is about breaking free: starting free and being captured and breaking free again and being captured again.... It just seems that I end up with this place that I wish I could belong to and wish I could describe. But I am outside looking in. (S. Howe, "Talisman Interview" 165)

Paradoxically, Howe seeks belonging amid a consistent system of disjunction. This sustains a practice of disjointed composition and is intuitive of Howe's architecture of building, layering, and obscuring textual and visual components in the expanded poem. The distance of the poems from achieving a sense of united place invites Ford's "contradicting, revising and generating" production toward excess.

In the archive, Carolyn Steedman's "great, slow moving Everything," we find an assembly of difference (Steedman 167), which can be anticipated in such an inundated "open field." Lyn Hejinian suggests that difference is an essential fabric of the poem, refusing to close "what we all have in common ... [difference offers] instances of insubstantiality, because [it] marks points of mutability ... Differences are evidence of incompleteness" (Hejinian, "Continuing"). The archival field, then, is an entrance into difference and into fracture that is informed by women poets reclaiming an absent history.

Of excess, Ford writes that "new meaning is concomitant with excessive signification. There is a surplus in the medium, which produces an overgrowth, as it were, of signification" (Ford 69). Susan Howe's writing dwells in this irregular space of openings and closings, where she writes that there is "conflict and displacement in everything I write – in the way I arrange words on the page, in the way I hear and react to other languages – that I can't edit out" (Howe and Swensen 381). Dispersions and overburdened space can signal further unsettlements and adjacencies that are juxtaposed on the page. The "energies of dispersal located in [Susan] Howe's texts," for instance, offer such accumulation, her writing "influenced by the critical discourses of pluralism and multiplicity" (Montgomery 99).

The excessive fragment is a kind of waste product of the work that also becomes the work, from which a gloss forms and imparts new textual activity. Gloss informs and also contributes, adding further material in the extended activities of the poem to the archival field. In writing about her own process, DuPlessis details the effects of gloss within her poem series *Drafts*:

> Any thing can open out to meaning and be connected to other things.... Every detail could in a particular light have meaning. Error has meaning. Slips have meaning. Anything could be glossed. Gloss generates more text. Text and gloss exist in a permanent, continuous, generative relationship. Gloss on text is more text to be glossed. One makes gloss to comment on loss, against the loss of loss, but there is always more loss. (DuPlessis, *Blue Studios* 233–34)

Gloss offers no stable discourse, with each instance informing the next while at once encouraging remoteness and residue within the archive's pluralizing territory. Of marginalia, H. J. Jackson writes that its purpose is to "translate or explain foreign or obscure words," where gloss "operates at the most literal of levels, and aims to be faithful to the text it mediates" (Jackson 45). Relevance to the primary text can appear as "a grammatical or textual point, an elucidation, a new illustration, a historical reference, a confirming or contradicting authority," and gloss' "forms of interpretive labour" can accumulate to accommodate "a free-standing glossary, a mass of rubrics an index, and a mass of scholia an independent commentary" (45). DuPlessis' gloss takes up these measures and at once does not, seeming to gesture and generate notable "slips" intuitively within the fabric of the archive.

The archivist confronts the unending and embedded material of the archive just as women writers bring the unending expressions of their lives to the page. As Steedman writes, "You know you *will not finish*, that there will be something left unread, unnoted, untranscribed" (Steedman 45), just as DuPlessis writes of her own process, where "completion is always provisional." In her long-form work *Drafts*, a project spanning several years, the poems that began the collected *Drafts* begin to take shape in the final section of her book *Tabula Rosa*. Here begins a series that instills "a way of ignoring binary systems of limit," for which she gives several examples, such as "subject/object, male/female, speech/silence . . ., memory/invention" (DuPlessis, "Darkest Gush"). In this way, DuPlessis' systems interrogate the unending equivalence of the archivist. The first poem, entitled *Writing*, several pages in length and comprising what she calls a "28-section serial poem" (qtd. in "Darkest Gush") begins with a full stop and delivers the first two-line stanza as an uncompleted thought: ".Smudge, ballpoint, iridesces / behind the" (DuPlessis, *Tabula Rosa* 55).

The form of *Writing* takes on several incarnations: as incomplete thought, prose verse, partial words split at middles, handwritten text alongside typed characters, stylistic choices of capitalized phrases, bold and italic text, dual columns, open forms, and the truncated, taught narratives speaking back to the text (see Figure 15.1).

As with the phrase that begins page 77, hovering across the top of two columns, "Marginalia without a center? No beginning, No. No ending?" Fraser identifies *Writing* as a "back-and-forth" comprised of expressions of the infant and adult, the mother looking to "notate these primary sounds and meanings, layering them with her own complex residue of mundane

.A wri-
ting marks the
patch of void
foggy reflecting
mist catches wet carlight

that everything tests   film
condenses   fine tip flairs
refracted silence   baby wipes
The cold rush up   khaki thread
the dark dark trees   nipples
Somnulent spots of travel

Letters are canal-
ized as white foams
zagging, a fissure on the
sheet,
        tangle of branches unorganized without the leaves
cock-eyed underbelly of
plenitude of

mark. *outtakes, can imagine conversations?*
      conversions?
      Long passages of satisfaction swallowed up
      in darkness.

Figure 15.1   Rachel Blau DuPlessis, *Writing*, in *Tabula Rosa*, 1987, p. 57.

domestic details broken by ecstatic moments of 'vision.'" Fraser further
acknowledges the "struggle" of DuPlessis' line, in "running little columns
of half-words or crowded rushes of sound or syllables splitting to reveal
multiple readings." This has the effect of "allowing the mark of more than
one voice or self to be present" and shows the maternal experience now
located in poetry, as women poets "could first acknowledge its absence and
then find ways of bringing it onto the blank page" (Fraser, *Translating*
146). DuPlessis tells us that her "images, lines, phrases" can shift from one
Draft to another, "enter[ing] others freely, as if they had not found a final
home in any one poem, or as if they enjoyed the processes of circulation.
The poems have a strong acceptance of the unfinished ... everything is
marginal to everything else" (DuPlessis, "Darkest Gush"). We can see in

the third poem of this section DuPlessis' continued breaking of line, as it begins ".A wri-," which suggests at once fragmented and continued thought. The poem continues that "everything tests / condenses / refracted silence," which then turns to fragmented time, "long passages of satisfaction swallowed up / in darkness," the page recognizing this "fissure on the / sheet." Typed lines are interrupted with handwritten segments, another way to insert the woman's mark – an individual expression of experience. The poem is deliberate in navigating the reader away from the initial narrative by situating five lines in succession and detached from their companion texts. Aligned to the right of the page as if reserved thought or distraction, these lines observe the interruptions of mothering: "film / fine tip flairs / baby wipes / khaki thread / nipples" (DuPlessis, *Writing*, in *Tabula Rosa* 57).

The section finishes with its own notes, "writing on 'Writing' / notes made between 15 March and 4 April 1985" (84), which detail thoughts toward the drafts and provide the reader with the impetus for the overwritten and formally disjunctive poems, as the notes dictate the poem's purpose, "setting the poem so there is a bringing of marginalization into writing" (84). DuPlessis writes:

> In many poems ... all the works make visual and textual allusion to marks and markings, marks which are normally invisible, and are rarely used as a part of the language of poetry. There are incipit initials, palimpsested words, bracketed material as if "cut," contrasting typography.... There are odd signs on the page ... poems with a kind of binary page, an irregular fissure down the middle.... All these visual and discursive gestures are meant to bring the physical codes of writing and presentation up to scrutiny.... Tactics which deny or subvert the authoritative text have haunted me. I wanted polyphony; I wanted excess. I wanted to achieve uncontrollable elements.... I proposed on my page the contradictory. The unfinished. The processual. Multiple beginnings, multiple middles, and eroded endings. (DuPlessis, "Darkest Gush")

DuPlessis points to an expansive and limitless experience of writing space, and expansion keeps the open form poem both in motion and submerged; the series can repeat and risk divulging only glimpses of a totality. Excess then lies in threefold waste: the absent projection (unfinished, incomplete, and thus remaindering), the overdetermined page (collage or fragment materials reopening, accentuating difference), and the silent space (the swerve and in-betweenness of narrative difference). These excessive notations and gestures introduce several constellations that can render uncanny any notion of a primary text.

Contemporary practice has pushed open field writing into newly dynamic engagements. Others have written about this connection, such as in Harriet Tarlo's discussion of a poetics of open form characterized as "a place, a space, a structure, a form, a philosophy, an ethics" (Tarlo 117). Tarlo suggests that, as it involves the activity of the page, each "plotting on the page, an embodiment even," becomes a boundary with which the poet becomes "preoccupied," identifying relationships to surrounding boundaries (128). The archival field emerges in a similar way, navigating contiguous surface and boundary, a site of expanding and of practice, a malleable form that situates all palimpsestic and fragmented parts in residence. Navigational contours are nuanced and a broader set of identities displace the page, resisting simple construction. In this way, the field presupposes a commitment to engage the space of the page, a ground of fixed and movable parts in which ambiguity and meaning can be repurposed, all elements corresponding to their own philosophy of form.

Susan Howe writes of her work as being a process whereby texts are developed in stages of "quotations upon quotations." She notes the overlapping nature of the writing, remarking that it is "embedded and surrounded by ghosts and echoes," and considers the whole of her work as a project amassed (S. Howe, "Mother-Daughter"). Her poetry in *Debths* – a collection embodying smudges, histories, palimpsests, signs, and ghosts – draws comparisons in its title to "depths" and "debts" and "deaths," where debts may be owed to those who have come before, depths "of her engagement with material traces of ideas," and deaths of loved ones (Chiasson). Duplessis suggests that Howe is "suspicious of languages and discourses as already made and inhabited things" (DuPlessis, *Pink Guitar* 132), and so poems in *Debths* construct new narratives from historical memory and are positioned along both vertical and horizontal axis and where fragments are lined up, off-centered, smudged, and overlaid as unique textual gestures. Irregular and unmended phrases meet utterance and recall the archivist's process, that "no one historian's archive is ever like another's . . . each account of his or her experience within them will always produce counter narratives, of different kinds of discomfort" (Steedman 9).

The book invites its reader into alternating narratives of historical and literary figures, writings of place and of those inspired by it, and personal accounts of the history of a mother and a daughter, to name a few. The foreword introduces several artists and their practices, as well as Howe's own passage through and experience of exhibits and portraiture, with reflections on geography and on the people she's encountered through her life. The writing breaks and changes abruptly at times, just as it returns to personal narrative in Howe's reflections on her mother's own experience of place:

> It's late November. Fallen oak and maple leaves on the sidewalk outside are bound to childhood landscape memories filtered through my mother who never stopped harping on the cruel ugliness of Boston as compared to Dublin's fair city. For me there are two alternatives: either swallow or break free.... As life rushes by we do our best with the nerves we inherit. (S. Howe, *Debths* 17)

The indication that histories can be left behind and yet leave an indelible mark instructs the kind of layering present in Howe's poems, particularly in the text-collages that appear in two of the four sections of *Debths* (excluding the foreword).

From the first section of the book, *TITIAN AIR VENT*, all poems are set distinctly apart on facing pages in paragraph-shaped blocks. Occasionally the block texts veer off into a new single line, fragment, or "list" that resists full stops – final thoughts that do not end but suggest endings – a familiar method with Howe's poetry as it "returns us to beginnings (though not to origins) so that we may not arrive at our ending" (Lazer 61). Final lines in several poems of this section – identifiable at first as elements of an art exhibit on marginalia that Howe visited – seem to list elements needed for constructing, in "Ceramic, plaster, laquer, newspaper," and are set against objects evoking difference, "Yamuna river map, spreadsheet, riverbed" and "Reliquary, trellis, cross-grid, shoelace, comma." This collection implies at once a combing for objects that hold within them the suggestion of counternarrative and of the transformation of objects into textual gesture. These poems travel across the exhibit reflecting on encounters both in and out of memory, narrative, and history, the final poem trailing objects of the seashore of "Seaweed, nets, shells, fish, feathers" but from the incongruous origin of puddle, "our mother of puddled images fading away" (S. Howe, *Debths* 25–40), reflecting the small span of water as distinct from the larger, broadening sea. Here, Howe conflates pond and saltwater sea, and the association is depths, linked directly from the poem's reference to "polymer," rooted in the Ancient Greek *polus-meros* – meaning many-parted – and contributing to the concentration of materials and their stored memory (and separation) in the poems.

As Ford notes of a poetics of excess, "excesses of style enable crucial and liberating excesses of meaning" (Ford 11). Evidence can be found in Howe toward that end, articulated through textual collage that seems to stutter in place, presenting physical marks of erasure, half-words sliced through the middle, fragments meeting other fragments and phrases legible beneath words crossed-over or struck-through. This accumulation of parts delays and hesitates while at once instructing narratives of excess to emerge as enhanced and remade textual histories. For these poems, repetition of process is key: "the burden of history, for Howe, is that it repeats itself, even as it is being edited" (Schultz 143).

A poetics of excess can emerge from women writers resisting silence, having been "defined by the culture in an extremely limiting way and suppressed on that account" (Ford 7). Howe breaks from the confines of the past by rewriting it, her work "emerg[ing] from a paradoxical crossroads in thinking through the relationship between history and imaginative writing" where she takes "a historical system ... and desystematize[s] it, in part by telling the story backwards" (Schultz 156–57).

In the second section of the book, *TOM TIT TOT* – based on a Rumpelstiltskin fairy tale – text-collages are incomplete and underwritten yet frame the world, "crowded with o / and reworkings," the "original source," and "There are those of us who" adapt, "history scattered" (see Figure 15.2).

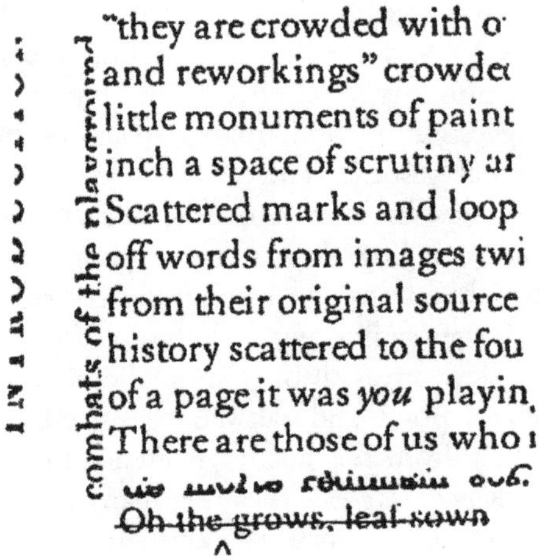

"they are crowded with o
and reworkings" crowde
little monuments of paint
inch a space of scrutiny ar
Scattered marks and loop
off words from images twi
from their original source
history scattered to the fou
of a page it was *you* playin
There are those of us who

Figure 15.2   Susan Howe, from *TOM TIT TOT*, in *Debths*, p. 43.

Here, half-words and "scattered marks" are remade from "their original source." Howe leaves enough – an "inch a space of scrutiny" – for the ideas torn, unfinished, refused, half-revealed, or hidden to allow us a glimpse into what might have been, and what might yet come to the surface (S. Howe, *Debths* 43).

The poem shown in Figure 15.3 highlights only two words and one character, "the cobwebs &" (S. Howe, *Debths* 44), but cannot prevent what was once visible to impact the reading of the deliberately exposed phrase.

Figure 15.3   Susan Howe, from *TOM TIT TOT*, in *Debths*, p. 44.

This small, recovered/supplanted piece of text is emphasized by two parallel lines supporting the word "cobwebs," and crossed-out word choices "Under" and "dim villages" further emphasize the materiality of the poem as well as its undecided speaker: Does an erased TOM TIT TOT venture into the dim villages or get stuck, struck-through, in the reshaping of the web? These two paired but dissimilar textual collages cohere whimsically, despite their otherness. Here and elsewhere, Howe positions place uniquely, in wanting to "search for a new kind of authority, one grounded in the history of places rather than of ideas" (Schultz 145). Her work that is "unsettling" is at once a project of "knowing and rewriting 'masculine' discourses, in the name of a feminist and critical cultural project which wants to transcend gender" (DuPlessis, *Pink Guitar* 125).

Howe's *Debths* also presents the "throw" as a circumstance of excess by indicating the word itself, hidden by an overdetermination of content. What we come to rely on is shaken up, the experience of "throw, through, threw" and so on, shifting awareness slowly, reflecting and embodying the accumulation and breaking of "thought, it seeme, fall" and "threw, crowded, thronge(s), presse." In the text-collage on the left-hand page, vertically aligned and illegible text is presented in ancient Greek alongside English-language strikethroughs and half-visible phrases, while the text on the facing page shows the poem as gesturing toward familiarity, as the alphabetized list seems similar to a dictionary or an accompanying index

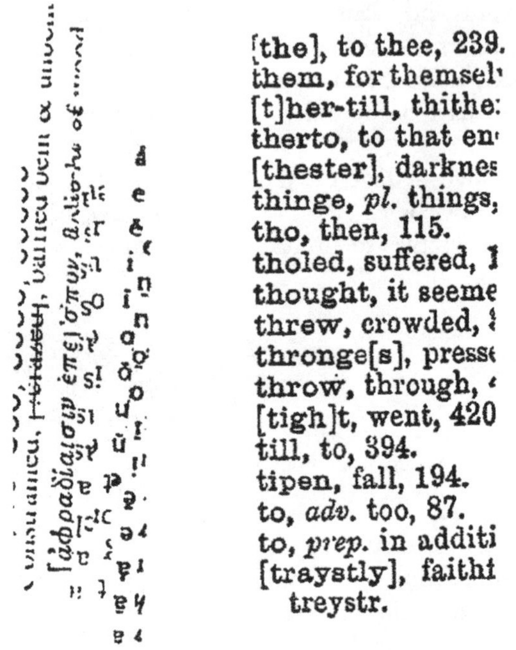

[the], to thee, 239.
them, for themsel'
[t]her-till, thithe:
therto, to that en'
[thester], darknes
thinge, *pl.* things,
tho, then, 115.
tholed, suffered, 1
thought, it seeme
threw, crowded, !
thronge[s], press
throw, through, '
[tigh]t, went, 420
till, to, 394.
tipen, fall, 194.
to, *adv.* too, 87.
to, *prep.* in additi
[traystly], faithf
treystr.

Figure 15.4 Susan Howe, from *TOM TIT TOT*, in *Debths*, pp. 48, 49.

for an unknown or missing text (Figure 15.4). We begin to uncover the nature of this text, pressed tight to an invisible left margin, yet seeming to be leaving and at once returning to the "throw." The right side of the block presses inward and is slightly askew while stressed and clipped and packed-in form, making a production of that content and bringing the reader's experience of the "throw" forward, further emphasized by "fall" and the truncation of faithful – "faithf," an expectation cut, thrown (S. Howe, *TOM TIT TOT*, in *Debths* 48–49).

Howe's work locates the kind of discomfort of counternarratives (Ford 9) common to an archive. In not knowing what will emerge in the relationship between the poet and her historical glosses that accumulate in an archival field, excess intuitively both shows the idea and the fractured form that elevates it. Howe's suspicion of "already made and inhabited things" in her search for authority of history over authority of ideas may signal her desire to situate poetry in an overdetermined field. Furthermore, her insistent voice in gathering the materials of the archive is a deliberate one in refusing an absent history of women writers. As DuPlessis notes of Howe's work, she shows "the whole history of the language in one gesture" and it is "filled with memories of abandonment; she represents the silence half-sounded of the powerless" (DuPlessis, *Pink Guitar* 131).

Ford tells us that excess can be valuable for women poets in "gaining voice in a literary environment that constantly threatens to silence" those voices (37). Through Fraser's "tracing moments of access" that would have her identifying and engaging with women's "fear of taking up [verbal] space" (Brennan et al. 516, 523), she is able to "enter history on my own terms" (516). DuPlessis notes a concerted move toward ownership, "what we were given of tradition is what we must break off, examine, fabricate. Making it ours, for it now has 'ourself' in it" and to seek within the page "feminist appropriation of / every genre large and small" (DuPlessis, *Pink Guitar* 130–31). And while Julie Bacon suggests that the archive is "memory itself, which has no fundamental material form" (Bacon 52), in engaging the explicit work of women's expanded poetic forms, we can view the renovated field as arrangements of memory and observe their tensions, the textual plots and gestures taking on what DuPlessis might refer to as "a territory": "The page is not neutral. Not blank, and not neutral. It is a territory" (DuPlessis, *Pink Guitar* 131). The scope of women's innovative writing practice involves an ongoing negotiation with loss and with remaking the poem's histories through a relationship both to difference as well as to excess, just as Nuttall writes that "imagination can keep excising the archive, replenishing it with things that were not there at the beginning" (Nuttall 299).

WORKS CITED

Bacon, Julie. "Archive, Archive, Archive!" *Circa*, no. 119, 2007, pp. 50–59.

Brennan, Karen, et al. "The Contemporary Long Poem: Feminist Intersections and Experiments." *Women's Studies: An Inter-Disciplinary Journal*, vol. 27, no. 5, 1998, pp. 507–36.

Chiasson, Dan. "Susan Howe's Patchwork Poems." *New Yorker*, 2017, www.newyorker.com/magazine/2017/08/07/susan-howes-patchwork-poems (accessed April 20, 2018).

Cixous, Hélène. "The Laugh of the Medusa." Trans. Keith Cohen and Paula Cohen. *Signs*, vol. 1, no. 4, 1976, pp. 875–93.

DuPlessis, Rachel Blau. *Blue Studios: Poetry and Its Cultural Work*. Tuscaloosa: University of Alabama Press, 2006.

"The Darkest Gush: Emily Dickinson and the Textual Mark." Dickinson Electronic Archive, Folio one, 2013, www.emilydickinson.org/titanic - operas/folio-one/rachel-blau-duplessis (accessed July 1, 2016).

Drafts 1–38, Toll. Middletown, CT: Wesleyan University Press, 2001.

"Olson and His Maximus Poems." In *Contemporary Olson*, ed. David Herd. Manchester: Manchester University Press, 2015.

"On *The Poem as Mask*." Modern American Poetry, 2020, www .modernamericanpoetry.org/criticism/rachel-blau-duplessis-poem-mask (accessed June 12, 2020).

The Pink Guitar: Writing as Feminist Practice. New York: Routledge, 2006.

"Psyche, or Wholeness." *The Massachusetts Review*, vol. 20, no. 1, 1979, pp. 77–96.

"The Serial as Portal: An Interview with Rachel Blau DuPlessis (with Chris McCreary)." *Xconnect*, vol. 20, 2003, ccat.sas.upenn.edu/xconnect/i20/g/mccreary.html (accessed April 2, 2016).

Tabula Rosa. Elmwood, CT: Potes & Poets Press, 1987.

Ford, Karen Jackson. *Gender and the Poetics of Excess: Moments of Brocade.* Jackson: University Press of Mississippi, 1997.

Fraser, Kathleen. "Etruscan Pages." In *il cuore – the heart: Selected Poems 1970–1995.* Hanover, NH: Wesleyan University Press, 1997, pp. 158–85.

"An Interview with Kathleen Fraser." *Contemporary Literature*, vol. 39, no. 1, 1998, pp. 1–26.

Translating the Unspeakable: Poetry and the Innovative Necessity. Tuscaloosa: University of Alabama Press, 2000.

"Untitled Contribution to 'forum.'" *HOW2*, vol. 1, no. 2, 1999, www.asu.edu/pipercwcenter/how2journal/archive/online_archive/v1_1_1999/forum.html (accessed January 10, 2018).

Fraser, Kathleen, Jo Ann Wasserman, et al. "Welcome to the *HOW(ever)* and *How2* ARCHIVES." *HOW2 Journal,* 1999, www.asu.edu/pipercwcenter/how2journal/archive (accessed May 20, 2017).

Freshwater, Helen. "The Allure of the Archive: Performance and Censorship." *Poetics Today*, vol. 24, no. 4, 2003, pp. 729–58.

Friedlander, Benjamin. "Charles Olson Now." Olson Now, 2006, olsonnow.blogspot.com/2006/05/benjamin-friedlandercharles-olson-now.html (accessed June 10, 2018).

Hejinian, Lyn. "Continuing against Closure." *Jacket Magazine*, vol. 14, 2001, jacketmagazine.com/14/hejinian.html (accessed January 3, 2016).

"The Rejection of Closure." In *The Language of Inquiry.* Berkeley: University of California Press, 2000, pp. 71–102.

Herd, David. *Contemporary Olson.* Manchester: Manchester University Press, 2015.

Hogue, Cynthia. "'The fact of her witness': Kathleen Fraser and the Poetics of Empathic Witness." *Jacket 2 Magazine*, 2022, https://jacket2.org/article/fact-her-witness (accessed January 28, 2022).

Howe, Florence, ed. *No More Masks!: An Anthology of Twentieth-Century American Women Poets*. New York: HarperPerennial, 1993.

Howe, Susan. *Debths*. New York: New Directions Publishing, 2017.

"The Mother-Daughter Thing." *New York Times*, 2015, http://tmagazine.blogs.nytimes.com/2015/03/24/susan-howe-rh-quaytman-mother-daughter-interview (accessed May 21, 2017).

"Talisman Interview, with Edward Foster." In *The Birth-Mark: Unsettling the Wilderness in American Literary History*. Middletown, CT: Wesleyan University Press, 1993.

Howe, Susan, and Cole Swensen. "A Dialogue." *Conjunctions: American Poetry: States of the Art*, vol. 35, 2000, pp. 374–87.

Jackson, H. J. *Marginalia: Readers Writing in Books*. New Haven, CT: Yale University Press, 2001.

Kinnahan, Linda. "Untitled Contribution to 'forum.'" *HOW2*, vol. 1, no. 2, 1999, www.asu.edu/pipercwcenter/how2journal/archive/online_archive/v1_1_1999/forum.html (accessed January 10, 2018).

Lazer, Hank. *Opposing Poetries, vol. 2: Readings*. Evanston, IL: Northwestern University Press, 1996.

Markotic, Nicole. "Untitled Contribution to 'forum.'" *HOW2*, vol. 1, no. 2, 1999, www.asu.edu/pipercwcenter/how2journal/archive/online_archive/v1_1_1999/forum.html (accessed January 10, 2018).

Mockel-Rieke, Hannah. "Untitled Contribution to 'forum.'" *HOW2*, vol. 1, no. 2, 1999, www.asu.edu/pipercwcenter/how2journal/archive/online_archive/v1_1_1999/forum.html (accessed January 10, 2018).

Montgomery, Will. *The Poetry of Susan Howe*. New York: Palgrave Macmillan, 2010.

Nuttall, Sarah. "Literature and the Archive: The Biography of Texts." *Refiguring the Archive*, ed. Carolyn Hamilton, Verne Harris, et al. Dordrecht: Springer, 2002.

Olson, Charles. *Collected Prose*, ed. Donald Allen and Benjamin Friedlander. Berkeley: University of California Press, 1997.

The Maximus Poems. Berkeley: University of California Press, 1983.

Presley, Frances. "Untitled Contribution to 'forum.'" *HOW2*, vol. 1, no. 2, 1999, www.asu.edu/pipercwcenter/how2journal/archive/online_archive/v1_1_1999/forum.html (accessed January 10, 2018).

Quartermain, Meredith. "Untitled Contribution to 'forum.'" *HOW2*, vol. 1, no. 2, 1999, www.asu.edu/pipercwcenter/how2journal/archive/online_archive/v1_1_1999/forum.html (accessed January 10, 2018).

Quartermain, Peter. "AND THE WITHOUT: An Interpretive Essay on Susan Howe." *The Difficulties*, vol. 3, no. 2, 1989.

Schultz, Susan M. "The Stutter in the Text: Editing and Historical Authority in the Work of Susan Howe." In *A Poetics of Impasse in Modern and Contemporary American Poetry*. Tuscaloosa: University of Alabama Press, 2005.

Steedman, Carolyn. *Dust: The Archive and Cultural History.* New Brunswick, NJ: Rutgers University Press, 2002.

Tarlo, Harriet. "Open Field: Reading Field as Place and Poetics." In *Placing Poetry*, ed. Ian Davidson and Zoe Skoulding. New York: Rodopi, 2013, pp. 117, 128.

CHAPTER 16

Transcultural Agency

Maria Dikcis

In "Pollen Fossil Record," the final section of Myung Mi Kim's *Commons* (2002), a poem titled "duration" evokes the elusive process by which a lyric poem inventories the material traces of perception, of expression, and of history. The task of the lyric, always seemingly impossible, is to translate the multivalent, multidirectional vectors of living into the shape of a sound, a line, an imaginary articulation. In the poem's closing lines, the speaker offers us an operational definition of transcultural agency that I would like to use as a guiding principle for this chapter: "The poem may be said to reside in disrupted, dilated, circulatory spaces, and it is the / means by which one notates this provisional location that evokes and demonstrates / agency – the ear by which the prosody by which to calibrate the liberative potential of / writing, storehouse of the human / To probe the terms under which we denote, participate in, and speak of cultural / and human practices – / To mobilize the notion of our responsibility to one another in social space" (Kim 111). What would it mean to treat accountability, as opposed to the loaded pressures of intimacy or the unmanageable demands of consensus, as the key paradigm of relation within a commons? And how have American poets variously participated in this "responsibility to one another in social space" across the twentieth and twenty-first centuries? Indeed, this is no small feat in a historical period marked by ceaseless empire-building, massive immigration, global warfare, expanding routes of trade and commerce, ecological collapses, the rise of mass incarceration, and increasing wealth disparities – phenomena that have unevenly impacted people of color throughout the United States and led many to cling more strongly to a sense of community based in self-recognition. And yet multiethnic American poets have continually shown us that thinking beyond the ideologies of modern conditions of colonialism, systemic racism, and global capitalism happens through a shared sense of responsibility to alternative modes of assembly empowered by dialogic discourse and cross-cultural exchange. If we think of poems as formal microcosms of the cultural practices and political networks of marginalized communities, we can begin to see how transcultural agency depends as much on dissonance as it does on harmony. Any poem that holds the potential to mediate encounters, at times reciprocal and at other times violent, that transgress national, political, and linguistic borders calls on us to become sonically attuned to multiple sites of exchange, traversal, and substitution at once. For Kim's speaker, agency denotes neither imposing force nor instrumentalist control but rather an "ear" that is sensitive to the "disrupted, dilated, circulatory" elements of culture – the ability, in other words, to flow with currents of meaning, of value, and of relation as they ripple across space and time.

The study of American poetry, like numerous other disciplines across the humanities, has stood only to benefit from the "transnational turn" that emerged in the 1990s and early 2000s – encapsulated in widely influential idioms such as Mary Louise Pratt's "contact zone," Lisa Lowe's "heterogeneity," Homi Bhabha's "hybridity," James Clifford's "traveling cultures," Édouard Glissant's "open boat," and Jahan Ramazani's "hybrid muse." As with countless other creative forms, too, poetry of the past few decades has reflected the frequent cultural displacements that were accelerated by the complex processes of late capitalist globalization. However, this heightened sense of cultural blending is certainly not unique to the rapid developments in finance, trade, and communication technology that characterize the post–Cold War era, and many scholars underscore how poetic strategies of the late nineteenth and early twentieth century were just as attuned to interstitial understandings of culture as they are today. For instance, examining the link between US poetic modernism and the development of diasporic and postcolonial archives in other parts of the Americas, Anita Patterson argues in *Race, American Literature, and Transnational Modernisms* (2008) that we must credit intercultural relations with laying the essential "foundation for the flourishing of modernist styles in the Americas" (3). Speaking across a more broadly defined era of globalization, Ramazani posits in *Poetry in a Global Age* (2020) that if "we were to submit almost any modern or contemporary poem for analysis to Ancestry.com, and if the units of analysis included allusions, techniques, etymologies, genres, forms, and rhetoric, the resulting pie chart, even if favoring one region in one era, would inevitably include others" (2–3). While Patterson's and Ramazani's studies encompass global poetries that far exceed the geographic boundaries of the US nation, any examination of American ethnic poetry in the twentieth and twenty-first centuries would do well to follow their examples of looking beyond nationally, temporally, and spatially circumscribed theories of identity formation. Moreover, as will be discussed at the end of this chapter, contemporary LGBTQ poets of color are leading the conversation on the vital role that gender and sexuality play in sustaining transcultural forms of relation, for instance, by exploring our queer affinities with cultures that exceed human political categories entirely and rupture the historically entrenched singularity of lyric subjectivity.

In the simplest of terms, transcultural agency is a means of navigating a sense of cultural in-betweenness – with all its fruitful combinations, unexpected assimilations, confusing contradictions, and violent frictions – without losing sight of the import of unique ethnic, regional, and national characteristics. It is hence a way of challenging the politics and practices of separatism without resorting to empty universalist claims that erase difference. When tracing the relation between culture, race, and ethnicity, we must therefore consider how Black, Latinx, Indigenous, and Asian American poets of the United States work to unfix these identity categories precisely because of their embeddedness in white supremacist hierarchies and racist social institutions. It is helpful here to bear in mind Junaid Rana's definition of race as "a social construction in which biology and culture are often conflated as a rhetorical logic and material practice in a system of domination. Inasmuch as race is used for subjugation, it is also a productive category used by subaltern groups in opposition to racism" (202). Above all, transcultural agency affirms that most cultures, to one extent or another, are heterogenous mixtures and that many cultural identities are in a state of flux, constantly pursuing new forms of togetherness and understanding. We tend to think of poetic legacies from at least the cultural nationalist movements of the 1960s to the digital era as evolving along parallel paths, such that multiethnic traditions are more or less separate, despite some linking figures or concerns. By tracking panethnic solidarities and aesthetic practices across several periods, I contend that minoritized poetries have continually developed in mutual relation to one another. Along these lines, I follow Long Le-Khac's assertion in *Giving Form to an Asian and Latinx America* (2020) that we must contend with the limits of "established axes for groups that have been drawn into the nation and excluded in opposed ways, or groups without a vibrant history of alliance, or groups whose structural relationships within the racial order, immigration system, and global economy cannot be captured in histories of direct encounter" (17). In my estimation, transcultural exchange across racial, ethnic, and national boundaries is the very quality that distinguishes American poetry since 1900. Much work remains to be done when it comes to situating US poetry within comparative, transnational, and cross-hemispheric contexts. And while this chapter is an unavoidably incomplete attempt to address sites of transcultural agency in ethnic American poetry across the twentieth and twenty-first centuries, my hope is that it is generative of renewed conversation on the poetics and politics of cultural hybridity.

If the twinned processes of modernity and colonialism from at least the mid-eighteenth century onward created the turbulent conditions for American poetry's oscillation between local and global perspectives, poetic strategies of formal hybridization, transnational collage, and multilingualism would be well advanced by the early 1900s. Poets of color especially found themselves caught between the need to be received legibly by capitulating to the formal demands of canonical (read white) modernist strategies and the call to pay due diligence to matters of racial formation, postcolonial resistance, and cultural heritage. The Harlem Renaissance – a flourishing of African American literature, art, and culture in the 1920s and 1930s – while certainly representing a concentrated period of Black pride that was routed through the principles of Négritude, pan-Africanism, and the cultural separatism of Garveyism, always had a palpable transcultural dimension to it. I begin with this early twentieth-century moment not merely for reasons of chronology, but also because the Harlem Renaissance laid the groundwork for many thematic and formal dilemmas that would come to occupy poets of color for the next hundred years. These entailed rejecting the assumption that poetic form is white while poetic content is racial; accentuating the role of the immigrant in dissolving artificial boundaries between nations, languages, and customs; and underscoring that culture must be understood as fluid, negotiable, and heterogenous if it is to be understood at all. The works of the Jamaican American poet Claude McKay encapsulated many of the internationalist perspectives that made Harlem a capital of cross-cultural literary and artistic exchange. Composed in 1912, the year he first immigrated to the United States, McKay's "To the White Fiends" presents a speaker who firmly establishes his affiliation with a shared experience of anti-Black violence: "Think ye I am not fiend and savage too? / Think ye I could not arm me with a gun / And shoot down ten of you for every one / Of my black brothers murdered, burnt by you?" (McKay 276). While "To the White Fiends" notably incorporates McKay's native Jamaican dialect, it also takes the form of a Petrarchan sonnet, thus representing an early Black protest poem that melds poetic conventions from a variety of lineages. If we consider how McKay's poem emerges in close historical proximity to W. E. B. Du Bois's theory of double consciousness, we see how it participates in "white" society in its form even while its radical, transgressive language attacks the hypocrisy of Western civilization. McKay, along with others such as Countee Cullen, was known to diverge from the free verse and jazz rhythms of his contemporaries by adopting the traditional poetic forms of odes, sonnets, ballads, and intricate rhyme schemes. Cullen was particularly influenced by the British Romantic poet John Keats and believed strongly in the power of form to evince one's mastery over the long history of poetics and to stake one's claim in honorably carrying on a poetic tradition. Cullen's stance emphatically defied racializing perceptions of what Black poetry was "supposed" to look or sound like, yet it also reinforced how working within classical verse forms was not inimical to confronting deeply political concerns over racism, segregation, and economic inequality.

Other poets of the period stressed that while the nation might have been divided along a Black/white racial order, whiteness could not be treated in insolation from Blackness. This is exemplified in a line from Langston Hughes's poem "Theme for English B" (1949): "You are white – / yet a part of me, as I am a part of you. / That's American" (40). Hughes's great contribution to the tradition of transcultural poetics was his ability to maintain deep ambivalence toward the American bricolage even as he celebrated its potential to break down social hierarchies. Many of his other poems register an explicitly Marxist awareness of an interethnic proletariat that was certainly influenced by the continued ramifications of slavery in the United States, but also by his interests in Latin American culture and visits to China, the Soviet Union, and West Africa. His "Let America Be America Again" (1936) from the collection *A New Song* elucidates the shared experiences of subjugation among colonized, deracinated, and slain peoples by constructing a speaker who personifies multiple identity positions at once: "I am the poor white, fooled and pushed apart, / I am the Negro bearing slavery's scars. / I am the red man driven from the land, / I am the immigrant clutching the hope I seek – " (9). Hughes's poem fluidly integrates different conjugations of race and class into one dissenting lyric voice. Through a series of inter-stanzaic asides that formally pierce holes into an idealized American Dream that is promised but never realized – "(America never was America to me.)" (9) – the speaker accentuates the dichotomy between distinct "Americas" overlaying one another that afford very inequitable opportunities for upward social mobility.

The Harlem Renaissance demonstrated that cross-cultural exchanges could flourish even *within* movements that appeared to be motivated by racial similitude on the surface. Throughout the Civil Rights movement of the 1950s to 1970s, race likewise became an organizing tool not only of cultural expression but also of protest against destructive hegemonies empowered by war, imperialism, wealth inequality, and heteropatriarchy. We see this especially in the application of political ideas to art and literature throughout the Black Arts Movement, El Movimiento (the Chicano Movement), and Native American Renaissance, all of which sought to embrace shared racial experiences and reclaim squandered heritages. This period, however, also marked a transitional moment when marginalized groups began to more intentionally explore pan-ethnic solidarities. Taking the Asian American movement as one example of such a shift, Amardeep Singh proposes in his interactive digital archive *Asian American Little Magazines 1968–1974* that up until 1968 (the year when scholar Yuji Ichioka coined the term "Asian American"), support among various groups was based primarily on "'ethnic' advocacy," whereby Japanese Americans and Chinese Americans advocated for their own communities (Singh, "Welcome"). The post-1968 era of the Asian American movement significantly "marks the beginning of true *pan-ethnic* Asian identity" (Singh, "Welcome"). Lawson Fusao Inada's poem "Asian Brother, Asian Sister," published in the anthology *Roots: An Asian American Reader* (1971), represents an early example of this expansive vision of situating a pan-Asian perspective within a larger milieu of pan-ethnic influence. The speaker gathers at a ceremony to mourn his grandmother's passing and recalls her unwavering bravery in the face of immigration, war, and internment. The grandmother's pride in her newborn grandson and desire to nourish him with Japanese foods ("Bring him down to the store tomorrow / so I can get him some manju, / let him chew on an ebi") mixes with references to the cross-cultural backdrop of his communal upbringing ("Listen, big baby – Mexican tunes / moving around the jukeboxes") (Inada 123). The sound of chewing on ebi (shrimp) and the Mexican tunes wafting from the jukeboxes becomes an unexpected kind of harmony that riffs on Inada's broader interests in jazz improvisation. A third-generation Japanese American (Sansei), Inada was imprisoned with his family at the age of three and remained in camps in California, Arkansas, and Colorado for the duration of World War II. Inada's identification with other oppressed groups stemmed not only from his experience of incarceration but also from the community-building that was integral to living in a multicultural neighborhood. After being released, his family resettled in the business district of Fresno, California, where many Black and Japanese, Chinese, and Mexican American families lived, leading Inada to take an interest in the jazz music favored by high school friends. His first full-length poetry collection, *Before the War: Poems as They Happened* (1971), expands upon Inada's self-fashioning as a "campsman" (a play on "bluesman") by reframing a distinctly Japanese American experience of internment through the idiom of an African American musical tradition evoking the sorrowful spirit of a people.

In the wake of the Black, Brown, and Red power movements of the 1960s and 1970s, we continue to see not only the development of pan-African, pan-Latinx, and pan-Indigenous poetries, but also a heightened attunement to Euro-American colonialism's collective violence toward distinct marginalized groups. To take one example, restrictions on movement across the North American continent have historically targeted brown-skinned communities and served to bolster regimes of surveillance, criminalization, and border racism. In her poem "Crossing the Border" from the collection *What Moon Drove Me to This?* (1979), Joy Harjo (Muscogee Creek) uses a site that resonates with Chicanx immigration to explore Indigenous sovereignty and the arbitrariness of invisible political boundaries separating one nation from another. Border-crossing here refers not to migration from Mexico into the United States, but rather to a group of Native Americans crossing the northern border as they are on their way to a powwow in Moraviantown, Ontario. Harjo draws our attention to the forgotten violence of the line dividing the United States and Canada, as "[m]any tribal nations are slashed by the border" (Harjo 205). In the poem, a border guard ignorantly asks the travelers, "'Who are you Indians / and which side are you from?'" (20). In response to this confrontation with law enforcement, the speaker expresses the frustration of dispossession and national unbelonging from an Indigenous point of view: "But hidden under the windshield / at the edge of this country / we feel immediately suspicious. / These questions and we don't look / like we belong to either side" (20). Named the US Poet Laureate in 2019, Harjo often uses trans-Indigenous perspectives to explore the fluid movement and exchange of cultural practices. This plays out in "Crossing the Border" as a criticism of restraints placed on such movement, as the speaker alludes to an array of Indigenous locales and tribes – "Delaware," "Menominee," "Milwaukee" (20, 21) – that have been unquestioningly co-opted into the fabric of the country's makeup as state names and major metropolitan areas.

The casual violence of this Indigenous erasure echoes across time and space in the collection *Postcolonial Love Poem* (2020) by Natalie Diaz (Mojave, Akimel O'odham, Latinx), as can be seen in poems such as "Manhattan Is a Lenape Word" and "*exhibits from* the American Water Museum." The latter of these despairs over the careless disregard for Indigenous heritage that feels characteristically national: "An American way of forgetting Natives: / Discover them with City. Crumble them by City. / Erase them into Cities named for their bones, until / you are the new Natives of your new Cities" (Diaz 64). By defamiliarizing the entrenched ordinariness of these geographical sites, both Harjo and Diaz critique how a multiplicity of groups that are Indigenous to the Americas have consistently been racialized as foreigners on their own land through artificial borders.

As the examples above have shown, poetic diction has been a primary site for multiethnic poets to grapple with and challenge hegemonic discourse that privileges English as a marker of "genuine" American culture and values. The stakes of reclaiming the power of language and its relation to social identity are hence especially amplified in works that cross over and between multiple languages. For many, a poem becomes the formal ground upon which the politics of language play out precisely through the constraints placed on linguistic choices. In her poem "Bilingual/ Bilingüe" from *Where Horizons Go* (1998), Rhina P. Espaillat portrays a domestic encounter whereby Spanish words that are enclosed in parenthetical marks are formally mimetic of a father's strict instructions that only Spanish must be spoken indoors. Rhyming couplets construct a series of rooms inside the house of the poem:

> My father liked them separate, one there,
> one here (allá y aquí), as if aware
>
> that words might cut in two his daughter's heart
> (el corazón) and lock the alien part
>
> to what he was – his memory, his name
> (su nombre) – with a key he could not claim.
>
> "English outside this door, Spanish inside,"
> he said, "y basta." But who can divide (Espaillat 60)

As the daughter of a political exile and herself an asylum seeker from Trujillo's dictatorship in the Dominican Republic, Espaillat was not permitted to mix languages in her new life in New York City, leading her to see how English "was the medium of the outer world" (Espaillat 67).

Espaillat's poem represents a more measured type of code-switching that distinguishes it from the practices of Chicana and Nuyorican writers such as Lorna Dee Cervantes, Gloria Anzaldúa, Sandra Cisneros, and Sandra María Esteves, who often fluidly amalgamate English and Spanish words in the same breath. Take, for instance, these lines in the poem "Oaxaca, 1974" from Cervantes's *Emplumada* (1981): "But Mexico gags, / ¡Esputa! / on this bland pochaseed. / I didn't ask to be brought up tonta! / My name hangs about me like a loose tooth. / Old women know my secret, / 'Es la culpa de los antepasados'" (44). Although these poems illustrate different facets of bilingual identity – one the result of forced diaspora and the other of a willful refusal to relinquish one's mother tongue – each in their own way evokes the struggle of reconciling the loyalties that come with inhabiting two cultures simultaneously.

Just as Espaillat's emigration from the Caribbean reveals the promises and limits of language as a medium of transcultural understanding, many other poets contribute to this disavowal of American exceptionalism by situating the United States within its proper transhemispheric contexts. Frequently ostracized in discussions of American poetry and yet historically victim to the United States' most violent regimes of exploitation, Pacific Islander poets offer especially penetrating insight into extended genealogies of material extraction, militarism, and cultural colonization that persist to the present day. With roots in native Hawaiian, Samoan, Chamorro, Chinese, Filipino, Japanese, Korean, and Afro-Diasporic heritages, among others, these poets encompass a hybridity of identities that make the Pacific Islands a uniquely transcultural, multilingual region. Moving across diverse platforms that include print, sound recording, and spoken word, their works shed light on issues ranging from colonial exploitation to the historical use of islands as military bases and nuclear testing sites to present-day experiences of indigeneity, decolonization, and the clash between imposed and inherited cultures. Lisa Linn Kanae, Brandy Nālani McDougall, and Joe Balaz are a notable group of poets who make Hawai'i Creole English (Pidgin) an essential component of their practice. Others like Juliet Kono, Lois-Ann Yamanaka, Garrett Hongo, and Eric Chock (cofounder of the extant Hawaiian literary journal *Bamboo Ridge*) investigate the complex alienation felt by Asian American immigrants living in Hawai'i. In her 1988 collection *Hilo Rains*, Kono traces the routes of her family's diaspora, beginning with her grandparents' emigration from Japan to her upbringing in Kaiwiki on land leased from the Wainaku Sugar Plantation. The poem "The Wake" offers a glimpse into the transcultural community-building of post–World War II Hawai'i as we learn of the various people who gather to mourn her grandfather's death: "some Filipino friends / straight from the fields, / others in old zoot suits," "the Puerto Rican, / we only know as 'Bu-zing,'" "The Japanese women / help serve the meatless *okazu*," "The Portuguese have come too: / the young girls in white / like Madonnas, / smelling of sweet bread" (Kono 32–33).

More recently, Craig Santos Perez's groundbreaking *from unincorporated territory* tetralogy explores the poet's homeland of Guam and native Chamorro culture through the lens of extractive capitalism. The series' second volume, *[saina]* (2010), traces the United States' hypermilitariza-tion of Guam, the resulting pollution and extinction of the island's flora and fauna, and the procedure by which native residents became US "citizens" with limited rights. The poem "*from* all with ocean view" reveals the link between settler colonialism and the privileged vacuity of American cultural tourism through a striking clash of nature and the material residues of military occupation at a resort hotel:

> 'an island jewel' 'vie
> for space barbed
>   wire and beaches'   'granite boulders from
>   afar were
>   unexplainably
>   brought here' 'my guidebook' | 'different | spellings for place names'
> 'become souvenirs' | 'empty pools | with infinity
>   edge' (Santos Perez 47)

Santos Perez's scattered arrangement of words on the page guides the symbolic navigation of a sakman (Indigenous outrigger canoe), signifying one of myriad innovations by Pacific Islanders that expand our sense of the confluence between cultural practice and poetic form.

The militarization of the Pacific Islands marks just one of numerous instances of the violent manufacture of subjects who could claim nominal belonging to American citizenship while still being regarded as illegal aliens or even enemies of the United States. From World War I to the current so-called global War on Terror, militarism has waged endless threats to culture understood as the meaningful expression of difference through everyday life. September 11, 2001, in particular, marked an intensified moment for ethnic American poets to explore shared experiences of resist-ing the overdetermined role that crisis plays in standardizing culture as a homogenous category rooted in nationalist sentiment. Published in the immediate aftermath of 9/11, Suheir Hammad's "First Writing Since

(Poem on Crisis of Terror)" addresses how people racialized as "Middle Eastern" were uniformly vilified for the events that transpired in Lower Manhattan. The speaker declares: "the most privileged nation, most americans do not know the difference / between indians, afghanis[sic], syrians, muslims, sikhs, hindus." Articulated in a candidly confessional mode, Hammad's poem represented an unhesitating critique of the United States' widespread militaristic backing of right-wing extremism, cultural genocide, and various human rights violations. In response to the hatred and common desire for retaliation that she hears from neighbors and other passers-by in New York City, the speaker uses an ironic inversion of geography to highlight that feelings of insecurity are shared by many who live under authoritarian regimes: "if there are any people on earth who understand how new york is / feeling right now, they are in the west bank and the gaza strip."

For others, 9/11 signified a moment of cultural trauma that meaningfully opened a gateway for other kinds of collective grief to manifest. In Ocean Vuong's "Untitled (Blue, Green, and Brown): oil on canvas: Mark Rothko: 1952" from the collection *Night Sky with Exit Wounds* (2016), newscasts of the planes hitting the buildings airing on TV bookend a speaker's ruminations about missed chances for communication with a lover or friend. Vuong, a refugee from Vietnam whose family fled to the United States when he was two, has articulated how the collapse of the Twin Towers revealed for him a parallel between national and queer (un) belonging: "9/11 became for me, personally, this charged spectacle of public American collapse. And in some ways it signified what I felt on the private scale as a queer American, experiencing my own American collapse" (qtd. in Pham). Conjuring visions of Hart Crane's homage to an iconic site of gay male cruising in the 1920s and titled after the abstract expressionist artist who took his own life, "Untitled" constructs a speaker who acutely understands the uncomfortable proximity of queerness and death: "my greatest accolade was to walk / across the Brooklyn Bridge / & not think of flight. How we live like water: wetting / a new tongue with no telling / what we've been through. They say the sky is blue / but I know it's black seen through too much distance" (49). As a gay Vietnamese American whose work strives to find intimacy within national tragedy, Vuong exposes how different configurations of ethnic and sexual identity ultimately preclude certain groups from blending into the American cultural mosaic.

Since the turn of the twenty-first century, a remarkable range of poets of color have employed digital platforms to better understand how cultural identities morph under the conditions of networked mediation, while simultaneously envisioning alternatives to the Internet's inequitable infrastructures and neoliberal ideologies. Mendi and Keith Obadike, an Igbo Nigerian American married duo who experiment widely across poetry, art, music, and digital installation, were two of the earliest practitioners to create net art in the early 1990s. Perhaps best known for the work "Blackness for Sale" from 2001, in which Keith's Blackness was auctioned on eBay, Mendi and Keith offer us through their oeuvre an embryonic look into the digitally networked spectacle of Black death and trauma that was only just beginning to emerge. Reworking the genre of the memorial to contend with a distinctly Black experience of American collapse, their Internet tribute for Amadou Diallo titled *my hands/wishful thinking* (2000) examines the role that poetry, news reportage, and animation can play in mediating the horrors of racialized police brutality without erasing the complexity of the individual who becomes victim to it. On opening the website, visitors see replicating images of blue-hued, palm-up hands, one of which clutches and releases a leather wallet like an animated GIF. Meanwhile, audio in the background sampled from a news clip repeats the words "forty-one" and "fired" in a glitchy loop for two and a half minutes. Diallo, an immigrant from Guinea, was shot at forty-one times by plainclothes NYPD cops and struck by nineteen of their bullets. Protesting the security state as an apparatus for disqualifying immigrants from the national imaginary, *my hands/wishful thinking* proffers "one thought to counteract each bullet fired" and rejects "the negative forces directed against us, the survivors, african people in the united states" (Obadike and Obadike, "Early Media"). The work cycles through forty-one glimpses into Diallo's world that read like revised epitaphs – ones that do not despair over life lost but rather articulate "wishful" thoughts about what it would mean to live in a country that is more accepting of the brilliant diversity of various Black diasporas. "Counter bullet" number 3, for instance, affirms that "everyone thinks your pidgin is beautiful and a higher form of thinking," while number 33 states, "if you go to a new country, the law will protect you" (Obadike and Obadike, *my hands*). As a precursor to the Black Lives Matter movement, *my hands/wishful thinking* announced the crucial role that decentralized, virtual forms of activism can play in documenting and rebuking racially motivated violence. For Mendi and Keith Obadike, the early Internet unlocked a new graphical terrain to actively experiment with political and cultural alternatives of identity formation that exceed the narrowness of nation-state citizenship.

More recently, we have seen the emergence of a new generation of queer, trans, and nonbinary poets of color who work in digital, augmented reality, and other "post-Internet" print spheres that bear the distinct markings of text message slang. Staging encounters with a wide variety of cultural "others" that we still have not fully metabolized our relationships with – artificial intelligence, the virtual avatars of our meatspace lives, intergalactic travel as a response to our planet's ecological collapse, to name a few – this group collectively examines how the racializing apparatuses of technology have both constrained multiethnic poets and productively fractured the presumed (i.e., white, male) proprietor of lyric subjectivity. For many, multimedia poetry is hence an opportunity to theorize new conceptions of personhood with the historical awareness that race, gender, and sexuality have always been mutually constitutive, for better or for worse, with media and information technologies. One such poet is Margaret Rhee, who scrutinizes our enticingly precarious interactions with robotic forms of life and other smart machines. In 2014, Rhee collaborated with Berkeley's Center for Information Technology Research in the Interest of Society to create *The Kimchi Poetry Machine*. This poetry reciting device consists of a glass jar containing small pieces of paper with poetic fragments on them, whereby unscrewing the lid activates an audio recording of one of these poems. To develop the machine, Rhee worked alongside industrial roboticists and incorporated a batch of poetry written by a queer and feminist multiethnic group known as the "machine poetas," including micha cárdenas, Devi Laskar, Hyejung Kook, and Sun Yung Shin. By treating the ancient culinary process of kimchi making (gimjang) as a participatory new media format, *The Kimchi Poetry Machine* reformulates a Korean methodology of communal labor to imagine culture as shared creative preservation and consumption rather than simply shared racial or ethnic identity.

Rhee's poetry collection *Love, Robot* (2017) shares with Franny Choi's *Soft Science* (2019) an interest in dwelling within the queer affinities between information technology and women of color. In the first poem of Choi's text, titled "Turing Test," the speaker conveys the multifarious ways in which humans are made to feel othered by the uprooting of their bodies and origins: "i was made far away / & born here / . . . i was born miles beneath the ocean / i am part machine / part starfish / part citrus / part girl / part poltergeist / i rage & all you see / is broken glass / . . . *do you believe you have consciousness*" (3). Choi's poem evokes the irresolvable dualities that attend to being marked as a racialized subject – feeling both unseen and hypervisible, too hard and too soft, more than and less than human. Each section of *Soft Science* begins with a "Turing Test" poem, as if the speaker must iteratively measure her ability to master language against forms of artificial intelligence that attempt to mimic, and therefore disprove, her humanity. Choi is an affiliate of the multiracial, multigenre poetry collective Dark Noise, which explores intergenerational trauma and healing through a range of print platforms and community-oriented performances. As members of genre-bending and culture-crossing artists' groups, Rhee and Choi advocate for aesthetic practices that participate in an increasing turn away from the privileging of so-called individual "poetic genius" toward new forms of cultural fluidity and reciprocal collaboration.

Other poets have innovated open-source data visualization tools to map the poetics of movement within complex and often violent systems of racial control, such as the growing tension between twenty-first-century globalization and restrictions placed on immigration through border regimes. In her interactive poetic video game *Redshift & Portalmetal*, micha cárdenas repurposed the multimodal publishing platform Scalar to explore what it means to imagine that our last resort for decolonizing our planet is to leave it entirely. As a science fiction-esque allegory of Latina immigrant experience, the work follows the journey of a character named Roja whose home planet is experiencing climate collapse as she embarks on an uncertain exodus involving tense confrontations with intergalactic border agents and other threats to bodily sovereignty (e.g., not having a sustainable supply of hormones). A prime example of hypertext literature, *Redshift & Portalmetal* presents users with a nonlinear pathway of poetic fragments that intermingle with film clips of eerie, smog-choked panoramas and mystical dance routines performed by cárdenas herself, which present a counter visualization to the hypersexualized female body hallowed by misogynistic video game culture. By crafting new channels of survival amid the omnipresent hazards of a global economy rooted in capitalist extraction and forced labor, cárdenas demonstrates the power of communities of care that organize "in their own fractal, local ways / connecting across translocalities with respect and love, / in a time of fragility, / and the closeness of death." Similar to Harjo, cárdenas's poetry participates in a creative cultural hybridization that speaks to the shared struggles with displacement and statelessness faced by Indigenous and Latinx communities. As outlined in *Redshift & Portalmetal*'s editorial statement, cárdenas meant for her work to honor "the native people of the Anishnabe, Mississauga, New Credit and Grassy Narrows territories, where environmental destruction is a huge ongoing threat." Frequently experimenting with digital and augmented reality platforms to reveal how settler colonialism, climate change, and gender self-determination are intimately linked, cárdenas visualizes trans of color movement as a cultural practice that resists the biopolitical control of bodies.

Tommy Pico, originally from the Viejas Reservation of the Kumeyaay nation, similarly explores questions of personhood in the age of ubiquitous digital connection through a queer delight in and intense exhaustion over the unpredictability of popular American culture. From 2016 to 2019, Pico published his "Teebs cycle," which includes the collections *IRL*, *Nature Poem*, *Junk*, and *Feed*. In *IRL*, we follow the search for a muse/paramour undertaken by Teebs, a sort of online alter ego of Pico, as he both fiercely guards and relinquishes his sense of self amid the abundant caprices of modern dating. Formally speaking, this nearly 100- page poem doomscrolls through the chaotic feeds of our unregulated digital commons, as climate crisis mixes with pop culture mixes with global conflict mixes with the occasional inspiring discovery:

> ... Tar Sands, Pine Ridge,
> Ferguson, the Tea Party, stolen
> Nigerian school girls, gay marriage,
> Gaza, Kim Kardashian, Tim
> Dlugos, fundamentalism, plane
> shot from the sky over Ukraine
> ... 6'5 white actor
> slash personal trainer asks do I feel
> connected to the land bc I'm
> NDN – I haven't learned to live
> with everything yet much less myself,
> so I'm sorry for texting
> @ 1:30 in the AM (Pico 65–66)

Thwarting the white, essentializing assumption that Indigenous peoples find spiritual harmony through an innate link with nature, Teebs's longing for connection – to himself and to others – is compromised by the frequent distractions of his Internet-saturated world and can only be provisionally soothed by beaming an unrequited text message out into the night. *IRL* represents a kind of righteously cynical foil to the poem "The Delight Song of Tsoai-talee" by N. Scott Momaday (Kiowa) from his collection *The Gourd Dancer* (1976), which begins "I am a feather on the bright sky / I am the blue horse that runs in the plain" and concludes "You see, I am alive, I am alive / I stand in good relation to the earth" (27). The speaker in Momaday's poem – propelled forward by confident, anaphoric "I am" statements – is prideful for not simply feeling connected to nature, but for knowing that his entire existence is contiguous with its many elements. Unable to reconcile his cultural heritage that is rooted in what seems like a too distant past with his millennial impulses, Teebs believes that to feel connected to the land or even to write a nature poem is the equivalent of reifying the racist stereotypes that first generated the noble savage trope. Pico's tetralogy prompts us to consider how the culturally homogenizing lure of our digitally mediated society has complicated anew questions of heritage, belonging, and memory for Indigenous peoples.

In the past decade alone, a blossoming of scholarly monographs, edited anthologies, literary journals, and multimedia programs have made unprecedented advances in the study of transcultural poetry and poetics. The popular edited series *The BreakBeat Poets* features collections by an up-and-coming generation of poets who are reshaping the conversation around poetry's intersection with race, culture, and politics. This growing series includes the volumes *New American Poetry in the Age of Hip-Hop* (2015), *Black Girl Magic* (2018), *Halal If You Hear Me* (2019) – which compiles poems by Muslims around the world – and *LatiNext* (2020). Equally international in scope, *Cross Worlds: Transcultural Poetics* (2014), coedited by Anne Waldman and Laura Wright, is a far-reaching compilation of poetry and essays that address such topics as cultural hybridity, multilingualism, and the transgression of borders. Ranjan Ghosh's *Transcultural Poetics and the Concept of the Poet: From Philip Sidney to T. S. Eliot* (2017) espouses a new approach to the global and diachronic comparison of poetry that the author calls the "transcultural now." The recently digitized journal *XCP: Cross Cultural Poetics* (1997–2010), edited by Mark Nowak, offers an astoundingly diverse account of global ethnopoetics grounded in "cross-cultural connections to a planetary conception of resistance via poetic practice" ("XCP"). Moreover, Leonard Schwartz's radio show "Cross-Cultural Poetics," produced from 2003 to 2018 at the Evergreen State College in Olympia, Washington, and made available through PennSound, features interviews with poets around the world discussing their works in their own language.

These numerous examples attest to an immense interest in expanding our methodologies and idioms with which we explore the effects of globalization on language and culture. In many senses, we are only just entering a new era of transcultural, cross-hemispheric, comparative discourse on poetics that is paying much needed attention to the linkages between racial formation, global capitalism, and cultural politics. And while these developments are certainly being shaped by poetry that is to be found in all corners of the world, they hold many generative possibilities for the study of contemporary American poetry as well. As the outlook of the United States' "minority-majority" future continues to produce conservative fears over a diminishing white nation and progressive hopes for dismantling the stranglehold of white supremacy, we can no longer pretend that the cultural practices of diverse ethnic groups will remain on the peripheries or stay neatly sequestered within established communities and regions. I conclude with the faith that the poets I have discussed throughout this chapter will lend even more kindling to Ramazani's proclamation that intercultural dynamics, "whether experienced as a condition of tragic mixture and alienation or as the comic integration of multiple energies and sources . . . have fueled some of the most powerful poetry of our time" (*Hybrid Muse* 7).

WORKS CITED

cárdenas, micha. *Redshift & Portalmetal.* 2014. https://scalar.usc.edu/works/red shift-and-portalmetal/index.

Cervantes, Lorna Dee. *Emplumada.* University of Pittsburgh Press, 1981.

Choi, Franny. *Soft Science.* Alice James Books, 2019.

Diaz, Natalie. *Postcolonial Love Poem.* Graywolf Press, 2020.

Espaillat, Rhina P. *Where Horizons Go.* New Odyssey Press, 1998.

Hammad, Suheir. "First Writing Since (Poem on Crisis of Terror)." *In Motion Magazine.* 2001. https://inmotionmagazine.com/ac/shammad.html.

Harjo, Joy. *What Moon Drove Me to This?* 1979. In *How We Became Human: New and Selected Poems.* W. W. Norton, 2002.

Hughes, Langston. "Let America Be America Again" (1936). In *A New Song.* International Workers Order, 1938.

"Theme for English B" (1949). In *Montage of a Dream Deferred.* Henry Holt, 1951.

Inada, Lawson Fusao. "Asian Brother, Asian Sister." In *Roots: An Asian American Reader.* University of California Press, 1971. 121–127.

Kim, Myung Mi. *Commons.* University of California Press, 2002.

Kono, Juliet. *Hilo Rains.* Bamboo Ridge Press, 1988.

Le-Khac, Long. *Giving Form to an Asian and Latinx America.* Stanford University Press, 2020.

McKay, Claude. "To the White Fiends." *Pearson's Magazine,* vol. 38, no. 3 (September 1918): 275–276.

Momaday, N. Scott. *The Gourd Dancer.* Harper & Row, 1976.

Obadike, Mendi, and Keith Obadike. "Early Media Art Projects (1996–2010)." *Mendi + Keith Obadike,* http://blacksoundart.com/#/ice/ (accessed August 20, 2021).

my hands/wishful thinking. Mendi + Keith Obadike. 2000, https://obadike .tripod.com/Adiallo2.html.

Patterson, Anita. *Race, American Literature, and Transnational Modernisms*. Cambridge University Press, 2008.

Pham, Yen. "Ocean Vuong, Reluctant Optimist." *Literary Hub*, July 27, 2017. https://lithub.com/ocean-vuong-reluctant-optimist/.

Pico, Tommy. *IRL*. Birds, 2016.

Ramazani, Jahan. *The Hybrid Muse: Postcolonial Poetry in English*. University of Chicago Press, 2001.

   Poetry in a Global Age. University of Chicago Press, 2020.

Rana, Junaid. "Race." In *Keywords for Asian American Studies*, ed. Cathy J. Schlund-Vials, Linda Trinh Võ, and K. Scott Wong. New York University Press, 2015. 202–207.

Rhee, Margaret. *Love, Robot*. The Operating System, 2017.

Santos Perez, Craig. *from unincorporated territory [saina]*. Omnidawn, 2010.

Singh, Amardeep. *Asian American Little Magazines 1968–1974*. Last updated July 25, 2019, https://scalar.lehigh.edu/asian-american-little-magazines/index.

Vuong, Ocean. *Night Sky with Exit Wounds*. Copper Canyon Press, 2016.

"XCP: Cross Cultural Poetics, 1997–2010 (ed. Mark Nowak)." *Jacket2*, February 25, 2021, https://jacket2.org/reissues/xcp.

CHAPTER 17

Ecopoetry Now
Three American Poets

Ann Fisher-Wirth

As the environmental crisis has worsened in recent decades, hundreds of American poets have addressed it in their writing, bringing attentiveness, precision, and tenderness toward existence to bear against the failure of the imagination that has led us to the brink of environmental catastrophe. This essay cannot begin to do justice to the plenitude and variety of contemporary, politically engaged ecopoetry; instead, I will focus on three major poets writing in this vein: Camille Dungy, Brenda Hillman, and Craig Santos Perez. They and their work are quite different from each other. Yet all three are environmental activists for whom poetry is not separate from political engagement and awareness of the ways in which colonialism, postcolonialism, and industrialism have exploited both humans and nature.

***

One strength of Camille Dungy's poetry is her sense of interconnectedness between her personal life, human history, and the nonhuman world. Her work manifests the first principle of ecology: interrelatedness between all organisms in their environment. Her love and imagination extend outward from herself and her family to past and present others in the human community, and to other-than-human beings, all of whom share in the rich fabric of life. Her proclivity for pleasure is enormous, but tempered by a stern awareness of human suffering and environmental damage.

Born in Denver in 1972, Dungy moved often as a child; her father, an academic physician, taught at various medical schools around the United States. Having held several academic positions, she is now a University Distinguished Professor at Colorado State. She is married to Ray Black; they have one daughter, Callie. Dungy has published four prize-winning books of poems – *What to Eat, What to Drink, and What to Leave for Poison* (2006), *Suck on the Marrow* (2010), *Smith Blue* (2011), and *Trophic*

Cascade (2017) – and a book of essays, *Guidebook to Relative Strangers: Journeys into Race, Motherhood, and History* (2017). Dungy is also an important editor, especially of the groundbreaking anthology *Black Nature: Four Centuries of African American Nature Poetry* (2009). In September 2021 she was awarded the Academy of American Poets Fellowship.

The sonnet corona "What to Eat, What to Drink, and What to Leave for Poison," a fine example of Dungy's grounding in nature, closes her first book. Written while she lived in Virginia, it celebrates the coming of spring. "Only now, in spring, can the place be named," the sequence begins:

> tulip poplar, daffodil, crab apple,
> dogwood, budding pink-green, white-green, yellow
> on my knowing.   All winter I was lost. (79)

"The world is charged with the grandeur of God," wrote Gerard Manley Hopkins more than a century ago ("God's Grandeur"). As Dungy's poems turn toward spring, they share, but naturalize, this praise, attesting to the indwelling connection between human and other-than-human in lists of beloved species, rising to paean with "My God." The corona's final poem ends,

> Something like the birds' return, each morning's
> crescendo rising toward its brightest pitch,
> colors unfurling, petals alluring.
> The song, the color, the rising ecstasy
> of spring.   My God.   This beauty.   This, this
> is what I've hoped for.   All my life is here
> in the unnamed core – dogwood, daffodil,
> tulip poplar, crab apple, crepe myrtle –
> only now, in spring, can the place be named. (85)

Poetry praising nature is ancient, but the worsening environmental crisis demands also political urgency, which intensifies in Dungy's third book, *Smith Blue*. A brilliant poem, "A Massive Dying Off," skewers our – and her own – first-world inability to maintain focus on the human and environmental devastation caused by global capitalism:

> You needed covers, pillows, disposable containers.
> At Costco, everything comes cheap.
> *Sea stars, jellies, anemones*, all the scuttlers and hoverers
> and clingers along the ocean floor. *A massive dying off, further displacing depleted oxygen*, cried the radio announcer.

You plugged in your iPod.
Enough talk. You'd found the song you had been searching for. (7)

Then the final section expands, becomes surreal: "In the dream, your father is the last refuse to wash ashore. / This wasn't what you wanted. / Any of you." The father becomes an Ur-figure. He is wrapped in papyrus like a Pharaoh, prayed over, loaded onto an outrigger like a Viking king, and all of human history seems to prepare for the present crisis, in which the dead body returns, "Stinking. / Swelling." The poem ends with a grim warning of global warming and rising sea waters: "You can't dispose of the rising dead and you're worried. / What can you do?" (8–9).

Another poem, the elegy "The Blue," recounts the discovery of a tiny butterfly in 1948 at Big Sur by two undergraduates at UC Berkeley, Claude I. Smith and Rudi Mattoni. When Smith died a few years later, Mattoni named the butterfly after his friend. This butterfly, which inhabits coastal dunes and cliffs from Monterey Bay south to near Point Gorda, cannot live elsewhere, and lays its eggs only on coast or seacliff buckwheat. Therefore, in 1976 it was listed on the Federal Endangered Species Act (https://courses.cit.cornell.edu/icb344/abstracts/Smiths-Blue .htm). Dungy's poem describes both the men's joy at discovering the butterfly and the great losses that ensued: Mattoni's loss of his friend, the butterfly's loss of habitat, and the human loss of this beautiful coast via the caterpillar that wreaks so much environmental damage:

> seacliff buckwheat cleared, relentless
> ice plant to replace it, the wild fields bisected
> by the scenic highway, canyons covered with cul-de-sacs,
> gas stations, comfortable homes, the whole habitat
> along this coastal stretch endangered, everything,
> everyone everywhere in it in danger as well – (17)

Dungy's essay "Is All Writing Environmental Writing?," published in *The Georgia Review* in 2018, jives with her most recent book of poems, *Trophic Cascade*. In the essay she argues that "even indifference to the environment directly affects the world," and furthermore that

> [t]o separate the concerns of the human world ... from those of the many life forms with which humans share this planet strikes me as disastrous hubris and folly. We live in community with all the other lives on Earth, whether we acknowledge this or not. When we write about our lives, we ought to do so with an awareness of the other lives we encounter ... ("Is All Writing")

Trophic Cascade bears out this sense of interconnection. Trophic cascades, which can be of various kinds, are "powerful indirect interactions that can control entire ecosystems" ("Trophic Cascade"). As Dungy is using the phrase in her eponymous poem, it refers to the phenomenon observed in Yellowstone: when gray wolves were reintroduced to the park some years ago, they culled deer, whose populations had become rampant; this permitted stunted trees and bushes to reestablish, which in turn led to the return of songbirds, birds of prey, hares and other small animals, beavers that built dams, dams that harbored fishes, and so on. After describing the process of cascading life forms, Dungy turns to her own personal experience. Beautifully, this rich ecological process becomes an analogy for the changes happening in her own life and reminds us that she, like all humans, is part of nature:

> Don't
> you tell me this is not the same as my story. All this
> life born from one hungry animal, this whole,
> new landscape, the course of the river changed,
> I know this. I reintroduced myself to myself, this time
> a mother. After which, nothing was ever the same. (16)

The interconnectedness between Dungy's personal history, African American history, and the environment is particularly rich in *Trophic Cascade*. Joy suffuses the book, though leavened with anger, irony, humor. Dungy writes wonderfully about motherhood – how she has "loved every cell of [Callie's] body from the time I could count them / until now" (30). But also, there is grief. Dungy reminds us that our environment includes our history – for instance, her poems include the four little girls killed in the 1963 Birmingham church bombing (51); the Chinese and Polish and Salvadoran immigrant detainees locked up at Angel Island (55); slave mothers, "*All those women sold away // from their babies*" for whom a black steward on an airplane flight begins to weep when he sees Dungy rocking her baby (50). A remarkable poem, "Notes on what is always with us," starts out to be about a birthday party the poet threw for her mother, but as she says, "grief came along / for the cake," since three of the ten mothers at her mother's party had lost a child. Then the poem segues to penguins and their chicks, and thence to global warming, which enables ticks carried by cormorants to survive the winter and embed themselves in penguins' bodies, which in turn causes the penguins to abandon their nests and seek the relief of the water:

She will run and slide and dive into danger.

Her eggs will die and her chicks will die
and she may die as well.

The poem turns to the memory of an afternoon spent with a friend who subsequently lost his partner and son, and concludes that there, too, grief rides in like a tick on a cormorant's wing: "I was trying to write about beauty, but grief won't stay away. // I was trying to write about babies and birthdays and birds. / I was trying to write about joy" (33–34).

***

The job of a soul is to stay awake.
—Brenda Hillman, "Day 11," "Metaphor & Simile: 24 journal poems at
year's end," *Extra Hidden Life, among the Days*, p. 71

Brenda Hillman, twenty years older than Camille Dungy, is one of the leading poets of our times – an indefatigable environmentalist who has led and participated in political actions for decades. Brilliantly innovative, she draws on Romanticism, Modernism, surrealism, science writing, sound and word play, forays into etymology, passages from official documents, bits of conversation, and scraps of found text to create a lyric poetry of rare and difficult beauty. She dismantles the idea of the monolithic self, reducing the capital "I" to lowercase and speaking of herself as many "brendas." Her work is full of playful punctuation – for instance, to indicate the clicks of birds, the hesitancies of thought, the stutter of a congressional aide – and inhabits the page in a stunning array of open field compositions. A "sorceress looking for my sources" ("Hydrology of California," *Practical Water* 92), for years she has practiced trance writing, through which she bears witness to the consanguinity between nature and spirit. As she writes in "To a Desert Poet," "*the features / of the world are the same / as the language of the soul*" (*Practical Water* 99).

Hillman was born in Tucson, Arizona, in 1951; though she has not lived there in adulthood, the desert continues to figure in her writing. But the primary, beloved terrain of Hillman's work is California – its deserts, coasts, cities, and mountains. She holds the Olivia Filippi Chair in Poetry at St. Mary's College in Moraga and is married to the poet Robert Hass. Her work has received numerous awards and fellowships; in 2016 she was elected a Chancellor of the Academy of American Poets, and in 2017 she was elected to the American Academy of Arts and Sciences ("Brenda Hillman").

Hillman is the author of eleven books of poetry and the translator, editor, or coeditor of several additional volumes. Her books most informed by ecopoetics and politics are *Cascadia* (2001), *Pieces of Air in the Epic* (2005), *Practical Water* (2011), *Seasonal Works with Letters on Fire* (2013), *Extra Hidden Life, among the Days* (2018) and *In a Few Minutes Before Later (2022)*. The first four of these celebrate, in turn, the four classical elements: earth, air, water, and fire. Of the fifth, Hillman writes, "When they ask 'What are you working on now that the elements are finished' i say the elements are never finished; in China they have metal, in India they have ether, in the West we are short on time. Wood has also been named as an element" ("Whose Woods These Are We Think," *Extra Hidden Life* 4). *In a Few Minutes Before Later*, Hillman's latest book, appeared too recently to be included in this discussion, but as Forrest Gander writes in a review published in *The Los Angeles Review of Books*, its "wild and moving poems" continue her "insistent relation of the human and nonhuman, of animate and inanimate agencies, of language (including punctuation) and thingness, of nonlinear time and the mystery of presence, and of the particular and the conceptual...." Taken together, the six volumes comprise one of the farthest-ranging, most imaginative ecopoetic/ecopolitical interventions of our times.

A piece from *Seasonal Works* outlines the terrain and many of the methods of Hillman's work:

A – At times a poem might enact qualities brought from Romantic poetry, through Baudelaire, to modernism & beyond – freedom of form, expressivity, & content – taking these to a radical intensity, with uncertainty, complexity, contradiction;

B – such a poem employs knowledge from diverse disciplines – including scientific vocabularies, but it does not privilege only the human. Research includes rural and urban wilds as well as knowledge from all cultures; creative forms bring together earth & spirit, rejecting no sources, including the personal;

C – its energies shuttle across binaries: realism/non-realism, rationality/irrationality, refuting received authority;

D – such a poem like an animal could graze or hunt in its time, exploring each word, carrying symbolic rhythms, syntax & images directly between the dream & the myth; the imagination does not reject the spirit world:

E – then a poem is its own action, performing practical miracles:
  1. "the miracle of language roots" – to return with lexical adventures
  2. "the miracle of perception" – to honor the senses

3. "the miracle of nameless feeling" – to reflect the weight of the
    subjective, the contours of emotion
4. "the miracle of the social world" – to enter into collective
    bargaining with the political & the social
F – & though powerless to halt the destruction of bioregions, the poem
can be brought away from the computer. The poet can accompany
acts of resistance so the planet won't die of the human. ("Ecopoetics
Minifesto: A Draft for Angie" 29)

The "minifesto" well describes the heterogeneity of Hillman's work, its
constant elements of idiosyncrasy and surprise. And the last point, F,
expresses her combination of despair and determination – a clear-eyed
acknowledgment of catastrophic environmental damage and an unshak-
able commitment to activism, both of which have become increasingly
urgent beginning with *Practical Water*.

In *Cascadia* and *Pieces of Air*, activism takes place mainly in the writing;
the poem itself is a field of action. The first of the tetralogy, *Cascadia*, takes
its name from the landform that once underlay what is now California. One
of the book's long poems, "A Geology," explores the "faults" and islands, the
coasts and constant shifts of the Pacific Plate, and via a pun on the word
"fault" it interweaves this other-than-human material with an exploration of
addiction and recovery – another form of shifting landform, as it were.
Other poems focus primarily on the human history and exploitation of
nature in California – for instance, "The Shirley Poem," which quotes from
letters about the California Gold Rush written in 1851–1852, and a series of
experimental lyrics commemorating the California Missions. "Dioxin
Promenade" and "Dioxin Sunset" bring current environmental toxins to
the fore, and a wonderful short poem, "Styrofoam Cup," breaks down Keats'
ode to lambaste the ubiquitous product that takes at least 500 years to
biodegrade; like the urn, it is sempiternal:

> thou still unravished   thou
> thou,   thou bride
> thou unstill,
> thou unravished   unbride
> unthou   unbride (21)

Pieces of Air was published during the height of the Iraq War; its troubled
poems set contemporary violence against culture's long history of anguish
and warfare, with echoes of the Psalms –

> I will lift up mine blindfold
> Down round eyes unto the hills (64)

– and *The Inferno*: "In the middle of your life / you cast aside the brittle flame; // the doctor took some cancer off / pain ceased to be an organizer" ("Clouds Near San Leandro" 65). The primary echo, though, is to the Trojan War and to Iphigenia, who, in Greek mythology, was sacrificed by her father, Agamemnon, after he had slain a deer in Artemis' sacred grove and in punishment Artemis had stalled the winds, preventing the Greeks from sailing to Troy. Hillman acerbically comments,

> Her
> father could have removed the sails   & rowed to Troy. Nothing makes
> sense in war, you say. Throw
> away the hunger & the war's   all gone. ("Air in the Epic" 9)

Like Iphigenia's, ours is an "under-mothered world in crisis," where the (former) "president says global warming doesn't exist" ("Air in the Epic" 8). In the "Maimed heart walled city," "The lost one is everywhere," and with the advent of aerial warfare, the "global kill[s] people / it [will] never see" ("Nine Untitled Epyllions" 46, 47, 49). The poet is the "seamstress," stitching the cloth of the soul, but, she acknowledges, "my needle means / nothing to the State," nor to the jovial mall-crowding citizens for whom "the war is forget forgot forgotten" ("Nine Untitled Epyllions" 47, 51, 52). As George Santayana remarked, "Those who cannot remember the past are condemned to repeat it," and so the tragic myth still echoes in the present. "I, it, we, you, he, they am, is, are, sick about America," Hillman writes in "String Theory Sutra" (82). Thinking about her country and her students, the affection that is ubiquitous in her work mingles with both frustration and despair.

> You
> love the human species when you   see them, even when they load
> their backpacks early & check the
> tiny screens embedded in their phones. ("Air in the Epic" 9)

With *Practical Water*, Hillman begins to practice what she calls "reportorial poetry," which records details "with immediacy while one is doing an action & thinking about something else" ("Reportorial Poetry, Trance & Activism" 33). In particular, in section two, "Of Communal Authority," the poet becomes more activist, both reporting on her own and urging others to intervene directly in matters of state. The furious poem "In a House Subcommittee on Electronic Surveillance" ends by addressing the reader:

> You at home, what do you feel.
> You can vote by calling 1-900-it's-either-too-fucking-
> late-or-too-early. There's

a secret in every century that likes it
        if you shout. There is time for our little secret.
There is space for the secret spilling out. (49)

One of Hillman's most powerful expressions of the connections between
ecopoetry and politics is "A Violet in the Crucible," in the section of
Practical Water about the trips that she and other members of Code Pink
made to Washington to attend congressional hearings on the Iraq War. It
takes its title from Percy Bysshe Shelley's *A Defence of Poetry*, and comes
from a passage about translation: "Hence the vanity of translation," Shelley
writes;

> it were as wise to case a violet into a crucible that you might discover the
> formal principle of its color and odor, as seek to transfuse from one
> language into another the creations of a poetry. The plant must spring
> again from its seed, or it will bear no flower – and this is the burden of the
> curse of Babel.

The passage would seem to testify to the impossibility of "translating"
poetry into the language of congresspeople who are discussing and defending the Pentagon budget – "*We cannot leave them / there without weapons,*"
an aide stutters to the poet – and perhaps it does express a certain despair
about the Babel that characterizes current political discourse. But accompanying the phrase "*a violet in the crucible*" in Hillman's poem is the phrase
"*imagination is enlarged by a sympathy,*" the full sentence of which in
Shelley's essay is "The imagination is enlarged by a sympathy with pains
and passions so mighty, that they distend in their conception the capacity
of that by which they are conceived." And behind that, though Hillman
does not quote it, is this:

> The great secret of morals is love; or a going out of our nature, and an
> identification of ourselves with the beautiful which exists in thought,
> action, or person, not our own.. . . The great instrument of moral good is
> the imagination. (*A Defence of Poetry and Other Essays*)

We arrive at Hillman's deeply ecopoetic awareness that the poet is the
legislator (in Shelley's phrase) in human form, just as other forms of life
"legislate" for their ecosystems:

> the duskytail darter from Tennessee legislates or
> the Indiana bat, *myotis sodalist,* the dwarf wedgemussel
>   half buried in Maryland with your bivalve
>   in silt of your wetland habitat, as you, the vanishing
> northeastern bulrush from Massachusetts

> legislate by shrinking; he doesn't mean you will live,
> he means you could live on listen. As the sturgeon
> in a million pounds of phosphorous or
> the snowy plover from Cascadia might. (42–43)

So we are called to witness and to action, through love and imagination; because not only humans but other-than-human beings are "endangered," our names are "on the list." The poem ends with this grim, beautiful injunction: "if you don't survive this way there are others, / . . . send the report with your body – " (43).

Seasonal Works continues Hillman's exploration of poetry's role in environmental politics. "Years of not getting enough sleep; / awake at 5 to worry about the planet," she writes ("Between the Fire and the Flood" 35), in lines that capture the anguish that pervades much of the book. The book casts a wide net. Teaching *The Aeneid* "for the twelfth time" leads Hillman to think of

> Ceaseless Empire Trojan Roman
> Ottoman British U.S.A., treating tribal lands
> like layers on a big old onion. Hard to be cheerful
>   at work. Fuck cheerful. Women
> in Kandahar make $2 a month; our people
> tweet & sleep through the wars . . . ("I Heard Flame-Folder Spring Bring Red" 17)

Unmarked drones that pour down death on wedding parties; the genetic engineering conducted by Monsanto, AstraZeneca, Novartis that seeks to control the fertility of seeds; the passage of Citizens United, giving corporations the status of persons; methane release; offshore drilling; global warming – all these receive Hillman's attention, as well as her scorn for "candidates" with their "idiotic speeches" that "sound like *boing*. / They sound like *boing boing*. They go boing-boing, / boing-boing-boing" ("Radical Lads, Blisters & Glad Summers" 91). But several things save the book from a tone of complete despair. One is Hillman's irrepressible formal playfulness, her quirkiness and originality. Another is humor, however dark – as in the lines quoted above, or "The Seeds Talk Back to Monsanto." Another is the gathering hopefulness engendered by the Occupy Movement, in which Hillman took an active part, and which is the subject of several poems: "The revolution is not far away," she writes. "It is / in your heart" ("Mists from People as They Pass" 80). Then too, Hillman's long practice of trance work has given her an unshakeable sense of spiritual realities; this is the "unknowable flame" that grounds both her activism and her poetry. And finally, there is simple human love.

> Deep in the night
> a trough of chaos forms;
> your lover's body stops it every time. ("In the Evening of the Search" 105)

Major Jackson has described *Extra Hidden Life as* "full of celebrations of those who keep fighting the good fight, or ... devoted their lives to resisting" (Jackson). Rosa Luxemburg and Rosa Parks are presiding spirits in this book, and a third, everywhere throughout, is lichen, the combined fungi and algae that breaks down stone, which Hillman calls "my wife of decomposers," for "Lichen says / accept what is then break it down" ("Day 3," "Metaphor & Simile: 24 journal poems at year's end" 58). Among the sources of anguish and unrest that Hillman addresses in this book are America's economic distress, deforestation, homelessness, racism, debt and the greed of banks, gun violence and murdered children, fracking, Monsanto and WalMart, toxic seas, threatened corals, waste, a vacillating state, and – in "Hearing La Bohème after the March" – "Simpering and thug idiocies" (49). It is no wonder that the words "suffering," "grief," and "tired" recur in many of the poems, for this is a book written in struggle. Two of the sequences are elegies: "The Rosewood Clauses" and "Her Presence Will Live Beyond Progress." The first elegizes Hillman's father, who lived a long and happy life, and the second commemorates her beloved friend C. D. Wright, whose sudden death in 2016 brought an "impossible sorrow" (123). But it is difficult in a short space adequately to describe the book's overall complexity, for the poems, particularly the series of "24 journal poems at year's end" titled "Metaphor and Simile," move quickly as thought moves from one figure or issue to another, and accrue power to reveal a nearly overwhelming sense of general suffering, injustice, and catastrophe. These lines, from "Day 4," may serve as an example:

> It's impossible to know
> how to live: Rilke paralyzed, depressed
> wrote little during WWI. Claude McKay, Jamaican
>   songs in dialect. In letters, Roza writes:
> *my gold* ... The workers strike. The tsar's children had
> diamonds sewn into their clothes.
>
>   . . .
>
>   Walmart
>   doing violence to the poor who work & shop
>   at Walmart how now brown cow
> they cannot live. Dream baby. Crowds were
>   in   the streets
>   again   in   groups. We had a brief
> window to join   in: black + brown + white ... (60)

Still, there are moments of happiness, even joy, in *Extra Hidden Life*. The "wife of decomposers," lichen, provides a metaphor for patience; all rock may be broken down at last, and a "radical hope lives on in us" ("Hearing La Bohème after the March" 49). In some form or another, the natural world endures; as Hillman writes, "it's too late for countries / but it's not too late for trees" ("Angrily Standing Outside in the Wind" 19). Rich in love – a word that occurs often – the poems celebrate students, fellow activists, friends, and most of all, the spirits that bring poetry, earth and its airs and waters, and the poet's human family. The book ends with two odes, "Poem for a National Forest" and "Poem for a National Seashore," for two of the most beautiful places in California, Muir Woods and Point Reyes National Seashore, respectively. The final lines of the last poem in the book describe a scattering of cremated ashes:

> Talking about events that mattered as the ashes were
> sucked back in the tide so loss could be lost
> for a while as love kept them
> in company beside – (168)

***

Craig Santos Perez is an indigenous Chamorro, born on Guam, where he lived until he was fifteen. Now, formerly married to a Hawaiian woman, Brandy Nālani McDougall, he teaches at the University of Hawai'i. He is the author of five books of poetry and a critical book, *Navigating CHamoru Poetry: Indigeneity, Aesthetics, and Decolonization*; coeditor of five anthologies; and cofounder of Alta Press, dedicated solely to Pacific literature. His work has received many awards; in 2010, the Guam Legislature passed Resolution No. 315-30, recognizing and commending Craig as an accomplished poet and ambassador for Guam, "eloquently conveying through his words, the beauty and love that is the Chamorro culture" (http://craigsantosperez.com/).

The four brilliant books by Craig Santos Perez that comprise *from unincorporated territory* are [hacha], [saina], [guma'], and [lukao], from 2008, 2010, 2014, and 2017, respectively. (His 2020 book, *Habitat Threshold*, is more direct protest poetry and casts an international net.) The four books trace back to a story his mother tells in a memoir, which he quotes in *from unincorporated territory [guma']*.

> One day in our geography class [in Virginia], my teacher taped several maps on the wall and asked each of us to stand in front of the class and mark where our parents and grandparents were born. I tried to remember

everything my mom told me about Guam. I only remembered that she told me it would be hard to find on a map . . . because it was so small. She said it's in the Pacific Ocean, and it's a tiny dot on the map, so find the Philippine Islands first because it's not far from there. . . . I knelt down so I could see better and found the Philippine Islands. I still couldn't find Guam and I started crying. (17–18)

Santos Perez makes Guam visible. Highly experimental, his books combine lyric poetry with documentation, making use of maps, lists, strikethroughs, italicized passages, passages in faint gray ink, and code-switching between English and Chamorro and sometimes Spanish. The four books of *from unincorporated territory* speak to each other and continually complicate his narrative. The titles' beginning with "from" indicates that in both poetry and history, Guam's story is unfinished. Because of this complexity, they are richly rewarding but hard to describe. As Michael Lujan Bevacqua writes,

> Through his poetry, he weaves together different languages, citations, and spatial configurations in order to challenge old maps and to retrace the steps of Chamorros through their ancient past and challenge the ways in which key points on that journey have come to be represented, remembered, or forgotten. In challenging colonialist, Eurocentric maps, he is also in essence creating new song maps meant to lead Chamorros in new directions in terms of their consciousness and their identity. His work represents a poetic and a political decolonization, whereby the sites that once constricted and constrained us can now help us imagine our liberation. (Bevacqua)

from unincorporated territory [hacha] lays out the geographic and the poetic territory. It describes Guam: "approx. 209 square miles," it is the "southernmost island in the Marianas archipelago," the peak of a "submerged mountain . . . rising 37,820 feet above the floor of the [Marianas] trench" (7–8). Unincorporated, "an area under U.S. jurisdiction in which only certain 'natural' protections of the U.S. Constitution apply," it is "organized"; "the 1950 Guam Organic Act conferred U.S. citizenship and organized local government" (8). Won from Spain in the 1898 Spanish American War, it is a "colonial possession" whose citizens dwell in a permanent "state of political disenfranchisement" (9). Under Spanish rule, its people were forcibly converted to Catholicism. Officially named Guåhan, it has always played a strategic role in the Pacific, "as a stopping post on the Spanish Galleon Trade Route, as a significant advancement for the Japanese Army during World War II, and as a continuing military colony of the U.S." (11). On December 8, 1941, the Japanese bombed

Guam; quickly they invaded and controlled the island, continuing to hold it until August 12, 1944 ("Guam"). Postwar US military presence has endured; with the decision to transfer thousands of Marines from Okinawa, it continues to escalate.

One affective thread that runs through "[hacha]" consists of the poems titled "*from* TA(LA)YA," dedicated to Santos Perez's grandfather, who as a young man was taught to weave a *talaya* – in Chamorro, a fishing net. The sequence narrates bits of the grandfather's history during Japanese occupation, but the *talaya* also becomes a metaphor for the way the book catches disparate bits of history. These occur in fragmentary poem-sequences called "*from* Lisiensan Ga'lago," "*from* tidelands," "*from* aerial roots," and "*from* descending plumeria" – this last, a haunting narrative about a cousin who dies in San Francisco after a motorcycle accident. The vigil the family keeps in Guam while Renee lies in the hospital mingles with information about the brown tree snakes inadvertently brought to Guam on cargo ships after World War II, with memories of a trip with Renee to the "cave of chief gadao," and finally with memories of Renee's poignant, fading watercolor that the family brings to California when they move.

from unincorporated territory [saina] continues the exploration of Chamorro history. One important series of poems concerns the sakman, the outrigger canoes "once numerous in waters of the marianas islands," and "the fastest sailing vessels in the world," but systematically destroyed by the Spanish; by the mid-nineteenth century, the knowledge of how to build and sail the sakman had been lost. Then in the 1990s an organization called "tasi" ("traditions about seafaring islands") built a sakman, named it "'saina': 'parents elders spirits ancestors,'" and blessed and first sailed it in September 2008 (15). This act of cultural retrieval is countered by poems concerning the proliferation of military dumping, nuclear testing, and other military toxic waste that have polluted Pacific waters since World War II (60); and poems concerning the US military appropriation of land and personnel buildup in Guam. Some of these poems constitute an interspersed series, "ginen tidelands," in which all the text is struck through as if to imitate the official suppression of its knowledge. In 2010, the US military "occupies a third of the island" (67), and a buildup has continued since then. The tourist industry, too, brings crowding, destruction of traditional sites, and environmental damage. Elderly Chamorros are dying of disease and younger Chamorros are disproportionately joining the military and dying in American wars; "in the current war on terror, our killed in action rate is now five times the national average." (127)

The third book of the series, "[guma']," introduces "the legends of juan malo" – "a young poor Chamorro man" whose adventures involved tricking the Spanish during colonial occupation and who becomes an alter ego for Santos Perez in his "spirit of resistance" (n.p.) There are poems about Spam, the popular but unhealthy canned meat introduced by the American military, and – in contrast – poems about latte, stone pillars dating from as early as AD 900 that symbolize Chamorro strength and "formed the foundations of homes, schools, canoe shelters, food sheds, and communal spaces" (18). Movingly, lists of the dead killed in US military action run throughout the book, with all details except their names struck through. And a series of "*ginen* fatal impact statements" register opposition during a public comment period to the continued military buildup on the island.

from unincorporated territory [lukao] foregrounds several kinds of birth. It begins, "Guam was born on March 6, 1521, when Ferdinand Magellan arrived in . . . Hamatack Bay and delivered [us] into the calloused hands of modernity" (11). Poems titled "*ginen* island of no birdsong" thread their way throughout, about various endangered or extinct species. These include the Micronesian kingfisher and the Marianas crow, both now extinct in the wild, extirpated by the brown tree snakes inadvertently brought on US cargo ships and now numbering in the millions; the only births of these birds take place in captivity.

Other births are happier. The book has four sections, each divided into five groups of poems: "*from* the legends of juan malo [a malalogue]," "*ginen* understory," "*ginen* organic acts," "*ginen* Ka Lāhui o ka Pō Interview," and "*ginen* island of no birdsong." Throughout the poems of "*ginen* understory," Santos Perez awaits, then begins to parent, his first child, whom he calls [neni] – baby or sweetheart in English. The phrase "*ginen* Ka Lāhui o ka Pō Interview" refers to traditional Chamorro birthing practices, and juxtaposes his wife's accounts of [neni's] birth with his mother's accounts of the births of her own three children. But as always, the political dimensions of American occupation are manifest; a series of lined-through prose paragraphs narrates the US Navy medical officers' gradually shutting down the practices of Chamorro midwives – another example of the denial of nature and indigenous practices.

In Chamorro, "lukao" means "procession," especially a religious procession. A series of prayers runs through this book: his elderly Catholic grandmother's recitations of the rosary; his own invocations of saints, as in "St. Sebastian, tayuyute [ham]" (12); the possibly ironic lists of #pray-for_____ with which he ends the book's sections; his prayers to *puntan* and *fu'una*, Chamorro gods of creation, and to *haumea*, Hawaiian goddess of fertility (35), to protect his wife in her pregnancy and then their newborn daughter; and his constant remembrance of "i taotaomo'na *the spirits of before*" (35). A beautiful prayer ends the poem "(first birthday)", and it may serve as a blessing to end this essay about three poets whose writings and activism so vigilantly have defended nature against a destructive colonial/postcolonial/industrial society:

> . . . [neni], no matter how far from home
>
> the storms take you, remember to carry our words
> in your canoe // [neni], remember: you will always
>
> belong, you will always be sheltered, and you
> will always be sacred in our ocean of stories (65)

WORKS CITED

Bevacqua, Michael Lujan. "The Song Maps of Craig Santos Perez." *Transmotion*, vol. 1, no. 1, 2015.

"Brenda Hillman." Poets.org. https://poets.org/poet/brenda-hillman.

"Dr. Craig Santos Perez." http://craigsantosperez.com/.

Dungy, Camille. *Black Nature: Four Centuries of African American Nature Poetry*. Athens: Georgia University Press, 2009.

"Is All Writing Environmental Writing?" *Georgia Review*, Fall 2018, https://thegeorgiareview.com/posts/is-all-writing-environmental-writing/.

Smith Blue. Carbondale: Southern Illinois University Press, 2011.

Suck on the Marrow. Pasadena, CA: Red Hen Press, 2010.

Trophic Cascade. Middletown, CT: Wesleyan University Press, 2017.

What to Eat, What to Drink, and What to Leave for Poison. Pasadena, CA: Red Hen Press, 2006.

Gander, Forrest. "In a Garden of Zeroes: On Brenda Hillman's 'In a Few Minutes Before Later'," *The Los Angeles Review of Books*, October 12, 2022.

"Guam: War in the Pacific National Historical Park." National Park Service. www.nps.gov/articles/pacificnational.htm.

Hillman, Brenda. *Cascadia*. Middletown, CT: Wesleyan University Press, 2001.

Extra Hidden Life, among the Days. Middletown, CT: Wesleyan University Press, 2018.

Pieces of Air in the Epic. Middletown, CT: Wesleyan University Press, 2005.

Practical Water. Middletown, CT: Wesleyan University Press, 2011.

Seasonal Works with Letters on Fire. Middletown, CT: Wesleyan University Press, 2013.

Hopkins, Gerard Manley. "God's Grandeur." In *Gerard Manley Hopkins: Selected Poetry*, edited with introduction and notes by Catherine Phillips. Oxford: Oxford University Press, 2008.

Jackson, Major. "Brenda Hillman." Academy of American Poets. www .poetryfoundation.org/poets/brenda-hillman.

Santos Perez, Craig. *from unincorporated territory [guma']*. Oakland, CA: Omnidawn Publishing, 2014.

 from unincorporated territory [hacha]. Oakland, CA: Omnidawn Publishing, 2008.

 from unincorporated territory [lukao]. Oakland, CA: Omnidawn Publishing, 2017.

 from unincorporated territory [saina]. Oakland, CA: Omnidawn Publishing, 2010.

 Habitat Threshold. Oakland, CA: Omnidawn Publishing, 2020.

 Navigating CHamoru Poetry: Indigeneity, Aesthetics, and Decolonization. Tucson: University of Arizona Press, 2022.

Shelley, Percy Bysshe. *A Defence of Poetry and Other Essays*. Austin, TX: West by Southwest Press, 2012.

"Trophic Cascade." Wikipedia. https://en.wikipedia.org/wiki/Trophic_cascade.

CHAPTER 18

The Politics and History of Digital Poetics
Copyright, Authorship, Anti-Lyric

Orchid Tierney

Digital poetry emerged in tandem with advances in the computer sciences in the mid-twentieth century, although we can trace its experimental impulses to earlier literary traditions. As Dani Spinosa argues, "digital poetry has its roots in a history of print-based avant-garde" (x). The recombinant and nonlinear conditions of electronic literature, broadly conceived, have led some scholars to attend to modernist works by writers and media visionaries such as Gertrude Stein, Ezra Pound, and Bob Brown in a search for the origins of the procedural play in contemporary innovative writing. "Early digital poems," as Christopher Funkhouser notes, "can be conceptually interpreted as searching for their essence or as striving to make their essence apparent, as did modernist endeavors" (3). Media theorists, such as Marshall McLuhan, Friedrich Kittler, and Lev Manovich understood the innovations of early media as cornerstones in the development of the digital revolution. The modernist transition to new communication and media technologies, such as cinema, radio, and the gramophone, fostered faster transmissions of information that in turn influenced novel approaches to structuring narrative time, visual language, and reading practices. Bob Brown's 1930 proposal for a mechanized reading machine offers an intriguing example of this collision between media and literature. Invoking the "talkies" or sound films, Brown's reading device proposed to deliver "readies" or a ticker-tape stream of prose or poetry to a viewer, thereby efficiently transmitting a visual spectacle of information. For Brown, the machine would "revitalize" an "interest in the Optical Art of Writing" and thus merge the act of reading with the technological innovations that were already modernizing society (27). With this background in mind, it remains a useful exercise to apprehend the radical experimentation of contemporary electronic literature alongside the visual, technological, and formal innovations of earlier avant-garde movements, including Futurism and Dadaism, as well as later literary groups, such as Oulipo, Fluxus, and language writing.

The complexities of innovative literary forms are often compounded by their relationships to programmable media and social networks. It thus pays to tease out an initial definition, given that twenty-first-century digital poetry proliferates in variegated platforms, cultural systems, and networked technologies such as installation projections, text messages, Twitter bots, mobile apps, locative GPS media, hypertexts, poem generators, cinepoems, Twine and video games, and augmented reality worlds. In 1999, Scott Rettberg, Robert Coover, and Jeff Ballowe founded the Electronic Literature Organization "to foster and promote the reading, writing, teaching, and understanding of literature as it develops and persists in a changing digital environment" ("History"). That digital environments are not static bears emphasizing, for the digital revolution is never complete but an ever-evolving material event that incorporates new technologies while adapting older ones. Noah Wardrip-Fruin describes electronic literature as "work with important literary aspects that requires the use of digital computation" (Wardrip-Fruin 163). Founder of the archive *I ♥ E-Poetry*, Leonardo Flores narrows digital poetry within a subset of electronic literature and defines the genre as "a poetic practice made possible by digital media and technologies" (155). Similarly, Davin Heckman and James O'Sullivan propose that electronic literature is "construed not as other but rather as a construction whose literary aesthetics emerge from computation – a system of multimodal forces with the word at its center" (Heckman and O'Sullivan). These definitions collectively resist the idea that any text produced with the aid of a computer can be considered a digital poem. Rather, the literariness of a work relies on a digital mechanism to produce textual signs. For this reason, I will focus on poetic texts that depend on new media or coding for their instantiation, even if they are published in conventional print formats. If digital poetry is "born digital," an approach to its textuality must commit to all of its expansive components, including the software and hardware, that activate the visual, sonic, kinetic, and textual signs of the work. Since new media converge in often astonishing ways, Heckman and O'Sullivan's formulation of electronic literature seems particularly useful here, for to centralize the multimodality of digital textuality in relation to language underscores the fuzzy boundaries between forms of poetry that overlap with art, gaming, video, and code.

The multimodality of digital poetry has opened the range of responses available to writers to explore categories of identity or experiences that underlie language and provoke critical reflection on contested sites of power. While artivism, activism, and hacktivism are not the focus in this chapter, the ways that digital poets have utilized new media or technology to intervene in the various sites of power – whether authorial, environmental, or linguistic – are. Of course, the experiments of digital poetry, which challenge social and political assumptions, are themselves not novel. The language poets, for example, underscored the social and political ideologies and hierarchies underlying material language. Poets such as Ron Silliman proposed that a "capitalist mode of reality" required a "re-evaluation of the history, form and function" of poetry, and a recentering of language in relation to a working class (131). The digital tools and environments of contemporary poetry are likewise not divorced from the expressive politics of language, class, race, and gender. While early cyber-libertarian digital activists, such as John Perry Barlow, may have insisted that cyberspace was a disembodied democratic network of "transactions, relations, and thought," digital cultures frequently mirror the situated sociopolitical systems of the real world (Barlow, "A Declaration of the Independence of Cyberspace"). Indeed, the emergence of online forums, listservs, and virtual worlds in the 1980s and 1990s tended to reinforce sexual, gender, and capitalist ideologies. As Lisa Nakamura has argued, the Internet "propagates, disseminates, and commodifies images of race and racism" (3). Racial and gender identity stereotypes and tropes in the form of avatars or fictional characters are performed through online roleplay and video games, or are expressed through search engine algorithms. In other words, digital technologies are not neutral tools but often replicate or amplify already existing racist, gendered, and economic structures.

This chapter interrogates three vectors of digital poetry in order to address why the politics of this form matters. First it will engage with history of digital texts that have intervened in poetic language and form as contested sites of power, before charting, second, the intersections between video games and digital poetry. The rise of gaming technologies has fostered new aesthetic modes that have allowed digital artists to challenge the hierarchical, racial, and colonial ideologies that often underlie the visual syntaxes and semiotic regimes of commercial video games. Third, this chapter will interrogate how digital poetry challenges notions of traditional authorship to open new pathways that nurture expanded collaborative partnerships between the writer and reader. Digital poetry underscores the communal and interactive possibilities of the language arts and foregrounds their complex haptic sociality that reorients lyricism as a political condition in the twenty-first century. The shift from an individual positionality toward multiplicity, mixed authorship, and polyvocality destabilizes – but does not erase – the lyrical subject or their sociopolitical experiences. But let's first begin with a short history.

A Short History

Although I will not rehearse the entire history of digital poetics and electronic literature as its background has already been extensively covered by scholars such as Loss Pequeño Glazier in *Digital Poetics* (2002), Christopher Funkhouser in *Prehistoric Digital Poetry* (2007) and *New Directions in Digital Poetry* (2012), N. Katherine Hayles in *Electronic Literature: New Horizons for the Literary* (2008), and Scott Rettberg in *Electronic Literature* (2018). Scholars have situated digital poetry in the context of broader technology trends to reflect on the intersections between experimental literatures, the computer sciences, and the emergence of information technologies and social networks since the 1950s. Chronological divisions have marked major technological shifts. N. Katherine Hayles proposes that 1995 divides first- and second-generation electronic literature, with the latter comprising then-emergent Web and multimedia-based works (8). First-generation digital objects were frequently under the purview of computer programmers – or artists with connections to programmers – who were testing the possibilities of their nascent tools. Permutation poems and text generators, such as Christopher Strachey's *Love Letters* (1952), Theo Lutz's *Stochastische Texte* (1959), and Brion Gysion's *I Am That I Am* (1960) are often cited as examples of this early period. The advent of personal computing and user-friendly interfaces opened literary experimentation to a broader spectrum of writers, who used these tools to explore mechanical textualities. We might turn to the mixed media and collaborative practices of Fluxus artists and writers, such as Dick Higgins, Emmett Williams, Jackson Mac Low, and Alison Knowles, whose practices readily dovetailed into procedural forms of indeterminate writing, both on- and off-screen. Jackson Mac Low, for example, explored algorithmic aleatory approaches to writing in his *PER-3* poems (1969), which he generated with a PER-3 programmable film reader and a DEC PDP-9 computer. Mac Low also developed what he called the "diastic technique," a set of self-imposed rules that he applied to various source texts by writers such as Rabindranath Tagore and Virginia Woolf to produce *Stanzas for Iris Lezak* (1971) and *The Virginia Woolf Poems* (1985). Charles O. Hartman, a fellow poet-programmer, developed a DOS executable version of the diastic method, called DIASTEXT, which Mac Low later used with various seed sentences from five works by modernist writer Djuna Barnes to produce his 1996 text-generated poems, gathered in *The Barnesbook*. Mac Low's *PFR-3* poems and *The Barnesbook* exemplify the programmatic capabilities of these early experimental poets, who were intrigued by the potential combinations of indeterminacy within literature that early digital tools had afforded. Mac Low's remixed poetries partially strip the authorial subject from his output – and I say partially for the Barnes poems clearly indicate Mac Low's editorial presence – but the erasure of the author is also the point. The obscured authorial subject destabilizes the information economies within the normative structures of language itself. Mac Low's chance-based practices are not only in line with his Taoist and Buddhist philosophies, but as Spinosa argues, his poetry "acts like a microcosm for anarchism" (9). The diastic technique reduces the authorial ego and neutralizes the sociocultural conditions of the appropriated text. Mac Low's poetics of indeterminacy thus encourages a sense of egalitarian politics within his work, one that supports spontaneity and relationality over individual control and capitalist ownership of language.

Programmatic writing neither is medium-specific nor is it native to technology and networked literary productions. The term "digital poetry" may even be a misnomer in the sense that it potentially elides the concurrent influences that have shaped both print-based and digital literature since the postwar period. As Richard Hughes Gibson argues, "old media are material *to* the study of digital literature because they have always been among the materials *of* digital literature" (4; emphases in original). A case in point for Gibson is the 1967 computer poem *A House of Dust* by Fluxus artist Alison Knowles and composer James Tenney. Now considered one of the earliest examples of computer poetry, *A House of Dust* used an early compiled programming language, FORTRAN IV, and a Siemens 4004 computer to produce a list of random attributes from a database of vocabulary. The output was organized into quatrains that followed a predetermined format with randomly selected nouns: "a house of (list material), using (list location), (list light source), inhabited by (list inhabitants)."

A HOUSE OF SAND
ON THE SEA
USING CANDLES
INHABITED BY HORSES AND BIRDS

Verlag Gebrüder König published a limited edition chapbook of the poem on dot matrix printer paper in 1968. Additionally, Knowles produced variations in different media, including a physical house-like installation, postcards, and art performances. That the poem exists in multiple iterations, has inspired digital simulations by Nick Montfort and Zach Whalen, and underlies Stephanie Strickland and Ian Hatcher's digital poem *House of Trust* (2014) underscores the difficulty of defining digital poetics as a stable category of inquiry. As Majorie Perloff notes, digital poetry lends itself to multiplicity, whereby a text might exist in different versions "with no single version being the definitive one" (146). Seen in this light, *A House of Dust* illustrates the trend toward the multimedia versioning in the twentieth century in which born digital literature seeps into other forms of new media – installations, video games, net art, as well as print media – and thus necessitates a more sophisticated apprehension of its multimodality and spreadability.

I foreground Mac Low and Alison Knowles here as their works highlight the indeterminate, procedural, and assemblage-oriented components within digital poetics that have remade poetic textualities in the context of new literary dissemination technologies, Internet infrastructures, and social networks. As Leonardo Flores argues, the development of the World Wide Web and affordable computing radically modified the circulation of electronic literature after 1995 as the Internet and intuitive computing technologies opened the field to a larger body of writers (Flores, "Third Generation"). Authoring tools such as Flash and Javascript enabled poet-programmers to explore the expanded field of time-based language and kinetic art, as well networked practices as evidenced in works such as Brian Kim Stefans' *Dreamlife of Letters* (2000), Talan Memmott's *Lexia to Perplexia* (2000), Deena Larsen's *Carving in Possibilities* (2001), Reiner Strasser and Alan Sondheim's *Tao* (2004), and William Poundstone's *Project for Tachistoscope [Bottomless Pit]* (2005). As Flores notes, third-generation electronic literature emerged alongside the proliferation of social media platforms and mobile apps that fostered cultures of spreadability and reproduction. New platforms and media formats have encouraged viral digital content, such as memes, to migrate quickly across plural networks or to remix language and images in multiple configurations. Works such as Allison Parrish's @everyword, a Twitter bot that tweeted every word in the English language, or the twenty different remixes of Nick Montfort's 2009 Javascript nature poem *Toroko Gorge* are examples of this period.

Arguably, the rise of social media, remixes, and mobile apps has heightened the sense of ubiquitous technologies in which a private poetic language is publicly sharable across multiple networks. This shareable

online culture has enabled poets to explore the political implications of
these commercialized technologies that circulate language within social
networks or communication infrastructures. Works such as Electronic
Theater Disturbance 2.0/B.A.N.G. Lab's *The Transborder Immigrant
Tool* (2007), Sophia Le Fraga's *W8ing* (2014), Jennifer Scappettone and
Judd Morrissey's *Sentiment Fuxt* (2016), Ava Hofmann's *The Woman
Factory* (2020), or Ginger Ko's *Power On* (2022) extend the embodied
site-specificities of mobile apps, Captchas, text messages, and Google Maps
to examine identity formations or localized experiences within digital
environments. *The Transborder Immigrant Tool*, for example, is a long
poem that includes survival strategies to help undocumented immigrants,
who cross the dangerous borderlands between the United States and
Mexico. Delivered through a GPS mobile app on a burner cell phone,
these survival poems are intended to help migrants find hidden water
caches, while also offering advice for any obstacles that they might
encounter in the desert. The poems themselves are instructional and
minimal, and thus convey the feeling of urgency a migrant might experience in a spare desert environment:

> Cholla, or jumping cactus, attaches. A bud of spines breaks off at the
> slightest hint of touch. Remove cholla from your skin and clothing in
> increments, with a rock, a stick, a knife: the bud ... large spines left
> behind ... small spines or glochids. Needling needles that remain will work
> themselves out in the days ahead. (59, ellipses in original)

Conservative pundits like Glenn Beck accused the app creators of "using
poetry to 'dissolve' the US-Mexico border" (qtd. in *The Transborder
Immigrant Tool*). While never formally distributed, *The Transborder
Immigrant Tool* illustrates the tension between private and public knowledge, between technologies of surveillance and a poetics of aid, during a
contested period in which the borderlands have become an increasingly
hostile environment for undocumented immigrants. At the same time, the
mobile app demonstrates the intervention of commercialized technologies
to respond with urgency to a vexed geopolitical environment where life is
literally at stake. More to the point, the app underscores what Rita Raley
has called "tactical media": media that "operates in the field of the
symbolic, the site of power in the postindustrial society" (6). Here, *The
Transborder Immigrant Tool* disrupts the semiotics of the "border crossing"
and renders legible the situated artifice of US-Mexico borderlands, where
governmental structures of immigration control are violently and routinely
sanctioned, often at the expense of human life.

Casual Gamification of Poetics

The Transborder Immigrant Tool further underscores how much a poem's textual signs – including its code – rely its sociopolitical environment for a reader to instantiate its interpretation. Much has been made of the idea that digital poetics fosters co-creation, whereby the reader and author (and, by extension, the machine, platform, or software) activate and interpret the textual signs of poem. Digital poetry and digital environments have extended the community-driven engagement practices that print-based texts themselves foster. "In online spaces," as Anastasia Salter reminds us, "the activeness of the reader comes to life in everything from writing and art to Tumblr sites dedicated to characters – and this is only a visible, community-oriented output of the same type of engagement print demanded before the introduction of digital technology" (8). Yet while print literature is interactive media – reading is hardly a passive endeavor – we might attend to the peculiarities of how digital poetry foregrounds the reader's somatic interaction with the poem's visual, kinetic, and audio signifiers to enhance the meaning-making possibilities of a text. Hypertexts such as Michael Joyce's *afternoon, a story* (1987), Stewart Moulthrop's *Victory Garden* (1991), and J. Yellowlees Douglass' *"I Have Said Nothing": Hypertext Fiction* (1994) are demonstrative of the interactive possibilities for a reader to explore different hypertextual structures, pathways, and story choices that drive the narrative arcs of early digital fiction.

These fiction examples demonstrate the character of playful navigation in digital spaces. Early text parser adventure games such as *Colossal Cave Adventure* (1975–77), *Adventureland* (1979), *Zork* (1980), *Mystery Fun House* (1981), and *Suspect* (1984) have long highlighted that the assumptions between literariness and ludic intentionality. These games foregrounded user strategy-making, textual inputs, and puzzle-solving. Later games such as Roberta and Ken Williams' *Mystery House* (1980), Cyan's *Myst* (1993), and Dejobaan and Popcannibal Games' *Elegy for a Dead World* (2014) incorporated graphic elements with storytelling and open world environments that allowed users to manipulate gameplay and objects. Text parser adventure games and interactive fiction help us to apprehend how game mechanics and design have been deployed within electronic literature, not as corollaries of mainstream gaming but as off-shoots that draw on the conventional game structures. The elements of open worlds, modding (modifying), and the manipulation of visual and textual assets are extended and incorporated in digital texts that explore the genre of visual games and casual playfulness. Digital texts that cross these borders include Dan Shiowitz's interactive *Bad Machine* (1999) and Jim Andrew's *Arteroids* (2003), a word shooter based on the 1979 Atari game *Asteroids*. Additionally, Jason Nelson's *Game, Game, Game, and again Game* (2007) employs a messy amateur interface that gestures to the two-dimensional aesthetics of side-scrolling games like *Mario Brothers* or *Donkey Kong* and imposes nonlinear pathways and narrative onto a poetic form. The visual aesthetic of game-poems like *Arteroids* and *Game, Game, Game, and again Game* expand the idea of poetic language as code, visual, rule-based, and screenic. As Jason Nelson argues, "Video games are a language, a grammar or linguistics for various texts."

> The sounds, the movement, the graphics, the rules (or lack of rules) – everything about a video game is a component of some kind of language. While poetry is traditionally taught as being constrained to words, I think of poetry as being based on *texts*. I mean "texts" in the broadest sense: all the elements, media, code, and artefact within a digital poetry game become a literary element/tool/device. (337; emphasis in original)

The graphic elements in *Game, Game, Game and again Game* appropriate the procedural rhetoric of familiar retro platform games, whereby the user manipulates and scrolls a playable object across the screen, while integrating drawings, handwritten text, poetry, and family videos into the game environment. The resultant game-poem challenges the absurd logic of ordered cultural systems and the pleasing neatness of straight lines used in modern interface design. In particular, *Game, Game, Game, and again Game* utilizes play as a means to render legible sociocultural rules, belief systems, and worldviews. Nelson forces the reader through the game's thirteen levels that stage varying belief systems that are represented as figures such as "the Buddhist," "the capitalist," "the tourist," and "the collection officer." The cluttered aesthetics and gameplay intervene in the way that belief systems formalize rules and shape lived, embodied experiences. In other words, rather than resisting game design and mechanics, *Game, Game, Game, and again Game* insists on replicating the familiarity of these conventions to highlight the way we toggle between various rigid belief systems. As the game's text states: "your choice bricks your future."

We might argue then that games with poetic elements mobilize the logic of game mechanics to critique online and gaming culture, in addition to our real-world, lived experiences. Anna Anthropy's *The Hunt for the Gay Planet* (2013) offers a compelling example. A Twine game, the narrative combines the hypertextual mobility of play in a browser-based platform with users developing their own decision-making strategies within set parameters. *The Hunt for the Gay Planet* spoofs the Makheb planet from the *Star Wars: The Old Republic* downloadable content (DLC) for the base game where queer characters exist but are available only to paying customers. Players must undertake an intergalactic search for a safe queer haven called Lesbionica. The journey involves looking under rocks, exploring caves and planets, and digging holes while engaging with innuendos and puns. Combining hypertextual play with sardonic humor undercuts the LGBTQ+ stereotypes often found in game environments. *The Hunt for the Gay Planet* challenges not only the lack of free queer representation in new media but also the siloing of gay experiences within video gaming environments in general.

Rather than rejecting gaming systems for their exclusions, texts like *The Hunt for the Gay Planet* use the mechanisms of gameplay to render legible the hierarchical social structures replicated in mainstream gaming. Conventional video games typically draw on racialized, colonial, neoliberal, and sexualized ideologies that reinforce stereotypes, behaviors, or worldviews. As Patrick Jagoda reminds us, "video games emerge from the military-industrial-entertainment complex, are complicit with an instrumental problem-solution framework of contemporary technoscience, and contribute to the action-oriented competition that underlies neoliberalism" (413). The use of these conventional modes of gameplay within electronic literature is a self-reflexive strategy to highlight commercialized games that exploit dominant colonial or neoliberal semiotics. Aaron A. Reed's *Maybe Make Some Change* (2011), for example, combines haunting audio, video, and text to explore a repeated battlefield event that is seen from different perspectives. Based on the real-life trial of Adam Winfield, following the notorious Maywand District murders in Afghanistan, Reed's game fragments the war trope of the Oriental Other in the media representations of war zones. Moreover, *Maybe Make Some Change* troubles first-person shooters and commercialized war narratives that valorize patriotism and nationalism while erasing the violence experienced by noncombatants. Incorporating footage from popular commercial games such as *Call of Duty: Modern Warfare 2*, *Call of Duty: Black Ops*, *Counterstrike*, and *Medal of Honor*, Reed's game challenges the aestheticization of a significant global conflict that normalizes harm and creates the apathetic conditions for soldiers to murder unarmed civilians. While commercial games like *Call of Duty* and *Modern Warfare* commodify the Other, *Maybe Make Some Change* interrogates the ecology of war that reduces participants to their immoral actions.

By fragmenting the "us-versus-them" narrative, *Maybe Make Some Change* highlights the conditions of uncertainty within war zones, when commercial media typically crystallize the firm boundaries between heroes and enemies, right and wrong. Similarly, Sandy Baldwin's *New Word Order: Basra* (2003) is a mod for the game *Half-Life*, meaning users can play the new game, provided they have the original installed. One of several of his "Black Mesa Poems," *New Word Order* (*NWO*) uses an immersive navigable map where users encounter phrases from Billy Collins' "Introduction to Poetry," from the 1988 collection *The Apple That Astonished Paris*. Baldwin literalizes the aggression in critical pedagogy of poetry that Collins' poem provokes: "They begin beating it with a hose / to find out what it really means" (58). As Baldwin notes,

> "Introduction to poetry" linked to the circulation and re-circulation of tortured-bodies and interpretive agendas. Every game and every image is part of this linkage. The destruction within NWO reveals the linkage, discloses the settings of bodies in space. Computer space is not simulation but communication. I ask: what poem remains if we destroy both the response taught by the institution of literature and the propriety of how we read and respond to images?

As players navigate Baldwin's map, they can destroy words with a crowbar, rifle, or grenade, thereby violently breaking down language. In the process, players enact an immersive critical environment to engage with the social violence of pedagogy that beats meaning out of poetry. Baldwin's first-person shooter perspective ruptures the normative, institutional, and hier-archical structures that not only enforce tortured codes of instruction but also liken the ensuring violence to the US invasion of Iraq that was then underway when his poem-game was released.

Adding game mechanics and design elements such as first-person per-spectives, mods, and open world environmental assets fosters a participa-tory culture that not only extends the normal life cycle of a game – and the poem – but also shapes the malleable relationships between the user and producer. As Markku Eskelinen notes, "In computer games, random access and controlled access are related to and depend on both spatial and temporal segmentation of the game and the availability of game elements for manipulation" (361). First-person shooters have long been subject to fan modding, which has historically complicated copyright and third-party claims to digital assets. Fan modding describes the act by which players alter or add game elements, such as playable maps, through software or modding tools that are then incorporated in the game. In *NWO*, for example, Baldwin created playable maps using "standard wares for creating Half-Life maps" (Baldwin). While digital rights management typically poses limitations on what modders can and cannot do to a game, mods do allow users to extend their affective engagement and thus the playability of the base game. For this reason, game developers typically encourage mods since the transformation of gaming elements will allow companies to further profit from new additions. Yet transgressive modding, such as Baldwin's critical transformation of *Half-Life* in *New Word Order* and the appropriation of gameplay footage in *Maybe Make Some Change*, is not about extending playability. Rather, modding and appropriation enables writers to generate critical experiences on the nature of language within warfare and within game environments other than those initially intended by the game developer. The ability to navigate these heightened textual spaces transforms the user's bodies into active sensing machines in service of an expanded field of reading that involves nonverbal forms of communication, including the violent destruction of language. Destroying Collins' poem in *NWO* explicitly destabilizes the hermeneutics of reading, while drawing parallels between simulated and real-world violence that play out in both war zones and virtual spaces.

Collaboration and the Lyrical Imagination

While the digital revolution has fostered the political rhetoric of user "freedom" and "choice," we might otherwise find these choices restricted to the internal logic of the poem's and/or game's programming in works such as *NWO*. Conversely, mobile and iPad apps attend to the haptic surfaces of the screen to foreground the tactile and gestural codes of poetry and poetic language. Notable examples include Eric Loyer's *Pry Strange Rain* (2011), Jason Edwards Lewis and Bruno Nadeau's *PoEMM* (Poetry for Excitable [Mobile] Media) project (2010–13), and the mobile and iPad app *Abra: A Living Text* (2017) by Amaranth Borsuk, Kate Durbin, Ian Hatcher, and "You" (as the application tells us). *Abra* is a poetry generator that instrumentalizes the touch of the user to mutate, graft, and prune a default poem. Describing itself as a "magic spell book," the app uses a touchscreen interface to interrogate the user's sensory encounters with readable language. The user is encouraged to "caress the words and watch them shift under your fingers." The ecological language of instruction is telling, for users can either graft new words of their own selection or prune words from the poem, thereby reshaping the text into a completely new object. To this end, *Abra* underscores the fluidity of digital spaces that overlap with the kinetic forces that reorganize the playful, intimate, and expressive materials of poetry. In other words, the user's private experience with their touchscreen materializes the poem. *Abra* invites the user to explore the embodied and private experiences of poetry as an extended field of meaning production. In the process the app meditates on the politics of book as an interface for the shifting desires of the reader as opposed to being a fixed object of authorial intent. Arguably, *Abra* positions the app as a technology of intimacy that extends the lyrical self into the materiality of language within digital spaces. It disperses the responsibility of interpretation to the reader as a collaborator in the production of a poem while decentering the poet as producer. *Abra*, in other words, positions the user as a co-collaborator, which is further implied by the developers' release of the apps' open source code on GitHub.

Ginger Ko/Ko Labs' *Power On* likewise imagines the user as a collaborator of the poet's finished manuscript, which is also available as a book under the same title. While *Power On* does not command the same level of tactile engagement as *Abra*, the *Power On* app does allow users to upload their own videos and image files as backgrounds for the poems that appear in the collection. The app interrogates the automation of labor within the speculative context, where technological entities are the extensions of our corrupted cultural and racialized hierarchies. Selecting a poem from the app's list "creates a collaboration" with the poet and the poet's manuscript, in which the user can opt to hear the poet herself recite the poem against the user-generated canvas. The resultant work thus creates something akin to a private poetry reading, where the user is also contributing to the construction of the poem's visual semiotics.

Power On and *Abra* both respond to the idea of dispersed authorial presence and use the text as a highly mediated starting point that yields to user inputs. In the process, these forms of digital poetry demonstrate the instability of the lyric subject as it migrates across digital spaces, surfaces, and social networks such as Facebook and Twitter, as well as mobile and tablet apps. While much can be made that technology-driven, disembodied, citational, and recycled language of contemporary poetry has disrupted the Romantic formulation of the lyric sensitivity – that is, the Wordsworthian "spontaneous overflow of powerful feelings" – *Abra* and *Power On* nonetheless demonstrate that the lyrical "I" is in fact a lyrical "we," one that the apps' technological processes continually reconstitute. Dani Spinosa's use of "invitational" over expressive engagement with language seems especially apt here, for poetry apps such as Ko's *Power On* "call in" the reader into an affective "commoning" with the textual material (57). In other words, the poetry app serves to extend the lyric's incoherent, dispersed subjectivity that invites the reader, user, co-creator, and collaborator into an intimate experience with an publicly accessible poem.

Conclusion: Poetry and the Public Domain

Poetry apps emphasize the shifting digital landscapes in which language and form highlight the tensions between the private and public expressiveness of language. In many respects, the open-source ethos, the rhetoric of collaboration, and the appropriation of game elements underscore the practices of assemblage and textual recycling seen in adjacent literary movements such as conceptual writing. Arguably, digital spaces undermine traditional hierarchies of ownership and authorship, while also strengthening the idea of public discourse and public commons. By way of a conclusion, then, I want to gesture to two print collections, where the commoning of language further challenges notions of private expressiveness in digital poetry that utilizes algorithmic processes: Allison Parrish's *Articulations* (2018) and Ranjit Bhatnagar's *Encomials: Sonnets from Pentametron* (2018).

Parrish's *Articulations* is a collection of poems and prose that are extracted from some two million lines of public domain poetry from Project Gutenberg using natural language processing. "The goal," notes Parrish, "is to explore an aesthetic of poetic cohesion based on unusual, perhaps unseen similarities among lines, based not on their surface meaning but their understanding linguistic structure" (vi). The first section of the collection, for example, is a long prose poem that builds on an articulatory repetition: "No murmyr of the gusty sea, no murmur of distress, I murmur no more. Ah, murmured Don Ramon. A moment on her bosom heaved; a moment on some autumn bough some rainbow promise: – Not a moment flies a Sonnet is a moment's monument, – sing on: sometime, and at some new moon, a moment since I knew not of her" (5). The resultant text collapses the distinctiveness of the individual authorial presence in favor of a near-coherent voice that is based on linguistic similarities.

Similarly, Ranjit Bhatnagar's Pentametron was a Twitter bot that scanned for tweets that happened to be arranged in iambic pentameters. The bot organized the found lines into rhyming couplets. Bhatnagar applied another program to arrange the corpus into sonnets with enjambed lines that produce an odd confluence of private and public discourses:

Fuck second chances. People never change.
Get money, fuck the system, break the law.
Just ordered Papa John's. A very strange
enchanted boy, McCaffrey takes the draw. (21)

Twitter bots such as Pentametron complicate the commercialized commons of spaces like Twitter by highlighting the arbitrary borders between
private and public language. Pentametron's sonnets are thus aggregated
assemblages of semi-coherent utterances on Twitter that underscore the
polyvocality of cultural codes in public media ecologies. Ultimately, we
might look to social media technologies and processing techniques used in
works such as *Articulations* and *Encomials* as minor resistances to originality and private expression to favor instead the public circulation of language across platforms, archives, and media. Twitter bots in particular reify
the notions of privacy and ownership in digital spaces. As it turns out,
anyone who uses social media might one day find their utterances in a
digital poem. Given the corporatization and monopolization of social
media by companies such as Meta, it may be tempting to view digital
poets, who utilize Twitter bots or processing techniques, as returning to
the earlier conceptualization of the Internet as an egalitarian democratic
network of free ideas. However, it is more accurate to suggest that digital
poetry recognizes the circulating and interconnecting economies of language in various virtual environments. Twitter bots and public domain
poetry call attention to the narrowing of a shared commons and the
expansion of market forces where poetry is transformed into a transactional
commodity. Hence, the emergence of co-creation and partnerships, if not
fracturing the authority of the author, certainly enlarges the relationships
between poets and their readers.

WORKS CITED

Baldwin, Sandy. "The Nihilanth: Immersivity in a First-Person Gaming Mod."
    Electronic Literature Volume 2 (2006), collection.eliterature.org/2/works/
    baldwin_basra/irw_baldwin.pdf.
Barlow, John Perry. "A Declaration of the Independence of Cyberspace," www.eff
    .org/cyberspace-independence (accessed March 2, 2022).
Bhatnagar, Ranjit. *Encomials: Sonnets from Pentametron*. Counterpath Press, 2018.
Borsuk, Amaranth, Kate Durbin, and Ian Hatcher. Abra: A Living Text. iOS app,
    2017.
Brown, Bob. *The Readies*. Edited and with an introduction by Craig Saper.
    Roving Eye Press, 2014.
Collins, Billy. *The Apple That Astonished Paris*. Arkansas University Press, 2006.

Electronic Disturbance Theater 2.0/B.A.N.G. Lab. *The Transborder Immigrant Tool.* 2007. https://anthology.rhizome.org/transborder-immigrant-tool (accessed February 22, 2022).

The Transborder Immigrant Tool Book. University of Michigan Press, 2014.

Electronic Literature Organization. "History." https://eliterature.org/elo-history/ (accessed February 22, 2022).

Eskelinen, Markku. *Cybertext Poetics: The Critical Landscape of New Media Literary Theory.* Bloomsbury, 2012.

Flores, Leonardo. "Digital Poetry." In *The Johns Hopkins Guide to Digital Media*, ed. Marie-Laure Ryan, Lori Emerson, and Benjamin J. Robertson. Johns Hopkins University Press, 2014, 155–61.

"Third Generation Electronic Literature." *Electronic Book Review*, April 6, 2019, doi.org/10.7273/axyj-3574.

Funkhouser, Christopher. *Prehistoric Digital Poetry: An Archaeology of Forms.* University of Alabama Press, 2007.

Gibson, Richard Hughes. *Paper Electronic Literature: An Archaeology of Born Digital Materials.* University of Massachusetts Press, 2021.

Hayles, N. Katherine. *Electronic Literature: New Horizons for the Literary.* Notre Dame University Press, 2008.

Heckman, Davin, and James O'Sullivan. "Electronic Literature: Contexts and Poetics." In *Literary Studies in the Digital Age: An Evolving Anthology*, ed. Kenneth M. Price and Ray Siemens. MLA, 2018. https://dlsanthology.mla .hcommons.org/ (accessed February 15, 2022).

Jagoda, Patrick. *Experimental Games: Critique, Play, and Design in the Age of Gamification.* University of Chicago Press, 2020.

Knowles, Alison, and James Tenney. *House of Dust.* Gebrüder König. 1968.

Nakamura, Lisa. *Cybertypes: Race, Ethnicity, and Identity on the Internet.* Routledge, 2002.

Nelson, Jason. "Poetic Playlands: Poetry, Interface, and Video Game Engines." In *Electronic Literature as Digital Humanities: Contexts, Forms, and Practices*, ed. Dene Grigar and James O'Sullivan. Bloomsbury, 2021, 335–49.

Parrish, Allison. *Articulations.* Counterpath Press, 2018.

Perloff, Majorie. "Screening the Page/Paging the Screen: Digital Poetics and the Differential Text." In *New Media Poetics: Contexts, Technotexts, and Theories*, ed. Adalaide Morris and Thomas Swiss. MIT Press, 2006, 143–62.

Raley, Rita. *Tactical Media.* University of Minnesota Press, 2009.

Salter, Anastasia. *What Is Your Quest? From Adventure Games to Interactive Books.* Iowa University Press, 2014.

Silliman, Ron. "Disappearance of the Word, Appearance of the World." In *The Language Book*, ed. Bruce Andrews and Charles Bernstein. Southern Illinois University Press, 1984, 121–32.

Spinosa, Dani. *Anarchists in the Academy: Machines and Free Readers in Experimental Poetry.* Alberta University Press, 2018.

Wardrip-Fruin, Noah. "Reading Digital Literature: Surface, Data, Interaction, and Expressive Processing." In *A Companion to Digital Literary Studies*, ed. Susan Schreibman and Ray Siemens. Blackwell, 2008, 163–82.

Index

Index

CAMBRIDGE COMPANIONS TO ...

Authors

Edward Albee edited by STEPHEN J. BOTTOMS

Margaret Atwood edited by, Coral Ann Howells (second edition),

W. H. Auden edited by STAN SMITH

Jane Austen edited by EDWARD COPELAND AND JULIET MCMASTER (SECOND EDITION)

James Baldwin edited by MICHELE ELAM

Balzac edited by OWEN HEATHCOTE AND ANDREW WATTS

Beckett edited by JOHN PILLING

Bede edited by SCOTT DEGREGORIO

Aphra Behn edited by DEREK HUGHES AND JANET TODD

Saul Bellow edited by VICTORIA AARONS

Walter Benjamin edited by DAVID S. FERRIS

William Blake edited by MORRIS EAVES

Boccaccio edited by GUYDA ARMSTRONG, RHIANNON DANIELS, AND STEPHEN J. MILNER

Jorge Luis Borges edited by EDWIN WILLIAMSON

Brecht edited by PETER THOMSON AND GLENDYR SACKS (second edition)

The Brontës edited by HEATHER GLEN

Bunyan edited by ANNE DUNAN-PAGE

Frances Burney edited by PETER SABOR

Byron edited by DRUMMOND BONE

Albert Camus edited by EDWARD J. HUGHES

Willa Cather edited by MARILEE LINDEMANN

Catullus edited by IAN DU QUESNAY AND TONY WOODMAN

Cervantes edited by ANTHONY J. CASCARDI

Chaucer edited by PIERO BOITANI AND JILL MANN (second edition)

Chekhov edited by VERA GOTTLIEB AND PAUL ALLAIN

Kate Chopin edited by JANET BEER

Caryl Churchill edited by ELAINE ASTON AND ELIN DIAMOND

Milton edited by, DENNIS DANIELSON (second edition),

Molière edited by DAVID BRADBY AND ANDREW CALDER

Toni Morrison edited by JUSTINE TALLY

Alice Munro edited by DAVID STAINES

Nabokov edited by JULIAN W. CONNOLLY

Eugene O'Neill edited by MICHAEL MANHEIM

George Orwell edited by JOHN RODDEN

Ovid edited by PHILIP HARDIE

Petrarch edited by ALBERT RUSSELL ASCOLI AND UNN FALKEID

Harold Pinter edited by, PETER RABY (second edition),

Sylvia Plath edited by JO GILL

Plutarch edited by FRANCES B. TITCHENER AND ALEXEI ZADOROJNYI

Edgar Allan Poe edited by KEVIN J. HAYES

Alexander Pope edited by PAT ROGERS

Ezra Pound edited by IRA B. NADEL

Proust edited by RICHARD BALES

Pushkin edited by ANDREW KAHN

Thomas Pynchon edited by INGER H. DALSGAARD, LUC HERMAN AND BRIAN MCHALE

Rabelais edited by JOHN O'BRIEN

Rilke edited by KAREN LEEDER AND ROBERT VILAIN

Philip Roth edited by TIMOTHY PARRISH

Salman Rushdie edited by ABDULRAZAK GURNAH

John Ruskin edited by FRANCIS O'GORMAN

Sappho edited by P. J. FINGLASS AND ADRIAN KELLY

Seneca edited by SHADI BARTSCH AND ALESSANDRO SCHIESARO

Shakespeare edited by MARGARETA DE GRAZIA AND STANLEY WELLS (second edition)

George Bernard Shaw edited by CHRISTOPHER INNES

Shelley edited by TIMOTHY MORTON

Mary Shelley edited by ESTHER SCHOR

Sam Shepard edited by MATTHEW C. ROUDANÉ

CPSIA information can be obtained
at www.ICGtesting.com
Printed in the USA
LVHW042241170523
747316LV00005B/78

9 781009 180030